SPECULATIONS

An Anthology for Reading, Writing, and Research

Edited by

Jason Landrum

Matthew Wynn Sivils

Constance Squires

KENDALL/HUNT PUBLISHING COMPANY
4050 Westmark Drive Dubuque, Iowa 52002

Acknowledgements

The editors wish to thank the Department of English, Oklahoma State University, for assistance with this project. Our particular thanks go to those who helped develop the text and see it to completion: Matt Carter, Deborah Carmichael, Paula Farca, Richard Frohock, Elizabeth Grubgeld, Miriam Love, Richard Paustenbaugh, Vicki Phillips, Scott Rogers, and Shelley Reid.

Contents

Chapter Four: What's in the Future?   259

CHAPTER ONE

How Does the Mind Work?

Introduction

The idea of Artificial Intelligence presupposes that we can understand enough of how the human mind works to duplicate it, and cloning aspires to the perfect duplication of a functioning human. So how does the mind work? At its most basic level, human consciousness must constantly mediate between itself and the world outside, between "me" and everything that is "not me." The subject of the fundamental barrier between these two worlds stands at the core of every selection in this section. As citizens, students, writers, readers, and consumers, all of us have probably at one time or another become aware of the impossibility of seeing the world outside ourselves without the mind imposing its own order on what it perceives.

We encounter this difficulty at every level, from the personal to the professional. It affects our thinking on many questions, from what kind of learning environment is best for different kinds of intelligence to whether or not the Internet changes how effectively we connect with other people. How does our ability to imagine walking a mile in someone else's shoes determine how we understand societal issues, and subsequently, how we vote? How do the stories we tell about ourselves form and sustain our sense of self? Do objective standards of art, culture, politics, or religion help us to understand our world, or do they artificially impose objective standards where there are none?

None of the pieces appearing in this section claims to settle the question of how the mind works. The writing in this section ranges from ancient philosophy to contemporary poetry and fiction, from modern philosophy to psychology and medicine. Each piece suggests the fascinating complexity of the human mind and offers ways of approaching the subject that will facilitate further exploration.

Wallace Stevens, "The Anecdote of the Jar"

Wallace Stevens was one of the foremost poets of the twentieth century. Winner of both the Pulitzer Prize and the National Book Award, Stevens lived a quiet life as the vice-president of the Hartford Accident and Indemnity Insurance Company in Hartford, Connecticut, where few of his colleagues or neighbors were aware of his celebrated reputation as a writer. Stevens died in 1955.

 Before You Read:

Most of us have heard the conundrum: "If a tree falls in the woods and no one is there to hear it, does it make a sound?" What does this conundrum point out about how we comprehend our world?

Anecdote of the Jar

I placed a jar in Tennessee,
And round it was, upon a hill.
It made the slovenly wilderness
Surround that hill.

The wilderness rose up to it,
And sprawled around, no longer wild.
The jar was round upon the ground
And tall and of a port in air.

It took dominion everywhere.
The jar was gray and bare.
It did not give of bird or bush,
Like nothing else in Tennessee.

For Discussion:

1. What does the jar do to the objects that surround it? Why Tennessee? How might the poem be different if the jar were a statue or a vase?
2. The jar seems to dominate its surroundings. What specific lines in the poem would lead you to think this has a positive or negative effect?
3. Imagine a scene or picture. Then imagine an object of some kind. Place the object in the scene you first envisioned. Which transforms which?

 For Fact-Finding, Research, and Writing:

1. Using a dictionary, define "anecdote," "story," and "allegory." How are these definitions different from the way these words are used by Stevens, Schank, and Plato?
2. Using a reliable website, read about the career of Wallace Stevens. Are the concerns of this poem representative of his career? With what literary movement is he usually aligned, and what are some of the defining traits of this movement? How do you know the website you chose is reliable?
3. Compare this poem to Plato's "Allegory of the Cave." Both provide metaphors for how the mind interacts with reality. How are they similar? How do they differ?

Carmella Braniger, "Pear in a Bottle"

Ohio native Camella Braniger holds a master's degree in Creative Writing from Johns Hopkins University and a doctorate in English from Oklahoma State University. Her poems have appeared in *Sycamore Review* and *Poems and Plays*. She is currently on the faculty of Millikin University of Illinois.

 Before You Read:

When do you think it's acceptable to alter nature? When is it not?

Carmella Braniger, "Pear in a Bottle"

Squeezed into the crowded liquor
store, aisles tight, air close, we pay
for our nectar of wine, a slender *Gris,*
and notice a new spirit's emergence.
I raise it to my brother's face showing
him a whole pear drawn to the bottom
of a tinted, narrow-necked container.
He asks how the bottle gulped a pear
into its belly through the tight throat.
The clerk explains. They place bottles
over buds before they well up into fruit.
She points us to a picture on the label,
glass bottles strapped to pear trees.
Fifty a tree perhaps. She's excited.
It's a long process and the pear can
grow only as large as the bottle's bulb.
My brother reminds me of Hairy Buffalo
parties. Over a hundred dollars in fruit
at the bottom of a fifty gallon tin tub,
soaked with vodka, everclear, rum,
the nearest transparent liquor available.
Out of rising memory he explodes,
pretends to pay the fifty dollars to free
the thick, stuck pear we have taken in.
After his birth, doctors discovered
a series of misnumbered vertebrae.
When they diagnosed scoliosis, said
he'd need to grow in a brace, to hold
his right shape until he drew to full
blossom, we laughed at the pretense
as we laugh now; viability will beguile,
into a mirror where *objects are closer,*
into a bottle at which a slightly confused
clerk keeps pointing, saying *look,*
the pear is smaller than it appears.

For Discussion:

1. In what ways does the speaker find the pear in the bottle reminiscent of her brother in a back brace?
2. The clerk is full of excitement and admiration for the process by which the pear in the bottle is produced. Do you think the speaker shares her enthusiasm? Which words and lines would you point to in answering that question?
3. "The Anecdote of the Jar" suggests that the presence of the jar changes everything around it. Do you think that the bottle, the tub of "transparent liquor," or the back brace completely change the pear, the fruit, or the boy? Which lines in "Pear in a Bottle" might support your interpretation?

 For Fact-Finding, Research, and Writing:

1. The brother and sister in the poem purchase a bottle of Gris, but that is not the liquor that kindles the speaker's memory and imagination. What is that liquor?
2. The most famous French producer of that liquor gives it an interesting name. How might that name relate to the condition of the speaker's brother? Or not? Use an on-line French-English dictionary if necessary.
3. What kinds of miniature plants and animals are cultivated around the world? How do their exponents explain the desirability of such products? Find two examples.
4. Think of this poem in light of Lauren Slater's essay about radical plastic surgery in Chapter Four. Do you feel differently about the alteration of plant forms than you do about the deliberate alteration of human forms?

Plato, "The Allegory of the Cave"

Plato (428–347 B.C.) lived in Athens and studied closely with Socrates. Much of Plato's writing is in the form of imagined dialogues between Socrates and Plato, with occasional questions from various students. After Socrates was sentenced to death in 399 B.C., Plato founded the Academy, an institution of learning that endured for almost a thousand years. Many of the practices and beliefs begun by Plato in the Academy are still visible in the basic organization and educational premises of most modern universities. "The Allegory of the Cave" models the belief that we cannot rely on our senses to tell us the truth about the world; it also suggests a relationship between our ability to understand what is outside ourselves and our ability to lead.

 Before You Read:

How do you know that what you perceive with your senses is real? Why might this be an important question? Or isn't it?

The Allegory of the Cave

Plato

NEXT, I SAID, compare the effect of education and the lack of it upon our human nature to a situation like this: imagine men to be living in an underground cave-like dwelling place, which has a way up to the light along its whole width, but the entrace is a long way up. The men have been there from childhood, with their neck and legs in fetters, so that they remain in the same place and can only see ahead of them, as their bonds prevent them turning their heads. Light is provided by a fire burning some way behind and above them. Between the fire and the prisoners, some way behind them and on a higher ground, there is a path across the cave and along this a low wall has been built, like the screen at a puppet show in front of the performers who show their puppets above it.—I see it.

See then also men carrying along that wall, so that they overtop it, all kinds of artifacts, statues of men, reproductions of other animals in stone or wood fashioned in all sorts of ways, and, as is likely, some of the carriers are talking while others are silent.—This is a strange picture, and strange prisoners.

They are like us, I said. Do you think, in the first place, that such men could see anything of themselves and each other[1] except the shadows which the fire casts upon the wall of the cave in front of them?—How could they, if they have to keep their heads still throughout life?

And is not the same true of the objects carried along the wall?—Quite.

If they could converse with one another, do you not think that they would consider these shadows to be the real things?—Necessarily.

What if their prison had an echo which reached them from in front of them? Whenever one of the carriers passing behind the wall spoke, would they not think that it was the shadow passing in front of them which was talking? Do you agree?—By Zeus I do.

Altogether then, I said, such men would believe the truth to be nothing else than the shadows of the artifacts?—They must believe that.

Consider then what deliverance from their bonds and the curing of their ignorance would be if something like this naturally happened to them. Whenever one of them was freed, had to stand up suddenly, turn his head, walk, and look up toward the light, doing all that would give him pain, the flash of the fire would make it impossible for him to see the objects of which he had earlier seen the shadows. What do you think he would say if he was told that what he saw then was foolishness, that he was now somewhat closer to reality and turned to things that existed more fully, that he saw more correctly? If one then pointed to each of the objects passing by, asked him what each was, and forced him to answer, do you not think he would be at a loss and believe that the things which he saw earlier were truer than the things now pointed out to him?—Much truer.

If one then compelled him to look at the fire itself, his eyes would hurt, he would turn round and flee toward those things which he could see, and think that they were in fact clearer than those now shown to him.—Quite so.

And if one were to drag him thence by force up the rough and steep path, and did not let him go before he was dragged into the sunlight, would he not be in physical pain and angry as he was dragged along? When he came into the light, with the sunlight filling his eyes, he would not be able to see a single one of the things which are now said to be true.—Not at once, certainly.

I think he would need time to get adjusted before he could see things in the world above; at first he would see shadows most easily, then reflections of men and other things in water, then the things themselves. After this he would see objects in the sky and the sky itself more easily at night, the light of the stars and the moon more easily than the sun and the light of the sun during the day.—Of course.

Then, at last, he would be able to see the sun, not images of it in water or in some alien place, but the sun itself in its own place, and be able to contemplate it.—That must be so.

After this he would reflect that it is the sun which provides the seasons and the years, which governs everything in the visible world, and is also in some way the cause of those other things which he used to see.—Clearly that would be the next stage.

What then? As he reminds himself of his first dwelling place, of the wisdom there and of his fellow prisoners, would he not reckon himself happy for the change, and pity them?—Surely.

And if the men below had praise and honours from each other, and prizes for the man who saw most clearly the shadows that passed before them, and who could best remember which usually came earlier and which later, and which came together and thus could most ably prophesy the future, do you think our man would desire those rewards and envy those who were honoured and held power among the prisoners, or would he feel, as Homer put it, that he certainly wished to be "serf to another man without possessions upon the earth"[2] and go through any suffering, rather than share their opinions and live as they do?—Quite so, he said, I think he would rather suffer anything.

Reflect on this too, I said. If this man went down into the cave again and sat down in the same seat, would his eyes not be filled with darkness coming suddenly out of the sunlight?—They certainly would.

And if he had to contend again with those who had remained prisoners in recognizing those shadows while his sight was affected and his eyes had not settled down—and the time for this adjustment would not be short—would he not be ridiculed? Would it not be said that he had returned from his upward journey with his eyesight spoiled, and that it was not worthwhile even to attempt to travel upward? As for the man who tried to free them and lead them upward, if they could somehow lay their hands on him and kill him, they would do so.—They certainly would.

This whole image, my dear Glaucon, I said, must be related to what we said before. The realm of the visible should be compared to the prison dwelling, and the fire inside it to the power of the sun. If you interpret the upward journey and the contemplation of things above as the upward journey of the soul to the intelligible realm, you will grasp what I surmise since you were keen to hear it. Whether it is true or not only the god knows, but this is how I see it, namely that in the intelligible world the Form of the Good is the last to be seen, and with difficulty; when seen it must be reckoned to be for all the cause of all that is right and beautiful, to have produced in the visible world both light and the fount of light, while in the intelligible world it is itself that which produces and controls truth and intelligence, and he who is to act intelligently in public or in private must see it.—I share your thought as far as I am able.

Come then, share with me this thought also: do not be surprised that those who have reached this point are unwilling to occupy themselves with human affairs, and that their souls are always pressing upward to spend their time there, for this is natural if things are as our parable indicates.—That is very likely.

Further, I said, do you think it at all surprising that anyone coming to the evils of human life from the contemplation of the divine behaves awkwardly and appears very ridiculous while his eyes are still dazzled and before he is sufficiently adjusted to the darkness around him, if he is compelled to contend in court or some other place about the shadows of justice or the objects of which they are shadows, and to carry through the contest about these in the way these things are understood by those who have never seen Justice itself?—That is not surprising at all.

Anyone with intelligence, I said, would remember that the eyes may be confused in two ways and from two causes, coming from light into darkness as well as from darkness into light. Realizing that the same applies to the soul, whenever he sees a soul disturbed and unable to see something, he will not laugh mindlessly but will consider whether it has come from a brighter life and is dimmed because unadjusted, or has come from greater ignorance into greater light and is filled with a brighter dazzlement. The former he would declare happy in its life and experience, the latter he would pity, and if he should wish to laugh at it, his laughter would be less ridiculous than if he laughed at a soul that has come from the light above.—What you say is very reasonable.

We must then, I said, if these things are true, think something like this about them, namely that education is not what some declare it to be; they say that knowledge is not present in the soul and that they put it in, like putting sight into blind eyes.—They surely say that.

Our present argument shows, I said, that the capacity to learn and the organ with which to do so are present in every person's soul. It is as if it were not possible to turn the eye from darkness to light without turning the whole body; so one must turn one's whole soul from the world of becoming until it can endure to contemplate reality, and the brightest of realities, which we say is the Good.—Yes.

Education then is the art of doing this very thing, this turning around, the knowledge of how the soul can most easily and most effectively be turned around; it is not the art of putting the capacity of sight into the soul; the soul possesses that already but it is not turned the right way or looking where it should. This is what education has to deal with.—That seems likely.

Now the other so-called virtues of the soul seem to be very close to those of the body—they really do not exist before and are added later by habit and practice—but the virtue of intelligence belongs above all to something more divine, it seems, which never loses its capacity but, according to which way it is turned, becomes useful and beneficial or useless and harmful. Have you never noticed in men who are said to be wicked but clever, how sharply their little soul looks into things to which it turns its attention? Its capacity for sight is not inferior, but it is compelled to serve evil ends, so that the more sharply it looks the more evils it works.—Quite so.

Yet if a soul of this kind had been hammered at from childhood and those excrescences had been knocked off it which belong to the world of becoming and have been fastened upon it by feasting, gluttony, and similar pleasures, and which like leaden weights draw the soul to look downward—if, being rid of these, it turned to look at things that are true, then the same soul of the same man would see these just as sharply as it now sees the things towards which it is directed.—That seems likely.

Further, is it not likely, I said, indeed it follows inevitably from what was said before, that the uneducated who have no experience of truth would never govern a city satisfactorily, nor would those who are allowed to spend their whole life in the process of educating themselves; the former would fail because they do not have a single goal at which all their actions, public and private, must aim; the latter because they would refuse to act, thinking that they have settled, while still alive, in the faraway lands of the blessed.—True.

It is often our task as founders, I said, to compel the best natures to reach the study which we have previously said to be the most important, to see the Good and to follow that upward journey. When they have accomplished their journey and seen it sufficiently, we must not allow them to do what they are allowed to do today.—What is that?

To stay there, I said, and to refuse to go down again to the prisoners in the cave, there to share both their labours and their honours, whether these be of little or of greater worth.[3]

Are we then, he said, to do them an injustice by making them live a worse life when they could live a better one?

You are again forgetting, my friend, I said, that it is not the law's concern to make some one group in the city outstandingly happy but to contrive to spread happiness throughout the city, by bringing the citizens into harmony with each other by persuasion or compulsion, and to make them share with each other the benefits which each group can confer upon the community. The law has not made men of this kind in the city in order to allow each to turn in any direction they wish but to make use of them to bind the city together.—You are right, I had forgotten.

Consider then, Glaucon, I said, that we shall not be doing an injustice to those who have become philosophers in our city, and that what we shall say to them, when we compel them to care for and to guard the others, is just. For we shall say: "Those who become philosophers in other cities are justified in not sharing the city's labours, for they have grown into philosophy of their own accord, against the will of the government in each of those cities, and it is right that what grows of its own accord, as it owes no debt to anyone for its upbringing, should not be keen to pay it to anyone. But we have made you in our city kings and leaders of the swarm, as it were, both to your own advantage and to that of the rest of the city; you are better and more completely educated than those others, and you are better able to share in both kinds of life. Therefore you must each in turn go down to live with other men and grow accustomed to seeing in the dark. When you are used to it you will see infinitely better than the dwellers below; you will know what each image is and of what it is an image, because you have seen the truth of things beautiful and just and good, and so, for you as for us, the city will be governed as a waking reality and not as in a dream, as the majority of cities are now governed by men who are fighting shadows and striving against each other in order to rule as if this were a great good." For this is the truth: a city in which the prospective rulers are least keen to rule must of necessity be governed best and be most free from strife, whereas a city with the opposite kind of rulers is governed in the opposite way.—Quite so.

Do you think that those we have nurtured will disobey us and refuse to share the labours of the city, each group in turn, though they may spend the greater part of their time dwelling with each other in a pure atmosphere?

They cannot, he said, for we shall be giving just orders to just men, but each of them will certainly go to rule as to something that must be done, the opposite attitude from that of the present rulers in every city.

That is how it is, my friend, I said. If you can find a way of life which is better than governing for the prospective governors, then a well-governed city can exist for you. Only in that city will the truly rich rule, not rich in gold but in the wealth which the happy man must have, a life with goodness and intelligence. If beggars hungry for private goods go into public life, thinking that they must snatch their good from it, the well-governed city cannot exist, for then office is fought for, and such a war at home inside the city destroys them and the city as well.—Very true.

Can you name, I said, any other life than that of true philosophy which disdains political office?—No, by Zeus.

And surely it is those who are no lovers of governing who must govern. Otherwise, rival lovers of it will fight them.—Of course.

What other men will you compel to become guardians of the city rather than those who have the best knowledge of the principles that make for the best government of a city and who also know honours of a different kind, and a better life than the political?—No one else.

Do you want us to examine how such men will come to be in our city, and how one will lead them to the light, as some are said to have gone up from the underworld to join the gods?—Of course I want it.

This is not a matter of spinning a coin[4] but of turning a soul from a kind of day that is night to the true day, being the upward way to reality which we say is true philosophy.—Quite so.

Notes

1. These shadows of themselves and each other are never mentioned again. A Platonic myth or parable, like a Homeric simile, is often elaborated in considerable detail. These contribute to the vividness of the picture but often have no other function, and it is a mistake to look for any symbolic meaning in them. It is the general picture that matters.
2. *Odyssey* 11, 489–90, where Achilles says to Odysseus, on the latter's visit to the underworld, that he would rather be a servant to a poor man on earth than king among the dead.
3. Plato does indeed require his philosopher to go back into the cave to help those less fortunate than himself, but only as a duty, not because he loves his neighbour or gets any emotional satisfaction from helping him.
4. A proverbial saying, referring to a children's game in which the players were divided into two groups. A shell or potsherd, white on one side and black on the other, was then thrown in the space between them to the cry of "night or day" (note the reference to night and day which immediately follows) and, according as the white or black fell uppermost, one group ran away pursued by the other. The meaning here is much the same as in our expression "spinning a coin," namely that this was not a matter to be settled in a moment or by chance.

 For Discussion:

1. Plato describes the process of education as similar to emerging from a cave. He considers the essential quality of an educated person to be tolerance of others. Consider your own education, both formal and informal. Does your own education agree with Plato's version of education?

2. Explain Plato's statement, "And surely it is those who are no lovers of govern-ing who must govern." What in his argument leads him to this conclusion? Do you agree?

3. Where do modern means of communication like television and the Internet fit into Plato's cave metaphor? Do they help us to apprehend the world outside of the cave, or do they act as the shadows on the wall inside the cave, or both?

4. If the material world is an illusion, as Plato asserts, how would over-reliance on materialism affect a person's decision-making ability?

 ## *For Fact-Finding, Research, and Writing:*

1. Plato believes that educated people owe a debt to their communities that should be paid by useful service to that community. Identify and provide basic background on two educational programs that strongly emphasize this service ethic today.

2. Using appropriate reference materials, identify the allusion to Plato's allegory in the writing of St. Paul.

3. Compare Plato's ideas on education to those of Russell or Gardner.

Roger Schank, "Where Stories Come From and Why We Tell Them"

Roger Schank is the Director of the Institute for Learning Sciences and John Evans Professor of Electrical Engineering and Computer Science, Psychology, and Education at Northwestern University. His publications include *The Creative Attitude: Learning to Ask and Answer the Right Questions, Narrative and Freedom: The Shadows of Time,* and *Tell Me A Story: Narrative and Intelligence,* from which "Where Stories Come From and Why We Tell Them" is excerpted. An expert in both education and computers, Schank explains how narratology (the study of how the mind organizes reality into stories) can provide a model of human thought processes useful in the development of Artificial Intelligence. In "Where Stories Come From and Why We Tell Them" Schank categorizes stories according to their goals.

Before You Read:

What are urban legends? How many can you name? Where did you learn them?

Where Stories Come from and Why We Tell Them

I WAS SITTING in my office one day when three people came in, one at a time, to talk to me. The first was a foreign student who was about to become a graduate student. He told me the following story.

> *In order to go to graduate school, I had to postpone going into the army. Ordinarily, three years of service are required, but my country decided that if I wanted to study for a Ph.D. now, I would owe them five years after I finish my studies. I agreed to this, but after I agreed, my country called and said I would owe six years of service. Again I agreed, and again I received a call saying that now they had decided seven years would be required. What should I do?*

The second person who entered my office was someone who worked for me. This was his story:

> *My ex-wife just called. She's moving back to town, and she's planning to put our child in public school here. She's had him in private school, but now she wants me to pay the tuition money to her instead. She isn't planning on working and is trying to get me to support her. I just called my lawyer to ask him what to do.*

The third person was a friend. He had been looking to change jobs and had negotiated a fine deal for himself in another town. This was his story:

> *I've been busy selling my house and otherwise preparing for the move. All of a sudden, my appointment has been stopped at the highest levels of the company. No one will tell me why, but I think someone who was my enemy in the past has a friend at the company. And I think she wrote a letter that prejudiced them against me. I'm very upset.*

Schank, Roger C. "Where Stories Come from and Why We Tell Them," from *Tell Me A Story: Narrative and Intelligence.* Evanston: Northwestern University Press, 1990, pp. 28–55.

Everyday human communication revolves around stories such as these. Where do we get stories to tell? Obviously, stories digest one's experiences. We tell what happened to us. But we also create stories. I, for example, had a story to tell at the end of that day about how people mistreat one another, and I needed to tell it.

When people talk to you, they can only tell you what they know. And the knowledge that people have about the world around them is really no more than the set of experiences that they have had. Now, of course, not every experience that someone has had is worth remembering, let alone telling to someone else. The experiences we do remember form the set of stories that constitute our view of the world and characterize our beliefs. In some sense, we may not even know what our own view of the world is until we are reminded of and tell stories that illustrate our opinion on some aspect of the world.

Types of Stories

With the exception of certain questions and some straightforward and factual answers, such as "What room is Jones in?" followed by "1244," everything people say regarding their opinions or experiences is a story of some sort. Some stories are too dull to worry about, but the process of search, retrieval, and adaptation of stories is the same whether the story is long or short. One question is where stories come from. We start life without stories, and we go through life acquiring them. Some are handed to us directly by others and some we invent for ourselves.

With respect to the issue of where stories come from, there are five basic types of stories:

1. official
2. invented (adapted)
3. firsthand experiential
4. secondhand
5. culturally common

OFFICIAL STORIES

Official stories are those we learn from an official place, such as school or church or a business or from the government. They are stories that have been told many times, and no one knows or cares who thought them up first. Governments and other official bodies have a kind of script for inventing them, and people in general know how much credence to give them. We know official stories about the creation of the universe, for example. Science has its versions, and religions have theirs. From time to time, we tell an official story because our job requires us to or because the official story is the only one we know.

Official stories are those that our boss, our government, our parents, or anyone in authority instructs us to tell. They are repeated as originally related. People can tell their own official stories. For example, Gary Hart in the 1987–1988 political campaign told an official story about his alleged lover Donna Rice that it seemed no one, not even he, could have believed. But it was the official story. One of my favorite official stories is about Sydney Biddle Barrows, the so-called Mayflower Madam. The following was taken from the *New York Post*:

MAYFLOWER MADAM SAILS INTO A NEW BUSINESS

The Mayflower Madam, a thirty-three-year-old blonde blueblood awaiting trial on charges of running a $1000-a-night prostitution ring, is back in business as the Makeover Madam. She has founded a house-call service for women who want to eat better, dress better, and look better, called We Can Work It Out. Sydney Biddle Barrows, the beautiful descendant of Mayflower pilgrims, will send training counselors to enforce tough diet and exercise regimens on middle-class women.

Her attorney and friend, Risa Dickstein, yesterday told of the project, still in its infancy. In a three-hundred-page motion filed in Manhattan Supreme Court, Mrs. Dickstein asked for a dismissal of the charges against Miss Barrows on grounds ranging from insufficient evidence to prosecutorial misconduct.

She painted a heartwarming picture of the woman accused of running a prostitution ring for high-class clients. She said Miss Barrows:

> *voluntarily reads to a blind college student and helps him with term papers in a program to aid the handicapped;*
> *instructed her employees to patronize an Upper West Side food store because it supplied free meals to the needy on Thanksgiving;*
> *doesn't drink, smoke, or take drugs—not even aspirin;*
> *has the support of her mother, stepfather, and siblings in her ordeal;*
> *lost the love of her natural father because of her arrest.*

Mrs. Dickstein said in her motion that Miss Barrows has a totally unblemished record. It is undisputed that she comes from a family which is well recognized not only as law-abiding but also for its commitment to public service. She is accurately viewed by those who know her well as a well-bred, well-educated, responsible citizen for her community.

The defense argues that the escort agencies run by Miss Barrows were legitimate businesses in which clients paid for companionship. Sex, when it took place, was indulged in freely by the escorts—and at no extra charge.

Official stories are ones that have been carefully constructed by one or more people to tell a version of events that is sanitized and presumed to be less likely to get anyone in trouble. Alternatively, official stories are often the position of a group that has a message to sell and treats that message independently of the facts. A rather grisly example of this was recently placed on a billboard overlooking I–95 in Bridgeport, Connecticut. The sign showed an iridescent skeleton crawling into a body bag.

The legend over the picture said: "AIDS—It's a Hop in the Sack." Such epithets are quite typical of official stories. The facts are made simple, often to the point of being wrong, so that a message can be made public. Official stories often leave out details that would make things clearer in order to portray situations as being less complicated than they are.

The overall intention of an official story is to make complex issues seem clearer than they otherwise might appear. When we don't have answers, official stories give us those answers. We learn these stories when we have no stories of our own for those particular situations. As soon as we do have a story of our own that we believe more than the official version, we tend to ignore the official story.

INVENTED STORIES

Obviously, people can make up stories, but the process of story creation and invention is one of adaptation rather than creation out of nothing. Official stories are made up by adapting real stories into appropriately sterilized stories. Invented stories can also, of course, be official stories. In any case, the processes behind the creation of these two story types are remarkably similar. Both of these story types tend to use a real story, that is, a firsthand experiential story, something that really happened to somebody, and then expand upon that story in some way.

The invented story expands upon an experience for the purpose of entertainment, sometimes leaving the original experience unrecognizable in the process. The official story is created in the same way, albeit for a different purpose. An official story tends to obscure the facts of the original experience for the purposes of eliminating culpability on the part of the actors in the story.

Invented stories are also created brand-new by authors, by parents, and often by people who pose a hypothetical case in order to make a point in an argument; however, even brand-new invented stories are usually adaptations of previous stories and frequently, but by no means always, have a point. They tend to be much less rich in detail at first, but their continued elaboration can make them very rich over time.

A good way to understand the story invention process is to observe it firsthand. Unfortunately, when people create a new story, we have difficulty knowing exactly how they found the various pieces of the story they are telling. We cannot easily know what has been invented out of thin air and what has been adapted from prior experiences or other stories. We can reasonably assume, however, that true creation can hardly exist with respect to stories. Every story we tell has to have its basis in something that we have already experienced. Of course, the better we are at telling stories, the better we are at giving them the appearance of being complete fiction. This can mean that even we as tellers see the story as fictional, not realizing the adaptation process that we ourselves have used. Even stories that are pure fantasy are adaptations of more realistic stories where certain constraints of the real world are relaxed. People can take past experiences, consciously or unconsciously, and modify them into stories where the original experience is completely hidden.

One way to see this is to observe a child who is learning to tell stories. When my daughter, Hana, was very little, I recorded some stories that she told at various ages. Here are some of them, taken from *Scripts, Plans, Goals and Understanding* (Roger Schank and Robert Abelson; Hillsdale, NJ: Lawrence Erlbaum Associates, 1977). Hana, age two years, eleven months:

PAPA: I met you in the plant store and then what happened?

HANA: I don't know.

PAPA: Oh, come on, I thought you were going to tell me a story.

HANA: I went on a bike and you drived, and you buckled me in and we went riding the park, and droved and went on one swing and then the other swing and two swings and then we, I went on two slides and then went in the sandbox and then I met somebody, and then I met, and then I went right on our bicycle, and took the thing off and and and we went on and you drived on and then you taked the one street and then you ride on the other side and then we were home and then we were opened, I opened, you opened, I opened the door and then I went right in and I take my jacket off and said hang up your coat and I hanged up my coat and said and went right in the kitchen and and was almost time to dinner.

PAPA: And then what happened?

HANA: I don't know.

PAPA: What happened after you took your coat off?

HANA: Then we went take a nap and you were and then we, you, we went to the plant store and then Nadine was at home and then at our home, and then she was clean, changed, cleared all the rugs, and then I wake woke up and then I I was . . . went into living room and there's something I didn't ask her and and then she I didn't want and watched and watched cartoons. I watched this, I watched, I did, when we got home I watched I watched TV um "Sesame Street." That's the end.

This is a story in the sense that it is what my daughter told when she was asked to tell a story. But obviously she has just recapped the day's experiences. By age four, Hana could really invent a new story. The story itself is invented in the sense that it didn't happen as such, but each individual event in the story did happen. Hana had experienced it all before; she just adapted the events for her use here. We lose coherence here because Hana hasn't yet learned standard coherent story forms that an adult might know. Other than that, though, the process of story creation is remarkably similar to the adult process.

PAPA: Tell me a story.

HANA: Once upon a time there was a little girl and she lived with her mother and father in a big house, not an apartment house, and she was born in California. She has her own passport, her brother has a passport, too. Everyone has a passport, you know that, 'cause they have to have passports for special reasons. They went out to London and they had a good time there. They went riding on horses and they had real good times. They played. They brang lots of toys to play with, even books. Well, books are not such things to play with, you read them. And so then they went out, and then they saw a rabbit and they said hi to the rabbit, and then they said would the rabbit be their pet. But the rabbit said it couldn't be their pet and then they came up to a kitten. They said to the kitten, "Could we have a kitten?" And then, after they had the kitten for their own, then they named it, Joan, Joe, and then they walked on. The kitten was almost in danger. It got struck by a big wolf came and almost tried to bite it and then eat it, but it finally chased the wolf out and Mama and Papa got danger, Hana helped, Joshua was too little, he just said "ah da" to the wolf. And then they came up to a great forest, they had lots of pine trees. And then they came up something shiny with bright eyes, another kitten, instead it was a mother. And so, they took good care of the two kittens and then rode back to where they were, and got, and then went to sleep, and often got dressed the next morning and went out to have their breakfast. They had Chinese breakfast, but Hana in case didn't bring the cat and left it outside by mistake, and Mama and Daddy, locked it in a cage. It was barking the next day, and meowing the next day, and then, away from danger, they saw balloons and then one bursted the balloon and then they got all the rest of the balloons. They had all the money that they needed for to buy a balloon. It was free. They didn't know that, so they paid some money. And then they got all the money that they paid. And then they went home to their own real house and wrote down that they had a good time and sended it to someone and everyone got a chance to read that. And then they had such good time, they had a jolly time here and from all you, this is telling the story. That's the end.

Story invention, for children or adults, is a process of the massaging of reality. How reality is massaged, how old stories are transformed into new ones, depends upon the goals of the teller. If the teller has something to hide, a fantasy to express, a political point to make, whatever, the original story can be changed in a variety of ways. Invention is not a process that comes from nowhere.

FIRSTHAND STORIES

People tell about their own experiences all the time, but they do not necessarily tell about the same experience in the same way every time. The telling process, even in the relating of a firsthand experience, can be a highly inventive process. That is, the art of storytelling involves finding good ways to express one's experiences in a way appropriate to the listener. A fine line exists, therefore, between invented stories and the relation of firsthand experiences. The entertainment factor exists in relating first-hand experiences just as it does in inventing stories. Nobody wants to listen to what happened to you today unless you can make what happened appear interesting. The process of livening up an experience can involve simply telling that experience in such a way as to eliminate the dullest parts, or it also can involve "jacking up" the dull parts by playing with the facts.

Firsthand experiential stories are the type of stories we talk about most. They represent our own personal experiences. Some of these experiences have been digested and analyzed so that we know their point or points and are reminded of them when those points come up. But many firsthand stories come up because of random associations, and many have no intended point; they are just stories about ourselves which have not necessarily been fully understood and from which no conclusions may have yet been drawn. Or more often firsthand stories are told because they relate information that is nonstandard in some way. We don't tell about experiences that we believe everyone else has also had. We tell about what we believe to be unusual. The more usual such an experience is, the less we want to tell about it. Good stories are about things that are unusual and could not have easily been predicted.

SECONDHAND STORIES

Secondhand stories are acquired secondhand. We often tell the stories of others. Telling secondhand experiences tends to be a much more straightforward process than telling firsthand stories, because the task is mostly an attempt at proper recall of the facts as they were heard. The problem, of course, is that we can't recall all the facts, even when the event being related is firsthand, much less when it is second-hand. Here again, "facts" are made up as needed to preserve coherence, although tellers may not actually be aware that they are making up part of the story. The parlor game of telephone relies upon the inability of people to recall and to relate properly what they have just heard.

Secondhand experiential stories are simply the firsthand stories of others that we have heard and remembered. Usually the indices to them are much less rich, much more specific. These stories often have clear points and are frequently remembered in terms of the points that they are intended to illustrate.

CULTURALLY COMMON STORIES

The culturally common story is not as obvious a category as the other four. We get culturally common stories from our environment. No one person tells them, and no one person makes them up. They are pervasive nevertheless. Below are two examples of culturally common stories, again taken from a movie, this time *Casablanca:*

YVONNE:	Will I see you tonight?
RICK:	I never make plans that far ahead.
CAPTAIN RENAULT:	And what in heaven's name brought you to Casablanca?
RICK:	My health. I came to Casablanca for the waters.
RENAULT:	Waters? What waters? We're in the desert.
RICK:	I was misinformed.

Both of the above statements by Rick are stories. Obviously, they are not your usual kind of story and to all outward appearances seem to be merely tag lines that are meant to be funny. But the reason one can speak in such a shorthand and humorous way and be understood not only by one's listener but also by a movie audience is that both statements are simply cryptic ways of referring to well-known stories, stories that the movie writers, in this instance, are assuming their audience knows.

Culturally common stories are usually referred to rather than told. For example, the following one-liner from the Woody Allen movie *Love and Death* is a reference to stories that we all know about insurance salesmen:

> *There are worse things in life than death—If you have ever spent an evening with an insurance salesman, you know what I mean.*

The commonality of our culture's views of insurance salesmen allows us to communicate in this way about insurance salesmen. The culturally common story here is simply that insurance salesmen are boring and painful to listen to.

To a large extent, a story's usefulness depends upon how much of the original detail has remained over time. An ossified story is useful as a rule applicable to many specific situations but not to all the situations which in its original form it might have been. A story still present in its full form in memory can be applied to a variety of situations but not necessarily as widely as a distilled story. Memory richness versus memory succinctness is a trade-off between multiple labels, or ways of referring to a story, with general applicability and few labels with specific applicability.

On the other hand, distilling a story sufficiently gives back its general applicability. A proverb is an ossified distilled story, but it has lost so much of its original detail that it needs the hearer to supply some detail. Thus a proverb can be seen to carry with it great wisdom because the hearer has supplied the specific referents to the general frame which is the proverb. This is the case with the *I Ching*, a collection of ossified distilled stories that seem to contain great wisdom when one adds one's own details. The following, a comment on the Hsu hexagram, is a passage from the *I Ching*:

2. The second line, undivided, shows its subject waiting on the sand (of the mountain stream). He will (suffer) the small (injury of) being spoken (against), but in the end there will be good fortune.

3. The third line, undivided, shows its subject in mud (close by the stream). He thereby invites the approach of injury.

4. The fourth line, divided, shows its subject waiting in (the place of) blood. But he will get out of the cavern.

In some sense, much of what we consider to be creativity is no more than the adaptation of a story from one domain for use in another. Taking a neutral story and adding detail can also be considered to be creative; indeed, many new stories for television are written in precisely this way. We are also creative when we understand the stories of others by adding details of our own lives that allow us to read more into a story than may have been put there by the author. In each case, the story adapted from the original is now a story in its own right and can be stored in memory with new indices.

The opposite side of the coin is that some stories get told in their least detailed form, making them understandable only to those who already know them. Such stories can become so short that they do not in any way appear to be stories, and in some obvious sense, they are not stories. Maybe the best way to illustrate what I mean here is by a well-known joke.

The prisoners in a maximum-security prison had little to entertain themselves with so they told jokes to each other. But they had long since run out of new jokes to tell, so they simply numbered the jokes and yelled out the numbers. A new prisoner hearing "forty-two," "sixty-four," "one hundred eight" being yelled down the hall with raucous laughter following each number asked about what was happening, and it was explained to him. He asked if he could try it, and his cellmate said sure. He hollered "thirty-six," and nothing happened. Next he tried "twenty-seven" and still nothing. The new prisoner finally asked his cellmate what was wrong, and he replied, "You didn't tell them so well."

Is "forty-two" a story? Of course it is, and it isn't. It doesn't sound like a story; it's more the name of a story, so to speak. In some sense, every story is simply the name of a longer story. No one tells all the details of any story, so each story is shortened. How much shortening has to take place until there is no story left? A story shortened so that it ceases to be understood is no longer a story, but what is understandable to one person may not be understandable to another, so it is clear that "story" is a relative term. In any case, as long as it *is* understood, it remains a story. For this reason, there are some very short stories.

One of my favorite short stories comes from the movie *Manhattan*:

YALE: She's gorgeous.

ISAAC: She's seventeen. I'm forty-two, and she's seventeen.

More needn't be said here because the point has been made without saying more. We all know stories or can imagine stories involving the complexity of a relationship between a forty-two-year-old man and a seventeen-year-old girl. Of course, the movie goes on to tell exactly that story. The referent here is to a story we all know which then serves as the basis for the new story we are about to hear.

Why We Tell Stories

People can be viewed in some sense as repositories of stories. Old people most obviously tell the same story again and again, but many people have a number of stories to tell and take the occasion to tell them whenever that opportunity arises. When we look at particular stories, we can think about the points that they express and attempt to understand why a given story may have come to mind at any specific point in a conversation, but particular stories don't really matter. The issue here is why do we tell stories at all? What is interesting about stories? What is the point of telling a story instead of just saying what we want to say directly? In order to understand why we tell stories, we must identify the goals that people have in a conversation. Because stories are usually told to someone and not to an empty room, no story commonly satisfies only one goal. Rather, tellers may have one goal for themselves and another goal for their listeners.

In broad terms, then, we usually have one of three basic reasons for telling stories. First, we may derive some satisfaction from telling a story. Second, we may derive satisfaction from the effect we believe, or convince ourselves to believe, that a story will have on our listener. Or third, we sometimes tell a story because of the effect we believe that the story will have on the conversation itself. We can categorize our intentions in storytelling as follows:

Category 1: Me-goals (the intentions that storytellers have with respect to themselves)

Category 2: You-goals (the intentions that storytellers have with respect to others)

Category 3: Conversational goals (the intentions that storytellers have with respect to the conversation itself)

ME-GOALS

The first category, me-goals, includes our intentions in telling stories to satisfy our own personal goals. When we tell stories to others, we often do so entirely because of our own goals for ourselves that are satisfied by the listener paying attention in the desired way. Tellers can have five intentions with respect to themselves: to achieve catharsis, to get attention, to win approval, to seek advice, or to describe themselves. Several intentions are frequently present at once. For example, imagine a man at a party where he sees a woman he wants to meet. He begins to tell a story that is designed immediately to get the attention of the group he is talking to and ultimately to get the woman's approval for his being sensitive. The story he chooses is self-descriptive and tells about a horrible situation that allows him to become emotional in the telling. As a result of telling the story, he feels better, but, more important, the woman in the group notices him, likes his emotional qualities, and feels that she can tell him something that will help him in his predicament. We can see that the teller's intentions fall into all categories.

In the following scene from the movie *The Apartment,* a character tells a story to prevent herself from committing suicide on Christmas. Her intention, in other words, is cathartic:

> *I think I'm going to give it all up. Why do people have to love people, anyway? I don't want it. What do you call it when somebody keeps getting smashed up in automobile accidents? That's me with men. I've been jinxed from the word go— first time I was ever kissed was in a cemetery. I was fifteen—we used to go there to smoke. His name was George—he threw me over for a drum majorette. I just have this talent for falling in love with the wrong guy in the wrong place at the wrong time. The last one was manager of a finance company, back home in Pittsburgh—they found a little shortage in his accounts, but he asked me to wait for him—he'll be out in 1965. So I came to New York and moved in with my sister and her husband—he drives a cab. They sent me to secretarial school, and I applied for a job with Consolidated—but I flunked the typing test—oh, I can type up a storm, but I can't spell. So they gave me a pair of white gloves and stuck me in an elevator—that's how I met Jeff—Oh, God, I'm so fouled up. What am I going to do now? Maybe he does love me—only he doesn't have the nerve to tell his wife.*

The teller of this story needs to explain why she has reached an emotional crisis and doesn't seem especially interested in how the listener feels about what she says. Of course, we can't know for sure what her attitude toward the listener is. She may intend to elicit an emotional response from him, and his reaction to her, if sympathetic, may affect how successfully cathartic the telling of her story is. But either way, telling her story attempts to accomplish the hoped-for catharsis.

In response to her story, the listener offers a story of his own which falls not into the me-goals but into the you-goals category, a story told to have an effect on someone else. He tells the story seemingly to display some kind of feeling—"We are in this together"—for the teller of the original story:

I know how you feel, Miss Kubelik. You think it's the end of the world—but it's not, really. I went through exactly the same thing myself. Well, maybe not exactly—I tried to do it with a gun. She was the wife of my best friend, and I was mad for her. But I knew it was hopeless—so I decided to end it all. I went to a pawnshop and bought a .45 automatic and drove up to Eden Park—do you know Cincinnati? Anyway, I parked the car and loaded the gun—well, you read in the papers all the time that people shoot themselves, but believe me, it's not that easy—I mean, how do you do it? Here or here or here [with cocked finger, he points to his temple, mouth, and chest]. You know where I finally shot myself? [Indicates knee.] Here. While I was sitting there, trying to make my mind up, a cop stuck his head in the car, because I was illegally parked—so I started to hide the gun under the seat, and it went off—pow! Took me a year before I could bend my knee—but I got over the girl in three weeks. She still lives in Cincinnati, has four kids, gained twenty pounds—she—Here's the fruitcake. [Shows it to her under Christmas tree.] And you want to see my knee?

Within the me-goal category, we also tell stories expressly to get attention. One way to grab attention is to tell stories that will interest the group one is involved with at the moment. The teller of attention-getting stories often wants to impress listeners as being very funny or sympathetic or honest or powerful, etc. The teller may have the allied intention of entertaining the listener so that the teller can continue telling stories and thus remain the center of attention. In the following story from Tennessee Williams's *The Glass Menagerie*, a woman tries to win the approval of a gentleman caller and in the process draw attention to the virtues of her exceedingly shy daughter:

It's rare for a girl as sweet an' pretty as Laura to be domestic! But Laura is, thank heavens, not only pretty but also very domestic. I'm not at all. I never was a bit. I never could make a thing but angel food cake. Well, in the South we had so many servants. Gone, gone, gone. All vestige of gracious living! Gone completely! I wasn't prepared for what the future brought me. All of my gentlemen callers were sons of planters and so of course I assumed that I would be married to one and raise my family on a large piece of land with plenty of servants. But man proposes—and woman accepts the proposal! To vary that old saying a little bit—I married no planter! I married a man who worked for the telephone company! That gallantly smiling gentleman over there! . . . A telephone man who fell in love with long-distance! Now he travels and I don't even know where!

We tell stories to describe ourselves not only so others can understand who we are but also so we can understand ourselves. Telling our stories allows us to compile our personal mythology, and the collection of stories we have compiled is to some extent who we are, what we have to say about the world, and tells the world the state of our mental health.

To some extent, our stories, because they are shaped by memory processes that do not always have their basis in hard fact, are all fictions. But these fictions are based on real experiences and are our only avenue to those experiences. We interpret reality through our stories and open our realities up to others when we tell our stories. We can also tell stories to escape reality, to paint a picture that is more like what we would like to have happened than what actually happened. But, it should be understood, this is to some extent what we do all the time with stories. The extent to which we can stretch reality and still be considered mentally healthy is not all that clear.

Our intentions in telling self-descriptive stories are often complex. Our goals with respect to ourselves and to others are sometimes complementary and sometimes contradictory. One might, for example, tell a story hoping to rekindle a friendship in the eyes of another but in reality attempting to manipulate the other for personal gain.

Because telling a self-descriptive story often satisfies at least two goals, me-goals and you-goals, and often the conversational-goal as well, the self-descriptive prototype is both common and important. People have a great many things to say about themselves for a great many reasons and thus have many stories to illustrate various aspects of their personalities, their points of view, and their hopes and their problems. As we saw in the story sequence from *The Apartment,* the description of the woman's problem reminded her listener of a similar problem in his own life. His quickness in telling the story suggests that he has told the story before. People love to match stories, communicating by having similar experiences to relate. For this reason, we tend to tell the same stories over and over until we fashion a stock story which illustrates a point about ourselves effectively. The man, however, also intended to make a further point to the woman about the resilience of human beings and thus to prevent her suicide.

In the following story from *Long Day's Journey into Night,* a man tries to justify choosing a low-cost state sanitarium for his ill son by recounting events from his own childhood that shaped his character. Again, his story seems to be well rehearsed to illustrate a basic point about himself:

We never had clothes enough to wear, nor food enough to eat. Well, I remember one Thanksgiving, or maybe it was Christmas, when some Yank in whose house Mother had been scrubbing gave her a dollar extra for a present, and on the way home she spent it all on food. . . . It was in those days I learned to be a miser. A dollar was worth so much then. And once you've learned a lesson, it's hard to unlearn it. You have to look for bargains. If I took this state farm sanitarium for a good bargain, you'll have to forgive me. The doctors did tell me it's a good place.

Another example, but much shorter, of telling a stock story to describe oneself occurs in the movie *A Thousand Clowns:*

MURRAY: You're going to have to stop crying.

SANDRA: I cry all the time, and I laugh at the wrong places in the movies.

The story—crying all the time, laughing at the wrong places in the movies—is an example of a personal myth derived from our experiences and confirmed again in the telling. Here, the story has been reduced again and again until only its essential message remains.

The next story from *All the President's Men* is another example of a self-descriptive narrative. Woodward and Bernstein are in their car, parked outside the house of yet another CREEP employee on their list. The frustrations of working for a newspaper are getting to Bernstein. He attempts to make sense of his present work by remembering an incident early on in his career:

> *My first day as a copyboy I was sixteen and wearing my only grown-up suit—it was cream colored. At two-thirty, the head copyboy comes running up to me and says, "My God, haven't you washed the carbon paper yet? If it's not washed by three, it'll never be dry for tomorrow." And I said, "Am I supposed to do that?" and he said, "Absolutely, it's crucial." So I run around and grab all the carbon paper from all the desks and take it to the men's room. I'm standing there washing it, and it's splashing all over me, and the editor comes in to take a leak, and he says, "What the fuck do you think you're doing?" And I said, "It's two-thirty. I'm washing the carbon paper."*
>
> *I'm beginning to feel like I never stopped.*

We also acquire personal myths from our parents, teachers, friends, enemies—in short, from anyone who tells us stories about ourselves. Listening to and telling these stories has an effect on memory which makes it almost impossible not to believe the stories that describe who we are. The following stories are examples of self-descriptive myths initiated by other family members; thus, the process of telling begins with a you-goal intention, and the retelling involves the me-goal intention. In the first example from Elizabeth Stone's *Black Sheep and Kissing Cousins*, Peter Mott, a nuclear physicist, attempts to explain why he and his sister defined themselves according to their mother's story.

> *My mother's father, whom she always saw as a comforter, had died. . . . Then her two sisters died—one of scarlet fever and the other of spilling boiling water on herself. Then my grandmother, my mother's mother, died of a heart attack. My mother was pregnant with my sister at this time, and so they named my sister Blanche, which had been my grandmother's name. In fact my grandmother's maiden name was Kane, and they named my sister Blanche Kane Mott. . . . My mother was in terrible shape. . . . She was hospitalized—she had a nervous breakdown—and there was a nursemaid to take care of my sister. . . . My mother could never bring herself to use the name Blanche with my sister, so she called her Missy.*

It was just too much, the death was too much and the daughter was too much. Perhaps my sister was just too much of a reminder. But anyhow, my sister was the one in the family who could do nothing right. As a consequence, she was raised as if she were dirt, or incompetent, or terrible. Growing up, I didn't consciously recognize how my sister was being devalued, but one of the most extraordinary aspects of all this family stuff is that for most of my adult life, I dealt with my sister as my mother had dealt with her. As for me . . . I was "the Golden Boy." The doctor told my mother to have another child to make her well. I was that child, and I could do no wrong.

In the following passage from *The Pawnbroker*, the narrator tells a story about himself, but he also has a conversational goal in telling the story—to respond to a question. Sol Nazerman has been a survivor of the death camps for twenty years. His wife and children died at Auschwitz. Before the war, he was a professor at the University of Cracow, but now he runs a pawnshop in Spanish Harlem. One evening, his apprentice asks Sol, "How come you people come to business so naturally?" Sol responds:

You begin . . . you begin with several thousand years during which you have nothing except a great bearded legend. Nothing else. You have not land to grow food on. No land on which to hunt. Not enough time in one place to have a geography, or an army, or a land-myth. You have only a little brain in your head and this bearded legend to sustain you . . . convince you there is something special about you, even in your poverty. But this little brain . . . that is the real key. With it you obtain a small piece of cloth, wool, silk, cotton—it doesn't matter. You take this cloth, and you cut it in two and sell the two pieces for a penny or two more than you paid for the one. With this money, then, you buy a slightly larger piece of cloth. Which perhaps may be cut into three pieces. And sold for three pennies profit. You must never succumb to buying an extra piece of bread at this point. Or a toy for your child. Immediately you must repeat the process. And so you continue until there is no longer any temptation to dig in the earth and grow food. No longer any desire to gaze at limitless land which is in your name. You repeat this process over and over for centuries. And then, all of a sudden, you discover you have a mercantile heritage. You are known as a merchant. You're also known as a man with secret resources, usurer, pawnbroker, a witch, or what have you.
But by then it is instinct. Do you understand?

We tell stories like this in order to express our feelings, to get out our anger, or to explain ourselves in some fundamental way. These stories become who we are and telling them allows us to feel these feelings that define us yet again. We avoid telling stories that evoke feelings that we do not care to relive.

YOU-GOALS

Obviously, the above story contains many unspoken stories, but unspoken stories, as other survivors of Auschwitz have testified, change substantively in memory or disappear altogether. The survivors of the Holocaust tell stories to preserve their memories for themselves and for their listeners. Their intentions in recounting what happened to them at the hands of the Nazis fall within both the me-goal and the you-goal categories.

As we have already seen, when we tell stories about ourselves our goals are often internal and difficult to determine, but when we tell stories intended for other people our goals tend to fall within five categories:

> to illustrate a point
> to make the listener feel some way or another
> to tell a story that transports the listener
> to transfer some piece of information in our head into the head of the
>   listener
> to summarize significant events

Most stories have a point, or at least are supposed to have one. What exactly a point is, is difficult to define, but we know when one is missing. In such cases, we ask *What's your point?* We tell stories, then, to illustrate points we wish to make or to help listeners achieve their goals. In an essay in which he reflects on the costs of personal success, Tennessee Williams illustrates his point with a story.

> *I lived on room service. But in this, too, there was disenchantment. Sometime between the moment when I ordered dinner over the phone and when it was rolled into my living room like a corpse on a rubber-wheeled table, I lost all interest in it. Once I ordered a sirloin steak and a chocolate sundae, but everything was so cunningly disguised on the table that I mistook the chocolate sauce for gravy and poured it over the sirloin steak. . . .*
>
> *I got so sick of hearing people say, "I loved your play!" that I could not say thank you anymore. I choked on the words and turned rudely away from the usually sincere person. I no longer felt any pride in the play itself but began to dislike it, probably because I felt too lifeless inside ever to create another. . . .*
>
> *This curious condition persisted about three months, till late spring, when I decided to have another eye operation mainly because of the excuse it gave me to withdraw from the world behind a gauze mask. . . .*
>
> *Well, the gauze mask served a purpose. While I was resting in the hospital the friends whom I had neglected or affronted in one way or another began to call on me and now that I was in pain and darkness, their voices seemed to have changed. . . .*

When the gauze mask was removed, I found myself in a readjusted world. I checked out of the handsome suite at the first-class hotel, packed my papers and a few incidental belongings, and left for Mexico, an elemental country where you can quickly forget the false dignities and conceits imposed by success, a country where vagrants innocent as children curl up to sleep on the pavements and human voices, especially when their language is not familiar to the ear, are soft as birds'. My public self, that artifice of mirrors, did not exist here and so my natural being was resumed.

A second reason for telling stories with you-goals is to make the listener feel some way or other, in other words, to tell an affective story. Trying to get someone to fall in love with you or to make a special exception in your pathetic case or simply to feel better is typical of the affective intention. We can, of course, have goals for both ourselves and others in a story we tell; sometimes the distinction can be confusing. However, stories that are intended to make somebody feel something are very common and very important. They may also make the teller feel something as well, often unintentionally.

In a passage from *Below the Line,* the narrator recalls telling an affective story that failed to achieve the effect he wanted:

One day—this is how I got in the worst trouble—my baby was crying. We didn't have no money, no food, so I went to the grocery store. I told the owner—he knew that I had boughten there before—I told the owner, I was crying, I told him, "Please can you do me a favor, give me a dozen eggs, a loaf of bread, a gallon of milk, and I'll pay you back in the morning." He told me no. So I went back home and I took out my gun and I went back. I said, "Now give it to me." Then I went back home. Within fifteen minutes they locked me up, but I didn't care. I did it for my kids.

For reasons similar to telling affective stories, we tell transportive stories to make others experience certain sensations, feelings, or attitudes vicariously. One way to achieve this effect is to be clever enough in our descriptive capabilities in order to make listeners come to view the scene the way we want them to. Usually, we have some additional purpose in mind when we tell a transportive story; nevertheless, stories are so often heavily laden with description of a transportive nature, we should recognize the transportive intention independently of other motivations. In the play *That Championship Season,* a high school basketball team gets together for a reunion with their old coach. The coach reminisces:

You were a rare and a beautiful thing, boys . . . a miracle to see people play beautifully together . . . like when I was a boy . . . long time past . . . the whole town would come together. We'd have these huge picnics, great feasts of picnics. My father ran the only bank in town. An elegant man. Bach was played in his house. He quoted Shakespeare, "To be or not to be, that's the question." Shoulders like a king . . . he carried me on his back into the freezing, God, yes, waters of the lake. So clear you could see the white pebbles on the bottom. Gone now, all gone, vanished. Lake, picnic grounds, gone now. All concrete and wires and glass now. Used car lots now. Phil's trucks came and took it away. . . . Jesus, I can still see buckets of ice cream . . . great red slabs of beef . . . kites, yes, the sky full of blue and red kites, men playing horseshoes, big silver pails of beer, in the late afternoon the men would dive from the high rocks, so high they made you dizzy to look down. I watched my father dive and turn and glisten in the sun, falling like a bird falls, and knife the water so clean as to leave only ripples.

We have similar intentions in telling stories that summarize significant events, i.e., historical synopses, and in telling stories that transfer information. Tellers want their listeners to know whatever it is they are telling them. Teachers want their students to know certain information; parents want children to know how to behave, how to play safely, etc.; and people who are talking to one another want their friends and associates to know about their lives or about various events in the world. All of them want to transfer some piece of knowledge in their heads into the heads of their listeners. Historical synopsis is a special case of transfer where the teller must reduce a tremendous amount of information into a form small enough to be absorbed.

CONVERSATIONAL GOALS

The above stories have been relayed without the context of a surrounding conversation. When we tell stories within a conversation, the goals that need to be satisfied are more complex. The following set of intentions, unlike the others we have discussed, has nothing to do with the content of the conversation. People do not always speak to communicate some specific piece of information or remark. Sometimes we speak solely to keep on being able to speak or simply to get the general topic of the story on the floor for discussion. For example, we might tell a story about a problem in a particular relationship if we wanted to discuss relationships in general. Our intention, then, would be *topic opening*. On the other hand, we might open a new topic in order to close off or avoid another; in this case, our intention would be *topic changing*. We also tell stories to revive conversation. For example, in airplanes two people seated next to each other often tell stories for the sole purpose of having something to do during the flight. When the conversation bogs down, one of the speakers will tell a story to *continue* the conversation. So that the conversational partner won't go away or talk to someone else, often the speaker tells a story just to keep the conversation going.

A more significant but still in essence structural part of the story-telling process in a conversation involves the relationship that exists between the partners in a conversation. When someone tells a story, he or she expects conversational politeness, a response of some sort. Therefore, when you tell a story in turn, you may have no point in mind other than to be *responsive.*

One of the goals of history synopsis is often conversational as well. Above, we saw an example of history synopsis told to satisfy the you-goals, but often these stories are responses to direct requests for stories, rather than spontaneous remindings. When we ask certain questions, we expect stories as answers. We associate stories with life events such as the story of our choosing a college, the story of our first job, the story of the birth of our child, the story of our first love, and the story of our marriage. Since these stories have usually been told many times, they often have rehearsed and well-planned versions. Sometimes we get the whole story, and sometimes we get partial or cryptic stories. Below is an example from *Manhattan* of a cryptic yet revealing shorthand depiction of an obviously much larger history.

MARY: Why did you get divorced?

ISAAC: My wife left me for another woman.

Another category of responsive story is the argument. When you tell a story that implies something is wrong with yourself, you may hope for a story that disputes your point. Sometimes, you make an assertion, however, without intending to stir an *argumentative* response but do so anyway. Of course, not all arguments are unfriendly; mutual storytelling, even in the form of an argument, can make the storytellers feel closer to each other.

Stories can also be used as a defense. Sometimes we tell a story to *distract* our listeners from what they want to discuss. Many times we tell stories to avoid whatever it is we should be talking about, as a defense against what other people are liable to say. We distract our conversational partners by giving them a range of other things to think about. Such stories are often made up on the fly, but sometimes they have been previously constructed and are retrieved because they relate superficially to the question at hand. The goal of such a story is to avoid telling a different story. The reasons for distraction/obfuscation may be as simple as maintaining conversational sociability to avoid an argument or a painful or perhaps embarrassing subject. Obversely, the reason may be psychologically complex. Someone with a checkered past might obfuscate when relating certain experiences if fearful of losing a friendship. Similarly, we may obfuscate to protect a family member or ourselves if we perceive a question as a threat. An example of this kind of story from *A Thousand Clowns* follows. In this story, Murray tells a joke to avoid being sad about something else, to avoid telling the story he should be telling:

SANDRA: Which job did you get?

MURRAY: I shall now leave you breathless with this strange and wondrous tale of this sturdy lad's adventures today in downtown Oz. Picture if you will, me. I am walking on East Fifty-first Street about an hour ago practicing how to say "I am sorry" with a little style.

SANDRA: Sorry about what?

MURRAY: Oh, not for anything—just rehearsing, you know how you are walking down the street talking to yourself, and suddenly you say something to yourself out loud? So I said: "I'm sorry"—and this fellow walking by, a complete stranger, said: "That's all right, Mac," and goes right on. He immediately forgave me. Now five o'clock rush hour in midtown, you could say "Sir, your hair is on fire," and they wouldn't even hear you. So I decided to test the whole thing out scientifically. I just stood there saying "I'm sorry" to everyone who came by. . . . Of course I got a few funny looks—but seventy-five percent of them forgave me. . . . I could run up on the roof right now, and I would say I'm sorry and a half a million people would say, "That's OK, just see that you don't do it again."

SANDRA: You didn't take any of the jobs.

MURRAY: I'm sorry. I'm very sorry. Damn it, lady, that was a beautiful apology. You got to love a guy who apologizes so well. I rehearsed it. Oh, Sandy, that's the most you should expect from life—a really good apology for all the things you won't get.

Conclusion

The various combinations of our intentions affect the processes that transform the gists of the stories that we have in our memories into the actual stories that we tell. We don't remember the stories that we tell or hear, in the sense that we cannot recall all the words. We extract gists when we listen to stories, and we recast gists when we transform them into actual stories. These memory processes—extraction of gists from stories for storage in memory and transformation of gists into stories that express an intention—are fundamental to the thinking process. How these processes work is the subject of later chapters.

I might add that the most you can expect from an intelligent being is a really good story. To get human beings to be intelligent means getting them to have stories to tell and having them hear and perhaps use the stories of others. Now, by stories here, recall that I mean having a set of interesting things that one has already thought up and stored, ready to say when necessary. There are other aspects to intelligence that come into play to finish the process to make something that is intelligent seem very intelligent. The first is storytelling ability. How a story is told greatly affects the receptivity of the listener. Good storytellers will make their stories seem interesting and that interestingness makes the stories more memorable and hence more useful to an understander. Good storytellers cause positive responses in their listeners. Thus, good storytellers seem very intelligent.

But intelligence is also manifest in the content of what one has to say. And new content, innovative ideas are seen by listeners as marking intelligence as well. We like inventive stories, even when told badly, because their new content excites us, and we deem the tellers of those stories to be intelligent as well.

Whatever the reason for telling a story, and whatever the origin of the content of the story, the concept here is a rather simple one. Intelligence means having stories to tell. If those stories are told well or are innovative in some way, so much the better, but a being must have a set of stories and tell them for the right reasons at the right time in order to be intelligent.

It would seem, then, that the cliché "Experience is the best teacher" is quite true. We learn from experience, or to put this more strongly, what we learn *are* experiences. The educational point that follows from this is that we must teach cases and the adaptation of cases by telling stories, not teach rules and the use of rules by citing rules. We may never find ourselves in a situation where the rules we were taught apply exactly. Ordinarily, we find answers for ourselves. Lots of stories and cases help, but methods of applying these stories and cases, especially in places where they weren't originally supposed to apply, help more.

 ### *For Discussion:*

1. What is a story? What isn't a story? What marks the boundary between a story and some other form of communicating information? Is there another form of communicating information?
2. What are some official stories you know? Do you remember learning them? How much of what you know about the world comes through official stories?
3. Is Schank right when he says, "Intelligence means having stories to tell"?

 ### *For Fact-Finding, Research, and Writing:*

1. Find two news stories on the same topic from opposing newspapers (for example, newspapers from different countries who oppose each other's policies). In what ways are stories used to support different interpretations of the event in question?
2. What does the progress between Hana's storytelling ability at age two and age four suggest about how we learn? Using an academic database, list two articles that deal with the importance of storytelling ability to cognitive development.
3. Research the differences and similarities between the use of storytelling in psychological therapy and storytelling as it is practiced on television talk shows.

4. Can storytelling occur in Artificial Intelligence? Find at least two other selections in this reader that suggest an answer to this question.

Howard Gardner, "A Rounded Version: The Theory of Multiple Intelligences"

Howard Gardner is the John H. and Elisabeth A. Hobbs Professor in Cognition and Education at the Harvard Graduate School of Education. Gardner has received numerous awards, including a MacArthur Prize Fellowship in 1981, the Grawemeyer Award in Education in 1990, and a Guggenheim Fellowship in 2000. The author of numerous books and articles, Gardner is best known for his theory of multiple intelligences. This theory, first published in *Frames of Mind* (1983), critiques the notion of a single intelligence that is measurable through standard testing, such as the intelligence quotient (IQ) test. This selection is excerpted from *Multiple Intelligences* (1993).

 Before You Read:

How do you define intelligence? How many different kinds of intelligences or ways of knowing can you categorize?

A Rounded Version: The Theory of Multiple Intelligences

Howard Gardner

TWO ELEVEN-YEAR-OLD children are taking a test of "intelligence." They sit at their desks laboring over the meanings of different words, the interpretation of graphs, and the solutions to arithmetic problems. They record their answers by filling in small circles on a single piece of paper. Later these completed answer sheets are scored objectively: the number of right answers is converted into a standardized score that compares the individual child with a population of children of similar age.

The teachers of these children review the different scores. They notice that one of the children has performed at a superior level; on all sections of the test, she answered more questions correctly than did her peers. In fact, her score is similar to that of children three to four years older. The other child's performance is average—his scores reflect those of other children his age.

A subtle change in expectations surrounds the review of these test scores. Teachers begin to expect the first child to do quite well during her formal schooling, whereas the second should have only moderate success. Indeed these predictions come true. In other words, the test taken by the eleven-year-olds serves as a reliable predictor of their later performance in school.

How does this happen? One explanation involves our free use of the word "intelligence": the child with the greater "intelligence" has the ability to solve problems, to find the answers to specific questions, and to learn new material quickly and efficiently. These skills in turn play a central role in school success. In this view, "intelligence" is a singular faculty that is brought to bear in any problem-solving situation. Since schooling deals largely with solving problems of various sorts, predicting this capacity in young children predicts their future success in school.

"Intelligence," from this point of view, is a general ability that is found in varying degrees in all individuals. It is the key to success in solving problems. This ability can be measured reliably with standardized pencil-and-paper tests that, in turn, predict future success in school.

What happens after school is completed? Consider the two individuals in the example. Looking further down the road, we find that the "average" student has become a highly successful mechanical engineer who has risen to a position of prominence in both the professional community of engineers as well as in civic groups in his community. His success is no fluke—he is considered by all to be a talented individual. The "superior" student, on the other hand, has had little success in her chosen career as a writer; after repeated rejections by publishers, she has taken up a middle management position in a bank. While certainly not a "failure," she is considered by her peers to be quite "ordinary" in her adult accomplishments. So what happened?

This fabricated example is based on the facts of intelligence testing. IQ tests predict school performance with considerable accuracy, but they are only an indifferent predictor of performance in a profession after formal schooling.[1] Furthermore, even as IQ tests measure only logical or logical-linguistic capacities, in this society we are nearly "brain-washed" to restrict the notion of intelligence to the capacities used in solving logical and linguistic problems.

To introduce an alternative point of view, undertake the following "thought experiment." Suspend the usual judgment of what constitutes intelligence and let your thoughts run freely over the capabilities of humans—perhaps those that would be picked out by the proverbial Martian visitor. In this exercise, you are drawn to the brilliant chess player, the world-class violinist, and the champion athlete; such outstanding performers deserve special consideration. Under this experiment, a quite different view of *intelligence* emerges. Are the chess player, violinist, and athlete "intelligent" in these pursuits? If they are, then why do our tests of "intelligence" fail to identify them? If they are not "intelligent," what allows them to achieve such astounding feats? In general, why does the contemporary construct "intelligence" fail to explain large areas of human endeavor?

In this chapter we approach these problems through the theory of multiple intelligences (MI). As the name indicates, we believe that human cognitive competence is better described in terms of a set of abilities, talents, or mental skills, which we call "intelligences." All normal individuals possess each of these skills to some extent; individuals differ in the degree of skill and in the nature of their combination. We believe this theory of intelligence may be more humane and more veridical than alternative views of intelligence and that it more adequately reflects the data of human "intelligent" behavior. Such a theory has important educational implications, including ones for curriculum development.

What Constitutes an Intelligence?

The question of the optimal definition of intelligence looms large in our inquiry. Indeed, it is at the level of this definition that the theory of multiple intelligences diverges from traditional points of view. In a traditional view, intelligence is defined operationally as the ability to answer items on tests of intelligence. The inference from the test scores to some underlying ability is supported by statistical techniques that compare responses of subjects at different ages; the apparent correlation of these test scores across ages and across different tests corroborates the notion that the general faculty of intelligence, g, does not change much with age or with training or experience. It is an inborn attribute or faculty of the individual.

Multiple intelligences theory, on the other hand, pluralizes the traditional concept. An intelligence entails the ability to solve problems or fashion products that are of consequence in a particular cultural setting or community. The problem-solving skill allows one to approach a situation in which a goal is to be obtained and to locate the appropriate route to that goal. The creation of a *cultural* product is crucial to such functions as capturing and transmitting knowledge or expressing one's views or feelings. The problems to be solved range from creating an end for a story to anticipating a mating move in chess to repairing a quilt. Products range from scientific theories to musical compositions to successful political campaigns.

MI theory is framed in light of the biological origins of each problem-solving skill. Only those skills that are universal to the human species are treated. Even so, the biological proclivity to participate in a particular form of problem solving must also be coupled with the cultural nurturing of that domain. For example, language, a universal skill, may manifest itself particularly as writing in one culture, as oratory in another culture, and as the secret language of anagrams in a third.

Given the desire of selecting intelligences that are rooted in biology, and that are valued in one or more cultural settings, how does one actually identify an "intelligence"? In coming up with our list, we consulted evidence from several different sources: knowledge about normal development and development in gifted individuals; information about the breakdown of cognitive skills under conditions of brain damage; studies of exceptional populations, including prodigies, idiots savants, and autistic children; data about the evolution of cognition over the millennia; cross-cultural accounts of cognition; psychometric studies, including examinations of correlations among tests; and psychological training studies, particularly measures of transfer and generalization across tasks. Only those candidate intelligences that satisfied all or a majority of the criteria were selected as bona fide intelligences. A more complete discussion of each of these criteria for an "intelligence" and the seven intelligences that have been proposed so far, is found in *Frames of mind*.[2] This book also considers how the theory might be disproven and compares it to competing theories of intelligence.

In addition to satisfying the aforementioned criteria, each intelligence must have an identifiable core operation or set of operations. As a neutrally based computational system, each intelligence is activated or "triggered" by certain kinds of internally or externally presented information. For example, one core of musical intelligence is the sensitivity to pitch relations, whereas one core of linguistic intelligence is the sensitivity to phonological features.

An intelligence must also be susceptible to encoding in a symbol system—a culturally contrived system of meaning, which captures and conveys important forms of information. Language, picturing, and mathematics are but three nearly worldwide symbol systems that are necessary for human survival and productivity. The relationship of a candidate intelligence to a human symbol system is no accident. In fact, the existence of a core computational capacity anticipates the existence of a symbol system that exploits that capacity. While it may be possible for an intelligence to proceed without an accompanying symbol system, a primary characteristic of human intelligence may well be its gravitation toward such an embodiment.

The Seven Intelligences

Having sketched the characteristics and criteria of an intelligence, we turn now to a brief consideration of each of the seven intelligences. We begin each sketch with a thumbnail biography of a person who demonstrates an unusual facility with that intelligence. These biographies illustrate some of the abilities that are central to the fluent operation of a given intelligence. Although each biography illustrates a particular intelligence, we do not wish to imply that in adulthood intelligences operate in isolation. Indeed, except for abnormal individuals, intelligences always work in concert, and any sophisticated adult role will involve a melding of several of them. Following each biography we survey the various sources of data that support each candidate as an "intelligence."

MUSICAL INTELLIGENCE

When he was three years old, Yehudi Menuhin was smuggled into the San Francisco Orchestra concerts by his parents. The sound of Louis Persinger's violin so entranced the youngster that he insisted on a violin for his birthday and Louis Persinger as his teacher. He got both. By the time he was ten years old, Menuhin was an international performer.[3]

Violinist Yehudi Menuhin's musical intelligence manifested itself even before he had touched a violin or received any musical training. His powerful reaction to that particular sound and his rapid progress on the instrument suggest that he was biologically prepared in some way for that endeavor. In this way evidence from child prodigies supports our claim that there is a biological link to a particular intelligence. Other special populations, such as autistic children who can play a musical instrument beautifully but who cannot speak, underscore the independence of musical intelligence.

A brief consideration of the evidence suggests that musical skill passes the other tests for an intelligence. For example, certain parts of the brain play important roles in perception and production of music. These areas are characteristically located in the right hemisphere, although musical skill is not as clearly "localized," or located in a specifiable area, as language. Although the particular susceptibility of musical ability to brain damage depends on the degree of training and other individual differences, there is clear evidence for "amusia" or loss of musical ability.

Music apparently played an important unifying role in Stone Age (Paleolithic) societies. Birdsong provides a link to other species. Evidence from various cultures supports the notion that music is a universal faculty. Studies of infant development suggest that there is a "raw" computational ability in early childhood. Finally, musical notation provides an accessible and lucid symbol system.

In short, evidence to support the interpretation of musical ability as an "intelligence" comes from many different sources. Even though musical skill is not typically considered an intellectual skill like mathematics, it qualifies under our criteria. By definition it deserves consideration; and in view of the data, its inclusion is empirically justified.

BODILY-KINESTHETIC INTELLIGENCE

Fifteen-year-old Babe Ruth played third base. During one game his team's pitcher was doing very poorly and Babe loudly criticized him from third base. Brother Mathias, the coach, called out, "Ruth, if you know so much about it, YOU pitch!" Babe was surprised and embarrassed because he had never pitched before, but Brother Mathias insisted. Ruth said later that at the very moment he took the pitcher's mound, he KNEW he was supposed to be a pitcher and that it was "natural" for him to strike people out. Indeed, he went on to become a great major league pitcher (and, of course, attained legendary status as a hitter).[4]

Like Menuhin, Babe Ruth was a child prodigy who recognized his "instrument" immediately upon his first exposure to it. This recognition occurred in advance of formal training.

Control of bodily movement is, of course, localized in the motor cortex, with each hemisphere dominant or controlling bodily movements on the contra-lateral side. In right-handers, the dominance for such movement is ordinarily found in the left hemisphere. The ability to perform movements when directed to do so can be impaired even in individuals who can perform the same movements reflexively or on a nonvoluntary basis. The existence of specific *apraxia* constitutes one line of evidence for a bodily-kinesthetic intelligence.

The evolution of specialized body movements is of obvious advantage to the species, and in humans this adaptation is extended through the use of tools. Body movement undergoes a clearly defined developmental schedule in children. And there is little question of its universality across cultures. Thus it appears that bodily-kinesthetic "knowledge" satisfies many of the criteria for an intelligence.

The consideration of bodily-kinesthetic knowledge as "problem solving" may be less intuitive. Certainly carrying out a mime sequence or hitting a tennis ball is not solving a mathematical equation. And yet, the ability to use one's body to express an emotion (as in a dance), to play a game (as in a sport), or to create a new product (as in devising an invention) is evidence of the cognitive features of body usage. The specific computations required to solve a particular bodily-kinesthetic *problem*, hitting a tennis ball, are summarized by Tim Gallwey:

> At the moment the ball leaves the server's racket, the brain calculates approximately where it will land and where the racket will intercept it. This calculation includes the initial velocity of the ball, combined with an input for the progressive decrease in velocity and the effect of wind and after the bounce of the ball. Simultaneously, muscle orders are given: not just once, but constantly with refined and updated information. The muscles must cooperate. A movement of the feet occurs, the racket is taken back, the face of the racket kept at a constant angle. Contact is made at a precise point that depends on whether the order was given to hit down the line or cross-court, an order not given until after a split-second analysis of the movement and balance of the opponent.
>
> To return an average serve, you have about one second to do this. To hit the ball at all is remarkable and yet not uncommon. The truth is that everyone who inhabits a human body possesses a remarkable creation.[5]

LOGICAL-MATHEMATICAL INTELLIGENCE

In 1983 Barbara McClintock won the Nobel Prize in medicine or physiology for her work in microbiology. Her intellectual powers of deduction and observation illustrate one form of logical-mathematical intelligence that is often labeled "scientific thinking." One incident is particularly illuminating. While a researcher at Cornell in the

1920s McClintock was faced one day with a problem: while *theory* predicted 50-percent pollen sterility in corn, her research assistant (in the "field") was finding plants that were only 25- to 30-percent sterile. Disturbed by this discrepancy, McClintock left the cornfield and returned to her office where she sat for half an hour, thinking:

> *Suddenly I jumped up and ran back to the (corn) field. At the top of the field (the others were still at the bottom) I shouted "Eureka, I have it! I know what the 30% sterility is!" . . . They asked me to prove it. I sat down with a paper bag and a pencil and I started from scratch, which I had not done at all in my laboratory. It had all been done so fast; the answer came and I ran. Now I worked it out step by step—it was an intricate series of steps—and I came out with [the same result]. [They] looked at the material and it was exactly as I'd said it was; it worked out exactly as I had diagrammed it. Now, why did I know, without having done it on paper? Why was I so sure?[6]*

This anecdote illustrates two essential facts of the logical-mathematical intelligence. First, in the gifted individual, the process of problem solving is often remarkably rapid—the successful scientist copes with many variables at once and creates numerous hypotheses that are each evaluated and then accepted or rejected in turn.

The anecdote also underscores the *nonverbal* nature of the intelligence. A solution to a problem can be constructed *before* it is articulated. In fact, the solution process may be totally invisible, even to the problem solver. This need not imply, however, that discoveries of this sort—the familiar "Aha!" phenomenon—are mysterious, intuitive, or unpredictable. The fact that it happens more frequently to some people (perhaps Nobel Prize winners) suggests the opposite. We interpret this as the work of theological-mathematical intelligence.

Along with the companion skill of language, logical-mathematical reasoning provides the principal basis for IQ tests. This form of intelligence has been heavily investigated by traditional psychologists, and it is the archetype of "raw intelligence" or the problem-solving faculty that purportedly cuts across domains. It is perhaps ironic, then, that the actual mechanism by which one arrives at a solution to a logical-mathematical problem is not as yet properly understood.

This intelligence is supported by our empirical criteria as well. Certain areas of the brain are more prominent in mathematical calculation than others. There are idiots savants who perform great feats of calculation even though they remain tragically deficient in most other areas. Child prodigies in mathematics abound. The development of this intelligence in children has been carefully documented by Jean Piaget and other psychologists.

LINGUISTIC INTELLIGENCE

At the age of ten, T. S. Eliot created a magazine called "Fireside" to which he was the sole contributor. In a three-day period during his winter vacation, he created eight complete issues. Each one included poems, adventure stories, a gossip column, and humor. Some of this material survives and it displays the talent of the poet.[7]

As with the logical intelligence, calling linguistic skill an "intelligence" is consistent with the stance of traditional psychology. Linguistic intelligence also passes our empirical tests. For instance, a specific area of the brain, called "Broca's Area," is responsible for the production of grammatical sentences. A person with damage to this area can understand words and sentences quite well but has difficulty putting words together in anything other than the simplest of sentences. At the same time, other thought processes may be entirely unaffected.

The gift of language is universal, and its development in children is strikingly constant across cultures. Even in deaf populations where a manual sign language is not explicitly taught, children will often "invent" their own manual language and use it surreptitiously. We thus see how an intelligence may operate independently of a specific input modality or output channel.

SPATIAL INTELLIGENCE

Navigation around the Caroline Islands in the South Seas is accomplished without instruments. The position of the stars, as viewed from various islands, the weather patterns, and water color are the only sign posts. Each journey is broken into a series of segments; and the navigator learns the position of the stars within each of these segments. During the actual trip the navigator must envision mentally a reference island as it passes under a particular star and from that he computes the number of segments completed, the proportion of the trip remaining, and any corrections in heading that are required. The navigator cannot see the islands as he sails along; instead he maps their locations in his mental "picture" of the journey.[8]

Spatial problem solving is required for navigation and in the use of the notational system of maps. Other kinds of spatial problem solving are brought to bear in visualizing an object seen from a different angle and in playing chess. The visual arts also employ this intelligence in the use of space.

Evidence from brain research is clear and persuasive. Just as the left hemisphere has, over the course of evolution, been selected as the site of linguistic processing in right-handed persons, the right hemisphere proves to be the site most crucial for spatial processing. Damage to the right posterior regions causes impairment of the ability to find one's way around a site, to recognize faces or scenes, or to notice fine details.

Patients with damage specific to regions of the right hemisphere will attempt to compensate for their spacial deficits with linguistic strategies. They will try to reason aloud, to challenge the task, or even make up answers. But such nonspatial strategies are rarely successful.

Blind populations provide an illustration of the distinction between the spatial intelligence and visual perception. A blind person can recognize shapes by an indirect method: running a hand along the object translates into length of time of movement, which in turn is translated into the size of the object. For the blind person, the perceptual system of the tactile modality parallels the visual modality in the seeing person. The analogy between the spatial reasoning of the blind and the linguistic reasoning of the deaf is notable.

There are few child prodigies among visual artists, but there are idiots savants such as Nadia.[9] Despite a condition of severe autism, this preschool child made drawings of the most remarkable representational accuracy and finesse.

INTERPERSONAL INTELLIGENCE

With little formal training in special education and nearly blind herself, Anne Sullivan began the intimidating task of instructing a blind and deaf seven-year-old Helen Keller. Sullivan's efforts at communication were complicated by the child's emotional struggle with the world around her. At their first meal together, this scene occurred:

> Annie did not allow Helen to put her hand into Annie's plate and take what she wanted, as she had been accustomed to do with her family. It became a test of wills—hand thrust into plate, hand firmly put aside. The family, much upset, left the dining room. Annie locked the door and proceeded to eat her breakfast while Helen lay on the floor kicking and screaming, pushing and pulling at Annie's chair. [After half an hour] Helen went around the table looking for her family. She discovered no one else was there and that bewildered her. Finally, she sat down and began to eat her breakfast, but with her hands. Annie gave her a spoon. Down on the floor it clattered, and the contest of wills began anew.[10]

Anne Sullivan sensitively responded to the child's behavior. She wrote home: "The greatest problem I shall have to solve is how to discipline and control her without breaking her spirit. I shall go rather slowly at first and try to win her love."

In fact, the first "miracle" occurred two weeks later, well before the famous incident at the pumphouse. Annie had taken Helen to a small cottage near the family's house, where they could live alone. After seven days together, Helen's personality suddenly underwent a profound change—the therapy had worked:

> My heart is singing with joy this morning. A miracle has happened! The wild little creature of two weeks ago has been transformed into a gentle child.[11]

It was just two weeks after this that the first breakthrough in Helen's grasp of language occurred; and from that point on, she progressed with incredible speed. The key to the miracle of language was Anne Sullivan's insight into the *person* of Helen Keller.

Interpersonal intelligence builds on a core capacity to notice distinctions among others; in particular, contrasts in their moods, temperaments, motivations, and intentions. In more advanced forms, this intelligence permits a skilled adult to read the intentions and desires of others, even when these have been hidden. This skill appears in a highly sophisticated form in religious or political leaders, teachers, therapists, and parents. The Helen Keller–Anne Sullivan story suggests that this interpersonal intelligence does not depend on language.

All indices in brain research suggest that the frontal lobes play a prominent role in interpersonal knowledge. Damage in this area can cause profound personality changes while leaving other forms of problem solving unharmed—a person is often "not the same person" after such an injury. ✱

Alzheimer's disease, a form of presenile dementia, appears to attack posterior brain zones with a special ferocity, leaving spatial, logical, and linguistic computations severely impaired. Yet, Alzheimer's patients will often remain well groomed, socially proper, and continually apologetic for their errors. In contrast, Pick's disease, another variety of presenile dementia that is more frontally oriented, entails a rapid loss of social graces.

Biological evidence for interpersonal intelligence encompasses two additional factors often cited as unique to humans. One factor is the prolonged childhood of primates, including the close attachment to the mother. In those cases where the mother is removed from early development, normal interpersonal development is in serious jeopardy. The second factor is the relative importance in humans of social interaction. Skills such as hunting, tracking, and killing in prehistoric societies required participation and cooperation of large numbers of people. The need for group cohesion, leadership, organization, and solidarity follows naturally from this.

INTRAPERSONAL INTELLIGENCE

In an essay called "A Sketch of the Past," written almost as a diary entry, Virginia Woolf discusses the "cotton wool of existence"—the various mundane events of life. She contrasts this "cotton wool" with three specific and poignant memories from her childhood: a fight with her brother, seeing a particular flower in the garden, and hearing of the suicide of a past visitor:

> These are three instances of exceptional moments. I often tell them over, or rather they come to the surface unexpectedly. But now for the first time I have written them down, and I realize something that I have never realized before. Two of these moments ended in a state of despair. The other ended, on the contrary, in a state of satisfaction.
>
> The sense of horror (in hearing of the suicide) held me powerless. But in the case of the flower, I found a reason; and was thus able to deal with the sensation. I was not powerless.
>
> Though I still have the peculiarity that I receive these sudden shocks, they are now always welcome; after the first surprise, I always feel instantly that they are particularly valuable. And so I go on to suppose that the shock-receiving ca-

pacity is what makes me a writer. I hazard the explanation that a shock is at once in my case followed by the desire to explain it. I feel that I have had a blow; but it is not, as I thought as a child, simply a blow from an enemy hidden behind the cotton wool of daily life; it is or will become a revelation of some order; it is a token of some real thing behind appearances; and I make it real by putting it into words.[12]

This quotation vividly illustrates the intrapersonal intelligence—knowledge of the internal aspects of a person: access to one's own feeling life, one's range of emotions, the capacity to effect discriminations among these emotions and eventually to label them and to draw upon them as a means of understanding and guiding one's own behavior. A person with good intrapersonal intelligence has a viable and effective model of himself or herself. Since this intelligence is the most private, it requires evidence from language, music, or some other more expressive form of intelligence if the observer is to detect it at work. In the above quotation, for example, linguistic intelligence is drawn upon to convey intrapersonal knowledge; it embodies the interaction of intelligences, a common phenomenon to which we will return later.

We see the familiar criteria at work in the intrapersonal intelligence. As with the interpersonal intelligence, the frontal lobes play a central role in personality change. Injury to the lower area of the frontal lobes is likely to produce irritability or euphoria; while injury to the higher regions is more likely to produce indifference, listlessness, slowness, and apathy—a kind of depressive personality. In such "frontal-lobe" individuals, the other cognitive functions often remain preserved. In contrast, among aphasics who have recovered sufficiently to describe their experiences, we find consistent testimony; while there may have been a diminution of general alertness and considerable depression about the condition, the individual in no way felt himself to be a different person. He recognized his own needs, wants, and desires and tried as best he could to achieve them.

The autistic child is a prototypical example of an individual with impaired intrapersonal intelligence; indeed, the child may not even be able to refer to himself. At the same time, such children often exhibit remarkable abilities in the musical, computational, spatial, or mechanical realms.

Evolutionary evidence for an intrapersonal faculty is more difficult to come by, but we might speculate that the capacity to transcend the satisfaction of instinctual drives is relevant. This becomes increasingly important in a species not perennially involved in the struggle for survival.

In sum, then, both interpersonal and intrapersonal faculties pass the tests of an intelligence. They both feature problem-solving endeavors with significance for the individual and the species. Interpersonal intelligence allows one to understand and work with others; intrapersonal intelligence allows one to understand and work with oneself. In the individual's sense of self, one encounters a melding of inter- and intrapersonal components. Indeed, the sense of self emerges as one of the most marvelous of human inventions—a symbol that represents all kinds of information about a person and that is at the same time an invention that all individuals construct for themselves.

Summary: The Unique Contributions of the Theory

As human beings, we all have a repertoire of skills for solving different kinds of problems. Our investigation has begun, therefore, with a consideration of these problems, the contexts they are found in, and the culturally significant products that are the outcome. We have not approached "intelligence" as a reified human faculty that is brought to bear in literally any problem setting; rather, we have begun with the problems that humans *solve* and worked back to the "intelligences" that must be responsible.

Evidence from brain research, human development, evolution, and cross-cultural comparisons was brought to bear in our search for the relevant human intelligences: a candidate was included only if reasonable evidence to support its membership was found across these diverse fields. Again, this tack differs from the traditional one: since no candidate faculty is *necessarily* an intelligence, we could choose on a motivated basis. In the traditional approach to "intelligence," there is no opportunity for this type of empirical decision.

We have also determined that these multiple human faculties, the intelligences, are to a significant extent *independent*. For example, research with brain-damaged adults repeatedly demonstrates that particular faculties can be lost while others are spared. This independence of intelligences implies that a particularly high level of ability in one intelligence, say mathematics, does not require a similarly high level in another intelligence, like language or music. This independence of intelligences contrasts sharply with traditional measures of IQ that find high correlations among test scores. We speculate that the usual correlations among subtests of IQ tests come about because all of these tasks in fact measure the ability to respond rapidly to items of a logical-mathematical or linguistic sort; we believe that these correlations would be substantially reduced if one were to survey in a contextually appropriate way the full range of human problem-solving skills.

Until now, we have supported the fiction that adult roles depend largely on the flowering of a single intelligence. In fact, however, nearly every cultural role of any degree of sophistication requires a combination of intelligences. Thus, even an apparently straightforward role, like playing the violin, transcends a reliance on simple musical intelligence. To become a successful violinist requires bodily-kinesthetic dexterity and the interpersonal skills of relating to an audience and, in a different way, choosing a manager; quite possibly it involves an intrapersonal intelligence as well. Dance requires skills in bodily-kinesthetic, musical, interpersonal, and spatial intelligences in varying degrees. Politics requires an interpersonal skill, a linguistic facility, and perhaps some logical aptitude. Inasmuch as nearly every cultural role requires several intelligences, it becomes important to consider individuals as a collection of aptitudes rather than as having a singular problem-solving faculty that can be measured directly through pencil-and-paper tests. Even given a relatively small number of such intelligences, the diversity of human ability is created through the differences in these profiles. In fact, it may well be that the "total is greater than the sum of the parts." An individual may not be particularly gifted in any intelligence; and yet, because of a particular combination or blend of skills, he or she may be able to fill some niche uniquely well. Thus it is of paramount importance to assess the particular combination of skills that may earmark an individual for a certain vocational or avocational niche.

Notes

1. Jencks, C. (1972). *Inequality.* New York: Basic Books. [Gardner's note]
2. Gardner, H. (1983). *Frames of mind: The theory of multiple intelligences.* New York: Basic Books. [Gardner's note]
3. Menuhin, Y. (1977). *Unfinished journey.* New York: Knopf. [Gardner's note]
4. Connor, A. (1982). *Voices from Cooperstown.* New York: Collier. (Based on a quotation taken from *The Babe Ruth story,* Babe Ruth & Bob Considine. New York: Dutton, 1948.) [Gardner's note]
5. Gallwey, T. (1976). *Inner tennis.* New York: Random House. [Gardner's note]
6. Keller, E. (1983). *A feeling for the organism* (p. 104). Salt Lake City: W. H. Freeman. [Gardner's note]
7. Soldo, J. (1982). Jovial juvenilia: T. S. Eliot's first magazine. *Biography,* 5. 25–37. [Gardner's note]
8. Gardner, H. (1983). *Frames of mind: The theory of multiple intelligences.* New York: Basic Books. [Gardner's note]
9. Selfe, L. (1977). *Nadia: A case of extraordinary drawing in an autistic child.* New York: Academic Press. [Gardner's note]
10. Lash, J. (1980). *Helen and teacher: The story of Helen Keller and Anne Sullivan Macy* (p. 52). New York: Delacorte. [Gardner's note]
11. Lash (p. 54). [Gardner's note]
12. Woolf, V. (1976). *Moments of being* (pp. 69–70). Sussex: The University Press. [Gardner's note]

 ## For Discussion:

1. How would you define intelligence, and why? Does Gardner's theory of multiple intelligences resemble or contrast to your own definition?
2. What is the relationship, for Gardner, between culturally constructed and biologically determined (innate) qualities? How do these two types of qualities help to define intelligence?
3. What is the difference between interpersonal and intrapersonal intelligence?
4. List Gardner's types of intelligence. How is each intelligence independent? In what ways do these intelligences work together?

For Fact-Finding, Research, and Writing:

1. The word "creative" is now frequently added to programs formerly titled "Gifted and Talented." When and why did this change occur?
2. Many universities (including the prestigious University of California) are abandoning standardized testing as an important criterion for admission. Find information about the controversy surrounding this decision. How does Gardner's thinking appear to have been influential in the reasoning offered for using or disregarding such tests?
3. Compare Gardner's theory of multiple intelligences with Plato's conception of knowledge or Russell's idea of wisdom. Are Plato's or Russell's ideas "traditional"? In what ways does either Plato's or Russell's theory extend beyond "logical-mathematical" intelligence?

Ron Carlson, "The Ordinary Son"

Long regarded as one of America's finest short story writers, Ron Carlson is Professor of English at Arizona State University in Scottsdale, Arizona. He has published five books of fiction. His short stories are regularly anthologized in *Best American Short Stories* and *The O. Henry Prize Stories,* and his work has appeared in *The New Yorker, Esquire, Harper's Gentlemen's Quarterly,* and *Tin House.* "The Ordinary Son" is taken from Carlson's latest short story collection *At the Jim Bridger,* published in 2002. It can also be found in *The Best American Short Stories 2000* and *The Pushcart Prize Anthology 2001.*

Before You Read:

Using any source that comes to mind (movies, television, sports) come up with as many examples of "genius" as you can and try to arrive at a working definition of the term.

The Ordinary Son

THE STORY OF my famous family is a story of genius and its consequences, I suppose, and I am uniquely and particularly suited to tell the story since genius avoided me—and I it—and I remain an ordinary man, if there is such a thing, calm in all weathers, aware of event, but uninterested and generally incapable of deciphering implication. As my genius brother Garrett used to say, "Reed, you're not screwed too tight like the rest of us, but you're still screwed." Now, there's a definition of the common man you can trust, and further, you can trust me. There's no irony in that or deep inner meaning or Freudian slips, any kind of slips really, simply what it says. My mother told me many times I have a good heart, and of course, she was a genius, and that heart should help with this story, but a heart, as she said so often, good as it may be, is always trouble.

Part of the reason this story hasn't come together before, the story of my famous family, is that no one remembers they were related. They all had their own names. My father was Duncan Landers, the noted NASA physicist, the man responsible for every facet of the photography of the first moon landing. There is still camera gear on the moon inscribed with this name. That is, Landers. He was born Duncan Lrsdyksz, which was changed when NASA began their public-relations campaigns in the mid-sixties; the space agency suggested that physicists who worked for NASA should have more vowels in their names. They didn't want their press releases to seem full of typographical errors or foreigners. Congress was reading this stuff. So Lrsdyksz became Landers. (My father's close associate Igor Oeuroi didn't get just vowels; his name became LeRoy Rodgers. After le Cowboy Star, my mother quipped.)

My mother was Gloria Rainstrap, the poet who spent twenty years fighting for workers' rights from Texas to Alaska; in one string she gave four thousand consecutive lectures in her travels, not missing a night as she drove from village to village throughout the country. It still stands as some kind of record.

Wherever she went, she stirred up the best kind of trouble, reading her work and then spending hours in whatever guest house or spare bedroom she was given, reading the poems and essays of the people who had come to see her. She was tireless, driven by her overwhelming sense of fairness, and she was certainly the primary idealist to come out of twentieth-century Texas. When she started leaving home for months, years at a time, I was just a lad, but I remember her telling my father, Duncan, one night, "Texas is too small for what I have to do."

This was not around the dinner table. We were a family of geniuses and did not have a dinner table. In fact, the only table we did have was my father's drafting table, which was in the entry so that you had to squeeze sideways to even get into our house. "It sets the tone," Duncan used to say. "I want anyone coming into our home to see my work. That work is the reason we have a roof, anyway." He said that one day after my friend Jeff Shreckenbah and I inched past him on the way to my room. "And who are these people coming in the door?"

"It is your son and his friend," I told him.

"Good," he said, his benediction, but he said it deeply into his drawing, which is where he spent his time at home. He wouldn't have known if the Houston Oilers had arrived, because he was about to invent the modern gravity-free vacuum hinge that is still used today.

Most of my father, Duncan Landers's, work was classified, top-secret, eyes-only, but it didn't matter. No one except Jeff Shreckenbah came to our house. People didn't come over.

We were geniuses. We had no television, and we had no telephone. "What should I do," my father would say from where he sat in the entry, drawing, "answer some little buzzing device? Say hello to it?" NASA tried to install phones for us. Duncan took them out. It was a genius household and not to be diminished by primitive electronic foo-fahs.

My older sister was named Christina by my father and given the last name Rossetti by my mother. When she finally fled from M.I.T. at nineteen, she gave herself a new surname: Isotope. There had been some trouble, she told me, personal trouble, and she needed the new name to remind herself she wouldn't last long— and then she asked me how I liked my half-life. I was twelve then, and she laughed and said, "I'm kidding, Reed. You're not a genius; you're going to live forever." I was talking to her on the "hot line," the secret phone our housekeeper, Clovis Armandy, kept in a kitchen cupboard.

"Where are you going?" I asked her.

"West with Mother," she said. Evidently, Gloria Rainstrap had driven up to Boston to rescue Christina from some sort of meltdown. "A juncture of some kind," my father told me. "Not to worry."

Christina said, "I'm through with theoretical chemistry, but chemistry isn't through with me. Take care of Dad. See you later."

We three children were eight years apart; that's how geniuses plan their families. Christina had been gone for years, it seemed, from our genius household; she barely knew our baby brother, Garrett.

Garrett and I took everything in stride. We accepted that we were a family of geniuses and that we had no telephone or refrigerator or proper beds. We thought it was natural to eat crackers and sardines months on end. We thought the front yard was supposed to be a jungle of overgrown grass, weeds, and whatever reptiles would volunteer to live there. Twice a year the City of Houston street crew came by and mowed it all down, and daylight would pour in for a month or two. We had no cars.

My father was always climbing into white Chevrolet station wagons, unmarked, and going off to the NASA Space Center south of town. My mother was always stepping up into orange VW buses driven by other people and driving off to tour. My sister had been the youngest student at M.I.T. My brother and I did our own laundry for years and walked to school, where by about seventh grade, we began to see the differences between the way ordinary people lived and the way geniuses lived. Other people's lives, we learned, centered fundamentally on two things: television and soft foods rich with all the versions of sugar.

By the time I entered junior high school, my mother's travels had kicked into high gear, and she hired a woman we came to know well, Clovis Armandy, to live in and to assist with our corporeal care. Gloria Rainstrap's parental theory and practice could be summed up by the verse I heard her say a thousand times before I reached the age of six: "Feed the soul, the body finds a way." And she fed our souls with a groaning banquet of iron ethics at every opportunity. She wasn't interested in sandwiches or casseroles. She was the kind of person who had a moral motive for her every move. We had no refrigerator because it was simply the wrong way to prolong the value of food, which had little value in the first place. We had no real furniture because furniture became the numbing insulation of drones for the economy, an evil in itself. If religion was the opiate of the masses, then home furnishings were the Novocain of the middle class. Any small surfeit of comfort undermined our moral fabric. *We live for the work we can do, not for things,* she told us. I've met and heard lots of folks who shared Gloria's posture toward life on this earth, but I've never found anyone who put it so well, presented her ideas so convincingly, beautifully, and so insistently. They effectively seduced you into wanting to go without. I won't put any of her poems in this story, but they were transcendent. The *Times* called her "Buddha's angry daughter." My mother's response to people who were somewhat shocked at our empty house and its unkempt quality was, "We're ego distant. These little things," she'd say, waving her hand over the litter of the laundry, discarded draft paper, piles of top-secret documents in the hallway, various toys, the odd empty tin of sardines, "don't bother us in the least. We aren't even here for them." I always loved that last and still use it when a nuisance arises: I'm not even here for it. "Ego distant," my friend Jeff Shreckeubah used to say; standing in our empty house, "which means your ma doesn't sweat the small stuff."

My mother's quirk, and one she fostered, was writing on the bottom of things. She started it because she was always gone, away for months at a time, and she wanted us to get her messages throughout her absence and thereby be reminded again of making correct decisions and ethical choices. It was not unusual to find ballpoint-pen lettering on the bottom of our shoes, and little marker messages on the bottom of plates (where she wrote in a tiny script), and anywhere that you could lift up and look under, she would have left her mark. These notes primarily confused us. There I'd be in math class and cross my legs and see something on the edge of my sneaker and read, "Your troubles, if you stay alert, will pass very quickly away."

I'm not complaining. I never, except once or twice, felt deprived. I like sardines, still. It was a bit of a pinch when we got to high school, and I noted with new poignancy that I didn't quite have the wardrobe to keep up. Geniuses dress plain but clean, and not always as clean as their ordinary counterparts, who have nothing better to do with their lives than buy and sort and wash clothes.

Things were fine. I turned seventeen. I was hanging out sitting around my bare room, reading books, the History of This, the History of That, dry stuff, waiting for my genius to kick in. This is what had happened to Christina. One day when she was ten, she was having a tea party with her dolls, which were two rolled pink towels, the next day she cataloged and diagrammed the amino acids, laying the groundwork for two artificial sweeteners and a mood elevator. By the time my mother, Gloria Rainstrap, returned from the Northwest and my father looked up from his table, the State Department "mentors" had been by and my sister, Christina, was on her way to the inner sanctums of the Massachusetts Institute of Technology. I remember my mother standing against my father's drafting table, her hands along the top. Her jaw was set and she said, "This is meaningful work for Christina, her special doorway."

My father dragged his eyes up from his drawings and said, "Where's Christina now?"

So the day I went into Garrett's room and found him writing equations on a huge scroll of butcher paper, which he had used until that day to draw battle re-creations of the French and Indian War, was a big day for me. I stood there in the gloom, watching him crawl along the paper, reeling out figures of which very few were numbers I recognized, most of the symbols being X's and Y's and the little twisted members of the Greek alphabet, and I knew that it had skipped me. Genius had cast its powerful, clear eye on me and said, "No thanks." At least I was that smart. I realized that I was not going to get to be a genius.

The message took my body a piece at a time, loosening each joint and muscle on the way up and then filling my face with a strange warmth, which I knew immediately was relief.

I was free.

I immediately took a job doing landscaping and general cleanup and maintenance at the San Jacinto Resort Motel on the old Hempstead Highway. My friend Jeff Shreckenbah worked next door at Alfredo's American Cafe, and he had told me that the last guy doing handiwork at the motel had been fired for making a holy mess of the parking lot with a paintbrush, and when I applied, Mr. Rakkerts, the short little guy who owned the place, took me on. These were the days of big changes for me. I bought a car, an act that would have at one time been as alien for me as intergalactic travel or applying to barber college. I bought a car. It was a four-door lime-green Plymouth Fury III, low miles. I bought a pair of chinos. These things gave me exquisite pleasure. I was seventeen and I had not known the tangible pleasure of having things. I bought three new shirts and a wristwatch with a leather strap, and I went driving in the evenings, alone south from our subdivision of Spring Woods with my arm on the green sill of my lime-green Plymouth Fury III through the vast spaghetti bowl of freeways and into the mysterious network of towers that was downtown Houston. It was my dawning.

Late at night, my blood rich with wonder at the possibilities of such a vast material planet, I would return to our tumbledown genius ranch house, my sister off putting new legs on the periodic table at M.I.T., my mother away in Shreveport showing the seaport workers there the way to political and personal power, my brother in his room edging closer to new theories of rocket reaction and thrust, my father sitting by the entry, rapt in his schematics. As I came in and sidled by his table and the one real light in the whole front part of the house, his pencilings on the space station hinge looking as beautiful and inscrutable to me as a sheet of music, he'd say my name as simple greeting. "Reed."

"Duncan," I'd say in return.

"How goes the metropolis?" he'd add, not looking up. His breath was faintly reminiscent of sardines; in fact, I still associate that smell, which is not as unpleasant as it might seem, with brilliance. I know he said *metropolis* because he didn't know for a moment which city we were in.

"It teems with industrious citizenry well into the night," I'd answer.

Then he'd say it, "Good," his benediction, as he'd carefully trace his lead-holder and its steel-like wafer of 5H pencil-lead along a precise new line deep into the vast white space. "That's good."

The San Jacinto Resort Motel along the Hempstead Highway was exactly what you might expect a twenty-unit motel to be in the year 1966. The many bright new interstates had come racing to Houston and collided downtown in a maze, and the old Hempstead Highway had been supplanted as a major artery into town. There was still a good deal of traffic on the four-lane, and the motel was always about half full, and as you would expect, never the same half. There were three permanent occupants, including a withered old man named Newcombe Shinetower, who was a hundred years old that summer and who had no car, just a room full of magazines with red and yellow covers, stacks of these things with titles like *Too Young for Comfort* and *Treasure Chest*. There were other titles. I was in Mr. Shinetower's room only on two occasions. He wore the same flannel shirt every day of his life and was heavily gone to seed. Once or twice a day I would see him shuffling out toward Alfredo's American Cafe, where Jeff told me he always ate the catfish. "You want to live to be a hundred," Jeff said, "eat the catfish." I told him I didn't know about a hundred and that I generally preferred smaller fish. I was never sure if Mr. Shinetower saw me or not as I moved through his line of sight. He might have nodded; it was hard to tell. What I felt was that he might exist on another plane, the way rocks are said to; they're in there but in a rhythm too slow for humans to perceive.

It was in his room, rife with the flaking detritus of the ages, that Jeff tried to help me reckon with the new world. "You're interested in sex, right?" he asked me one day as I took my break at the counter of Alfredo's. I told him I was, but that wasn't exactly the truth. I was indifferent. I understood how it was being packaged and sold to the American people, but it did not stir me, nor did any of the girls we went to school with, many of whom were outright beauties and not bashful about it. This was Texas in the sixties. Some of these buxom girls would grow up and try to assassinate their daughters' rivals on the cheerleading squad. If sex was the game, some seemed to say, deal me in. And I guess I felt it was a game, too, one I could sit out. I had begun to look a little closer at the ways I was different from my peers, worrying about anything that might be a genius tendency. And I took great comfort in the unmistakable affection I felt for my Plymouth Fury III.

"Good," he said. "If you're interested, then you're safe; you're not a genius. Geniuses"—here he leaned closer to me and squinted his eyes up to let me know this was a ground-breaking postulate—"have a little trouble in the sex department."

I liked Jeff; he was my first "buddy." I sat on the round red Naugahyde stool at Alfredo's long Formica counter and listened to his speech, including, "sex department," and I don't know, it kind of made sense to me. There must have been something on my face, which is a way of saying there must have been nothing on my face, absolutely nothing, a blank blank, because Jeff pulled his apron off his head and said, "Meet me out back in two minutes." He looked down the counter to where old Mr. Shinetower sucked on his soup. "We got to get you some useful information."

Out back, of course, Jeff led me directly around to the motel and Mr. Shinetower's room, which was not unlocked, but opened when Jeff gave the doorknob a healthy rattle. Inside in the sour dark, Jeff lit the lamp and picked up one of the old man's periodicals.

Jeff held the magazine and thumbed it like a deck of cards, stopping finally at a full-page photograph that he presented to me with an odd kind of certainty. "There," he said. "This is what everybody is trying for. This is the goal." It was a glossy color photograph, and I knew what it was right away, even in the poor light, a shiny shaved pubis, seven or eight times larger than life size. "This makes the world go round."

I was going along with Jeff all the way on this, but that comment begged for a remark, which I restrained. I could feel my father in me responding about the forces that actually caused and maintained the angular momentum of the earth. Instead I looked at the picture, which had its own lurid beauty. Of course, what it looked like was a landscape, a barren but promising promontory in not this but another world, the seam too perfect a fold for anything but ceremony. I imagined landing a small aircraft on the tawny slopes and approaching the entry, stepping lightly with a small party of explorers, alert for the meaning of such a place. The air would be devoid of the usual climatic markers (no clouds or air pressure), and in the stillness we would be silent and reverential. The light in the photograph captivated me in that it seemed to come from everywhere, a flat, even twilight that would indicate a world with one or maybe two distant polar suns. There was an alluring blue shadow that ran along the cleft the way a footprint in snow holds its own blue glow, and that aberration affected and intrigued me.

Jeff had left my side and was at the window, on guard, pleased that I was involved in my studies. "So," he said. "It's really something, isn't it?" He came to me, took the magazine and took one long look at the page the way a thirsty man drinks from a jug, and he set it back on the stack of Old Man Shinetower's magazines.

"Yes," I said. "It certainly is." Now that it was gone, I realized I had memorized the photograph, that place.

"Come on. Let's get out of here before he gets back." Jeff cracked the door and looked out, both ways. "Whoa," he said, setting the door closed again. "He's coming back. He's on the walk down about three rooms." Jeff then did an amazing thing: he dropped like a rock to all fours and then onto his stomach and slid under the bed. I'd never seen anyone do that; I've never seen it since. I heard him hiss: "Do something. Hide."

Again I saw myself arriving in the photograph. Now I was alone. I landed carefully and the entire venture was full of care, as if I didn't want to wake something. I had a case of instruments and I wanted to know about that light, that shadow. I could feel my legs burn as I climbed toward it step by step.

What I did in the room was take two steps back into the corner and stand behind the lamp. I put my hands at my side and my chin up. I stood still. At that moment we heard a key in the lock and daylight spilled across the ratty shag carpet. Mr. Shinetower came in. He was wearing the red-and-black plaid shirt that he wore every day. It was like a living thing; someday it would go to lunch at Alfredo's without him.

He walked by me and stopped for a moment in front of the television to drop a handful of change from his pocket into a mason jar on top, turn on the television until it lit and focused, and then he continued into the little green bathroom, and I saw the door swing halfway closed behind him.

Jeff slid out from the bed, stood hastily, his eyes whirling, and opened the door and went out. He was closing it behind him when I caught the edge and followed him into the spinning daylight. When I pulled the door, he gasped, so I shut it and we heard it register closed, and then we slipped quickly through the arbor to the alley behind the units and then ran along the overgrown trail back to the bayou and sat on the weedy slope. Jeff was covered with clots of dust and hairy white goo-gah. It was thick in his hair and I moved away from him while he swatted at it for a while. Here we could smell the sewer working at the bayou, an odd, rich industrial silage, and the sky was gray, but too bright to look at, and I went back to the other world for a moment, the cool perfect place I'd been touring in Mr. Shinetower's magazine, quiet and still, and offering that light. Jeff was spitting and pulling feathers of dust from his collar and sleeves. I wanted so much to be stirred by what I had seen; I had stared at it and I wanted it to stir me, and it had done something. I felt something. I wanted to see that terrain, chart it, understand where the blue glow arose and how it lay along the juncture, and how that light, I was certain, interfered with the ordinary passage of time. Time? I had a faint headache.

"That was close," Jeff said finally. He was still cloaked with flotsam from under Mr. Shinetower's bed. "But it was worth it. Did you get a good look? See what I'm talking about?"

"It was a remarkable photograph," I said.

"Now you know. You've seen it, you know. I've got to get back to work. Let's go fishing this weekend, eh?" He rose and, still whacking soot and ashes and wicked whatevers from his person, ran off toward Alfredo's.

"I've seen it," I said, and I sat there as the sadness bled through me. Duncan would have appreciated the moment and corrected Jeff the way he corrected me all those years. "Seeing isn't knowing," he would say. "To see something is only to establish the first terms of your misunderstanding." That I remembered him at such a time above the rife bayou moments after my flight over the naked photograph made me sad. I was not a genius, but I would be advised by one forevermore.

Happily, my work at the motel was straightforward and I enjoyed it very much. I could do most of it with my shirt off, cutting away the tenacious vines from behind each of the rooms so that the air-conditioning units would not get strangled, and I sweated profusely in the sweet humid air. I painted the pool fence and enameled the three metal tables a kind of turquoise blue, a fifties turquoise that has become tony again just this year, a color that calls to the passerby: Holiday! We're on holiday!

Once a week I poured a pernicious quantity of lime into the two manholes above the storm sewer, and it fell like snow on the teeming backs of thousands of albino waterbugs and roaches that lived there. This did not daunt them in the least. I am no expert on any of the insect tribes nor do I fully understand their customs, but my association with those subterranean multitudes showed me that they looked forward to this weekly toxic snowfall.

Twice a week I pressed the enormous push broom from one end of the driveway to the other until I had a wheelbarrow full of gravel and the million crushed tickets of litter people threw from their moving vehicles along the Hempstead Highway. It was wonderful work. The broom alone weighed twenty pounds. The sweeping, the painting, the trimming braced me; work that required simply my back, both my arms and both my legs, but neither side of my brain.

Mr. Leeland Rakkerts lived in a small apartment behind the office and could be summoned by a bell during the night hours. He was just sixty that June. His wife had passed away years before and he'd become a reclusive little gun nut, and had a growing gallery of hardware on a pegboard in his apartment featuring long-barreled automatic weaponry and at least two dozen huge handguns. But he was fine to me, and he paid me cash every Friday afternoon. When he opened the cash drawer, he always made sure that be you friend or foe, you saw the .45 pistol that rested there, too. My mother would have abhorred me working for him, a man she would have considered the enemy, and she would have said as much, but I wasn't taking the high road, nor the low road, just a road. That summer, the upkeep of the motel was my job, and I did it as well as I could. I'd taken a summer job and was making money. I didn't weigh things on my scale of ethics every ten minutes, because I wasn't entirely sure I had such a scale. I certainly didn't have one as fully evolved as my mother's.

It was a bit like being in the army: when in doubt, paint something. I remeasured and overpainted the parking lot where the last guy had drunkenly painted a wacky series of parentheses where people were supposed to park, and I did a good job with a big brush and five gallons of high mustard yellow, and when I finished I took the feeling of satisfaction in my chest to be simply that: satisfaction. Even if I was working for the devil, the people who put their cars in his parking lot would be squared away.

Getting in my Plymouth Fury III those days with a sweaty back and a pocketful of cash, I knew I was no genius, but I felt—is this close?—like a great guy, a person of some command.

That fall my brother, Garrett Lrsdyksz (he'd changed his name back with a legal kit that Baxter, our Secret Service guy, had got him through the mail), became the youngest student to matriculate at Rice University. He was almost eleven. And he didn't enter as a freshman; he entered as a junior. In physics, of course. There was a little article about it on the wire services, noting that he had, without any assistance, set forward the complete set of equations explaining the relationship between the rotation of the earth and "special atmospheric aberrations most hospitable to exit trajectories of ground-fired propulsion devices." You can look it up and all you'll find is the title because the rest, like all the work he did his cataclysmic year at Rice, is classified, top-secret, eyes-only. Later he explained his research this way to me: "There are storms and then there are storms, Reed. A high-pressure area is only a high-pressure area down here on earth; it has a different pressure on the other side."

I looked at my little brother, a person forever in need of a haircut, and I thought: He's mastered the other side, and I can just barely cope with this one.

That wasn't exactly true, of course, because my Plymouth Fury III and my weekly wages from the San Jacinto Resort Motel allowed me to start having a little life, earthbound as it may have been. I started hanging out a little at Jeff Shreckenbah's place, a rambling hacienda out of town with two out-buildings where his dad worked on stock cars. Jeff's mother called me Ladykiller, which I liked, but which I couldn't hear without imagining my mother's response; my mother who told me a million times, "Morality commences in the words we use to speak of our next act."

"Hey, Ladykiller," Mrs. Shreckenbah would say to me as we pried open the fridge looking for whatever we could find. Mr. Shreckenbah made me call him Jake, saying we'd save the last names for the use of the law-enforcement officials and members of the Supreme Court. They'd let us have Lone Star long-necks if we were staying, or Coca-Cola if we were hitting the road. Some nights we'd go out with Jake and hand him wrenches while he worked on his cars. He was always asking me, "What's the plan?" an opening my mother would have approved of.

"We're going fishing," I told him, because that's what Jeff and I started doing. I'd greet his parents, pick him up, and then Jeff and I would cruise hard down Interstate 45 fifty miles to Galveston and the coast of the warm Gulf of Mexico, where we'd drink Lone Star and surf-cast all night long, hauling in all sorts of mysteries of the deep. I loved it.

Jeff would bring along a pack of Dutch Masters cigars and I'd stand waist deep in the warm water, puffing on the cheap cigar, throwing a live shrimp on a hook as far as I could toward the equator, the only light being the stars above us, the gapped two-story skyline of Galveston behind us, and our bonfire on the beach, tearing a bright hole in the world.

When fish struck, they struck hard, waking me from vivid daydreams of Mr. Leeland Rakkerts giving me a bonus for sweeping the driveway so thoroughly, a twenty so crisp it hurt to fold it into my pocket. My dreams were full of crisp twenties. I could see Jeff over there, fifty yards from me, the little orange tip of his cigar glowing, starlight on the flash of his line as he cast. I liked having my feet firmly on the bottom of the ocean standing in the night. My brother and sister and my mother and father could shine their lights into the elemental mysteries of the world; I could stand in the dark and fish. I could feel the muscles in my arm as I cast again; I was stronger than I'd been two months ago, and then I felt the fish strike and begin to run south.

Having relinquished the cerebral, not that I ever had it in my grasp, I was immersing myself in the real world the same way I was stepping deeper and deeper into the Gulf, following the frenzied fish as he tried to take my line. I worked him back, gave him some, worked him back. Though I had no idea what I would do with it, I had decided to make a lot of money, and as the fish drew me up to my armpits and the bottom grew irregular, I thought about the ways it might be achieved. Being no genius, I had few ideas.

I spit out my cigar after the first wavelet broke over my face, and I called to Jeff, "I got one."

He was behind me now, backing toward the fire, and he called, "Bring him up here and let's see."

The top half of my head, including my nose, and my two hands and the fishing pole were all that were above sea level when the fish relented and I began to haul him back. He broke the surface several times as I backed out of the ocean, reeling as I went. Knee deep, I stopped and lifted the line until a dark form lifted into the air. I ran him up to Jeff by the fire and showed him there, a two-pound catfish. When I held him, I felt the sudden shock of his gaffs going into my finger and palm.

"Ow!" Jeff said. "Who has got whom?" He took the fish from me on a gill stick.

I shook my stinging hand.

"It's all right," he assured me, throwing another elbow of driftwood onto the fire and handing me an icy Lone Star. "Let's fry this guy up and eat him right now. I'm serious. This is going to be worth it. We're going to live to be one hundred years old, guaranteed."

We'd sit, eat, fish some more, talk, and late late we'd drive back, the dawn light gray across the huge tidal plain, smoking Dutch Masters until I was queasy and quiet, dreaming about my money, however I would make it.

Usually this dream was interrupted by my actual boss, Mr. Leeland Rakkerts, shaking my shoulder as I stood sleeping on my broom in the parking lot of the hot and bothered San Jacinto Resort Motel, saying, "Boy! Hey! Boy! You can take your zombie fits home or get on the stick here." I'd give him the wide-eyed nod and continue sweeping, pushing a thousand pounds of scraggly gravel into a conical pile and hauling it in my wheelbarrow way out back into the thick tropical weeds at the edge of the bayou and dumping it there like a body. It wasn't a crisp twenty-dollar bill he'd given me, but it was a valuable bit of advice for a seventeen-year-old, and I tried to take it as such.

Those Saturdays after we'd been to the Gulf beat in my skull like a drum, the Texas sun a thick pressure on my bare back as I moved through the heavy humid air skimming and vacuuming the pool, rearranging the pool furniture though it was never, ever moved because no one ever used the pool. People hadn't come to the San Jacinto Resort Motel to swim. Then standing in the slim shade behind the office, trembling under a sheen of sweat, I would suck on a tall bottle of Coca-Cola as if on the very nectar of life, and by midafternoon as I trimmed the hedges along the walks and raked and swept, the day would come back to me, a pure pleasure, my lime-green Plymouth Fury III parked in the shady side of Alfredo's American Cafe, standing like a promise of every sweet thing life could offer.

These were the days when my brother, Garrett, was coming home on weekends, dropped at our curb by the maroon Rice University van after a week in the research dorms, where young geniuses from all over the world lived in bare little cubicles, the kind of thing somebody with an I.Q. of 250 apparently loves. I had been to Garrett's room on campus and it was perfect for him. There was a kind of pad in one corner surrounded by a little bank of his clothing and the strip of butcher paper running the length of the floor, covered with numbers and letters and tracked thoroughly with the faint gray intersecting grid of sneaker prints. His window looked out onto the pretty green grass quad.

It was the quietest building I have ever been in, and I was almost convinced that Garrett might be the only inmate, but when we left to go down to the cafeteria for a sandwich, I saw the other geniuses in their rooms, lying on their stomachs like kids drawing with crayons on a rainy day. Then I realized that they were kids and it was a rainy day and they were working with crayons; the only difference was that they were drawing formulas for how many muons could dance on a quark.

Downstairs there were a whole slug of the little people in the dining hall sitting around in the plastic chairs, swinging their feet back and forth six inches off the floor, ignoring their trays of tuna-fish sandwiches and tomato soup, staring this way and then that as the idea storms in their brains swept through. You could almost see they were thinking by how their hair stood in fierce clusters.

There was one adult present, a guy in a blue sweater vest who went from table to table urging the children to eat: Finish that sandwich, drink your milk, go ahead, use your spoon, try the soup, it's good for you. I noticed he was careful to register and gather any of the random jottings the children committed while they sat around doodling in spilled milk. I guess he was a member of the faculty. It would be a shame for some nine-year-old to write the key to universal field theory in peanut butter and jelly and then eat the thing.

"So," I said as we sat down, "Garrett. How's it going?"

Garrett looked at me, his trance interrupted, and as it melted away and he saw me and the platters of cafeteria food before us, he smiled. There he was, my little brother, a sleepy-looking kid with a spray of freckles up and over his nose like the crab nebula, and two enthusiastic front teeth that would be keeping his mouth open for decades. "Reed," he said. "*How's it going?* I love that. I've always liked your acute sense of narrative. So linear and right for you." His smile, which took a moment and some force to assemble, was ancient, beneficent, as if he both envied and pitied me for something, and he shook his head softly. "But things here aren't going, kid." He poked a finger into the white bread of his tuna sandwich and studied the indentation like a man finding a footprint on the moon. "Things here *are*. This is it. Things . . ." He started again. "Things aren't bad, really. It's kind of a floating circle. That's close. Things aren't going; they float in the circle. Right?"

We were both staring at the sandwich; I think I might have been waiting for it to float, but only for a second. I understood what he was saying. Things existed. I'm not that dumb. Things, whatever they might be, and that was a topic I didn't even want to open, had essence, not process. That's simple; that doesn't take a genius to decipher. "Great," I said. And then I said what you say to your little brother when he sits there pale and distracted and four years ahead of you in school, "Why don't you eat some of that, and I'll take you out and show you my car."

It wasn't as bad a visit as I'm making it sound. We were brothers; we loved each other. We didn't have to say it. The dining room got me a little until I realized I should stop worrying about these children and whether or not they were happy. Happiness wasn't an issue. The place was clean; the food was fresh. Happiness, in that cafeteria, was simply beside the point.

On the way out, Garrett introduced me to his friend Donna Li, a ten-year-old from New Orleans, whom he said was into programming. She was a tall girl with shiny hair and a ready smile, eating alone by the window. This was 1966 and I was certain she was involved somehow in television. You didn't hear the word *computer* every other sentence back then. When she stood to shake my hand, I had no idea of what to say to her and it came out, "I hope your programming is floating in the circle."

"It is," she said.

"She's written her own language," Garrett assured me, "and now she's on the applications."

It was my turn to speak again and already I couldn't touch bottom, so I said, "We're going out to see my car. Do you want to see my car?"

Imagine me in the parking lot then with these two little kids. On the way out I'd told Garrett about my job at the motel and that Jeff Shreckenbah and I had been hanging out and fishing on the weekends and that Jeff's dad raced stock cars, and for the first time all day Garrett's face filled with a kind of wonder, as if this were news from another world, which I guess it was. There was a misty rain with a faint petrochemical smell in it, and we approached my car as if it were a sleeping Brontosaurus. They were both entranced and moved toward it carefully, finally putting their little hands on the wet fender in unison. "This is your car," Garrett said, and I wasn't sure if it was the *your* or the *car* that had him in awe.

I couldn't figure out what floats in the circle or even where the circle was, but I could rattle my keys and start that Plymouth Fury III and listen to the steady sound of the engine, which I did for them now. They both backed away appreciatively.

"It's a large car," Donna Li said.

"Reed," Garrett said to me. "This is really something. And what's that smell?"

I cocked my head, smelling it, too, a big smell, budging the petrocarbons away, a live, salty smell, and then I remembered: I'd left half a bucket of bait shrimp in the trunk, where they'd been ripening for three days since my last trip to Galveston with Jeff.

"That's rain in the bayou, Garrett."

"Something organic," Donna Li said, moving toward the rear of the vehicle.

"Here, guys," I said, handing Garrett the bag of candy, sardine tins, and peanut-butter-and-cheese packs I'd brought him. I considered for half a second showing him the pile of rotting crustaceans; it would have been cool and he was my brother. But I didn't want to give the geniuses the wrong first impression of the Plymouth.

"Good luck with your programming," I told Donna Li, shaking her hand. "And Garrett, be kind to your rocketry."

Garrett smiled at that again and said to Donna, "He's my brother."

And she added, "And he owns the largest car in Texas."

I felt bad driving my stinking car away from the two young people, but it was that or fess up. I could see them standing in my rearview mirror for a long time. First they watched me, then they looked up, both of them for a long time. They were geniuses looking into the rain; I counted on their being able to find a way out of it.

For Discussion:

1. Identify a few of the recurring images or phrases found in the story. How do these contribute to the story?
2. Do you believe Reed, the narrator, when he says he is not a genius? Does Gardner's "Linguistic Intelligence" category explain Reed? Examine the story for cues as to whether we are to believe or doubt the narrative voice.
3. What do you think Garrett means when he says to Reed, "*How's it going?* I love that. I've always loved your acute sense of narrative."

 For Fact-Finding, Research, and Writing:

1. Are there any governmental or educational institutions that define genius? Find at least two and evaluate the credibility of the definition.
2. How is funding for Gifted and Talented programs in the state of Oklahoma established? By the state? Local school districts? Go to government websites to uncover this information. Will it be cut in this current year? Who makes such decisions?
3. Consider "The Ordinary Son" in light of Schank's theory of narrative. How might Schank assess its goals and its place within the categories he establishes?
4. How do the stages of education described by Plato in "The Allegory of the Cave" help to explain Reed's experiences through the course of the story?

Temple Grandin, "Thinking in Pictures"

Temple Grandin is Associate Professor of Animal Science at Colorado State University and the author of numerous articles and several books on animal welfare and handling. Her designs for livestock-handling facilities have been implemented in several countries. She became well known to general readers following the 1996 publication of *An Anthropologist on Mars,* in which author Oliver Sacks offers a vivid and empathetic portrait of her life and mind.

Before You Read:

How would you describe your own way of thinking and learning? Do you use words? Pictures? Sounds? Or are you most comfortable with numbers? Or do you mostly think by doing? How has this practice affected your life and the ways others perceive you?

Thinking in Pictures

I THINK IN PICTURES. Words are like a second language to me. I translate both spoken and written words into full-color movies, complete with sound, which run like a VCR tape in my head. When somebody speaks to me, his words are instantly translated into pictures. Language-based thinkers often find this phenomenon difficult to understand, but in my job as an equipment designer for the livestock industry, visual thinking is a tremendous advantage.

Visual thinking has enabled me to build entire systems in my imagination. During my career I have designed all kinds of equipment, ranging from corrals for handling cattle on ranches to systems for handling cattle and hogs during veterinary procedures and slaughter. I have worked for many major livestock companies. In fact, one third of the cattle and hogs in the United States are handled in equipment I have designed. Some of the people I've worked for don't even know that their systems were designed by someone with autism. I value my ability to think visually, and I would never want to lose it.

One of the most profound mysteries of autism has been the remarkable ability of most autistic people to excel at visual spatial skills while performing so poorly at verbal skills. When I was a child and a teenager, I thought everybody thought in pictures. I had no idea that my thought processes were different. In fact, I did not realize the full extent of the differences until very recently. At meetings and at work I started asking other people detailed questions about how they accessed information from their memories. From their answers I learned that my visualization skills far exceeded those of most other people.

I credit my visualization abilities with helping me understand the animals I work with. Early in my career I used a camera to help give me the animals' perspective as they walked through a chute for their veterinary treatment. I would kneel down and take pictures through the chute from the cow's eye level. Using the photos, I was able to figure out which things scared the cattle, such as shadows and bright spots of sunlight. Back then I used black-and-white film, because twenty years ago scientists believed that cattle lacked color vision. Today, research has shown that cattle can see colors, but the photos provided the unique advantage of seeing the world through a cow's viewpoint. They helped me figure out why the animals refused to go in one chute but willingly walked through another.

Every design problem I've ever solved started with my ability to visualize and see the world in pictures. I started designing things as a child, when I was always experimenting with new kinds of kites and model airplanes. In elementary school I made a helicopter out of a broken balsa-wood airplane. When I wound up the propeller, the helicopter flew straight up about a hundred feet. I also made bird-shaped paper kites, which I flew behind my bike. The kites were cut out from a single sheet of heavy drawing paper and flown with thread. I experimented with different ways of bending the wings to increase flying performance. Bending the tips of the wings up made the kite fly higher. Thirty years later, this same design started appearing on commercial aircraft.

Now, in my work, before I attempt any construction, I test-run the equipment in my imagination. I visualize my designs being used in every possible situation, with different sizes and breeds of cattle and in different weather conditions. Doing this enables me to correct mistakes prior to construction. Today, everyone is excited about the new virtual reality computer systems in which the user wears special goggles and is fully immersed in video game action. To me, these systems are like crude cartoons. My imagination works like the computer graphics programs that created the lifelike dinosaurs in *Jurassic Park*. When I do an equipment simulation in my imagination or work on an engineering problem, it is like seeing it on a videotape in my mind. I can view it from any angle, placing myself above or below the equipment and rotating it at the same time. I don't need a fancy graphics program that can produce three-dimensional design simulations. I can do it better and faster in my head.

I create new images all the time by taking many little parts of images I have in the video library in my imagination and piecing them together. I have video memories of every item I've ever worked with—steel gates, fences, latches, concrete walls, and so forth. To create new designs, I retrieve bits and pieces from my memory and combine them into a new whole. My design ability keeps improving as I add more visual images to my library. I add video-like images from either actual experiences or translations of written information into pictures. I can visualize the operation of such things as squeeze chutes, truck loading ramps, and all different types of livestock equipment. The more I actually work with cattle and operate equipment, the stronger my visual memories become.

I first used my video library in one of my early livestock design projects, creating a dip vat and cattle-handling facility for John Wayne's Red River feed yard in

Arizona. A dip vat is a long, narrow, seven-foot-deep swimming pool through which cattle move in single file. It is filled with pesticide to rid the animals of ticks, lice, and other external parasites. In 1978, existing dip vat designs were very poor. The animals often panicked because they were forced to slide into the vat down a steep, slick concrete decline. They would refuse to jump into the vat, and sometimes they would flip over backward and drown. The engineers who designed the slide never thought about why the cattle became so frightened.

The first thing I did when I arrived at the feedlot was to put myself inside the cattle's heads and look out through their eyes. Because their eyes are on the sides of their heads, cattle have wide-angle vision, so it was like walking through the facility with a wide-angle video camera. I had spent the past six years studying how cattle see their world and watching thousands move through different facilities all over Arizona, and it was immediately obvious to me why they were scared. Those cattle must have felt as if they were being forced to jump down an airplane escape slide into the ocean.

Cattle are frightened by high contrasts of light and dark as well as by people and objects that move suddenly. I've seen cattle that were handled in two identical facilities easily walk through one and balk in the other. The only difference between the two facilities was their orientation to the sun. The cattle refused to move through the chute where the sun cast harsh shadows across it. Until I made this observation, nobody in the feedlot industry had been able to explain why one veterinary facility worked better than the other. It was a matter of observing the small details that made a big difference. To me, the dip vat problem was even more obvious.

My first step in designing a better system was collecting all the published information on existing dip vats. Before doing anything else, I always check out what is considered state-of-the-art so I don't waste time reinventing the wheel. Then I turned to livestock publications, which usually have very limited information, and my library of video memories, all of which contained bad designs. From experience with other types of equipment, such as unloading ramps for trucks, I had learned that cattle willingly walk down a ramp that has cleats to provide secure, nonslip footing. Sliding causes them to panic and back up. The challenge was to design an entrance that would encourage the cattle to walk in voluntarily and plunge into the water, which was deep enough to submerge them completely, so that all the bugs, including those that collect in their ears, would be eliminated.

I started running three-dimensional visual simulations in my imagination. I experimented with different entrance designs and made the cattle walk through them in my imagination. Three images merged to form the final design: a memory of a dip vat in Yuma, Arizona, a portable vat I had seen in a magazine, and an entrance ramp I had seen on a restraint device at the Swift meat-packing plant in Tolleson, Arizona. The new dip vat entrance ramp was a modified version of the ramp I had seen there. My design contained three features that had never been used before: an entrance that would not scare the animals, an improved chemical filtration system, and the use of animal behavior principles to prevent the cattle from becoming overexcited when they left the vat.

The first thing I did was convert the ramp from steel to concrete. The final design had a concrete ramp on a twenty-five-degree downward angle. Deep grooves in the concrete provided secure footing. The ramp appeared to enter the water gradually, but in reality it abruptly dropped away below the water's surface. The animals could not see the drop-off because the dip chemicals colored the water. When they stepped out over the water, they quietly fell in, because their center of gravity had passed the point of no return.

Before the vat was built, I tested the entrance design many times in my imagination. Many of the cowboys at the feedlot were skeptical and did not believe my design would work. After it was constructed, they modified it behind my back, because they were sure it was wrong. A metal sheet was installed over the nonslip ramp, converting it back to an old-fashioned slide entrance. The first day they used it, two cattle drowned because they panicked and flipped over backward.

When I saw the metal sheet, I made the cowboys take it out. They were flabbergasted when they saw that the ramp now worked perfectly. Each calf stepped out over the steep drop-off and quietly plopped into the water. I fondly refer to this design as "cattle walking on water."

Over the years, I have observed that many ranchers and cattle feeders think that the only way to induce animals to enter handling facilities is to force them in. The owners and managers of feedlots sometimes have a hard time comprehending that if devices such as dip vats and restraint chutes are properly designed, cattle will voluntarily enter them. I can imagine the sensations the animals would feel. If I had a calf's body and hooves, I would be very scared to step on a slippery metal ramp.

There were still problems I had to resolve after the animals left the dip vat. The platform where they exit is usually divided into two pens so that cattle can dry on one side while the other side is being filled. No one understood why the animals coming out of the dip vat would sometimes become excited, but I figured it was because they wanted to follow their drier buddies, not unlike children divided from their classmates on a playground. I installed a solid fence between the two pens to prevent the animals on one side from seeing the animals on the other side. It was a very simple solution, and it amazed me that nobody had ever thought of it before.

The system I designed for filtering and cleaning the cattle hair and other gook out of the dip vat was based on a swimming pool filtration system. My imagination scanned two specific swimming pool filters that I had operated, one on my Aunt Brecheen's ranch in Arizona and one at our home. To prevent water from splashing out of the dip vat, I copied the concrete coping overhang used on swimming pools. That idea, like many of my best designs, came to me very clearly just before I drifted off to sleep at night.

Being autistic, I don't naturally assimilate information that most people take for granted. Instead, I store information in my head as if it were on a CD-ROM disc.

When I recall something I have learned, I replay the video in my imagination. The videos in my memory are always specific; for example, I remember handling cattle at the veterinary chute at Producer's Feedlot or McElhaney Cattle Company. I remember exactly how the animals behaved in that specific situation and how the chutes and other equipment were built. The exact construction of steel fenceposts and pipe rails in each case is also part of my visual memory. I can run these images over and over and study them to solve design problems.

If I let my mind wander, the video jumps in a kind of free association from fence construction to a particular welding shop where I've seen posts being cut and Old John, the welder, making gates. If I continue thinking about Old John welding a gate, the video image changes to a series of short scenes of building gates on several projects I've worked on. Each video memory triggers another in this associative fashion, and my daydreams may wander far from the design problem. The next image may be of having a good time listening to John and the construction crew tell war stories, such as the time the backhoe dug into a nest of rattlesnakes and the machine was abandoned for two weeks because everybody was afraid to go near it.

This process of association is a good example of how my mind can wander off the subject. People with more severe autism have difficulty stopping endless associations. I am able to stop them and get my mind back on track. When I find my mind wandering too far away from a design problem I am trying to solve, I just tell myself to get back to the problem.

Interviews with autistic adults who have good speech and are able to articulate their thought processes indicate that most of them also think in visual images. More severely impaired people, who can speak but are unable to explain how they think, have highly associational thought patterns. Charles Hart, the author of *Without Reason,* a book about his autistic son and brother, sums up his son's thinking in one sentence: "Ted's thought processes aren't logical, they're associational." This explains Ted's statement "I'm not afraid of planes. That's why they fly so high." In his mind, planes fly high because he is not afraid of them; he combines two pieces of information, that planes fly high and that he is not afraid of heights.

Another indicator of visual thinking as the primary method of processing information is the remarkable ability many autistic people exhibit in solving jigsaw puzzles, finding their way around a city, or memorizing enormous amounts of information at a glance. My own thought patterns are similar to those described by A. R. Luria in *The Mind of a Mnemonist.* This book describes a man who worked as a newspaper reporter and could perform amazing feats of memory. Like me, the mnemonist had a visual image for everything he had heard or read. Luria writes, "For when he heard or read a word, it was at once converted into a visual image corresponding with the object the word signified for him." The great inventor Nikola Tesla was also a visual thinker. When he designed electric turbines for power generation, he built each turbine in his head. He operated it in his imagination and corrected faults. He said it did not matter whether the turbine was tested in his thoughts or in his shop; the results would be the same.

Early in my career I got into fights with other engineers at meat-packing plants. I couldn't imagine that they could be so stupid as not to see the mistakes on the drawing before the equipment was installed. Now I realize it was not stupidity but a lack of visualization skills. They literally could not see. I was fired from one company that manufactured meat-packing plant equipment because I fought with the engineers over a design which eventually caused the collapse of an overhead track that moved 1,200-pound beef carcasses from the end of a conveyor. As each carcass came off the conveyor, it dropped about three feet before it was abruptly halted by a chain attached to a trolley on the overhead track. The first time the machine was run, the track was pulled out of the ceiling. The employees fixed it by bolting it more securely and installing additional brackets. This only solved the problem temporarily, because the force of the carcasses jerking the chains was so great. Strengthening the overhead track was treating a symptom of the problem rather than its cause. I tried to warn them. It was like bending a paper clip back and forth too many times. After a while it breaks.

Different Ways of Thinking

The idea that people have different thinking patterns is not new. Francis Galton, in *Inquiries into Human Faculty and Development,* wrote that while some people see vivid mental pictures, for others "the idea is not felt to be mental pictures, but rather symbols of facts. In people with low pictorial imagery, they would remember their breakfast table but they could not see it."

It wasn't until I went to college that I realized some people are completely verbal and think only in words. I first suspected this when I read an article in a science magazine about the development of tool use in prehistoric humans. Some renowned scientist speculated that humans had to develop language before they could develop tools. I thought this was ridiculous, and this article gave me the first inkling that my thought processes were truly different from those of many other people. When I invent things, I do not use language. Some other people think in vividly detailed pictures, but most think in a combination of words and vague, generalized pictures.

For example, many people see a generalized generic church rather than specific churches and steeples when they read or hear the word "steeple." Their thought patterns move from a general concept to specific examples. I used to become very frustrated when a verbal thinker could not understand something I was trying to express because he or she couldn't see the picture that was crystal clear to me. Further, my mind constantly revises general concepts as I add new information to my memory library. It's like getting a new version of software for the computer. My mind readily accepts the new "software," though I have observed that some people often do not readily accept new information.

Unlike those of most people, my thoughts move from video-like, specific images to generalization and concepts. For example, my concept of dogs is inextricably linked to every dog I've ever known. It's as if I have a card catalogue of dogs I have seen, complete with pictures, which continually grows as I add more examples to my video library. If I think about Great Danes, the first memory that pops into my head is Dansk, the Great Dane owned by the headmaster at my high school. The next Great Dane I visualize is Helga, who was Dansk's replacement. The next is my aunt's dog in Arizona, and my final image comes from an advertisement for Fitwell seat covers that featured that kind of dog. My memories usually appear in my imagination in strict chronological order, and the images I visualize are always specific. There is no generic, generalized Great Dane.

However, not all people with autism are highly visual thinkers, nor do they all process information this way. People throughout the world are on a continuum of visualization skills ranging from next to none, to seeing vague generalized pictures, to seeing semi-specific pictures, to seeing, as in my case, in very specific pictures.

I'm always forming new visual images when I invent new equipment or think of something novel and amusing. I can take images that I have seen, rearrange them, and create new pictures. For example, I can imagine what a dip vat would look like modeled on computer graphics by placing it on my memory of a friend's computer screen. Since his computer is not programmed to do the fancy 3-D rotary graphics, I take computer graphics I have seen on TV or in the movies and super-impose them in my memory. In my visual imagination the dip vat will appear in the kind of high-quality computer graphics shown on *Star Trek*. I can then take a specific dip vat, such as the one at Red River, and redraw it on the computer screen in my mind. I can even duplicate the cartoonlike, three-dimensional skeletal image on the computer screen or imagine the dip vat as a videotape of the real thing.

Similarly, I learned how to draw engineering designs by closely observing a very talented draftsman when we worked together at the same feed yard construction company. David was able to render the most fabulous drawings effortlessly. After I left the company, I was forced to do all my own drafting. By studying David's drawings for many hours and photographing them in my memory, I was actually able to emulate David's drawing style. I laid some of his drawings out so I could look at them while I drew my first design. Then I drew my new plan and copied his style. After making three or four drawings, I no longer had to have his drawings out on the table. My video memory was now fully programmed. Copying designs is one thing, but after I drew the Red River drawings, I could not believe I had done them. At the time, I thought they were a gift from God. Another factor that helped me to learn to draw well was something as simple as using the same tools that David used. I used the same brand of pencil, and the ruler and straight edge forced me to slow down and trace the visual images in my imagination.

My artistic abilities became evident when I was in first and second grade. I had a good eye for color and painted watercolors of the beach. One time in fourth grade I modeled a lovely horse from clay. I just did it spontaneously, though I was not able to duplicate it. In high school and college I never attempted engineering drawing, but I learned the value of slowing down while drawing during a college art class. Our assignment had been to spend two hours drawing a picture of one of our shoes. The teacher insisted that the entire two hours be spent drawing that one shoe. I was amazed at how well my drawing came out. While my initial attempts at drafting were terrible, when I visualized myself as David, the draftsman, I'd automatically slow down.

Processing Nonvisual Information

Autistics have problems learning things that cannot be thought about in pictures. The easiest words for an autistic child to learn are nouns, because they directly relate to pictures. Highly verbal autistic children like I was can sometimes learn how to read with phonics. Written words were too abstract for me to remember, but I could laboriously remember the approximately fifty phonetic sounds and a few rules. Lower-functioning children often learn better by association, with the aid of word labels attached to objects in their environment. Some very impaired autistic children learn more easily if words are spelled out with plastic letters they can feel.

Spatial words such as "over" and "under" had no meaning for me until I had a visual image to fix them in my memory. Even now, when I hear the word "under" by itself, I automatically picture myself getting under the cafeteria tables at school during an air-raid drill, a common occurrence on the East Coast during the early fifties. The first memory that any single word triggers is almost always a childhood memory. I can remember the teacher telling us to be quiet and walking single-file into the cafeteria, where six or eight children huddled under each table. If I continue on the same train of thought, more and more associative memories of elementary school emerge. I can remember the teacher scolding me after I hit Alfred for putting dirt on my shoe. All of these memories play like video-tapes in the VCR in my imagination. If I allow my mind to keep associating, it will wander a million miles away from the word "under," to submarines under the Antarctic and the Beatles song "Yellow Submarine." If I let my mind pause on the picture of the yellow submarine, I then hear the song. As I start humming the song and get to the part about people coming on board, my association switches to the gangway of a ship I saw in Australia.

I also visualize verbs. The word "jumping" triggers a memory of jumping hurdles at the mock Olympics held at my elementary school. Adverbs often trigger inappropriate images—"quickly" reminds me of Nestle's Quik—unless they are paired with a verb, which modifies my visual image. For example, "he ran quickly" triggers an animated image of Dick from the first-grade reading book running fast, and "he walked slowly" slows the image down. As a child, I left out words such as "is," "the," and "it," because they had no meaning by themselves. Similarly, words like "of" and "an" made no sense. Eventually I learned how to use them properly, because my parents always spoke correct English and I mimicked their speech patterns. To this day certain verb conjugations, such as "to be," are absolutely meaningless to me.

When I read, I translate written words into color movies or I simply store a photo of the written page to be read later. When I retrieve the material, I see a photocopy of the page in my imagination. I can then read it like a TelePrompTer. It is likely that Raymond, the autistic savant depicted in the movie *Rain Man,* used a similar strategy to memorize telephone books, maps, and other information. He simply photocopied each page of the phone book into his memory. When he wanted to find a certain number, he just scanned pages of the phone book that were in his mind. To pull information out of my memory, I have to replay the video. Pulling facts up quickly is sometimes difficult, because I have to play bits of different videos until I find the right tape. This takes time.

When I am unable to convert text to pictures, it is usually because the text has no concrete meaning. Some philosophy books and articles about the cattle futures market are simply incomprehensible. It is much easier for me to understand written text that describes something that can be easily translated into pictures. The following sentence from a story in the February 21, 1994, issue of *Time* magazine, describing the Winter Olympics figure-skating championships, is a good example: "All the elements are in place—the spotlights, the swelling waltzes and jazz tunes, the sequined sprites taking to the air." In my imagination I see the skating rink and skaters. However, if I ponder too long on the word "elements," I will make the inappropriate association of a periodic table on the wall of my high school chemistry classroom. Pausing on the word "sprite" triggers an image of a Sprite can in my refrigerator instead of a pretty young skater.

Teachers who work with autistic children need to understand associative thought patterns. An autistic child will often use a word in an inappropriate manner. Sometimes these uses have a logical associative meaning and other times they don't. For example, an autistic child might say the word "dog" when he wants to go outside. The word "dog" is associated with going outside. In my own case, I can remember both logical and illogical use of inappropriate words. When I was six, I learned to say "prosecution." I had absolutely no idea what it meant, but it sounded nice when I said it, so I used it as an exclamation every time my kite hit the ground. I must have baffled more than a few people who heard me exclaim "Prosecution!" to my downward-spiraling kite.

Discussions with other autistic people reveal similar visual styles of thinking about tasks that most people do sequentially. An autistic man who composes music told me that he makes "sound pictures" using small pieces of other music to create new compositions. A computer programmer with autism told me that he sees the general pattern of the program tree. After he visualizes the skeleton for the program, he simply writes the code for each branch. I use similar methods when I review scientific literature and troubleshoot at meat plants. I take specific findings or observations and combine them to find new basic principles and general concepts.

My thinking pattern always starts with specifics and works toward generalization in an associational and nonsequential way. As if I were attempting to figure out what the picture on a jigsaw puzzle is when only one third of the puzzle is completed, I am able to fill in the missing pieces by scanning my video library. Chinese mathematicians who can make large calculations in their heads work the same way. At first they need an abacus, the Chinese calculator, which consists of rows of beads on wires in a frame. They make calculations by moving the rows of beads. When a mathematician becomes really skilled, he simply visualizes the abacus in his imagination and no longer needs a real one. The beads move on a visualized video abacus in his brain.

Abstract Thought

Growing up, I learned to convert abstract ideas into pictures as a way to understand them. I visualized concepts such as peace or honesty with symbolic images. I thought of peace as a dove, an Indian peace pipe, or TV or newsreel footage of the signing of a peace agreement. Honesty was represented by an image of placing one's hand on the Bible in court. A news report describing a person returning a wallet with all the money in it provided a picture of honest behavior.

The Lord's Prayer was incomprehensible until I broke it down into specific visual images. The power and the glory were represented by a semicircular rainbow and an electrical tower. These childhood visual images are still triggered every time I hear the Lord's Prayer. The words "thy will be done" had no meaning when I was a child, and today the meaning is still vague. Will is a hard concept to visualize. When I think about it, I imagine God throwing a lightning bolt. Another adult with autism wrote that he visualized "Thou art in heaven" as God with an easel above the clouds. "Trespassing" was pictured as black and orange NO TRESPASSING signs. The word "Amen" at the end of the prayer was a mystery: a man at the end made no sense.

As a teenager and young adult I had to use concrete symbols to understand abstract concepts such as getting along with people and moving on to the next steps of my life, both of which were always difficult. I knew I did not fit in with my high school peers, and I was unable to figure out what I was doing wrong. No matter how hard I tried, they made fun of me. They called me "workhorse," "tape recorder," and "bones" because I was skinny. At the time I was able to figure out why they called me "workhorse" and "bones," but "tape recorder" puzzled me. Now I realize that I must have sounded like a tape recorder when I repeated things verbatim over and over. But back then I just could not figure out why I was such a social dud. I sought refuge in doing things I was good at, such as working on reroofing the barn or practicing my riding prior to a horse show. Personal relationships made absolutely no sense to me until I developed visual symbols of doors and windows. It was then that I started to understand concepts such as learning the give-and-take of a relationship. I still wonder what would have happened to me if I had not been able to visualize my way in the world.

The really big challenge for me was making the transition from high school to college. People with autism have tremendous difficulty with change. In order to deal with a major change such as leaving high school, I needed a way to rehearse it, acting out each phase in my life by walking through an actual door, window, or gate.

When I was graduating from high school, I would go and sit on the roof of my dormitory and look up at the stars and think about how I would cope with leaving. It was there I discovered a little door that led to a bigger roof while my dormitory was being remodeled. While I was still living in this old New England house, a much larger building was being constructed over it. One day the carpenters tore out a section of the old roof next to my room. When I walked out, I was now able to look up into the partially finished new building. High on one side was a small wooden door that led to the new roof. The building was changing, and it was now time for me to change too. I could relate to that. I had found the symbolic key.

When I was in college, I found another door to symbolize getting ready for graduation. It was a small metal trap door that went out onto the flat roof of the dormitory. I had to actually practice going through this door many times. When I finally graduated from Franklin Pierce, I walked through a third, very important door, on the library roof.

I no longer use actual physical doors or gates to symbolize each transition in my life. When I reread years of diary entries while writing this book, a clear pattern emerged. Each door or gate enabled me to move on to the next level. My life was a series of incremental steps. I am often asked what the single breakthrough was that enabled me to adapt to autism. There was no single breakthrough. It was a series of incremental improvements. My diary entries show very clearly that I was fully aware that when I mastered one door, it was only one step in a whole series.

April 22, 1970

Today everything is completed at Franklin Pierce College and it is now time to walk through the little door in the library. I ponder now about what I should leave as a message on the library roof for future people to find.

I have reached the top of one step and I am now at the bottom step of graduate school.

For the top of the building is the highest point on campus and I have gone as far as I can go now.

I have conquered the summit of FPC. Higher ones still remain unchallenged.

Class 70

I went through the little door tonight and placed the plaque on the top of the library roof. I was not as nervous this time. I had been much more nervous in the past. Now I have already made it and the little door and the mountain had already been climbed. The conquering of this mountain is only the beginning for the next mountain.

The word "commencement" means beginning and the top of the library is the beginning of graduate school. It is human nature to strive, and this is why people will climb mountains. The reason why is that people strive to prove that they could do it.

*After all, why should we send a man to the moon? The only real justifica-
tion is that it is human nature to keep striving out. Man is never satisfied with
one goal he keeps reaching. The real reason for going to the library roof was to
prove that I could do it.*

During my life I have been faced with five or six major doors or gates to go
through. I graduated from Franklin Pierce, a small liberal arts college, in 1970, with
a degree in psychology, and moved to Arizona to get a Ph.D. As I found myself getting less interested in psychology and more interested in cattle and animal science,
I prepared myself for another big change in my life—switching from a psychology
major to an animal science major. On May 8, 1971, I wrote:

*I feel as if I am being pulled more and more in the farm direction. I walked
through the cattle chute gate but I am still holding on tightly to the gate post. The
wind is blowing harder and harder and I feel that I will let go of the gate post
and go back to the farm; at least for a while. Wind has played an important part
in many of the doors. On the roof, the wind was blowing. Maybe this is a symbol
that the next level that is reached is not ultimate and that I must keep moving
on. At the party [a psychology department party] I felt completely out of place and
it seems as if the wind is causing my hands to slip from the gate post so that I
can ride free on the wind.*

At that time I still struggled in the social arena, largely because I didn't have a
concrete visual corollary for the abstraction known as "getting along with people."
An image finally presented itself to me while I was washing the bay window in the
cafeteria (students were required to do jobs in the dining room). I had no idea my
job would take on symbolic significance when I started. The bay window consisted
of three glass sliding doors enclosed by storm windows. To wash the inside of the bay
window, I had to crawl through the sliding door. The door jammed while I was washing the inside panes, and I was imprisoned between the two windows. In order to get
out without shattering the door, I had to ease it back very carefully. It struck me that
relationships operate the same way. They also shatter easily and have to be approached carefully. I then made a further association about how the careful opening of doors was related to establishing relationships in the first place. While I was
trapped between the windows, it was almost impossible to communicate through the
glass. Being autistic is like being trapped like this. The windows symbolized my feelings of disconnection from other people and helped me cope with the isolation.
Throughout my life, door and window symbols have enabled me to make progress
and connections that are unheard of for some people with autism.

In more severe cases of autism, the symbols are harder to understand and often
appear to be totally unrelated to the things they represent. D. Park and P. Youderian
described the use of visual symbols and numbers by Jessy Park, then a twelve-year-old

autistic girl, to describe abstract concepts such as good and bad. Good things, such as rock music, were represented by drawings of four doors and no clouds. Jessy rated most classical music as pretty good, drawing two doors and two clouds. The spoken word was rated as very bad, with a rating of zero doors and four clouds. She had formed a visual rating system using doors and clouds to describe these abstract qualities. Jessy also had an elaborate system of good and bad numbers, though researchers have not been able to decipher her system fully.

Many people are totally baffled by autistic symbols, but to an autistic person they may provide the only tangible reality or understanding of the world. For example, "French toast" may mean happy if the child was happy while eating it. When the child visualizes a piece of French toast, he becomes happy. A visual image or word becomes associated with an experience. Clara Park, Jessy's mother, described her daughter's fascination with objects such as electric blanket controls and heaters. She had no idea why the objects were so important to Jessy, though she did observe that Jessy was happiest, and her voice was no longer a monotone, when she was thinking about her special things. Jessy was able to talk, but she was unable to tell people why her special things were important. Perhaps she associated electric blanket controls and heaters with warmth and security. The word "cricket" made her happy, and "partly heard song" meant "I don't know." The autistic mind works via these visual associations. At some point in Jessy's life, a partly heard song was associated with not knowing.

Ted Hart, a man with severe autism, has almost no ability to generalize and no flexibility in his behavior. His father, Charles, described how on one occasion Ted put wet clothes in the dresser after the dryer broke. He just went on to the next step in a clothes-washing sequence that he had learned by rote. He has no common sense. I would speculate that such rigid behavior and lack of ability to generalize may be partly due to having little or no ability to change or modify visual memories. Even though my memories of things are stored as individual specific memories, I am able to modify my mental images. For example, I can imagine a church painted in different colors or put the steeple of one church onto the roof of another; but when I hear somebody say the word "steeple," the first church that I see in my imagination is almost always a childhood memory and not a church image that I have manipulated. This ability to modify images in my imagination helped me to learn how to generalize.

Today, I no longer need door symbols. Over the years I have built up enough real experiences and information from articles and books I have read to be able to make changes and take necessary steps as new situations present themselves. Plus, I have always been an avid reader, and I am driven to take in more and more information to add to my video library. A severely autistic computer programmer once said that reading was "taking in information." For me, it is like programming a computer.

Visual Thinking and Mental Imagery

Recent studies of patients with brain damage and of brain imaging indicate that visual and verbal thought may work via different brain systems. Recordings of blood flow in the brain indicate that when a person visualizes something such as walking through his neighborhood, blood flow increases dramatically in the visual cortex, in parts of the brain that are working hard. Studies of brain-damaged patients show that injury to the left posterior hemisphere can stop the generation of visual images from stored long-term memories, while language and verbal memory are not impaired. This indicates that visual imagery and verbal thought may depend on distinct neurological systems.

The visual system may also contain separate subsystems for mental imagery and image rotation. Image rotation skills appear to be located on the right side of the brain, whereas visual imagery is in the left rear of the brain. In autism, it is possible that the visual system has expanded to make up for verbal and sequencing deficits. The nervous system has a remarkable ability to compensate when it is damaged. Another part can take over for a damaged part.

Recent research by Dr. Pascual-Leone at the National Institutes of Health indicates that exercising a visual skill can make the brain's motor map expand. Research with musicians indicates that real practice on the piano and imagining playing the piano have the same effect on motor maps, as measured by brain scans. The motor maps expand during both real piano playing and mental imagery; random pushing of the keys has no effect. Athletes have also found that both mental practice and real practice can improve a motor skill. Research with patients with damage to the hippocampus has indicated that conscious memory of events and motor learning are separate neurological systems. A patient with hippocampal damage can learn a motor task and get better with practice, but each time he practices he will have no conscious memory of doing the task. The motor circuits become trained, but damage to the hippocampus prevents the formation of new conscious memories. Therefore, the motor circuits learn a new task, such as solving a simple mechanical puzzle, but the person does not remember seeing or doing the puzzle. With repeated practice, the person gets better and better at it, but each time the puzzle is presented, he says he has never seen it before.

I am fortunate in that I am able to build on my library of images and visualize solutions based on those pictures. However, most people with autism lead extremely limited lives, in part because they cannot handle any deviation from their routine. For me, every experience builds on the visual memories I carry from prior experience, and in this way my world continues to grow.

About two years ago I made a personal breakthrough when I was hired to remodel a meat plant that used very cruel restraint methods during kosher slaughter. Prior to slaughter, live cattle were hung upside down by a chain attached to one back leg. It was so horrible I could not stand to watch it. The frantic bellows of terrified cattle could be heard in both the office and the parking lot. Sometimes an animal's back leg was broken during hoisting. This dreadful practice totally violated the humane intent of kosher slaughter. My job was to rip out this cruel system and replace it with a chute that would hold the animal in a standing position while the rabbi performed kosher slaughter. Done properly, the animal should remain calm and would not be frightened.

The new restraining chute was a narrow metal stall which held one steer. It was equipped with a yoke to hold the animal's head, a rear pusher gate to nudge the steer forward into the yoke, and a belly restraint which was raised under the belly like an elevator. To operate the restrainer, the operator had to push six hydraulic control levers in the proper sequence to move the entrance and discharge gates as well as the head- and body-positioning devices. The basic design of this chute had been around for about thirty years, but I added pressure-regulating devices and changed some critical dimensions to make it more comfortable for the animal and to prevent excessive pressure from being applied.

Prior to actually operating the chute at the plant, I ran it in the machine shop before it was shipped. Even though no cattle were present, I was able to program my visual and tactile memory with images of operating the chute. After running the empty chute for five minutes, I had accurate mental pictures of how the gates and other parts of the apparatus moved. I also had tactile memories of how the levers on this particular chute felt when pushed. Hydraulic valves are like musical instruments; different brands of valves have a different feel, just as different types of wind instruments do. Operating the controls in the machine shop enabled me to practice later via mental imagery. I had to visualize the actual controls on the chute and, in my imagination, watch my hands pushing the levers. I could feel in my mind how much force was needed to move the gates at different speeds. I rehearsed the procedure many times in my mind with different types of cattle entering the chute.

On the first day of operation at the plant, I was able to walk up to the chute and run it almost perfectly. It worked best when I operated the hydraulic levers unconsciously, like using my legs for walking. If I thought about the levers, I got all mixed up and pushed them the wrong way. I had to force myself to relax and just allow the restrainer to become part of my body, while completely forgetting about the levers. As each animal entered, I concentrated on moving the apparatus slowly and gently so as not to scare him. I watched his reactions so that I applied only enough pressure to hold him snugly. Excessive pressure would cause discomfort. If his ears were laid back against his head or he struggled, I knew I had squeezed him too hard. Animals are very sensitive to hydraulic equipment. They feel the smallest movement of the control levers.

Through the machine I reached out and held the animal. When I held his head in the yoke, I imagined placing my hands on his forehead and under his chin and gently easing him into position. Body boundaries seemed to disappear, and I had no awareness of pushing the levers. The rear pusher gate and head yoke became an extension of my hands.

People with autism sometimes have body boundary problems. They are unable to judge by feel where their body ends and the chair they are sitting on or the object they are holding begins, much like what happens when a person loses a limb but still experiences the feeling of the limb being there. In this case, the parts of the apparatus that held the animal felt as if they were a continuation of my own body, similar to the phantom limb effect. If I just concentrated on holding the animal gently and keeping him calm, I was able to run the restraining chute very skillfully.

During this intense period of concentration I no longer heard noise from the plant machinery. I didn't feel the sweltering Alabama summer heat, and everything seemed quiet and serene. It was almost a religious experience. It was my job to hold the animal gently, and it was the rabbi's job to perform the final deed. I was able to look at each animal, to hold him gently and make him as comfortable as possible during the last moments of his life. I had participated in the ancient slaughter ritual the way it was supposed to be. A new door had been opened. It felt like walking on water.

For Discussion:

1. How have Grandin's visual gifts allowed her to create new cattle equipment? What obstacles has she encountered in the process?
2. How does Grandin describe her process of creation? What is the correlation between imagination and memory?
3. Explain the difference between logical and associative thinking, using your own examples.

For Fact-Finding, Research, and Writing:

1. Locate a book or article that engages the topic of animal intelligence. How have researchers attempted to define animal intelligence? How do their methods and conclusions compare to ways that theorists attempted to define human intelligence?
2. Provide a professionally accepted definition of autism. How do you know your source is reliable? Are there any ongoing disputes over the definition?
3. Do Grandin's abilities fit into one or more of Howard Gardner's types of intelligence? After reading Grandin, can you think of intelligences that should be recognized besides those listed by Gardner?
4. Compare Grandin's description of her memory to Schacter's account of memory. Do they overlap in any ways?

Daniel L. Schacter, "Building Memories: Encoding and Retrieving the Present and the Past"

Schacter is Chair of the Department of Psychology at Harvard University. His publications are concerned with the psychological and biological aspects of memory and amnesia. He has authored several books, including *Searching for Memory: The Brain, the Mind, and the Past,* from which this selection is taken.

 Before You Read:

Write down one or two metaphors that describe how memory works. Then make up one of your own.

"Building Memories: Encoding and Retrieving the Present and the Past"

Daniel L. Schacter

ONE OF MY favorite places is the Museum of Modern Art in midtown Manhattan. A native New Yorker, I have made regular pilgrimages to this mecca of art since high school days, and have come to regard many of the paintings there as wise and familiar old friends. Like close friends, however, they cannot always be there when you want them. More than once I have returned to a favorite spot, eagerly anticipating another look at an esteemed painting by de Chirico, Hopper, or Klee, only to learn that it was away on extended loan. Although the painting's absence is disappointing, I sometimes attempt to make up for it by conducting an informal study of my own memory for the piece: What objects and people does the painting include, and how are they located relative to one another? How big is the work? What are the dominant colors and important themes? I can check the accuracy of my answers by locating a reproduction in the museum shop.

    The French artist Sophie Calle wondered what aspects of a painting linger in the memories of viewers who are familiar with it. To find out, she conducted a kind of naturalistic memory experiment with an artistic twist. Calle asked a cross section of museum personnel to describe their recollections of several paintings that had been removed from their usual locations at the Museum of Modern Art. She proceeded to create a "memory ghost" for each missing painting—exhibiting the exact words used by the museum workers to describe their recollections of the piece. The most striking outcome was the sheer variety of recollections that her inquiry elicited. Some people recalled only an isolated color or object; others remembered at length subtle nuances of form, space, people, and things.

Calle's observations imply that different people retain and recollect very different aspects of their everyday environments. Why would this be so? Scientists agree that the brain does not operate like a camera or a copying machine. Then what aspects of reality do remain in memory once an episode has concluded? These kinds of questions have dogged every philosopher, psychologist, and neuroscientist who has thought seriously about the nature of remembering and forgetting. Throughout much of the history of scholarly thinking about memory, dating back to the Greeks, people have approached these questions by adopting a spatial metaphor of the mind. The Greek philosophers held that memory is like a wax tablet on which experiences are imprinted, perhaps forever; centuries later, Sigmund Freud* and William James** both conjectured that memories are like objects placed in rooms of a house. One pundit compared memory to a garbage can that contains a random assortment of objects.[1]

The cognitive psychologist Ulric Neisser called the idea that faithful copies of experience are kept in the mind, only to reappear again at some later time pretty much in their original form, the "reappearance hypothesis." Neisser proposed instead that only bits and pieces of incoming data are represented in memory. These retained fragments of experience in turn provide a basis for reconstructing a past event, much as a paleontologist is able to reconstruct a dinosaur from fragments of bone. "Out of a few stored bone chips," reflected Neisser, "we remember a dinosaur."[2]

A visual analogue of Neisser's reflections is found in the work of the Israeli artist Eran Shakine. Shakine has explored his personal past by making collaged paintings in which fragments of old photographs and text are submerged in layers of milky white paint as exemplified by his painting "Hadassah." Shakine struggles with the seeming paradox that our sense of self, the foundation of our psychological existence, depends crucially on these fragmentary and often elusive remnants of experience. What we believe about ourselves is determined by what we remember about our pasts. If memory worked like a video recorder, allowing us to replay the past in exact detail, we could check our beliefs about ourselves against an objective record of what happened in our lives. We must make do instead with the bits and pieces of the past that memory grants us.

The general idea that memories are built from fragments of experience can help us understand key aspects of the rememberer's recollective experience, as

*Sigmund Freud: (1856–1939), Austrian neurologist and the founder of modern psychoanalysis.
**William James: (1842–1910), American psychologist and philosopher.

well as memory distortions and effects of implicit memory. . . . For now, it is important to understand something more about how the fragments are constructed and reconstructed.

Bubbles P. and the Nature of Encoding

Bubbles P., a professional gambler from Philadelphia, spends virtually all his time making bets: shooting craps at local gaming clubs, dealing cards in illegal poker games, attempting to come up with new systems to beat the numbers. He is not a highly educated man—Bubbles claims to have read only two books in his entire life—but he is capable of certain feats of memory that are well beyond the abilities of even the most erudite Ph.D.s. Most people have difficulty recalling in correct order a string of more than seven digits immediately after seeing or hearing them. When the task is to repeat them backward, most people remember even fewer digits. But Bubbles P.'s digit memory is usually spectacular in either direction.[3] To appreciate his ability, inspect each of the digits at the end of this sentence for one second each, then look away from the page and immediately try to recall them in reverse order: 43902641974935483256. I suspect that by the time you worked your way back to 8, 4, or 5, you were already having problems going any further, and I would be willing to place a bet that nobody made it to 0, much less all the way back to the beginning. Bubbles P., however, can rattle off in correct backward order every one of the twenty numbers in this sequence and similar ones. How does he do it? Has he simply been gifted with an extraordinary, perhaps photographic, memory?

The answer likely resides in the same process that contributes to constructing fragments of experience. Psychologists refer to it as an *encoding* process—a procedure for transforming something a person sees, hears, thinks, or feels into a memory. Encoding can be thought of as a special way of paying attention to ongoing events that has a major impact on subsequent memory for them.

Psychologists first recognized the importance of encoding processes during debates about short-term memory that raged in the 1960s. Short-term memories last for only seconds. Nowadays, researchers believe that such temporary records depend on a specialized system, called *working memory,* that holds small amounts of information for brief time periods, as in the backward recall task you just performed. Everyone is familiar with the operation of working memory from experiences in day-to-day life. Imagine that you need to look up a friend's number in the phone book. You find the number, then walk across the room to make the call, all the while madly repeating the digits to yourself as rapidly as you can. If you are distracted for even a moment during your walk to the phone, you will need to consult the book again; if you punch in the number successfully, you will probably forget it almost immediately. Why are such memories so fleeting?

Part of the answer is that working memory depends on a different network of brain structures than long-term memory systems do. Some patients with damage to

the inner part of the temporal lobes in the center of the brain have little or no difficulty retaining a string of digits for several seconds, yet they have great difficulty
forming and explicitly remembering more enduring memories. Other patients who
have suffered damage to a specific part of the parietal lobe on the cortical surface
can form long-term memories but cannot hold and repeat back a string of digits.
They lack a specific part of working memory, known as the *phonological loop*, that most
of us rely on when we need to hold a small amount of linguistic information in mind
for several seconds.[4]

This is where the concept of encoding comes in. By relying on your phonological loop to repeat a phone number madly to yourself, you encode it only superficially. To establish a durable memory, incoming information must be encoded much
more thoroughly, or deeply, by associating it meaningfully with knowledge that already exists in memory. You must do more than simply recycle the information in
the phonological loop. Suppose that instead of just repeating the phone number—
555-6024—to yourself over and over, you attempt to make the number meaningful
in some way. For example, if you play golf (as I do), you might encode the number
by thinking that 555 is the yardage of a par-5 hole and that 6024 is the length of a
relatively short 18-hole course. You have now carried out a deep encoding and
should be able to remember the information much longer and more accurately than
if you merely repeat it. This is known in the psychological literature as a "depth of
processing" effect.[5]

The same sort of effect is probably at work in cases like that of Bubbles P.
Bubbles is knowledgeable about numbers and seems able to segregate effortlessly a
long string of them into meaningful units or chunks. Rather than frantically recy-
cling them, as most of us do, Bubbles uses the skill he has developed with numbers
through years of gambling to link incoming digits to knowledge already in his
memory. Bubbles does not have a generally extraordinary memory: his memory for
words, faces, objects, and locations—anything other than numbers—is no better than
average.

ELABORATIVE ENCODING

Memory researchers have tried to devise special techniques to gain control over the
encoding operations that a person performs, and these operations have played a
crucial role in the unfolding story of memory and amnesia research during the past
twenty years.[6] Suppose I tell you that an hour from now, I will test your ability to recall the following words: floor, car, tree, cake, shirt, flower, cup, grass, dog, table. You
might try to remember the words by conjuring up visual images, by simply repeating the words again and again, or by making up a story that connects the words to
one another. As long as I leave you to your own devices, I cannot learn much about
how encoding processes influence memory. I need to come up with some way of
controlling how you think about the to-be-remembered items.

Memory researchers have solved this problem by using what is known as an orienting task. Instead of allowing people to memorize the target items in any manner they please, an orienting task guides encoding by requiring a person to answer a specific question about the target. For example, I could induce you to carry out a deep, semantic encoding of target words by asking for a yes or no answer to questions such as, "Is *shirt* a type of clothing?" You cannot answer this question accurately without thinking about the meaning of the word *shirt*. To induce you to engage in shallow, nonsemantic encoding of the word, I could ask you to answer a question such as, "Does *shirt* contain more vowels or more consonants?" You can answer this question easily without attending to the meaning of the word. If I later test your ability to recollect *shirt* and other words on the list, I can be fairly confident that you will be able to recall or recognize many of the words that you encoded semantically and few of the words that you encoded nonsemantically.

This finding may not seem particularly surprising; everyday experience suggests that something that is meaningful will be more easily remembered than something that is not. But it turns out that only a certain kind of semantic encoding promotes high levels of memory performance—an *elaborative* encoding operation that allows you to integrate new information with what you already know. For example, if I induce you to encode one of our study list words by posing the question, "Is *shirt* a type of insect?" you must pay attention to the meaning of the word in order to provide the correct answer. As you formulate a response to this question, however, you do not integrate the target word with your preexisting knowledge of shirts—that is, you do not carry out an effective elaboration of the word *shirt*. If I test you after you have answered this kind of orienting question, you will show surprisingly poor memory for whether the word *shirt* was on the list.[7]

In our everyday lives, memory is a natural, perhaps automatic, byproduct of the manner in which we think about an unfolding episode. If we want to improve our chances of remembering an incident or learning a fact, we need to make sure that we carry out elaborative encoding by reflecting on the information and relating it to other things we already know. Laboratory studies have shown that simply intending to remember something is unlikely to be helpful, unless we translate that intention into an effective elaborative encoding. For example, when preparing for an exam, a good student may make a special effort to form meaningful mental associations among the study materials, whereas the same student may not bother engaging in such elaborative encoding if she is not going to be tested. In my earlier example, carrying out the orienting task—answering the question, "Is *shirt* a type of clothing?"—ensures that you have already made effective use of elaborative encoding processes; "trying to remember" adds nothing beyond that.

The issue can be turned around, too: most experiences that we recall effortlessly from our day-to-day existence—yesterday's important lunch date, the big party last weekend, last year's summer vacation—are not initially encoded with any particular intention to remember them. Occasionally, the apparent significance of an event may prompt us to make a special effort to encode it deeply. However, day-to-day existence would be precarious and probably unmanageable if we had to make an intentional effort to encode each and every episode from our daily lives in order to be able to recollect it later. Instead, a kind of natural selection drives us. What we already know shapes what we select and encode; things that are meaningful to us spontaneously elicit the kind of elaborations that promote later recall. Our memory systems are built so that we are likely to remember what is most important to us.

Carrying out a deep, elaborative encoding influences not only the quantity of what can be remembered but also the quality of our recollective experience. . . . When we meet a new person and encode information elaboratively, we are more likely later to "remember" the episode; if we do not elaborate, we are more likely to "just know" that the person seems familiar. Elaborative encoding is a critical and perhaps necessary ingredient of our ability to remember in rich and vivid detail what has happened to us in the past.[8]

But the dependence of explicit memory on elaboration has a downside, too: if we do not carry out elaborative encoding, we will be left with impoverished recollections. Experiments have shown that people are surprisingly poor at remembering what is on the front and back of a penny, despite seeing and handling pennies all the time.[9] It is likely, however, that we encode the features of a penny quite superficially, because using pennies in everyday life requires only that we notice the general shape and color of the coin. The encoding process can halt once we have extracted the necessary information; there is no need to carry out a more elaborate analysis of the coin. In this example, we are behaving like experimental volunteers who perform shallow or superficial orienting tasks, and later recall little or nothing of what they have seen. If we operate on automatic pilot much of the time and do not reflect on our environment and our experiences, we may pay a price by retaining only sketchy memories of where we have been and what we have done.

ENCODING AND MNEMONIC DEVICES

Elaborative encoding is a critical component of virtually all popular memory-improvement techniques. The oldest example of a memory-improvement strategy is visual imagery mnemonics, first developed by the Greek orator Simonides in 477 B.C. As the story goes, Simonides, a poet, was called to recite verse at a large banquet. During the course of the evening, he was unexpectedly summoned outside to meet two young men; the moment he left, the roof of the banquet hall collapsed, crushing and mutilating beyond recognition all the guests. Simonides became a hero because he was able to reconstruct the guest list by imagining each location around the table, which brought to mind the person who had been sitting there.

He accomplished this feat by using a system of mnemonics he had developed known as the method of *loci*, which became famous in ancient Greece after this incident. The method involves encoding information into memory by conjuring up vivid mental images and mentally placing them in familiar locations. Later, at the time of attempted recall, one consults the locations, just as Simonides did.[10] If, for example, you wanted to remember to buy beer, potato chips, and toothpaste, you could use rooms in your home as locations, and imagine your bedroom afloat in beer, your kitchen stuffed from top to bottom with bags of potato chips, and your living room slathered with toothpaste. Upon arriving at the store, you could then take a mental walk around your house and "see" what is in each room.

Modern practitioners use the method of loci and other related imagery techniques to perform such feats as remembering all the names and numbers listed in good-sized telephone books. These accomplishments are nothing new, however. Greek orators used mnemonics to memorize speeches of extraordinary length, and Roman generals used them to remember the names of tens of thousands of men in their command. During the Middle Ages, scholastics used mnemonics to aid in the learning of interminable religious tomes. In fact, throughout the Middle Ages, mnemonics played a major role in society, exerting a large influence on artistic and religious life.[11]

By the fifteenth and sixteenth centuries, Simonides' relatively simple method of loci had been superseded by increasingly baroque "memory theaters" that were conceived and drawn by some of Europe's most inventive minds. These intricate and sometimes beautiful structures consisted of hundreds of locations, each containing ideas and precepts that were frequently mystical. Learning all the locations and precepts in a memory theater—into which one could later mentally deposit new to-be-remembered information—was itself an arduous, sometimes impossible task. The excesses of mnemonic systems eventually created a backlash against them.[12]

My central point is that the core cognitive act of visual imagery mnemonics—creating an image and linking it to a mental location—is a form of deep, elaborate encoding. Mnemonic techniques produce rich and detailed encodings that are tightly linked to preexisting knowledge, yet are distinctively different from other items in memory. It also seems likely, in light of my earlier discussion about the importance of visual reexperiencing in conscious recollection, that the visual format of imagery mnemonics enhances its usefulness as an aid to explicit remembering.[13] . . .

THE MUSEUM TEST

The notion of elaboration also provides interesting perspectives on the recollections of the Museum of Modern Art personnel in the project I mentioned earlier. Several of them were asked to recall the Magritte painting, "The Menaced Assassin" (Fig. 1). Their memory reports are revealing:

1. There's a lot of pink flesh, red blood, guys in black. The background is blue with French ironwork on the balcony, the bedroom is beige, but the only striking color is that blood painted red that looks like ketchup.
2. It's a painting with a smooth surface, an easy one to spot check. It is approximately five feet high and seven feet long. It is framed in a plain, dark, walnut-

stained molding, something austere. I never liked it. I don't like stories in painting. I don't like trying to figure them out. That's why I never gave it any time.

3. It has a film noir sort of feel, a mystery novel look to it. The puzzle is there. You have all those little clues that will probably lead you nowhere; there are men dressed in dark coats, and black bowler hats, the way Albert Finney was dressed in *Murder on the Orient Express,* placed in a room with a dead body. In the center, the one who seems to be the perpetrator is lifting the needle of a phonograph. Two weird-looking individuals are hiding to the side. There is a face looking from the balcony, almost like a sun on the horizon. And, when you look at her carefully, you realize that the towel probably conceals a decapitated head.

4. I think it's just a murder scene. Men in dark suits, a pale woman and dashes of red blood. That's all I remember.[14]

Based on what they recollected, I feel I can make reasonably confident guesses about their identities: Comment #4 probably belongs to a security guard or other nonprofessional staff, as does #1, which focuses solely on the physical features of the painting. Comment #2, which describes the work's exact measurements and properties of its frame, likely comes from someone charged with maintaining the painting. And the thematically rich set of memories in #3 no doubt belong to a curator or similar art professional. The rationale for these educated guesses is simple. What people remember about a painting is heavily influenced by how they think about or encode it, and exactly which aspects of a painting are elaborated depends on what kind of knowledge is already available in one's long-term memory.

Encoding and remembering are virtually inseparable. But the close relationship between the two can sometimes cause problems in our everyday lives. We remember

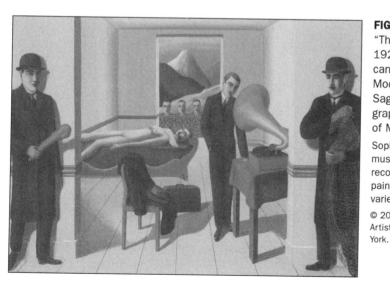

FIGURE 1 René Magritte, "The Menaced Assassin," 1926. 59¼" x 6' 4⅞". Oil on canvas. The Museum of Modern Art, New York. Kay Sage Tanguy Fund. Photograph © 1996 The Museum of Modern Art, New York.

Sophie Calle, an artist, queried museum personnel about their recollections of Magritte's painting, and elicited a wide variety of memories.

© 2003 C. Herscovici, Brussels/ Artists Rights Society (ARS), New York.

only what we have encoded, and what we encode depends on who we are—our past experiences, knowledge, and needs all have a powerful influence on what we retain. This is one reason why two different people can sometimes have radically divergent recollections of the same event. . . .

Historical Interlude

THE STORY OF RICHARD SEMON

The study of memory, like that of any scientific endeavor, has a history full of pioneering figures whose achievements are recognized and honored by researchers active in the field today. As a graduate student, I became intrigued by Richard Semon, who played an unappreciated role in the history of memory research. My curiosity was sparked by tantalizing comments from some of the twentieth century's most towering intellects, such as the philosopher Bertrand Russell* and the physicist Erwin Schrödinger,** concerning the great value of his work. Hardly anyone working on memory in 1977 had heard of him, but I soon discovered that his ideas were both original and important.[15]

Semon was born in Berlin in 1859, the same year that Charles Darwin published *The Origin of Species*. As a young man, Semon fell under the spell of this innovative approach to understanding evolution, and he went off to study at the University of Jena with the most famous German proponent of the new theory, the controversial biologist Ernst Haeckel. Semon received his Ph.D. and became a rising young professor at the University of Jena, a major European center for evolutionary research. Then, in 1897, he fell in love with the wife of an eminent colleague, Maria Krehl, who eventually left her husband to live with Semon. The two were vilified, Semon resigned his professorship, and the pair moved to Munich, where they were married. Semon, working on his own as private scholar, developed a theory of memory.

In 1904, he published a monograph, *Die Mneme*, that attempted to unite the biological analysis of heredity with the psychological and physiological analysis of memory. Semon argued that heredity and reproduction could be thought of as memory that preserves the effects of experience across generations. *Mneme*, a term Semon created in allusion to the Greek goddess of memory, Mnemosyne, refers to a fundamental process that he believed sub-serves both heredity and everyday memory. He conceived it as an elemental elasticity of biological tissue that allows the effects of experience to be preserved over time.

Semon distinguished three aspects or stages of Mneme that he deemed crucial to understanding both everyday memory and hereditary memory. Because he believed that ordinary language has too many potentially misleading connotations to

*__Bertrand Russell:__ Bertrand Arthur William Russell (1872–1970), English mathematician and philosopher.
**__Erwin Schrödinger:__ (1887–1961), American physicist.

be useful scientifically, Semon described the three stages with terms of his own invention: *engraphy* is Semon's term for encoding information into memory; *engram* refers to the enduring change in the nervous system (the "memory trace") that conserves the effects of experience across time; and *ecphory* is the process of activating or retrieving a memory.

Semon's unusual terminology and his emphasis on the memory/heredity analogy elicited a torrent of disapproval from prominent experts of the time. Yet precisely because of this controversy, his ideas about the operation of everyday memory tended to be overlooked. Only one reviewer of *Die Mneme*, the American psychologist Henry J. Watt, looked beyond the issues of heredity that so mesmerized biologists and picked out the single most important aspect of Semon's theory. "The most valuable part of the book is the concept of the ecphoric stimulus," reflected Watt. "However, Semon in his attempt to find something common in the reproduction of the organism and in the reproduction in the sense of memory, has lost sight of his own objective (the discovery of the nature of the ecphoric stimulus) and has gone astray."[16]

What exactly was Watt driving at? Psychologists at the time showed scant interest in memory-retrieval processes. Most of them believed that the likelihood of remembering an experience is determined entirely by the strength of associations that are formed when the information is initially encoded into memory. According to this view, if strong associations are formed—because the information is particularly vivid, or is repeated frequently enough—memory will later be good; if weak associations are formed, memory will later be poor. Semon, in contrast, argued that memory does not depend solely on the strength of associations. He contended that the likelihood of remembering also hinges on the ecphoric stimulus—the hint or cue that triggers recall—and how it is related to the engram, or memory trace, that was encoded initially. Watt realized that Semon had pinpointed a key aspect of memory that had been given short shrift, and wished that Semon had focused more extensively on it.

In 1909, Semon published a book that must have made Watt exceedingly happy. Entitled *Die Mnemischen Empfindungen (Mnemic Psychology)*, it was entirely about everyday memory, leaving aside the contentious issues of heredity in *Die Mneme*. Semon elaborated his theory of ecphory (retrieval processes) and applied it to a host of critical issues. Sadly for Semon, however, the new book aroused slight interest among researchers and had no detectable impact on the study of memory. Psychologists had little use for Semon's iconoclastic views on retrieval processes; in fact, they misunderstood his ideas. In addition, Semon's status as a scientific isolate, without prestigious institutional affiliations, did not enhance his cause. He was accorded the same kind of treatment given to flat-earth theorists, believers in perpetual-motion machines, and other cranks who exist at the fringes of science: he was ignored.

In 1918, Semon's wife died of cancer. Later that year, he placed a German flag on his wife's bed and shot himself through the heart.

Despite his nagging despair over the neglect of his work, Semon believed that his ideas would soon achieve widespread recognition among researchers. His hopes went largely unrealized, with the exception of one of his terminological inventions: the engram. The great neuroscientist Karl Lashley wrote a paper in 1950 entitled "In Search of the Engram," which summarizes Lashley's unsuccessful attempts to find the engram (the representation of a memory in the brain) in any single, restricted location. Because the paper became a classic in the field and contains the first prominent invocation of the term *engram,* most scientists have assumed that Lashley invented the word—and he did not even cite, much less discuss, Semon's prior use of the term.

Engrams are the transient or enduring changes in our brains that result from encoding an experience. Neuroscientists believe that the brain records an event by strengthening the connections between groups of neurons that participate in encoding the experience. A typical incident in our everyday lives consists of numerous sights, sounds, actions, and words. Different areas of the brain analyze these varied aspects of an event. As a result, neurons in the different regions become more strongly connected to one another. The new pattern of connections constitutes the brain's record of the event: the engram. This idea was first suggested by the Canadian psychologist Donald Hebb, and has since been worked out in considerable detail.[17]

Engrams are important contributors to what we subjectively experience as a memory of something that has happened to us. But, as we have seen, they are not the only source of the subjective experience of remembering. As you read these words, there are thousands, maybe millions, of engrams in some form in your brain. These patterns of connections have the potential to enter awareness, to contribute to explicit remembering under the right circumstances, but at any one instant most of them lie dormant. If I cue you by asking you to remember the most exciting high school sports event you ever attended, a variety of engrams that only seconds ago were in a quiescent state become active as you sift through candidate experiences; if I ask you to remember what you ate the last time you had dinner at an Italian restaurant, a very different set of engrams enters into awareness. Had I not just posed these queries to you, the relevant engrams might have remained dormant for years.

Semon appreciated that, engrams being merely potential contributors to recollection, an adequate account of memory depends on understanding the influences that allow engrams to become manifest in conscious awareness: What properties of a cue allow it to "awaken" a dormant engram? Why are some cues effective in eliciting recollection whereas others are not? Semon argued that any given memory could be elicited by just a few select cues—parts of the original experience that a person focused on at the time the experience occurred. Thus, only a fraction of the original event need be present in order to trigger recall of the entire episode.

To recollect the most exciting high school sports event you ever attended, you need not reinstate all the cues that were present initially. Only a subset must be available, those that are closely related to your encoding of the event. Your original encoding and elaboration of the event—say, a football game in which the quarterback made a series of miraculous plays to pull off an unexpected victory—focused heavily on the role of the quarterback. Years later, the mere mention of the quarterback's name, or even a glance at his face, may bring to your mind the game, the participants, and how your team won. But if you do not encounter the critical cues, you will not recall the experience. A friend may ask if you recall the time your team beat the school with the young coach who went on to a career with a professional team. You may be puzzled about what game he is referring to, and have only a fuzzy recollection of the coach. But as soon as he says that it was the game in which your quarterback threw two long touchdown passes in the final minutes, you can retrieve the memory easily. Thus, if encoding conditions are not adequately reinstated at the time of attempted recall, retrieval will fail—even if an event has received extensive elaborative encoding. . . .

Because our understanding of ourselves is so dependent on what we can remember of the past, it is troubling to realize that successful recall depends heavily on the availability of appropriate retrieval cues. Such dependence implies that we may be oblivious to parts of our pasts because we fail to encounter hints or cues that trigger dormant memories. This may be one reason why encountering acquaintances we have not seen for years is often such an affecting experience: our old friends provide us with cues and reminders that are difficult to generate on our own, and that allow us to recollect incidents we would ordinarily fail to remember. . . .

We must not, however, confuse these ideas with the notion that all experiences are recorded somewhere in our brains, only awaiting the appropriate retrieval cue to be brought into awareness. While controlled research has demonstrated over and over that cues and reminders can lead to recall of experiences that have seemingly disappeared, it does not necessarily follow that all experiences are preserved and potentially recallable. Sometimes we forget because the right cues are not available, but it is also likely that sometimes we forget because the relevant engrams have weakened or become blurred.[18]

Retrieval cues are a bit like the portable metal detectors that scavengers sometimes use to try to recover coins on a beach. If coins are hidden somewhere beneath the sands, then the scavenger needs the detector to find them. But if no coins remain in the sand, then even the most powerful detector will turn up nothing. Our brains include some beaches with hidden coins and others that are barren. Like the scavenger seeking money, we do not know before searching which are which.

Neil

RETRIEVAL PROCESSES AND THE BRAIN

In 1988, a fourteen-year-old English boy named Neil began radiation treatment for a tumor hidden deep within the recesses of his brain. Neil had been a normal child until the expanding tumor began to interfere with his vision and memory and to create a host of other medical problems. Chemotherapy was eventually successful, but Neil suffered heavy cognitive losses. He was virtually unable to read and could no longer name common objects on sight. Neil was able to recount most of his life prior to the operation, but he had great difficulty remembering his ongoing, day-to-day experiences.

Curiously, however, Neil performed reasonably well at school, especially in English and mathematics. The psychologists who tested his memory wondered how he managed to do so well. To find out, they asked him some questions about an audiotaped book he had been studying, *Cider with Rosie,* by Laurie Lee. He remembered nothing. Noting Neil's frustration, and realizing that his class performance was based on written responses, the examiner asked Neil to write down his answers, beginning with anything that he could recall from the book. After a while he wrote: "Bloodshot Geranium windows Cider with Rosie Dranium smell of damp pepper and mushroom-growth." "What have I written?" he then asked, unable to read his own handwriting but able to speak normally. The examiner, who was familiar with the book, immediately recognized that the phrases came directly from its pages.

Intrigued by Neil's ability to write down information that he could not express orally, the examiner asked whether Neil could write anything about incidents related to his hospitalization some two years earlier, which he had been unable to remember when asked to talk about them. "A man had Gangrene," he wrote, correctly recalling the ailment of another man in the ambulance that brought Neil to the hospital.

Neil's parents asked him to write down the names of the children in his class. He produced a long list, which turned out to be accurate. When his mother asked him what had happened at school that day, Neil wrote, "Mum I saw tulips on the way home." This was the first time in two years that Neil had been able to relate to his mother a memory of something that had happened to him in her absence.

Neil's parents equipped him with a small notebook, and he began to communicate regularly about incidents in his everyday life. Yet he remained unable to recount these episodes orally. When he wrote them down, Neil was unable to read them, and often expressed surprise when someone told him what he had written. After an afternoon's excursion to several familiar locations, Neil was unable to remember anything when asked. But when told to write down what had happened, he provided a succinct, and accurate, summary of the afternoon's activities: "We went to the museum, and we had some pizza. Then we came back, we went onto the Beach and we looked at the sea. Then we came home."

This case is unprecedented in the annals of psychology, psychiatry, or neurology.[19] Neil's tumor did damage his brain, including some structures that are known to be important for memory. But nothing about the condition of his brain provides specific clues to how or why he could retrieve recent episodic memories through writing but not speaking.

There are other indications that the brain uses different systems for retrieving written and spoken information. The neuropsychologist Alfonso Caramazza has described two patients who suffered strokes in different regions of the left hemisphere that are usually associated with language impairments. Both patients subsequently had special problems producing English verbs (they could produce nouns normally). One patient had problems writing verbs but not saying them, whereas the other had problems saying verbs but not writing them.[20]

Caramazza's findings still leave us a long way from understanding how Neil could recall his recent experiences through writing but not speaking. But these strange cases of disruptions of retrieval raise questions that are essential to understanding memory: Exactly how does the retrieval process work? What goes on in my mind/brain that allows the cue "What did you do during your summer vacation?" to evoke in me the subjective experience of remembering beautiful sunlit days of hiking and swimming at Lake Tahoe? We do not understand precisely how the retrieval process works, but some clues are beginning to emerge.[21] . . .

Constructing Memories

THE ROLE OF THE RETRIEVAL ENVIRONMENT

Findings and ideas concerning brain mechanisms of retrieval are absolutely crucial to understanding memory's fragile power. But it is still important to develop an adequate conceptualization of retrieval at the psychological level. How are we to think about what is retrieved when we recall a past experience? Does the act of retrieval simply serve to activate, or bring into conscious awareness, a dormant memory?

Suppose, for example, that I provide a retrieval cue such as "tell me about last year's Thanksgiving dinner." It may take you a few seconds to recollect where it occurred and who was there, but by the time you reach the end of this sentence there is a good chance that you will recall some of the basic information. How did this subjective experience of remembering come about? The simplest account is that the cue somehow activated a dormant engram of the event, and that your subjective experience of remembering the event, however incomplete, is a straightforward reflection of the information that had been quiescent in your mind: a lightbulb that had been turned off is suddenly turned on.

But memory retrieval is not so simple. I have already suggested an alternative possibility, rooted in Neisser's analogy that retrieving a memory is like reconstructing a dinosaur from fragments of bone. For the paleontologist, the bone chips that are recovered on an archaeological dig and the dinosaur that is ultimately reconstructed from them are not the same thing; the full-blown dinosaur is constructed by combining the bone chips with other available fragments, in accordance with general knowledge of how the complete dinosaur should appear. Similarly, for the rememberer, the engram (the stored fragments of an episode) and the memory (the subjective experience of recollecting a past event) are not the same thing. The stored fragments contribute to the conscious experience of remembering, but they are only part of it. Another important component is the retrieval cue itself. Although it is often assumed that a retrieval cue merely arouses or activates a memory that is slumbering in the recesses of the brain, I have hinted at an alternative: the cue combines with the engram to yield a new, emergent entity—the recollective experience of the rememberer—that differs from either of its constituents. This idea was intimated in some of Proust's writings, in which memories emerge from comparing and combining a present sensation with a past one, much as stereoscopic vision emerges from combining information from the two eyes. . . .

MARCEL PROUST: INVOLUNTARY MEMORY

No single work of literature is more closely associated with human memory than Marcel Proust's *À la recherche du temps perdu (In Search of Lost Time).*[22] The depth of Proust's obsession with recapturing the past is difficult to over-state. The eight volumes that constitute *À la recherche* were written over a period of nearly fifteen years, beginning around 1908 and concluding several months before his death in November 1922. The entire treatise exceeds three thousand pages, most concerned in one way or another with personal recollections or meditations on the nature of memory. Proust may have become so single-minded because he had largely withdrawn from society by the time he began writing his opus. He confined himself to his room throughout much of the writing, suffering from illness and exhaustion, and in so doing substituted a world of time for the world of space. But his obsession with the past also reflects Proust's passionate conviction that the truth of human experience could be grasped only through an understanding of memory and time.

In the most dramatic memory-related incident of the novel, the narrator, Marcel, is visiting his mother, who serves him tea and pastries known as *petites madeleines*. After dipping a madeleine into the tea and imbibing the mixture, he is overcome by an unexpected, overwhelming, and entirely mysterious sense of well-being. "Whence could it have come to me, this all-powerful joy?" he asks. "I sensed that it was connected with the taste of the tea and the cake, but that it infinitely transcended those savours, could not, indeed, be of the same nature. Whence did it come from? What did it mean? How could I seize and apprehend it?"[23] He tries to induce the experience again by tasting several more mouthfuls of the potent mixture, but each experience is weaker than the previous one, leading him to conclude that the basis of the effect "lies not in the cup but in myself." He surmises that the tea and cake have somehow activated a past experience, and wonders whether he will be able to recall it consciously.

Then comes the extraordinary instant when the mystery is resolved: "And suddenly the memory revealed itself. The taste was that of the little crumb of madeleine which on Sunday mornings at Combray [the fictional name of Proust's childhood town] when I went to say good morning to her in her bedroom, my aunt Leonie used to give me, dipping it first in her own cup of tea." Marcel notes that he had never elsewhere encountered the combination of smells and tastes that characterized the episode at his aunt's house, thus making them uniquely effective cues for an elusive but powerful memory: "But when from a long-distant past nothing subsists, after the people are dead, after the things are broken and scattered, taste and smell alone, more fragile but more enduring, more immaterial, more persistent, more faithful, remain poised for a long time, like souls, remembering, waiting and hoping, amid the ruins of all the rest; and bear unflinchingly, in the tiny and almost impalpable drop of their essence, the vast structure of recollection."

The moment when the madeleine memory revealed itself was the moment when the narrator saw that memory could be both fragile and powerful. Memories that can be elicited only by specific tastes and smells are fragile: they can easily disappear because there are few opportunities for them to surface. But those that survive are also exceptionally powerful: having remained dormant for long periods of time, the sudden appearance of seemingly lost experiences cued by tastes or smells is a startling event.

The madeleine episode also highlights that reexperiencing one's personal past sometimes depends on chance encounters with objects that contain the keys to unlocking memories that might otherwise be hidden forever. But Marcel's recognition that *involuntary* recollections are fleeting, lasting only several seconds, and depend on rare confrontations with particular smells or sights, leads him to alter the focus of his quest for the past. As the novel progresses, his quest for self-understanding depends increasingly on the active, *voluntary* retrieval of his past.[24] He explores the self-defining role of voluntary recollection in one of the key scenes from the final novel in the series, *Time Regained.* At a gathering of old friends whom Marcel has not seen for many years, he strains to recall their identities and to place them in the context of his remembered experiences. In so doing he achieves a synthesis of past and present that heightens his appreciation of his own identity.

Proust also draws on concepts and analogies from the science of optics to develop an analogy of time and memory, which he made explicit in a 1922 letter. "The image (imperfect as it is) which seems to me best suited to convey the nature of that special tense," Proust wrote, "is that of a telescope, a telescope pointed at time, for a telescope renders visible for us stars invisible to the naked eye, and I have tried to render visible to the consciousness unconscious phenomena, some of which, having been entirely forgotten, are situated in the past."[25]

Proust further develops his optical analogy. The experience of remembering a past episode, Proust contends, is not based merely on calling to mind a stored memory image. Instead, a feeling of remembering emerges from the comparison of two images: one in the present and one in the past. Just as visual perception of the three-dimensional world depends on combining information from the two eyes, perception in time—remembering—depends on combining information from the present and the past. The renowned Proust scholar Roger Shattuck explains: "Proust set about to make us *see time.* . . . Merely to remember something is meaningless unless the remembered image is combined with a moment in the present affording a view of the same object or objects. Like our eyes, our memories must see double; these two images then converge in our minds into a single heightened reality."[26] Foreshadowing scientific research by more than a half-century, Proust achieved the penetrating insight that feelings of remembering result from a subtle interplay between past and present.

Notes

1. Roediger (1980) reviews spatial metaphors of memory, and Landauer (1975) describes the "garbage can" analogy. Koriat and Goldsmith (in press) contrast the storehouse metaphor of memory to an alternative metaphor that emphasizes how well remembered events correspond to the original experiences.
2. Neisser (1967), p. 285.
3. Ceci, DeSimone, and Johnson (1992) describe the case of Bubbles P. and report a series of experiments concerning his memory abilities. The importance of the "magic number" seven was described by Miller (1956).
4. Research concerning working memory has been pioneered by Baddeley (1986) and colleagues. Baddeley fractionates working memory into several subsystems: a central executive or limited capacity workspace and two "slave" subsystems, the phonological loop and a visuospatial sketch pad that temporarily holds nonverbal information. For studies of patients with damage to the phonological loop, see Vallar and Shallice (1990).
5. The term *depth of processing,* synonymous with *levels of processing,* was introduced to the psychological literature in a classic paper by Craik and Lockhart (1972).
6. For a discussion of these special techniques, known as *orienting tasks,* see Craik and Tulving (1975).
7. This finding was first reported by Craik and Tulving (1975). Other early experiments documenting the importance of elaborative encoding included those by Stein and Bransford (1979), which revealed that even subtle differences in the exact kind of elaboration that people perform can have a major impact on subsequent memory performance.
8. See Gardiner and Java (1993) for elaborative encoding and experiences of remembering and knowing.
9. See Nickerson and Adams (1979).
10. This rendition of the story of Simonides is based on Yates (1966), who provides a definitive history of the origins of mnemonics.
11. The story of mnemonics and the Middle Ages is beautifully told by Carruthers (1990). Scholarly discussions of visual imagery mnemonics and memory improvement can be found in Bellezza (1981) and Bower (1972). A popular treatment of how to use mnemonics to enhance memory function has been provided by Lorayne and Lucas (1974), among many others. Herrmann, Raybeck, and Gutman (1993) focus specifically on improving memory performance in students.
12. For the backlash against mnemonics, see J. Spence (1984), pp. 4 and 12.
13. For wide-ranging discussions of imagery, mind, and brain, see Kosslyn (1981, 1994).
14. The quoted texts are from Storr (1992), p. 6.
15. For an overview of Semon's theory of memory, see Schacter, Eich, and Tulving (1978); for a broader treatment that delves into Semon's life and ideas in the context of the history and sociology of science, see Schacter (1982). For English translations of his work on memory, see Semon (1921, 1923).
16. Watt (1905), p. 130.

17. See Hebb (1949) for the original statement of what has come to be known as "Hebbian learning." For a modern treatment, see McNaughton and Nadel (1989), and for a review of recent evidence, see Merzenich and Sameshima (1993).
18. For a review of evidence from people and animals on retrieval of seemingly forgotten memories in response to cues and reminders, see Capaldi and Neath (1995).
19. Neil's case is described in detail by Vargha-Khadem, Isaacs, and Mishkin (1994). Quotes are from pp. 692–693 of that article. The tumor was in the pineal region of the third ventricle. Although it was treated successfully, MRI scans after treatment revealed abnormalities in structures thought to be important for memory, including the left hippocampal formation, parts of the diencephalon, and the fornix, which connects the hippocampus and diencephalon.
20. Caramazza and Hillis (1991).
21. For a readable discussion of possible cellular bases of memory retrieval, see Johnson (1991). For psychological and computational theories of retrieval, see McClelland (1995) and Metcalfe (1993).
22. Proust's collection of novels is best known in English as *Remembrance of Things Past*. My reading and all quotes are based on D. J. Enright's recent revision of earlier translations by C. K. Scott Moncrief and then Terence Kilmartin. In the Enright translation (Proust, 1992), the series is titled *In Search of Lost Time.*
23. This quote and the following ones are from the most recently revised translation of *Swann's Way* (Proust, 1992, pp. 60–63).
24. This point is made eloquently in Shattuck's (1983) superb analysis of the role played by memory and time in Proust's work.
25. The letter is quoted in ibid., p. 46.
26. Ibid., pp. 46–47.

Selected Bibliography

Baddeley, A. (1986). *Working memory.* Oxford: Clarendon.

Bellezza, F. S. (1981). Mnemonic devices: Classification, characteristics, and criteria. *Review of Educational Research, 51,* 247–275.

Bower, G. H. (1972). Mental imagery and associative learning. In L. Gregg (Ed.) Cognition and learning and memory. New York: Wiley.

Capaldi, E. J., & Neath, I. (1995). Remembering and forgetting as context discrimination. *Learning and Memory, 2,* 107–132.

Caramazza, A., & Hillis, A. E. (1991). Lexical organization of nouns and verbs in the brain. *Nature, 349,* 788–790.

Carruthers, M. J. (1990). *The book of memory: A study of memory in medieval culture.* New York: Cambridge University Press.

Ceci, S. J., DeSimone, M., & Johnson, S. (1992). Memory in context: A case study of "Bubbles P.," a gifted but uneven memorizer. In D. J. Herrmann, H. Weingartner, A. Searleman, & C. McEvoy (Eds.), *Memory improvement: Implications for memory theory* (pp. 169–186). New York: Springer-Verlag.

Craik, F. I. M., & Lockhart, R. S. (1972). Levels of processing: A framework for memory research. *Journal of Verbal Learning and Verbal Behavior, 11,* 671–684.

Craik, F. I. M., & Tulving, E. (1975). Depth of processing and the retention of words in episodic memory. *Journal of Experimental Psychology: General, 104,* 268–294.

Freud, S. (1899). Screen Memories. In J. Strachey (Ed. and Trans.), *The standard edition of the complete psychological works of Sigmund Freud* (Vol. 3). London: Hogarth Press.

Freud, S. (1926/1959). Inhibitions, symptoms, and anxiety. In J. Strachey (Ed. and Trans.), *The standard edition of the complete psychological works of Sigmund Freud* (Vol. 20). London: Hogarth Press.

Freud, S., & Breuer, J. (1966). *Studies on hysteria.* (J. Strachey, Trans.). New York: Avon.

Gardiner, J. M., & Java, R. I. (1993). Recognising and remembering. In A. F. Collins, S. E. Gathercole, M. A. Conway, & P. E. Morris (Eds.), *Theories of memory* (pp. 163–188). Hove, United Kingdom: Erlbaum.

Hebb, D. O. (1949). *The organization of behavior.* New York: Wiley.

Hermann, D., Raybeck, D., & Gutman, D. (1993). *Improving student memory.* Seattle, WA: Hogrefe & Huber.

James, W. (1890). *The principles of psychology.* New York: Holt.

Johnson, G. (1991). *In the palaces of memory: How we build the worlds inside our heads.* New York: Knopf.

Koriat, A., & Goldsmith, M. (in press). Memory metaphors and the everyday-laboratory controversy: The correspondence versus the storehouse conceptions of memory. *Behavioral and Brain Sciences.*

Landauer, T. K. (1975). Memory without organization: Properties of a model with random storage and undirected retrieval. *Cognitive Psychology, 7,* 495–531.

Lorayne, H., & Lucas, J. (1974). *The memory book.* New York: Ballantine.

McClelland, J. L. (1995). Constructive memory and memory distortions: A parallel-distributed processing approach. In D. L. Schacter, J. T. Coyle, G. D. Fischbach, M.-M. Mesulam, & L. E. Sullivan (Eds.), *Memory distortion: How minds, brains and societies reconstruct the past* (pp. 69–90). Cambridge, MA: Harvard University Press.

Metcalfe, J. (1993). Novelty monitoring, metacognition and control in a composite holographic associative recall model: Implications for Korsakoff amnesia. *Psychological Review, 100,* 3–22.

Miller, G. A. (1956). The magical number seven, plus or minus two: Some limits on our capacity for processing information. *Psychological Review, 63,* 81–96.

Neisser, U. (1967). *Cognitive psychology.* New York: Appleton-Century-Crofts.

Neisser, U., & Harsch, N. (1992). Phantom flashbulbs: False recollections of hearing the news about *Challenger.* In E. Winograd & U. Neisser (Eds.), *Affect and accuracy in recall: Studies of "flashbulb memories"* (pp. 9–31). Cambridge: Cambridge University Press.

Neisser, U., Winograd, E., Bergman, E. T., Schreiber, C. A., Palmer, S. E., & Weldon, M. S. (in press). Remembering the earthquake: Direct experience vs. hearing the news. *Memory.*

Nickerson, R. S., & Adams, M. J. (1970). Long-term memory for a common object. *Cognitive Psychology, 11,* 287–307.

Proust, M. (1992). *In search of lost time: Swann's way* (Moncrieff, C. K. S., Kilmartin, T., & Enright, D. J., Trans.). New York: The Modern Library.

Roediger, H. L., III (1980). Memory metaphors in cognitive psychology. *Memory & Cognition, 8,* 231–246.

Schacter, D. L. (1982). *Stranger behind the engram: Theories of memory and the psychology of science.* Hillsdale, NJ: Erlbaum.

Schacter, D. L., Eich, J. E., & Tulving, E. (1978). Richard Semon's theory of memory. *Journal of Verbal Learning and Verbal Behavior, 17,* 721–743.

Semon, R. (1904/1921). *The mneme.* London: George Allen & Unwin.

Semon, R. (1909/1923). *Mnemic psychology.* London: George Allen & Unwin.

Shattuck, R. (1983). *Proust's binoculars: A study of memory, time, and recognition in "A La Recherche du Temps Perdu."* Princeton: Princeton University Press.

Spence, J. (1984). *The memory palace of Matteo Ricci.* New York: Viking.

Stein, B. A., & Bransford, J. D. (1979). Constraints on effective elaboration: Effects of precision and subject generation. *Journal of Verbal Learning and Verbal Behavior, 18,* 769–777.

Storr, R. (1992). *Dislocations.* New York: The Museum of Modern Art.

Vallar, G., & Shallice, T. (1990). *Neuropsychological impairments of short-term memory.* Cambridge: Cambridge University Press.

Vargha-Khadem, F., Isaacs, E., & Mishkin, M. (1994). Agnosia, alexia and a remarkable form of amnesia in an adolescent boy. *Brain, 117,* 683–703.

Watt, H. J. (1905). Review of *Die Mneme. Archiv für die Gesamte Psychologie, 5,* 127–130.

Yates, F. A. (1966). *The art of memory.* Chicago: University of Chicago Press.

For Discussion:

1. Explain the difference between working memory and long-term memory. Why does some information become encoded in long-term memory while other information is forgotten?
2. How does Schacter explain why some people remember the same event differently than others do? What does this theory suggest about the possibility of recovering a "true" past?
3. What role do the stories of Bubbles P., Neil, and Richard Semon play in Schacter's argument? How does the function of each story differ?
4. What are some ordinary, everyday objects that we see every day but do not notice? List a few. Why, according to Schacter, do we fail to notice them?

 For Fact-Finding, Research, and Writing:

1. What are mnemonics? What is Simonides's method of loci? Explain how you came up with the answers.
2. Locate Eran Shakine's painting "Hadassah." After examining the painting, add your ideas to Schacter's analysis of how Shakine represents the past.
3. Schacter argues that "our understanding of ourselves is . . . dependent on what we can remember of the past." Investigate the legal controversy surrounding "recovered memory."
4. Introductory science education used to depend on rote memory. How does the new trend toward inquiry-based science education reflect Schacter's argument about memory?

Bertrand Russell, "University Education"

Bertrand Russell (1872–1970) is a British philosopher best known for his ground-breaking work in mathematical logic. He is considered a founder of modern analytic philosophy. Russell was also, however, an outspoken social critic. Founding president of the Campaign for Nuclear Disarmament, he was a courageous voice for pacifism even at great personal and professional cost. Because of his opposition to the First World War, he was dismissed from his faculty position at Cambridge University, fined by the government, and endured the confiscation of his library. After almost thirty-years without an academic position, Russell was appointed to the faculty of the College of the City of New

York, but opposition to his political and social views led to his dismissal. In 1944 he regained his position at Cambridge and six years later received the Nobel Prize.

 Before You Read:

What do you think is the purpose of a university education?

University Education

EDUCATION IS A vast and complex subject involving many problems of great difficulty. I propose, in what follows, to deal with only one of these problems, namely, the adaption of university education to modern conditions.

Universities are an institution of considerable antiquity. They developed during the twelfth and thirteenth centuries out of cathedral schools where scholastic theologians learned the art of dialectic. But, in fact, the aims which inspired universities go back to ancient times. One may say that Plato's Academy was the first university. Plato's Academy had certain well-marked objectives. It aimed at producing the sort of people who would be suitable to become Guardians in his ideal Republic. The education which Plato designed was not in his day what would now be called "cultural." A "cultural" education consists mainly in the learning of Greek and Latin. But the Greeks had no need to learn Greek and no occasion to learn Latin. What Plato mainly wished his Academy to teach was, first, mathematics and astronomy, and, then, philosophy. The philosophy was to have a scientific inspiration with a tincture of Orphic mysticism. Something of this sort, in various modified forms, persisted in the West until the Fall of Rome. After some centuries, it was taken up by the Arabs and, from them, largely through the Jews, transmitted back to the West. In the West it still retained much of Plato's original political purpose, since it aimed at producing an educated élite with a more or less complete monopoly of political power. This aim persisted, virtually unchanged, until the latter half of the nineteenth century. From that time onwards, the aim has become increasingly modified by the intrusion of two new elements: democracy and science. The intrusion of democracy into academic practice and theory is much more profound than that of science and much more difficult to combine with anything like the aims of Plato's Academy.

Universal education, which is now taken for granted in all civilized countries, was vehemently opposed, on grounds which were broadly aristocratic, until it was seen that political democracy had become inevitable. There had been ever since ancient times a very sharp line between the educated and the uneducated. The educated had had a severe training and had learnt much, while the uneducated could not read or write. The educated, who had a monopoly of political power, dreaded the extension of schools to the "lower classes." The President of the Royal Society in the year 1807 considered that it would be disastrous if working men could read, since he feared that they would spend their time reading Tom Paine. When my grandfather established an elementary school in his parish, well-to-do neighbours were outraged, saying that he had destroyed the hitherto aristocratic character of the neighbourhood. It was political democracy—at least, in England—that brought a change of opinion in this matter. Disraeli, after securing the vote for urban working men, favoured compulsory education with the phrase, "We must educate our masters." Education came to seem the right of all who desired it. But it was not easy to see how this right was to be extended to university education; nor, if it were, how universities could continue to perform their ancient functions.

The reasons which have induced civilized countries to adopt universal education are various. There were enthusiasts for enlightenment who saw no limits to the good that could be done by instruction. Many of these were very influential in the early advocacy of compulsory education. Then there were practical men who realized that a modern state and modern processes of production and distribution cannot easily be managed if a large proportion of the population cannot read. A third group were those who advocated education as a democratic right. There was a fourth group, more silent and less open, which saw the possibilities of education from the point of view of official propaganda. The importance of education in this regard is very great. In the eighteenth century, most wars were unpopular; but, since men have been able to read the newspapers, almost all wars have been popular. This is only one instance of the hold on public opinion which authority has acquired through education.

Although universities were not directly concerned in these educational processes, they have been profoundly affected by them in ways which are, broadly speaking, inevitable, but which are, in part, very disturbing to those who wish to preserve what was good in older ideals.

It is difficult to speak in advocacy of older ideals without using language that has a somewhat old-fashioned flavour. There is a distinction, which formerly received general recognition, between skill and wisdom. The growing complexities of technique have tended to blur this distinction, at any rate in certain regions. There are kinds of skill which are not specially respected although they are difficult to acquire. A contortionist, I am told, has to begin training in early childhood, and, when proficient, he possesses a very rare and difficult skill. But it is not felt that this skill is socially useful, and it is, therefore, not taught in schools or universities. A great many skills, however, indeed a rapidly increasing number, are very vital elements in the wealth and power of a nation. Most of these skills are new and do not command the respect of ancient tradition. Some of them may be considered to minister to wisdom, but a great many certainly do not. But what, you will ask, do you mean by "wisdom"? I am not prepared with a neat definition. But I will do my best to convey what I think the word is capable of meaning. It is a word concerned partly with knowledge and partly with feeling. It should denote a certain intimate union of knowledge with apprehension of human destiny and the purposes of life. It requires a certain breadth of vision, which is hardly possible without considerable knowledge. But it demands, also, a breadth of feeling, a certain kind of universality of sympathy. I think that higher education should do what is possible towards promoting not only knowledge, but wisdom. I do not think that this is easy; and I do not think that the aim should be too conscious, for, if it is, it becomes stereotyped and priggish. It should be something existing almost unconsciously in the teacher and conveyed almost unintentionally to the pupil. I agree with Plato in thinking this the greatest thing that education can do. Unfortunately, it is one of the things most threatened by the intrusion of crude democratic shibboleths into our universities.

The fanatic of democracy is apt to say that all men are equal. There is a sense in which this is true, but it is not a sense which much concerns the educator. What can be meant truly by the phrase "All men are equal" is that in certain respects they have equal rights and should have an equal share of basic political power. Murder is a crime whoever the victim may be, and everybody should be protected against it by the law and the police. Any set of men or women which has no share in political power is pretty certain to suffer injustices of an indefensible sort. All men should be equal before the law. It is such principles which constitute what is valid in democracy. But this should not mean that we cannot recognize differing degrees of skill or merit in different individuals. Every teacher knows that some pupils are quick to learn and others are slow. Every teacher knows that some boys and girls are eager to acquire knowledge, while others have to be forced into the minimum demanded by authority. When a group of young people are all taught together in one class, regardless of their greater or lesser ability, the pace has to be too quick for the stupid and too slow for the clever. The amount of teaching that a young person needs depends to an enormous extent upon his ability and his tastes. A stupid child will only pay attention to what has to be learnt while the teacher is there to insist upon the subject-matter of the lesson. A really clever young person, on the contrary, needs opportunity and occasional guidance when he finds some difficulty momentarily insuperable. The practice of teaching clever and stupid pupils together is extremely unfortunate, especially as regards the ablest of them. Infinite boredom settles upon these outstanding pupils while matters that they have long ago understood are being explained to those who are backward. This evil is greater the greater the age of the student. By the time that an able young man is at a university, what he needs is occasional advice (not orders) as to what to read and an instructor who has time and sympathy to listen to his difficulties. The kind of instructor that I have in mind should be thoroughly competent in the subject in which the student is specializing, but he should be still young enough to remember the difficulties that are apt to be obstacles to the learner, and not yet so ossified as to be unable to discuss without dogmatism. Discussion is a very essential part in the education of the best students and requires an absence of authority if it is to be free and fruitful. I am thinking not only of discussion with teachers but of discussion among the students themselves. For such discussion, there should be leisure. And, indeed, leisure during student years is of the highest importance. When I was an undergraduate, I made a vow that, when in due course I became a lecturer, I would not think that lectures do any good as a method of instruction, but only as an occasional stimulus. So far as the abler students are concerned, I still take this view. Lectures as a means of instruction are traditional in universities and were no doubt useful before the invention of printing, but since that time they have been out of date as regards the abler kind of students.

It is, I am profoundly convinced, a mistake to object on democratic grounds to the separation of abler from less able pupils in teaching. In matters that the public considers important no one dreams of such an application of supposed democracy. Everybody is willing to admit that some athletes are better than others and that movie stars deserve more honour than ordinary mortals. That is because they have a kind of skill which is much admired even by those who do not possess it. But intellectual ability, so far from being admired by stupid boys, is positively and actively despised; and even among grown-ups, the term "egg-head" is not expressive of respect. It has been one of the humiliations of the military authorities of our time that the man who nowadays brings success in war is no longer a gentleman of commanding aspect, sitting upright upon a prancing horse, but a wretched scientist whom every military-minded boy would have bullied throughout his youth. However, it is not for special skill in slaughter that I should wish to see the "egg-head" respected.

The needs of the modern world have brought a conflict, which I think could be avoided, between scientific subjects and those that are called "cultural." The latter represent tradition and still have, in my country, a certain snobbish preeminence. Cultural ignorance, beyond a point, is despised. Scientific ignorance, however complete, is not. I do not think, myself, that the division between cultural and scientific education should be nearly as definite as it has tended to become. I think that every scientific student should have some knowledge of history and literature, and that every cultural student should have some acquaintance with some of the basic ideas of science. Some people will say that there is not time, during the university curriculum, to achieve this. But I think that opinion arises partly from unwillingness to adapt teaching to those who are not going to penetrate very far into the subject in question. More specifically, whatever cultural education is offered to scientific students should not involve a knowledge of Latin or Greek. And I think that whatever of science is offered to those who are not going to specialize in any scientific subject should deal partly with scientific history and partly with general aspects of scientific method. I think it is a good thing to invite occasional lectures from eminent men to be addressed to the general body of students and not only to those who specialize in the subject concerned.

There are some things which I think it ought to be possible, though at present it is not, to take for granted in all who are engaged in university teaching. Such men or women must, of course, be proficient in some special skill. But, in addition to this, there is a general outlook which it is their duty to put before those whom they are instructing. They should exemplify the value of intellect and of the search for knowledge. They should make it clear that what at any time passes for knowledge may, in fact, be erroneous. They should inculcate an undogmatic temper, a temper of continual search and not of comfortable certainty. They should try to create an awareness of the world as a whole, and not only of what is near in space and time. Through the recognition of the likelihood of error, they should make clear the importance of tolerance. They should remind the student that those whom posterity honours have very often been unpopular in their own day and that, on this ground, social courage is a virtue of supreme importance. Above all, every educator who is engaged in an attempt to make the best of the students to whom he speaks must regard himself as the servant of truth and not of this or that political or sectarian interest. Truth is a shining goddess, always veiled, always distant, never wholly approachable, but worthy of all the devotion of which the human spirit is capable.

 For Discussion:

1. What reasons does Russell cite in favor of compulsory education? Can you think of other reasons why a democratic society requires a certain level of education?
2. What is the difference between skill and wisdom, for Russell? Do you agree with his distinction? Does your university foster "not only knowledge, but wisdom"? In what ways?
3. For Russell, what is the value of discussion? Of lecture? What purpose does each serve?

 For Fact-Finding, Research, and Writing:

1. What goals are highlighted in your school's mission statement? How do they correlate to or differ from Russell's ideal education? Do you think your education fulfills the university's stated mission?

2. Using the Statistical Universe database, find out how many Oklahomans have no post-secondary education and how many have attended or graduated from a four-year university. Use the most recent facts available and contrast those recent figures with figures from the 1960s.
3. Russell argues that in his culture the "egg-head" is not respected. Is this true in American culture? Drawing from your own knowledge or Gardner's multiple intelligences, define the intelligence that is most valued in American society.
4. Explain how Russell's idea of education draws on Plato's. Do the two theories of knowledge and learning differ in any ways?
5. Devise a university curriculum that Russell would approve. What would the aim of this type of education be? How might this curriculum be further altered to allow for Gardner's theory of multiple intelligences?

CHAPTER TWO

Who Controls Knowledge?

Introduction

Do you own your body? Does everything in it belong to you? Are you *sure?* Do you download music from the Internet or make copies of CDs? Is that theft, or is it fair use? Are the CD and its contents your property? Or do you merely lease them for a one-time fee? Have you ever thought about how the information retrieved by a search engine gets to you? How do the search engines "know" what you're looking for? And who controls those search engines? Who controls the information contained in the human genome, and who decides whether genome research should continue? Who controls our access to information, and who decides what is to be considered knowledge?

In the last twenty years, we have been witness to unprecedented technological and scientific advancements. We have mapped the human genome, and can now manipulate the human body at a genetic level. The explosive growth of the Internet has made available to nearly anyone an immense store of information on seemingly every topic imaginable. Data can be reproduced digitally with no loss of quality. But with these rapid advancements have come a series of difficult questions about the control of information. Should people of all ages have access to the same kind of information? Should governments be able to sequester controversial information as "classified" documents? How do we represent multiple perspectives when we must decide on the content of national curricular standards or college entrance exams?

We live in an age where our actions, more often than not, result in information about us being stored in vast databases—and that information can, if its collector wishes, be sold to others who would use it to study our lives. In a world such as this, what is private and what is not? Where do we draw the line between what is intellectual property and what is not? How is the exchange of this information to be regulated? Are the measures currently in place for the regulation of information, all of which have their origins in print information, sufficient for this new electronic medium? If they are not, will anyone bother to innovate? How can we best protect ourselves against the misuse of information? These questions about privacy, property and the control of information are the crucial questions of this century, and how we answer them will determine far more than just how much spam we receive in our e-mail in-boxes.

 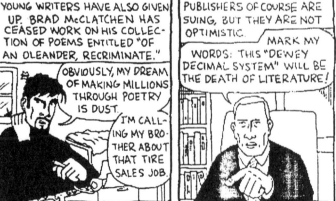 

Wil S. Hylton, "Who Owns This Body?"

Wil S. Hylton is a feature writer for *Esquire*, a magazine aimed at an educated male audience with an interest in fashion, ideas, and current affairs. Before joining *Esquire* at the age of 23, he worked for the Baltimore newspaper, *The Sun*, and for *Baltimore* magazine. This essay originally appeared in the June 2001 issue of *Esquire*.

Before You Read:

How do you define "private property"? Should all invented techniques, ideas, and objects be the property of their inventors, or should there be exceptions?

Who Owns This Body?

Wil S. Hylton

THE SYMPTOMS CRASHED down like an avalanche, and John Moore didn't know what to think. Bruises all over his body, bleeding gums, and the roll of flesh around his waist that he'd always figured for fat had gotten lumpy and red and sore.

He didn't know much about cancer, but when he finally dragged himself to a doctor in Anchorage in the summer of 1976, he learned more than he wanted to know. For one thing, he learned that he had it. For another, he found out his type was rare, something called hairy-cell leukemia. The doctor said it was attacking his spleen, so instead of absorbing aging blood cells the way a normal spleen does, his spleen was absorbing *all* his blood cells, cannibalizing him, swelling up in his gut and smashing his other organs against the walls of his body. The doctor said there wasn't much hope, but Moore wanted to give it a fight. He found a specialist at UCLA and flew down for a consultation.

Right off the bat, he liked Dr. Golde, who made such a point of cutting through bullshit that he let his patients call him Goldie. Moore trusted that, and when Goldie suggested that he should have his spleen taken out, he didn't hesitate. The surgery took three hours. A normal spleen weighs about fourteen ounces. Moore's spleen weighed fourteen pounds.

Within a few weeks, he was back on his feet, ready for a fresh start, and Seattle seemed as good a place as any. He was just thirty at the time, broad and strong, and it wasn't long before he found a nice girl there, married her, bought a ranch near the coast, and got himself a job as a salesman in the oyster industry. He tried to forget about the leukemia, the bruises, the bleeding gums, the cannibal spleen. For the most part, he did. The only reminders were his follow-up visits to see Goldie. They seemed never to end.

At first, Moore didn't think much of flying down to L. A. for his regular checkups. He knew cancer is something to keep an eye on. But after four years of it, he'd had enough. He didn't see why he had to travel a thousand miles every few months just to give blood and sperm samples. He offered to have the blood drawn in Seattle and shipped down to Goldie's lab, but Goldie said that wouldn't work. He mentioned that the price of the airfare was starting to hurt his pocketbook, but Goldie offered to pay for the flights. He brought up the fact that his folks were moving away from Pasadena and he wouldn't have anywhere to stay near L. A., but Goldie offered to get him a room at the Beverly Wilshire. Moore thought Goldie seemed mighty eager, but he agreed to keep coming down.

Then, after seven years of regular visits, Goldie's nurse brought him a contract to sign. Moore looked at it awhile, trying to figure out what the hell it was. Something about surrendering "any and all rights." Moore didn't like the sound of that, so he circled the box that said, "DO NOT" consent and gave it back. But when Moore got home to Seattle, he found another copy of the contract in his mailbox. This time, it had a Post-it note attached, with an arrow pointing to the word "DO." He looked at the contract again. Again, it seemed strange. Again, he didn't sign it. A few weeks later, yet another contract arrived by mail. This time, there was a nasty letter attached, Goldie telling Moore to stop being obtuse and sign the damned thing. He didn't like Goldie's attitude. Something was fishy, and he decided to find out what. He sent the contract to a lawyer.

Moore was at home when his lawyer called him back with some news. Turned out that Goldie had a few things going on behind Moore's back. Even before the surgery, Goldie had suspected that leukemia researchers would love to run experiments on Moore's spleen. So the doctor had instructed his surgical staff to remove some cells from Moore's spleen and make a culture. Then Goldie brought the culture back to his lab and kept Moore's cells alive, kept them reproducing, a tiny portion of Moore's body living inside a dish. Goldie took out a patent on Moore's cells in 1984, and then, without mentioning it to anyone, he shopped them around to a few pharmaceutical companies, eventually finding a taker. A company named Genetics Institute offered him seventy-five thousand shares of stock, worth about $1.5 million, for Moore's cells.

Moore nearly fell over when his lawyer told him about that transaction. Later, after the shock wore off, he was just plain pissed. Not that he minded his cells being used in research. He minded being lied to and treated like a sucker. He minded being invaded and ripped off. Goldie hadn't ever told him about any cell line, or any patent, or any million and a half bucks, and Moore was starting to feel like a fool. He figured his best recourse was a lawsuit.

But when his case went before the California Supreme Court in July of 1990, the judges weren't impressed. As far as they were concerned, Moore didn't have any right to sue Goldie for stealing his cells because the cells didn't belong to Moore in the first place. They might have come from his body, and they might have contained his DNA, but that didn't mean they were *his*. On the contrary. According to the judges, Moore's cells couldn't belong to him because if they did belong to him, then Goldie couldn't have a patent on them. "Moore's allegations that he owns the cell line and the products derived from it are inconsistent with the patent," the majority wrote, adding that he "neither has title to the property, nor possession thereof" and concluding that "the patented cell line and the products derived from it cannot be Moore's property."

John Moore didn't own his own body.

Neither do you. Not your body, not your blood, not even your genes. Not unless you've got a patent. And it's too late to get a patent on some parts of your body. They've already been sold.

Like, for example, the gene called BRCA1. There's a chance you have that gene. There's an even better chance your wife has it, or your sister or your mom, because that's the gene for breast cancer. If you could test yourself for BRCA1 right now, or if you could test your wife or your sister or your mom, you probably would, right? Just to be on the safe side. But you can't test yourself because you don't know how, and your doctor can't test you because he's not allowed—at least, not without permission from the person who owns the gene. And that person isn't you. It might be in your body, but it doesn't belong to you. It belongs to a company called Myriad Genetics in Salt Lake City. So if you want to know whether you have the gene for breast cancer, you're going to have to call somebody for permission. Then you're going to have to pay for the cost of the doctor's visit, plus a $2,500 fee to Myriad Genetics just to access its gene, the gene inside your body. Those are the rules of the patent game. That's what a patent means: exclusive access. And the last time somebody broke those rules, the last time somebody ran a test for BRCA1 without permission, Myriad Genetics went after them. And Myriad Genetics made them stop. And that was a university.

And that's just BRCA1. There are about a thousand other human genes that have been patented. Some of them are in your body, and many of them are important, like the one for Alzheimer's disease and the one for epilepsy and the one for brain cancer. If you happen to have one of those genes, it might interest you to know that researchers are paying to access them, too, sometimes millions of dollars just to continue the work of looking for a cure.

It's not just genes, either. There's a patent on the blood inside every human umbilical cord. So if, by chance, your newborn baby needs that blood, don't expect to get it for free. There's also a Swiss company called Novartis that has a patent on the stem cells in your American bone marrow. Don't expect to access those cells if you ever need a transplant, either, unless you're prepared to pay.

Some companies have patents on entire species of animals, like the species of mice and pigs that belong to DuPont. You can patent people, too, and not just John Moore. These days, you can get a patent on just about anybody; a patent issued in 1995 to the U.S. Department of Health covered the cell line of an unsuspecting member of the Hagahai tribe in Papua, New Guinea, whose resistance to certain diseases made him valuable to researchers. Other patents filed by the U.S. government at around the same time covered indigenous people from the Solomon Islands and from the Guaymi tribe in Panama.

As a matter of constitutional law, all of this is highly suspect. There's never been a vote by Congress to approve the patenting of human or animal life, there's never been an executive order by any president, and there's never been a decision by the U.S. Supreme Court on the patenting of any animal larger than a microorganism. In fact, just twenty-five years ago, you couldn't patent any of it: genes, cells, blood, marrow, even a clipped fingernail. Back then, the U.S. patent code looked a lot more like the code Thomas Jefferson wrote, the code that was designed to protect inventions—think cotton gins, whoopee cushions, Twinkies!—made on American soil. But that hasn't slowed down the patent code, which not only applies to U.S. soil but now lays claim to ninety foreign countries, and even to "any object made, used, or sold in outer space."

If you're starting to get the impression that the U.S. patent laws have gotten out of hand, if you're starting to wonder how they got that way, how they stretched so wide so quickly without any public debate or government approval, the first question you ought to ask yourself is why you never thought about it before. The answer, most likely, is that you didn't know. You didn't know because nobody knew. Nobody knew because nobody cared. Life went on, oblivious.

And that's how it happened.

Jim Watson saw the whole mess coming. Not at first, of course. At first, he was in awe of the biological revolution, just as the rest of the world was. After all, it was his revolution, his discovery that sparked it, his insight, made in his lab, his glimpse into the mind of God. And so, for a short while, he put aside his natural cynicism and basked in the glow of his accomplishment.

It wasn't that nobody had ever seen DNA, it was that nobody knew what it was, or what it did, or even what it looked like. Microscopes had never been able to get closer than a blurry smudge, and as far as anyone knew for sure, that smudge might have been irrelevant cellular garbage. It took Jim Watson and his partner, Francis Crick, to figure out that DNA mattered.

Watson might have made the discovery even sooner, but it took him a few years to get through school. Not many years, just a few. He started college at fifteen, received his doctorate at twenty-two, began his career at twenty-three, and when he and Crick solved the riddle of DNA in 1953, he was just twenty-four, a pale, gawky kid from Chicago with a long neck and a narrow head of wispy black hair. He was an ambitious bastard, too, already thinking about the Nobel prize that his work would bring.

Watson and Crick had solved the first riddle of DNA. They had figured out that it was shaped like a string, or, rather, like two strings twisted together, a Twizzler-like structure they called the double helix. They had also discovered that those strings were made out of billions of tiny particles, called nucleotides, all linked together in a chain, one by one, in a very specific order. The trick that lay ahead was to understand the precise order of those nucleotides, why they were aligned in that specific way.

The discovery carried certain risks, however, the most obvious of which was that the order of nucleotides could be tinkered with, changing a person's genetic instructions and thereby rearranging his or her body or mind. Such modifications might do good in some cases, with the potential to cure hereditary diseases or deformations, but they could also take nature down a new and unseemly path. They could replace natural selection with a kind of deliberate genetic art.

At the very least, it was clear from the outset that genetic science had a special responsibility, and one of the earliest voices of caution was none other than Jim Watson. By 1975, he had established himself as officially dubious, and when he arrived at the Asilomar Conference on Genetic Ethics that year, he stood before an assembly of his colleagues and announced, "We can't even measure the fucking risks."

Watson was still just forty-five years old, but he was already disenchanted with his own success. Instead of pursuing fame and fortune on the cutting edge of his field, he had retreated in 1968 to an obscure laboratory in Cold Spring Harbor, New York, where he assumed the title of director and spent most of his time fundraising for the lab's endowment. In a few interviews and public appearances, he voiced contempt for the scientific community, issuing proclamations like the one he made in his memoirs: "A goodly number of scientists are not only narrow-minded and dull but also just stupid."

The truth was, Watson's retreat from the front lines *had* left a vacuum of creative ambition. In the three decades following his discovery of the DNA structure, not a single effort had been launched to produce a map of human DNA. Such a map would be essential for the budding field of genetics to blossom. It would provide a complete list of the nucleotides along the DNA strand, making it easier for scientists to locate and isolate specific genes. Because that's not easy to do. A gene does not have a distinct shape or contour, is not even a physically independent structure. In fact, the word *gene* is really just scientific jargon that describes a segment of DNA, a portion of the double-helix strand that happens to produce a protein. Each "gene" starts on a particular nucleotide and ends on another nucleotide further down the strand. Since there's no dramatic marker to announce the beginning or end of a gene, and since there are roughly thirty thousand genes in human DNA, you can imagine how hard it is to locate them without a good map.

By the late 1980s, it was beginning to look as though nobody would ever draw that map. The project seemed dauntingly, if not impossibly, huge. Even with computers mapping one nucleotide per second, it would take one hundred years to finish the job. But if anything was predictable about Jim Watson, it was that he would do the unexpected, and just when he had been counted out of the game, he emerged from his twenty-year slumber. Standing before Congress in 1987, he received a hero's welcome and a starting budget of $30 million to launch the Human Genome Project, a new division of the National Institutes of Health. He predicted a complete DNA map by the year 2005.

It wasn't long, however, before Watson's prickly nature caused a clash with his colleagues, most notably with a young scientist named Craig Venter. Like Watson, Venter was unusually blunt-spoken for a molecular biologist. A Vietnam vet who spent most of his teen years smoking pot and surfing the California coast, Venter had about as much respect for authority as he did for scientific convention. If anything, he and Watson were too much alike. Watson had solved the DNA riddle in less than eighteen months, and Venter was in just as big a hurry to map the human genome. He wasn't interested in plodding along, one nucleotide at a time: He was developing a way to isolate genes along the DNA strand. He had found markers on the double helix that gave clues about the locations of genes, and by focusing on those markers, he could identify the most important parts of the genome without wasting time on extraneous nucleotides.

The only problem with Venter's approach was that Jim Watson didn't like it. He didn't like the science, and he didn't like Venter, and he wanted to get rid of both. But Venter had friends in high places at the NIH. His approach to DNA mapping was faster than any other, and that had value in itself. By the early nineties, the patent code had already swollen, through a bizarre series of loop-holes and judicial mistakes, to cover John Moore and maybe even raw human DNA. To the NIH, that spelled opportunity. The sooner Venter could locate genes, the sooner the NIH could patent them. And patents meant money. Big money. Money from pharmaceutical companies, from biotechnology companies, even from small laboratories hoping to do genetic research. Craig Venter meant more patents more quickly, and more patents meant more money, and that gave him a special cachet.

To Watson, the specter of genetic patents only made Craig Venter more distasteful. Watson complained to NIH administrators that they were privatizing nature, and when that didn't work, he took his beef to Capitol Hill, where, speaking to a roomful of senators in 1991, he blasted Venter's work as something that "could be run by monkeys." Venter and the NIH fought back, saying Watson was old news, old science, and that patents were the future of biotechnology. Heads butted and ideals clashed in a battle that history will remember as the inevitable conflict of two brilliant, unharnessable minds. But in the end, it was either Venter or Watson, patent or no patent, and in April of 1992, Jim Watson was asked to resign from the Human Genome Project. He returned to the Cold Spring Harbor Laboratory to resume his duties as director, the man who had unlocked the secret of DNA, who had led the charge to decode it, pushed aside by the commercial forces that would eventually consume biology.

"What is this? It looks like an artificial anus." Craig Venter is grinning now. His tiny eyes gleam beneath the tangled mass of eyebrows that protrude like fingers from his brow. He is mostly bald, with a friar's ring of hair grown longer than most men would dare, and he's running a hand over the dome, looking at a record cover with a picture of a trumpet mouthpiece on it. *"Uuunngh,"* he grunts, tossing the record aside.

This is Craig Venter, fifty-four, the man who mapped the human genome and who has been accused of attempting to own it, the man who left the NIH in order to compete with it, the man who has been called the "next Hitler" and who has, more than anyone else in the world, become the face of gene patents. This is Craig Venter at work, slung back in an executive chair, with his bare ankles crossed in front of him, surrounded by three black standard poodles, all barking and wrestling one another on the carpeted floor while three of his employees stand around the desk, all talking at once, to him and to one another, about three entirely different topics, with Venter listening to none of them and also to all three of them, responding occasionally to each of them, even while reading the mail and looking at the album cover and playing with the dogs and gazing out the window and generally giving the false impression that he is distracted, which he is not and rarely ever is.

Someone in the room is talking about Mount Everest. Someone else is talking about antibiotics. Venter picks up a pamphlet that he commissioned to announce the completed human-genome map, the second great secret of DNA, the one he unlocked, the reason he will probably win a Nobel prize. Venter unfolds the pamphlet, turns it over, then back. "Do I have any spare time tomorrow?" he asks an assistant who has, until now, been talking about a symposium in Europe.

She pauses, switching gears. "It's going to be a crazy day."

Venter shrugs. "They're all crazy." He tilts an ear toward a publicist on the other side of his desk, who has switched from the subject of Mount Everest and has begun prepping Venter for an upcoming press conference. He listens for a moment, then turns back to the assistant. "See if we can make time to call Umberto Eco," he says. "Just to make sure he's going to be at the symposium."

Refolding the pamphlet, he turns back to his publicist. "Who's going to be at this press conference?" he asks.

The phone is ringing. His cell phone.

"People like *The Guardian*," the publicist says, raising her eyebrow as she says the name of the left-wing British newspaper. The British press has been especially hostile toward Venter.

"Why would I want to talk to *them*?" asks Venter, reaching for the still-ringing cell phone.

"Well . . ." says the publicist.

A senior researcher steps into the room, a short man with neatly parted hair and a perfectly trimmed mustache.

Venter nods hello, yanks the phone from his hip, but doesn't hold it to his ear. "Okay," he says to the publicist as the researcher returns his nod. Venter wags the phone like a scolding finger. "I'll talk to the assholes, but you're coming with me."

The researcher smiles, acknowledged.

The publicist sighs, exasperated. "You're going to have to clone me," she says.

Venter on the phone: "Hello? Yeah. Just put in the estimation. The average accuracy. 99.96. Yeah, percent."

Lowering the phone to his thigh, he hands the pamphlet to the researcher. "Hey, check this out."

Then to the assistant, "Who's this guy from Disney speaking at the symposium?"

Back on the phone: "Sure, and Jim said there's a listing in the table that there's no yeast seven-transmembrane receptors."

The researcher looking at the pamphlet: "Cool."

The assistant shuffling papers: "I printed out his bio."

On the phone: "That's a mistake. There are at least two in yeast." The dogs barking, Venter squinting his eyes, reaching under the desk to grab one of them by the snout while still on the phone, saying, "There's yeast-mating factor," the assistant digging for the bio, the researcher reading the pamphlet out loud, the publicist asking the assistant questions, the dogs breaking away into another snarling roughhouse, the desk phone beginning to ring. . . .

Outside the room, stillness. Silence. The atmosphere you might fairly expect from a giant white building in a just-built Washington, D. C., suburb known as the Technology Corridor. There is the scent of detergent, of plastics and paint. Clean, whispering fluorescent lights. Prim young women and men walking briskly down the halls, giving artificial smiles and officious little nods to one another. It could be a law office or a dentist's waiting room except for the glass tunnel at the far end of the hall, spanning a landscaped garden, leading to one of the largest civilian supercomputers in the world.

He built that thing over there. He left the Human Genome Project in 1992 to build it. They wouldn't build it for him, so he built it for himself. His own human-genome project, his own genome processor, his own goddamn institute of health. Floor after floor of microprocessors, hard drives, alpha servers, you name it, all linked together, firing and rifling through more than 100 terrabytes of memory. This is Celera Genomics, Incorporated, the hardware of Craig Venter's imagination.

Because his imagination needed more room to breathe. Because the government computers were too small, and so were the government minds. Because they had liked him early on, until he needed more funding, more machines, more power. Because nobody—not even a fellow maverick like Jim Watson—believed him when he said there was a way to automate and accelerate the whole process. Because there were plenty of computer experts in the world, and plenty of mathematicians, and there were plenty of molecular biologists, some better in the field than he. But he was the one with the capacity to juggle all those fields in his mind, the algebra and biology and computational logic and probability and industrial sequencing, to keep all those mix-matched balls in the air long enough to see how they moved together. He was the one who drew inside and outside the lines of all those disciplines, who understood that a big enough computer and exactly the right algorithm and the forces of probability and logic and statistics could mesh together, allowing the computer to do the work for you, could let you sit back and drink a margarita while the human genome cracked open.

Maybe he didn't wire the supercomputer himself. And maybe he didn't write the software. Maybe he didn't devise the combinatorial algorithm for the data. But he was the one who woke up sweaty with the vision bashing through his skull, the train wreck of all those disciplines yielding an epiphany in the night: The human genome could be mapped in less than one year's time.

That's why he left the government project, and that's why the line formed behind him: a Nobel laureate named Hamilton O. Smith; some of the world's foremost computer-science geeks, including Gene Myers, the preeminent author of DNA-sequencing algorithms; even the director of the National Cancer Institute, Samuel L. Broder, all dropping out of their respective limelights, out of their various prestigious gobbledygook to form a technical-support group in Craig Venter's lab. It wasn't the money that brought them. Money never could. Besides, the moneymen were right there in line with the rest of the hangers-on, all clinging to Venter for the same reason: They bought his vision and wanted to see it happen.

Now Sam Broder stops in the glass passageway to explain why he did it, why he left one of the most coveted positions in the scientific world for this. A little man with downturned eyes and a faint, squeaky lisp, Broder is more the proper image of a biologist than his boss is.

"When I read in the newspapers that Craig was going to do the human genome," he says, his round eyes blinking proudly behind dense glasses, "I said, I've gotta do this. It was one of those areas where I knew that I would regret it the rest of my life if I didn't. Ten years from now, I would've looked back and said, I should've done it. The truth is, you can't go back. You don't get a second chance. I said to myself, I gotta do this. I gotta do this, because if I don't do it, I'll hate myself later."

Broder stops, smiles, gulps. His eyes are misty. "He's a genius. You can tell right away when you meet him. From the way he is. He's fearless. He's not like most scientists." Another employee enters at the far end of the passageway, and Broder's eyes dart to the floor. He waits for the man to pass, then looks up again. "You know, Craig gets a lot of criticism." A vaguely defiant smile, lips pressed together. "There have been people with very weird ideas about him, but I think in his heart . . ." The voice trails off again.

"If he had stayed at the NIH, his enemies would have slowed him down," Broder says finally. "So now we have to be a business to do the science we want to do."

The business of science is not exactly a thrill sport. Not to most people. Most people, for example, probably weren't paying very close attention when the Plant Patent Act was proposed in 1930. Most people were probably more concerned about, oh, say, the Great Depression than a law that would allow botanists to patent plants. But in Congress, the bill was a subject of fierce debate. This was about more than just plants, after all. At heart, it was about patenting life, and that required some consideration.

Until that point, living things had always been off-limits to the patent code, if for no other reason than that they were products of nature and products of nature cannot be claimed as inventions. For example, while it's okay to patent a method of purifying tungsten, it is not legal to patent the element itself. Tungsten is not an invention. The same had always been assumed about plants, but by 1930, the distinctions were beginning to blur. After all, nature may have invented the rose, but it certainly never produced the Betty Prior Hybrid Polyantha, a full-bodied rosebush that was bred for its resistance to disease and cold. Congress wanted to reward growers who were developing new strains, but it also knew that patenting plants was the beginning of a very slippery slope. You could start with the best intentions, but if you weren't careful, if you didn't pen the letter of the law just right, you could grease the way right down that slope into bizarre new territory—the patenting of hybrid insects, perhaps. Maybe even mammals. Maybe people.

To make sure that didn't happen, to plug any possible loophole in the law, Congress revisited the Plant Patent Act in 1970, adding a clause that specifically excluded bacteria. It had taken lawmakers forty years, but they had drawn a clear boundary on life patents: A plant could be seen as an invention, but other organisms could not.

Two years later, a scientist from General Electric showed up at the U.S. Parent and Trademark Office with an application for "a bacterium from the genus *Pseudomonas*." The application was quickly rejected. But GE wouldn't take no for an answer. As far as the company was concerned, the *Pseudomonas* bacterium was not just any bacterium; it was an invention; just as much as any hybrid rose. It had been genetically bred in a laboratory, did not exist in nature, and had a commercial function: It could eat oil out of salt water and could be used to clean up oil spills. GE decided to sue the patent office in hopes of changing the decision.

The courtroom was nearly empty when that case went before the U.S. Supreme Court on Saint Patrick's Day in 1980. The business of science is not exactly a thrill sport, and the national press was nowhere to be found. Arguments were brief and to the point. General Electric insisted that, no matter what the patent office said, its bacterium was an invention and should be protected by the patent code. The U.S. Patent and Trademark Office countered that, in spite of General Electric's marvelous bacterium, the laws of the United States were a clear and final authority that said bacteria were not patentable.

The decision that emerged from the judges' quarters nearly three months later would usher in a new era in American patent law. "The fact that microorganisms are alive is without legal significance," the majority wrote. "Respondent's microorganism plainly qualifies as patentable subject matter. His claim is not to a hitherto unknown natural phenomenon, but to a nonnaturally occurring manufacture or composition of matter—a product of human ingenuity having a distinctive name, character, and use."

Not only was the U. S. Supreme Court overruling Congress with its verdict, it was also overruling the U.S. Constitution, which states that only Congress has the power to change patent laws, a detail noted by Justice Brennan in his dissent: "It is the role of Congress, not this Court, to broaden or narrow the reach of the patent laws," he wrote. "Congress specifically excluded bacteria from the coverage of the 1970 Act."

Still, the majority had ruled, and the GE patent became official on a hot summer day in 1980. Here was the future, laid bare. Here was the Supreme Court making it legal to patent not only a bacterium but a whole new species of them. Here was the Supreme Court declaring a species of animal to be an invention. Here was the Supreme Court writing a new definition of life. Not that most people noticed or cared. Not that most people were even paying attention to the business of science. Not that a microorganism really counts as an animal, anyway. Not like it was a monkey or a fish or a mouse.

Jeff Green built a better mouse. Or, to be precise, he built a worse mouse, but he did it on purpose. He invented a mouse with cancer.

"What we did was overexpress oncogenes," he says, standing slightly stooped in a white turtleneck and faded black jeans, his longish brown hair and beard just unkempt enough to appear professorial. "We developed the first transgenic mouse model for prostate cancer doing this, and it turned out that we also developed an excellent model for breast cancer."

He's standing in a tiny government office on the campus of the National Cancer Institute in Bethesda, Maryland, an underfunded and overcrowded laboratory with research supplies stacked on the floors and counters. Behind him, there is a cartoon of a man holding a sign that says, WILL WORK FOR HEFTY SALARY AND PRE-IPO STOCK. At his feet is a small cardboard box. He reaches down to pick it up. "I think there might be one in here," he says, shaking the box lightly near his ear, setting it on a countertop and popping it open. A fat white mouse is inside, lying on its stomach, legs spread, with a peanut-sized hump on its shoulder. It doesn't move. Not a whisker. "Okay, so she's not very active," says Green. "But can you see that lump? That's a mammary gland. It's a female. This is what one of our mice looks like after the tumors progress." He studies it some more. "This animal is probably five or six months old. She's close."

Closing the box, Green takes a deep breath, sighs, and squares his shoulders. "We've essentially generated a new kind of animal," he says. "We've changed the genetics in a very defined way, so now we can breed these animals and predictably get the same kind of cancer in later generations. That's why it's a powerful tool; you don't have to go back and generate it again. It becomes incorporated into their genome."

That's the upside: that Jeff Green has plenty of mice with cancer, which is helpful when you study cancer, because mice get sick and die in a way that's similar to the way humans die, so if you watch the mice deteriorate, you can learn something about how cancer works. The downside, the thing that Jeff Green can't quite understand, is that somebody else already owns his mice, that somebody else has a patent on them, that even though he invented the mice and even though nobody has ever created mice quite like them, the mice are not his property and he cannot legally use them in his research because they belong to somebody else.

That somebody is Philip Leder, a genetic scientist at Harvard University. In the early 1980s, Leder invented his own cancerous mouse and named it OncoMouse. Much like Jeff Green's mouse, the OncoMouse had an overexpressed oncogene, and, also like Green's mouse, it got cancer. Those are the only significant similarities between Jeff Green's mouse and Leder's OncoMouse. They do not have the same genetic mutation or the same genetic code, they are not the same subspecies of mutated mouse, and they do not get the same type of cancer. But Leder was clever when he invented the OncoMouse. He knew that a few years earlier, GE's oil-eating bacterium had been patented and that the Supreme Court decision had left room for larger animals, so when Leder applied for the patent on the OncoMouse in 1984, he stretched that loop-hole to the limits. His attorney wrote the patent application so broadly that it covered not only the OncoMouse itself, a specific genetic creation, but also every other "non-human mammal" with an overexpressed oncogene.

In an earlier era, Leder's bloated patent application would almost certainly have been denied. But at the time he filed his application, the U.S. Parent Office was still reeling from the GE bacteria verdict, revising its laws, struggling to figure out where to draw the line on animal patents, and, somehow, in the midst of the confusion, Leder's patent was granted. Now it was possible to patent not only a species of bacteria, not only a subspecies of mouse, but even a group of animals that wasn't in the same species, or even the same genus. Leder's patent was so broad that, in addition to covering mice, it also covered pigs, horses, monkeys, cattle—anything with an overexpressed oncogene. So broad that it covered Jeff Green's mice, the first mice with prostate cancer, before Jeff Green even invented them. Before they even existed.

Now, all things being equal, Leder might have been willing to let it slide, since he's generally a nice guy and since, after all, Jeff Green works for the government, not for profit. Problem was, by the time Green invented his mouse, Leder had already licensed the OncoMouse patent to DuPont, and DuPont wasn't eager to extend any professional courtesies to Jeff Green or the government or anybody else. DuPont wanted to charge fifty dollars for every animal ever created or born with an overexpressed oncogene, and they had a legal right to do it.

"The mouse we made technically falls under that patent," Green shrugs. His work, for years, has skirted the law. If he had discovered a cure for cancer, the cure would have belonged to DuPont. Because the government didn't have permission to use those mice, didn't have permission from DuPont to continue with cancer research. Fortunately, says Green, just last year, after years of haggling, DuPont finally gave the government permission. Now the government can use mice for cancer research without being sued by DuPont. Now the government can, but a lot of research companies still can't.

"Other drug companies will stay away from using these mice," says Green. "If they use this technology or animals that were generated with this technology, then DuPont may have a legal right to their work." He shakes his head and laughs a laugh of disbelief, of polite disgust. "It would be nice if the system was revised."

The first time you ever heard John Moore's story, he was sitting at a bar in Seattle, telling a tale about a doctor stealing his cells, and you gaped at the sheer audacity. Now you know enough not to be surprised. Now you know about thousands of doctors and companies and government agencies doing the same thing, or worse, all clutching at Craig Venter's human-genome map as if it were a guide to pirates' treasure.

What amazes you now is not the patenting itself; it's that the whole thing passed you by, that life was being parceled out while your life went on, oblivious. But one man has been there through it all. Before Craig Venter mapped his first gene, before the oil-eating bacterium went to court, even before Jim Watson's big return, one man was keeping an eye on the business of science. He is a small and aging radical with a few tricks still up his sleeve, and you find him in his tidy office at the Foundation on Economic Trends in Washington, D. C., near Chinatown, a buttoned-down and squared-away old yippie with a neatly trimmed mustache and a cheap gray suit.

"Okay," he says, jumping up from behind a desk to shake your hand vigorously. The words come quick, in bursts. "Have you read *The Biotech Century*? What have you read? What do you think?"

The bookshelves, pressed against the wall of the adjoining room, are lined with his books. The first, *Who Should Play God?*, published in 1977, predicted things like surrogate wombs and test-tube babies and the commercialization of the gene pool, things that sounded absurd at the time, so absurd that Jeremy Rifkin quickly earned a reputation as an alarmist. Now he is taken more seriously. Now he speaks on the radio and wears suits to the office. Today, he has just returned from the World Economic Forum in Davos, Switzerland, where he was a featured speaker.

"There's a philosophical issue here that's the deepest of all issues, but it's never talked about," he says. His voice is narrow and thin and high. "In the last century, we fought over whether you can have a human being as property. Slavery. We abolished it. The Thirteenth Amendment." His eyes are dark and wide, his hands small. He spreads them. "So you can't own a whole human being, but now you *can* own all the parts. Genes, cells, chromosomes, organs, tissues, and whole organisms. What happens if we patent all the building blocks of life? What role is there for faith and theology, or even a concept of nature as being independent and a priori? What happens if kids grow up in a world where the government says life is an invention?"

But the truth is that these days, even Jeremy Rifkin is saying that life is an invention. These days, even Rifkin is playing within the system. After twenty years of agitating against the business of science, he has learned that the way to slow its momentum is not by protest but by patent. He has seen the power of DuPont's OncoMouse patent, its potential to slow down research on prostate cancer, and he has seen the power of Myriad Genetics' patent on BRCA1 and how it could slow down research on breast cancer, and seeing that power has given Rifkin an insight: It's the same power he wants to wield—the power to stop power.

And so in 1997 he applied for a patent on all human-animal hybrids, a patent that would give him the exclusive right to determine who can mix human and animal DNA, the next frontier of genetic research. Already, it's a frontier in fast development. There's a company called Nextran mixing human DNA with that of pigs, hoping to mutate pig livers into something a person could use. There's another group of scientists at the University of Bath in England experimenting with frog DNA, hoping to create sustainable systems of human organs that can be harvested for transplants. Rifkin's patent would cover both of those experiments, and he would wield his patent like a weapon, stopping anybody from doing any research whatsoever with human-animal hybrids.

So far, the prospects for his application don't look promising. Actually, it was denied last year. But to an agitator like Rifkin, rejection is where the fun starts. "We have a challenge in the patent office now," he says eagerly. "Then it's going to the Patent Board, the U.S. Court of Appeals, and then probably the Supreme Court."

Outside, traffic is moving down the busy street, but you can't hear it, and you have to wonder if anybody out there can hear Jeremy Rifkin. Or if anybody would hear him even if they could. If they even should hear him now, talking about his rejected patent and his efforts to force it through. Life is being parceled out while, at the same time, life goes on, oblivious. Outside, traffic is moving down the busy street. Inside, even the radicals are filing patent applications.

It would be hard to find something more unpatentable than a gene. Genetic materials do not meet the criteria for a patent. They are not new; their function, for the most part, is unknown; and while it may be true that some living things, like the OncoMouse or the *Pseudomonas* bacterium, were invented by humans, the same cannot be said about the one thousand human genes that have been found in nature and patented that way. They are, in the words of the Supreme Court bacteria decision, "a hitherto unknown natural phenomenon," which should make them unpatentable, like tungsten. They just don't fit the specs.

And yet, in the race to privatize life, the fact that genes should not be patentable makes them all the more important to patent. They have become the ultimate symbol: If a gene can be patented, anything can be. And so the bricks of life have come to mark the end, not the beginning, of the slippery slope.

The great irony of all this is that most of the early patents on genetic data were not filed by big business at all but by the government's Human Genome Project in

1992. And Jim Watson wasn't the only one to protest. The biggest opponent at the time was the Industrial Biotechnology Association, a consortium of private companies concerned about the effects gene patents would have on the flow of knowledge and research. It was only after the NIH defended gene patents that big business jumped into the game.

Even today, one of the most prolific patenters of human genes is the NIH. But big business is fast catching up. Companies like Incyte Genomics and Human Genome Sciences have filed for patents on hundreds of thousands of DNA sequences over the past five years, mostly on random patches of DNA that may or may not even contain genes. Incyte alone has applied for patents on more than one hundred thousand partial gene sequences, just hoping that somewhere along the stretch of DNA they have claimed there will be a few useful genes that they can hoard for themselves or sell. There will surely be money in licensing genes to researchers, but nowhere near the windfall these companies will collect when one of "their" genes is used to cure a disease like cancer or cystic fibrosis or Alzheimer's or Parkinson's or Huntington's, all of which are associated with patented genes.

To get a sense of just what these patents may be worth, you don't have to look any further than the reports of investment banks. "We maintain our long-term buy on Incyte," says J. P. Morgan's equity research report. "Given its early position in gene finding and patenting, and genomics databases, it has carved out a large, very valuable, and largely irreversible position."

Or Robertson Stephens on Human Genome Sciences: "HGS has one of the broadest portfolios of gene/protein targets in the industry . . . and an impressive patent estate to protect its discoveries. This translates into one of the largest intellectual property positions in the industry."

In fact, the one genetics company that doesn't brag about its patent collection is the company you'd probably expect to have the biggest collection of all: Celera. But the fact is, Craig Venter doesn't hold any gene patents. Not one. There was a time, a few years ago, when he did, when he applied for and was granted *provisional* patents on several thousands of gene fragments he had discovered. But they expire after one year, and Venter never upgraded them into full, twenty-year patents. He does plan to hold patents in the future, but the number of genes he'll patent will be in the low hundreds, not the hundreds of thousands like his competitors. He'll patent just the genes he wants to research himself so he won't have to pay a competitor for access. But, for the most part, patents aren't important to his business plan. Venter's goal is not to own the genes or even to provide access to them. His plan is to offer the best available analysis of the whole DNA strand, a running stream of information and insight, much like a trade magazine. Subscribers to his service won't get access to patented genes; they'll be exposed to a fresh collection of ideas and the most complete data available, including comparisons between the human genetic code and those of several other species.

Venter thinks of gene patents as a necessary evil, a way for researchers to recoup their financial investments without keeping their discoveries secret. "Patents are not secrecy," Venter says. "The patent law is basically there to encourage people *not* to hold trade secrets. When you patent, the information gets published." But the reason Venter has become a lightning rod in the growing debate is not because of his specific point of view or because he holds any gene patents. It's because he's one of the only people in the private sector who's willing to debate the issue at all. Actually, he's more than willing, even more willing than many academics. He's eager to engage the debate over gene patents, gene testing, gene discrimination, and anything else genetic. Because he's sick of hearing the eggheads do all the talking, and he's sick of the mentality that the business of science should be kept under wraps. He wants the public to know what's going on in the biotech revolution, and he wants to have an open debate about it, to confront not only its promises but also its threats. And so Craig Venter may be the only person in the whole field of genetics who's hungry for that discussion, who's so anxious to get a lively debate going that he's willing to fly around the world, often on his own tab, just to fan the flames.

Tonight, you can find him in the Gothic marble admitting room of a five-hundred-year-old hospital in France, a room that has been filled with a dozen round tables, each one holding ten place settings. His flight arrived from D. C. this morning, and he's flying back tomorrow morning, and it's been thirty-six hours without sleep so far, maybe a few more, which means that Venter, who is famous among his staff for being indefatigable, is just now starting to get tired. You can see the day in the droop of his eyebrows, less wild and lively than usual, sinking and then jerking back up, snapping to as he twirls his spoon around in his three-fish soup and tries to make conversation with his tablemates.

He's been a celebrity all day at a conference on genetics in Lyons, surrounded by a sea of autograph seekers, and he's brought a CD-ROM to the event tonight. The cover has a picture of Da Vinci's man and says "The Human Genome Map." The disc inside is blank. Venter's planning on leaving it behind at the end of the night, just to mess with the mind of some dummy.

He's finding ways to amuse himself, but he looks bored tonight, in an expensive blue suit that couldn't possibly fit worse over his slouchy, disinterested frame. The painkillers he took this afternoon have worn off, no longer blunting the edge of his exhaustion, and although he asked around for some pot, he wasn't able to find any, so he has been forced to rely on wine—the third bottle's almost empty—which is muting the pain but, unfortunately, dulling his wit as well. He's fading. He's drifting. He's something that Craig Venter rarely is: shot.

Suddenly, a voice comes blaring through the speaker system, and Venter snaps to attention. "Now that we've fed the senses in this beautiful hall, and we've fed the stomach, we come to feeding the mind and the imagination," the voice announces. Venter wipes his eyes, trying to spruce himself up. "We've got a really wonderful lineup of contributors this evening. We have Denis Hochstrasser, from the University of Geneva, a pioneer in proteomics. We have Jean-Marie Lehn, a Nobel laureate based at the Collège de France in Paris. We have Gert-Jan van Ommen, from the

University of Leiden. And we have a bloke who I'm not sure if anybody has ever heard of, Craig Venter from Celera Genomics. So I think it's a great group of people to get together and kick some ideas around."

Hearing his cue, Venter rises, shuffles to the front of the room, and climbs on stage where the other scientists are converging, greeting one another with niceties. Venter gives them all a quick nod, then flops down in a chair, shifting uncomfortably in his seat as each member of the panel introduces himself with a long-winded autobiography and a personal mission statement. Venter can barely suppress his yawns, and when it's his turn to make an opening statement, he leans into the microphone and mumbles, "Well, I've consumed a lot of wine, and I want to make sure I save some comments for later," then he leans back, done.

A flurry of hands leap from the crowd with questions, and the moderator invites a young man to be first. "I'd like to address a topic to anyone on the panel," he says, "and that's the issue of ownership versus free access."

Venter rolls his neck, reaching for the microphone. This is what he was hoping for, a lively debate, right from the start, something to help wake him up. "I think it is a difficult challenge in terms of deciding where to draw the line," he says, "and I think the legal system has been slow to respond to the front lines of science."

"Would you say that certain segments of the genome are not available to everyone?" the guy asks.

Venter shakes his head. In a few days, he will publish the entire genome map online; anyone will be able to see the nucleotide sequence for free. Anyone will be able to see the collection of all human genes, including dozens of new, unpatented ones. Of course, the patented genes will still be restricted in commercial research, but there will be no secrets about where or what they are.

"No offense," Venter says, "but that's the number-one fallacy I hear from people. When you submit a patent application, it gets published by the patent office. Patents are the opposite of secrecy."

At that, van Ommen leans forward, the spitting image of a young Einstein, with his brow in a bunch. "But patenting does create problems for the scientist," he says in a thick Dutch accent. "When you find something, you want to publish it in *Nature* right away, but you can't. You first have to call a patent lawyer."

Venter gives him an annoyed look. Van Ommen raises his eyebrows. Venter takes a sip of water. The debate is under way. Another guy stands up in the audience, asking why Venter won't publish his DNA map, with some analysis, in a scientific journal. Venter assures him that he's got an article in the upcoming issue of *Science*. There's a young woman from Glasgow who's worried about the prospect of genetic discrimination, and Venter nods, saying, yeah, it's a concern of his, too, that he's lobbying Congress in the U. S. to set a global example with some kind of bill to stop genetic discrimination before it starts. There's a guy who wants to know how hospitals in the Third World will ever be able to afford the licensing fees to screen for patented genes, and Venter says it's a fair question, reminding the crowd that he doesn't hold any patents himself, but admitting that he thinks companies should create a flexible pricing system, offering better deals to poorer nations. But just as the discussion is really starting to roll, a man stands up in the center of the room and brings it to a quick end.

"My two children suffer from a rare disease," he says. "I'm just a father. I got involved in this four years ago. I started a research foundation." His voice cracks. He catches himself, gives a slight smile. "I'm nervous," he says, swallowing. "Anyway, we found the gene, and we cloned an animal model." His voice breaks again. Again, he catches himself. "Whew," he says. "My hope and my expectation is that I will save my children's vision loss, and the six thousand other patients' that I represent. And I think it's just . . . I think we all kind of get buried in the minutiae of patents and so forth, and I think it's important to recognize the power of this technology to solve and to protect human existence. We have to remember to think positive thoughts and focus on the difference this technology can make in people's lives."

Silence. A cough splits off the marble walls, and for the first time today, all eyes are off Venter. The moment lingers, the room hushed in support of this speaker, this father, this man announcing his hope, his calm confidence that genetics will better the world. The room is still, and Venter endures it as he has endured the stillness and silence for so long. As we have all endured the blind optimism that allowed business to consume science, that allowed life to be parceled out, even as life went on. Oblivious.

 ## *For Discussion:*

1. How were companies allowed to patent parts of the human body?
2. If patents serve as a means of protecting a company's investment and intellectual property, should companies be able to patent the techniques used to access certain genes? Why should companies be expected to expend billions in researching these techniques, only to turn over their findings for free?
3. Should companies be allowed to mix human and non-human DNA? What kinds of arguments against such processes might be made? What kinds of arguments in favor of such processes might be made?

 ## *For Fact-Finding, Research, and Writing:*

1. Find the actual text of federal laws governing gene patenting. Summarize one of them.
2. What exactly is the Human Genome Project?
3. Compare the issues raised by Hylton to those raised by Clement or Lessig. What complex questions do these texts raise about the nature of private property?

4. Compare Hylton's description of Venter's work, and the issues associated with it, to the essay on cloning in chapter four. Hylton raises primarily questions of biomedical ethics and private property; how do the ethical issues in the debate over cloning affect your reading of Hylton? Or vice-versa?

5. Using the Web of Science database, find two articles on the issue of patenting the content of stem cells.

Douglas Clement, "Was Napster Right?"

Douglas Clement is a senior writer for *The Region,* a publication of the Federal Reserve Bank of Minneapolis. He has written widely on economic issues and has been a contributor to *Fedgazette,* a newspaper devoted to reporting on the economy of the Ninth District, and *Reason,* a publication of the Reason Foundation. This essay appeared in the September, 2002 issue of *The Region,* following a series of lawsuits between Napster and the music industry. Napster, the largest and one of the first music-sharing services to become popular on the Internet, eventually declared bankruptcy, and its assets were acquired by Roxio in 2002. In early 2003, Roxio announced plans to re-launch Napster as a fee-based service, this time with the blessing of many major music companies.

 Before You Read:

Do you download music from the Internet or make copies of CDs? Why or why not? Do you think that copyrights and patents promote or stifle innovation?

Was Napster Right?

Douglas Clement

FALLING IN THE emotional wake of the terrorist attacks on the World Trade Center and Pentagon, this year's Grammy awards ceremony had a solemn tone. More than a dozen moving performances recognized the mood of a nation seeking to heal its wounds. Tony Bennett crooned "New York State of Mind" in a duet with Billy Joel.

Nelly Furtado soared with "I'm Like a Bird." The Rev. Al Green and CeCe Winans gave a powerful gospel finale.

The most forceful performance of the evening, however, was the speech delivered by Michael Greene. As president of the National Academy of Recording Arts & Sciences, he spoke gravely of "serious risk" and warned of worldwide threat. "Embrace this life and death issue," he implored the audience. The menace is "pervasive, out of control and oh so criminal."

But Greene was not referring to the events of Sept. 11. The sinister threat he spoke of was neither Al Qaeda nor anthrax. "The most insidious virus in our midst," said Greene, with a very stern face, "is the illegal downloading of music on the Net."

If it seems just a bit overwrought to imply that pulling a Britney Spears song off the Web is the greatest threat since international terrorism, the tenor of Greene's sermon was a clear indication of the music world's fear. New technology has loosened the industry's hold over product replication and distribution. Their profits, their business model, their very existence is under siege.

And the music business is not alone in this worry. Over the past decade, the captains of many other industries—movies, publishing, software, pharmaceuticals—have railed against "piracy" that they feel afflicts their profits. The copyright and patent protection conferred by government to protect their intellectual property has been breached by new technologies that easily and quickly copy and distribute their products to mass markets. And as quickly as a producer figures a way to encrypt a DVD or software program to prevent duplication, some hacker in Seattle, Reykjavik or Manila figures a way around it.

So if Greene's tirade was tone-deaf, his concern was understandable. His industry and others feel threatened because they can no longer control their product. The music industry has tried to squelch the threat, most conspicuously by suing Napster, the wildly popular Internet service that matched up patrons with the songs they wanted, allowing them to download digital music files without charge. Napster, of course, lost the lawsuit and, as this goes to press, is heading toward liquidation.

But the struggle between Napster and the music industry has given high profile to a much broader question: How does an economy best promote innovation? Do patents and copyrights stifle innovation rather than nurture it? Have we gone too far in protecting intellectual property? Is a society served better by the unfettered exchange of ideas and information than by granting creators and inventors the right to control the distribution and future uses of their products? More succinctly: Was Napster right?

In a paper that has gained wide attention—and caught serious flak—because it challenges conventional wisdom on the matter, economists Michele Boldrin and David Levine have begun to answer that question in the affirmative. Copyrights, patents and similar government-granted rights over ideas and innovations serve only to reinforce monopoly control, with its attendant damages of inefficiently high prices, low quantities and stifled future innovation, said Boldrin and Levine in "Perfectly Competitive Innovation," a Minneapolis Fed staff report [minneapolisfed.org/research/sr/sr303.html]. And more to the point, they argued, economic theory shows that perfectly competitive markets are entirely capable of rewarding (and thereby stimulating) innovation, making copyrights and patents superfluous and wasteful.

Reactions to the paper have been predictably disparate. Robert Solow, the Massachusetts Institute of Technology economist who won a Nobel in 1987 for his pioneering work on growth theory, wrote them a letter calling the paper "an eye-opener" and making suggestions for further refinements. Danny Quah, a professor of economics at the London School of Economics, called their analysis "an important and profound development" that "seeks to overturn nearly half a century of formal economic thinking on intellectual property. . . ."

But UCLA economist Benjamin Klein finds their work "unrealistic," and Paul Romer, a Stanford University economist whose pathbreaking development of new growth theory is the focus of much of Boldrin and Levine's critique, considers their logic flawed and their assumptions implausible.

It is a measure of the depth and ambition of the paper that the authors absorb these criticisms and continue to consider their work sound and its implications far-reaching. "To avoid being humble when it is not needed," joked Boldrin in an e-mail from Madrid, where he is currently on sabbatical, "we are actually challenging IO [industrial organization] and IT [international trade] theories, beside NGT [new growth theory]." Yet he also noted in an earlier interview, "We're not claiming to have invented anything new, really. We're recognizing something that we think has been around ever since there has been innovation. In fact, patents and copyrights are a very recent distortion." But even if that's true, Boldrin and Levine are working against a well-established conventional wisdom that has sanctioned if not embraced intellectual property rights, and theirs is a decidedly uphill battle.

A Long Heritage

So, what is that conventional wisdom? In the 1950s, Solow showed that technological change was a primary source of economic growth, but his growth models viewed that change as exogenous, a given determined by elements beyond pure economic forces. In the 1960s, Kenneth Arrow, Karl Shell and William Nordhaus delved further into this source of economic growth, analyzing the relationship between free markets and technological change. They concluded that free markets might fail to bring about optimal levels of innovation.

"[T]hree of the classical reasons for the possible failure of perfect competition to achieve optimality in resources allocation: indivisibilities, inappropriability, and uncertainty . . . all . . . hold in the case of invention," wrote Arrow in a landmark 1962 article. "We expect a free enterprise economy to underinvest in invention and research (as compared with an ideal) because it is risky, because the product can be appropriated only to a limited extent, and because of increasing returns in use."

The uncertainty associated with creation and invention seems a clear roadblock to investment in technological change: Will all the hours and dollars spent on research and development result in a profitable product? Is the payoff worth the risk? The uncertainty of success diminishes the desire to try. Much of Arrow's article examined economic means of dealing with uncertainty, none of them completely successful.

The second problem, what economists call inappropriability, is the divergence between social and private benefit—in this case, the difference between the benefit reaped by society from an invention, and the benefit reaped by the inventor. Will I try to invent the wheel if all humankind would benefit immeasurably from my invention, but I'd only get $1,000? Maybe not. Property rights, well defined, help address this issue.

And the third obstacle to innovation, indivisibility, is the concept that the act of invention involves a substantial upfront expenditure (of time or money) before a single unit of the song, the formula or the book exists. But thereafter, copies can be made at a fraction of the cost. Such indivisibilities result in dramatically increasing returns to scale: If a $1 million investment results in just one unit of an invention, the prototype, a $2 million expenditure could result in the prototype plus thousands or millions of duplicates.

This is a great problem to have, but perfect competition doesn't deal well with increasing returns to scale. With free markets and no barriers to entry, products are priced at their marginal cost (the cost of the latest copy), and that price simply won't cover the huge initial outlay. Inventors will have no financial incentive for bringing their inventions to reality, and society will be denied the benefits.

Increasing returns therefore seem to argue for some form of monopoly, and in the late 1970s, Joseph Stiglitz and Avinash Dixit developed a growth model of monopolistic competition—that is, limited competition with increasing returns to scale. It's a model in which many firms compete in a given market but none is strictly a price-taker. It's a growth model, in other words, without perfect competition. The Dixit-Stiglitz model is widely used today, with the underlying assumption that economic growth requires technological change, which implies increasing returns, which means imperfect competition.

New (Endogenous) Growth Theory

Much of this work was formalized in the 1980s and 1990s by Romer in what he called a theory of endogenous growth. It was the idea that technological change—innovation—should be modeled as part of an economy, not external to it as Solow had done. And the policy implication was that economic variables like interest and tax rates, as well as subsidies for research and technical education, could influence the rate of innovation.

Romer refined the ideas of Arrow and others, developing new terms, integrating the economics of innovation and extending the Dixit-Stiglitz growth model into what he called "new growth theory." In a parallel track, Robert Lucas, Nobel laureate at the University of Chicago, elucidated the importance of human capital to economic growth. And just prior to all this growth theory work, Paul Krugman, Elhanan Helpman and others integrated increasing returns theory with international trade economics, creating "new trade theory." Similar theories became the bedrock of industrial organization economics.

Central to Romer's theory is the idea of nonrivalry, a property he considers inherent to invention, designs and other forms of intellectual creation. "A purely nonrival good," wrote Romer, "has the property that its use by one firm or person in no way limits its use by another." A formula, for example, can be used simultaneously and equally by a hundred people, whereas a wrench cannot. The formula is a nonrival good, the wrench is rivalrous.

Nonrivalrous goods are inherently subject to increasing returns to scale, said Romer. "Developing new and better instructions is equivalent to incurring a fixed cost," he wrote. "Once the cost of creating a new set of instructions has been incurred, the instructions can be used over and over again at no additional cost." But if this is true, then "it follows directly that an equilibrium with price taking cannot be supported." In other words, economic growth—and the technological innovation that it requires—isn't possible under perfect competition; it requires some degree of monopoly power.

Undermining Convention

Economists prize economic growth but distrust monopoly, and to accept the latter to obtain the former is a Faustian bargain at best. With "Perfectly Competitive Innovation," Boldrin and Levine vigorously reject the contract. "It may not be an exaggeration to assert that a meaningful treatment of endogenous innovation and growth is commonly believed to be impossible under competitive conditions," they wrote. "We aim at disproving this belief."

They point to the historical record. Innovation, they argue, has occurred in the past without substantial protection of intellectual property. "Historically, people have been inventing and writing books and music when copyright did not exist," noted Boldrin. "Mozart wrote a lot of very beautiful things without any copyright protection."

(The publishers of music and books, on the other hand, sometimes did have copyrights to the materials they bought from their creators. But as University of London economist Arnold Plant argued in a classic 1934 review of the copyright history, "The copyright monopoly, like patent monopoly" isn't necessary to remunerate authors and inventors, it restricts supply, and it doesn't produce better products than those "which [emerge] . . . from the competitive bidding of the open market.")

Contemporary examples, said Boldrin and Levine, are also plentiful. The fashion world—highly competitive, with designs largely unprotected—innovates constantly and profitably. True also in modern art. The financial securities industry makes millions by developing and selling complex securities and options without

PERFECTLY COMPETITIVE SUPERSTARS

WHY DO THEY MAKE SO MUCH MONEY?
A THEORY OF SIMILAR SKILLS BUT VERY DIFFERENT PAYCHECKS

Is Texas Rangers shortstop Alex Rodriguez worth $25.2 million a year? How about NBC news personality Katie Couric. Does she deserve her $13 million to $15 million salary, perhaps three times what veteran journalist Mike Wallace makes? And why did the members of Aerosmith have to split a paltry $25 million last year, while U2's crew shared earnings of $69 million?

Mere economists will probably never fully fathom such profound mysteries, but it's not because huge celebrity salaries have escaped their attention. The question of why superstars are paid so much more than the average person in their field—far more, indeed, than their close competitors—was the focus of a 1981 paper "The Economics of Superstars" by University of Chicago economist Sherwin Rosen.

About numerous professions—from comedians to economists to classical musicians—Rosen made two key observations. First, "performers of the first rank . . . have very large incomes." Second, there are "substantial differences in income between them and those in the second rank, even though most consumers would have difficulty detecting more than minor differences. . . ." Standard economic theory provides no explanation for these observations, he noted. "Competitive theory is virtually silent about any special role played by either the size of the total market or the amount of it controlled by any single person" because products are assumed to be virtually identical.

But Rosen provided a careful and complex explanation focusing on two things: imperfect substitution among different sellers and scale economies of joint consumption technologies. The first simply means that lesser talent is a poor substitute for greater talent. "Hearing a succession of mediocre singers does not add up to a single outstanding performance," wrote Rosen.

The second notion is that certain technologies allow very few sellers to service the entire market. Before the advent of the phonograph, your town's local singing star might be the best you'd ever hear; with Edison's invention, the voice of Enrico Caruso could spread across the globe.

"When the joint consumption technology and imperfect substitution features of preferences are combined," Rosen observed, "the possibility for talented persons to command both very large markets and very large incomes is apparent."

Does Competitive Innovation Diminish Superstars?

Twenty years later, Boldrin and Levine pick up where Rosen left off. In a short section of "Perfectly Competitive Innovation," they apply their theory of innovation to the phenomenon of superstars. One might suspect that superstar salaries have something to do with monopoly power, they observe, but that needn't be the case. Superstars will emerge even under perfect competition because of the impact of reproduction technology on prices paid to laborers of varying quality.

"Our model predicts that superstars should abound in industries where the main product is information which can be cheaply reproduced and distributed on a massive scale," wrote Boldrin and Levine. "Such is the case for the worlds of sport, entertainment, arts and letters, which coincides with the penetrating observations that motivated Rosen's original contribution." (They note that their idea is just one of a number of possible explanations for the super-salary phenomenon, but they suggest it is simpler, more elegant and more realistic than other theories that have been offered.)

Their model shows that if there are indivisibilities, technological changes in reproduction that lower prices and broaden markets will initially be beneficial to all entertainers. Real wages will increase at a uniform rate for all types of labor. "Eventually, though, further improvements in the reproduction technology lead to a 'crowding out' of the least efficient . . .," they wrote. As reproductive capacity increases still further, the superstar will capture the entire market and gain disproportionately high wages.

Thus, even very small differences in skill are magnified by technology that copies and distributes information with increasing ease. "Our theory," concluded Boldrin and Levine, "predicts that the increased reproducibility of information will continue generating large income disparities among individuals of very similar skills and in a growing number of industries."

The irony, of course, is that rapid innovation in information technology—championed by the underdogs at Napster and elsewhere—may result in an expanded galaxy of superstars and a growing gap between their salaries and ours.

—Douglas Clement

benefit of intellectual property protection. Competitors are free to copy a firm's security package, but doing so takes time. The initial developer's first-mover advantage secures enough profit to justify "inventing" the security.

As for software, Boldrin refers to a Massachusetts Institute of Technology working paper by economists Eric Maskin and James Bessen. Maskin and Bessen wrote that "some of the most innovative industries today—software, computers and semiconductors—have historically had weak patent protection and have experienced rapid imitation of their products."

Moreover, U.S. court decisions in the 1980s that strengthened patent protection for software led to less innovation. "Far from unleashing a flurry of new innovative activity," wrote Maskin and Bessen, "these stronger property rights ushered in a period of stagnant, if not declining R & D among those industries and firms that patented most." Industries that depend on sequential product development, they argued, are likely to be stifled by stronger intellectual property regimes.

"So examples abound," said Boldrin. "That's the empirical point: Evidence shows that innovators have enough of an incentive to innovate." But he and Levine are not, by nature or training, empiricists. They build mathematical models to describe economic theory. And in the case of intellectual property, they contend, evidence contradicts theory: Current theory says innovation won't happen unless innovators receive monopoly rights, but the evidence says otherwise. "So what we do is to develop the theoretical point to explain the evidence," said Boldrin.

Rivalry over Nonrivalry

Central to their argument is a closer look at nonrivalry. A fundamental tenet of current conventional wisdom is that knowledge-based innovations are subject to increasing returns because ideas are non-rivalrous: One person's use of an idea (or song, movie, book, software, etc.) doesn't diminish anyone else's. As Thomas Jefferson put the same concept (more eloquently): "He who receives an idea from me, receives instruction himself without lessening mine; as he who lights his taper at mine, receives light without darkening me."

But Boldrin and Levine argue that in an economy, this has no relevance. While pure ideas can be shared without rivalry in theory, the economic application of ideas is inherently rivalrous because ideas "have economic value only to the extent that they are embodied into either something or someone." What is relevant in the economic realm is not an abstract concept or formula—no matter how beautiful—but its physical embodiment. Calculus is economically valuable only insofar as engineers and economists know and apply it. "Only ideas embodied in people, machines or goods have economic value," they wrote. And because of their physical embodiment, "valuable ideas . . . are as rivalrous as commodities containing no ideas at all, if such exist."

A novel is valuable only to the extent that it is written down (if then). A song can be sold only if it is sung, played or written by its creator. A software program—once written—might seem costless, but "the prototype [of a program] does not sit on thin air," wrote Boldrin and Levine. "To be used by others it needs to be copied, which requires resources of various kinds, including time. To be usable it needs to reside on some portion of the memory of your computer. . . . When you are using that specific copy of the software, other people cannot simultaneously do the same. . . . Once again, there is no free lunch."

In each instance, development of the initial prototype is far more costly than production of all subsequent copies, admit Boldrin and Levine. But because copying takes time—a limited commodity—and materials (e.g., paper, ink, hard disk space), it is not entirely costless. "Consider the paradigmatic example of the wheel," they wrote. "Once the first wheel was produced, imitation could take place at a cost orders of magnitude smaller. But even imitation cannot generate free goods: to make a new wheel, one needs to spend some time looking at the first one and learning how to carve it."

The first wheel is far more valuable than all others, of course, but that "does not imply that the wheel, first or last that it be, is a nonrivalrous good. It only implies that, for some goods, replication costs are very small."

Economic theorists have generally assumed that the dramatic difference between development and replication costs can be modeled as a single process with increasing returns to scale: a huge fixed cost (the initial investment) followed by costless duplication.

Boldrin and Levine said this misrepresents reality: There are two distinct processes with very different technologies. Development is one production process involving long hours, gallons of coffee, sweaty genius and black, tempestuous moods. At the end of this initial process (hopefully), the prototype exists and the effort and money that produced it are a sunk cost, an expense in the past.

Thereafter, a very different production process governs replication: Replicators study the original, gather flat stones, round off corners, bore center holes and prune tree limbs into axles. Stone wheels roll off the antediluvian assembly line. In this second process, the economics of production are the same as for any other commodity, usually with constant returns to scale.

The Candle's Flicker

As Boldrin and Levine develop the mathematical model that describes this, they assume only that "as in reality," copying takes time and there is a limit (less than infinity) on the number of copies that can be produced per unit of time. These "twin assumptions" introduce a slim element of rivalry. After it's created, the prototype can be either consumed or used for copying in the initial time period. (Technically, it could be used for both, but not as easily as if it were used for just one or the other.)

While others have simply assumed, with Romer, that the prototype of an intellectual product is nonrivalrous, Boldrin and Levine argue that this tiny amount of cost undermines the conventional model. It's as if Jefferson's candle flickered when it was used to light another: The wax, wick and air that embody the flame are production factors, and sharing the flame actually does incur a drop of wax, a bit of wick and a wisp of oxygen. And when this is the case, find Boldrin and Levine, production is not subject to increasing returns and competitive markets can work. "Even a minuscule amount of rivalry," they wrote, "can turn standard results upside down."

Incenting Invention

Still, the central question is whether innovators will have enough incentive to go through the arduous, expensive invention process. Since the 1400s, when the first patent systems emerged in Venice, governments have tried to provide incentive by granting inventors sole rights to their creations for limited periods. The U.S. Constitution, for example, gives Congress the power "to promote the Progress of Science and useful Arts, by securing for limited Times to Authors and Inventors the exclusive Right to their respective Writings and Discoveries."

Economists have long recognized that those exclusive rights give creators limited monopolies, allowing them to set prices and quantities that may not be socially optimal. But conventional thinking has said these costs are the necessary trade-off for bringing forth creative genius, for lighting the candle. "Modern economic literature reflects our reality," wrote Steven Shavell of Harvard Law School and Tanguy van Ypersele of the University of Namur, in a recent article, "and takes the general optimality of intellectual property rights largely as a given." Today, the legal realities and economic conventions have assumed the air of incontrovertible fact: If inventors can be "ripped off"—copied as soon as they create—why would they bother? We must grant them rights.

In arguing for competitive innovation, rather than the monopolistic variety, Boldrin and Levine emphasize that they are not saying creators don't have property rights. On the contrary, they stress that innovators should be given "a well defined right of first sale." (Or more technically, "we assume full appropriability of privately produced commodities.") And creators should be paid the full market value of their invention, the first unit of the new product. That value is "the net discounted value of the future stream of consumption services" generated by that first unit, which is an economist's way of saying it's worth the current value of everything it's going to earn in the future.

Britney Gets Her Due

So, if Britney Spears records a new song, she should be able to sell the initial recording for the sum total of whatever music distributors think her fans will pay for copies of the music over the next century or so. Distributors know her songs are in demand, and she knows she can command a high price. As in any other market, the buyer and seller negotiate a deal. The same for a novelist who writes a book, a software programmer who generates code or a physicist who develops a useful formula. They get to sell the invention in a competitive market. They're paid whatever the market will bear, and if the market values copies of their song, book, code or formula, the initial prototype will be quite precious, and they'll be well paid.

In fact, said Boldrin, "in a competitive market, the very first few copies are very valuable because those are the instruments which the imitators—the other people who will publish your stuff—will use to make copies. They're more capital goods than consumption goods. So the initial copies will be sold at a very high price, but then very rapidly they will go down in price."

But what creators won't get, in Boldrin and Levine's world, is the right to "rent" their intellectual property—that is, the legal right to impose downstream licensing agreements that prevent customers from reproducing the product or modifying it or using it as a stepping stone to the next innovation. They can't, in brief, prevent their customers from competing with them.

"Britney will get her dues the same way Monteverdi, Mozart, Vivaldi and Co. did," wrote Boldrin in an e-mail. "Same for writers. All they have to do is follow in the footsteps of Homer and Shakespeare." Boldrin isn't proposing that Spears approach the King of Prussia for patronage, but he is saying that the market will take care of her; monopolies aren't necessary.

But will the market pay enough? That depends on the opportunity costs of the inventor. If the price likely to be paid for an invention's first sale exceeds the opportunity costs of the inventor, then yes, the inventor will create. If a writer spends a year on a book, and could have earned $30,000 during that year doing something else, then her opportunity cost is $30,000. Only if she guesses she can sell her book for at least that much is she likely to sit down and write.

"What we show in the technical paper is that the amount [a book publisher] gives me is positive, and in fact, it can be large," said Boldrin. "Then it's up to me to figure out if what society is paying me is enough to compensate for my year of work."

But more startling is the next implication of the Boldrin and Levine model. What happens as reproduction technologies improve, as printing presses get faster or as software and the Internet allow teenagers to share music files faster and farther—the scenario that so horrified Michael Greene at the Grammy ceremony? Won't that drive authors and musicians into utter poverty by ripping them off even more quickly?

In fact, the opposite should occur. Increasing rates of reproduction will drop marginal production costs and, therefore, prices. If demand for the good is elastic (if demand rises disproportionately when prices drop), then total revenue will increase. And since creators with strong rights of first sale are paid the current value of future revenue, their pay will climb. "The point we're making is the invention of things like the Napster or electronic publishing and so on, are actually creating more opportunities for writers, musicians, for people in general to produce intellectual value, to sell their stuff and actually make money," said Boldrin. "The costs I suffer to write down one of my books or songs have not changed, so overall we actually have a bigger incentive, not smaller incentive."

Static Efficiency vs. Dynamic Growth

Part of the conventional wisdom about economic growth and monopoly protection for innovation is that monopoly rights do impose short-term costs on an economy. They give an undue share of the economic pie to those who own copyrights and patents; they misallocate resources toward some uses by allowing innovators to command too high a price; and they allow innovators to produce less than the societally optimal level of the new invention. But these costs are all considered reasonable because innovation creates economic growth: The static costs are eclipsed by dynamic development. The pie grows. It is part of the Schumpeterian concept of "creative destruction," that future growth demands a sacrifice of static efficiency.

But again, Boldrin and Levine say this is a false dilemma. Monopoly rights are not only unnecessary for innovation, they may stifle it, particularly when an innovation reduces the cost of expanding production. "Monopolists as a rule do not like to produce much output," they wrote. "Insofar as the benefit of an innovation is that it reduces the cost of producing additional units of output but not the cost of producing at the current level, it is not of great use to a monopolist." Monopolists, after all, can set prices and quantities to maximize their profits; they have no incentive to find faster reproduction technologies if they won't enhance profits.

More broadly, producers are likely to engage in what economists call "rent-seeking behavior"—efforts to protect or expand turf (and profits) by fighting for government-granted monopoly protection—and that behavior is likely to stifle innovation. Expensive patent races, defensive patenting (in which firms create a wall of patents to prevent competitors from coming up with anything remotely resembling their product) and costly patent infringement battles are common functions of corporate law departments. Many observers say this kind of activity chokes off creative efforts by others, particularly small and middle-sized firms that are typically more innovative. "Rent-seeking behaviors induced through government grants of monopoly," wrote Boldrin and Levine, "are likely to hinder rather than promote innovation."

The Critics

Like any radical innovation, Boldrin and Levine's argument seems to have shocked many mainstream economists, at least initially. There's "a lot of 'that can't possibly be true' followed later by 'that actually seems to make some sense,'" said Levine. "We've been presenting it in quite a few key places, and I have to admit that every time there was a riot," said Boldrin. "There was a riot at Stanford last Thursday. It was a huge riot at Chicago two weeks ago. I know it was a riot at Toulouse when David presented it."

A "riot" among economists might not call for crowd control, but the paper does evoke strong reactions. Klein at UCLA said the paper is "unrealistic modeling with little to do with the real world." Specifically (in a paper with Kevin Murphy of the University of Chicago and Andres Lerner of Economic Analysis LLC), Klein wrote that Boldrin and Levine's model works only under the "arbitrary demand assumption" that demand for copies is elastic, so that as price falls over time output increases more than proportionately and profit rises. In the case of Napster and the music industry (the focus of the Klein-Murphy-Lerner paper) this "clearly conflicts with record company pricing. That is, if Boldrin and Levine were correct, why are record companies not pricing CDs as low as possible?"

Romer has a broader set of objections. As a co-author and graduate school classmate of Levine's and a former teacher of Boldrin's at the University of Rochester, Romer has no desire to brawl with his respected colleagues. Moreover, he agrees that property rights for intellectual goods are sometimes too strong; in some cases, society might benefit from weaker restrictions. Music file-sharing, for example, might increase social welfare even if it hurts the current music industry. And he stresses that alternative mechanisms for bringing forth innovation might well be superior to copyrights and patents: government support for technology education, for example, reward systems or public funding for research and development. Nonetheless, Romer does have serious problems with the theory that Boldrin and Levine espouse.

First of all, the property rights Boldrin and Levine would assign to innovators "would truly be an empty promise," said Romer. In their model, if a pharmaceutical firm discovers a new compound, it can sell the first pills but not restrict their downstream use. A generic drug manufacturer could then buy one pill, analyze it and start stamping out copies.

"So what Boldrin and Levine call 'no downstream licensing' is instant generic status for drugs" and while they argue that the inventor "can sell a few pills for millions of dollars" this conclusion is unrealistic if everyone who buys a pill can copy it. "You can make a set of mathematical assumptions so that this is all logically consistent," said Romer, "but those assumptions are wildly at odds with the underlying facts in the pharmaceutical industry."

If Boldrin and Levine are unrealistic about appropriability, they are even more at sea regarding rivalry, said Romer. While it's true that ideas must be embodied to be economically useful, it's false to say that there is no distinction between the idea and its physical instantiation. A formula must be written down, but the formula is far more valuable than the piece of paper on which it's written. In a large market, the formula could be so valuable that "the cost of the extra paper is trivial—so small that it is a reasonable approximation to neglect it entirely."

If Romer's approximation is right—if it truly is reasonable to neglect that "trivial" cost—then the slim element of rivalry that Boldrin and Levine use to overturn conventional wisdom disappears.

Romer also objects to Boldrin and Levine's contention that competition can deal well with sunk costs. "This claim is simply false," he said. And he suggests that Boldrin and Levine are wrong to object to copyright restriction of downstream use of products, since perfect competition optimally allows sellers and buyers to enter contracts that limit downstream use. "What justification is there," said Romer, "for preventing consenting adults from writing contracts that limit subsequent or downstream uses of a good?"

Boldrin's quick e-mail response: "We never say anything like that! Patents and copyrights are NOT private contracts; they are monopoly rights given by governments."

And Romer countered: "The legal system creates an opportunity for an owner to write contracts that limit how a valuable good can be used. . . . The proposal from Boldrin and Levine would deprive a pharmaceutical company or the owner of a song of the chance to write this kind of contract with a buyer."

What to Believe?

The discussion thickens rapidly. Even a master of abstruse theory like Lucas confesses in response to an onerous *Region* query about the Boldrin and Levine paper, "If the questions get too abstract (as in some of your questions and some of their paper!) I get lost."

Still, says Lucas, "there is no question that Boldrin and Levine have their theory worked out correctly. The issue is where it applies and where it doesn't." The strongest examples for Boldrin and Levine, according to Lucas, are Napster and the music industry. "If we do not enforce copyrights to music, will people stop writing and recording songs?" he asks rhetorically. "Not likely, I agree. If so, then protection against musical 'piracy' just comes down to protecting monopoly positions: something economists usually oppose, and with reason."

But Lucas cautions that their theory may not apply everywhere. "What about pharmaceuticals?" he says, in an echo of Romer. "Here millions are spent on developing new drugs. Why do this if the good ideas can be quickly copied?"

Solow suggests that Boldrin and Levine should enrich their "very nice paper" by testing its robustness. What happens if the time interval between invention and copying is shrunk? "It would be interesting to look at the limiting behavior," he wrote. And "does anything special happen if you introduce some uncertainty about the outcome of an investment in innovation?" Solow is raising here one of the key obstacles to competitive innovation that Arrow pointed out in 1962, an obstacle Boldrin and Levine "ruled out by considering a deterministic environment."

Replicating the Past

Curiously, much of this debate parallels an extensive controversy in Europe a century and a half ago. European critics of the patent system in the mid-1800s said it hindered further innovation and harmed consumers through unduly high prices. Other opponents said inventors themselves received little of the profit generated— the companies to which they sold rights made the big money—which implied that patents weren't necessary. Being first to market was often enough incentive, said other observers, as was the prestige associated with invention. "Many economists disapproved of the patent system," wrote Shavell and van Ypersele. Indeed, in 1863, the Congress of German Economists noted that "patents hinder rather than further the progress of invention, . . . hamper [their] prompt general utilization . . . [and] cause more harm than benefit to the inventors themselves."

The Dutch repealed their patent system in 1869. Switzerland rejected legislation to adopt a patent system in 1863. Bismarck called for its abolition in Prussia in 1868. The British established three commissions between 1850 and 1870 to investigate and reform their system and several members of Parliament proposed total abolition. But the depression of the 1870s created a backlash against the era's free-trade movement and patents again gained favor. "Europe ultimately embraced patent," wrote Shavell and van Ypersele, "but for reasons that may perhaps be regarded as more politically accidental than indicative of a substantive policy judgment favoring that system."

If the current debate repeats history, the controversy won't soon be resolved, but at least policymakers have begun again to discuss the issues. Announcing an extensive series of hearings held between February and May 2002 on antitrust policy and intellectual property rights, Timothy Muris, chairman of the Federal Trade Commission, noted that during the 1970s, antitrust lawyers tended not to appreciate the importance of intellectual property. Now, he said, the pendulum has swung, and some observers say "perhaps it is intellectual property doctrine that is not showing a proper appreciation for the innovation that competition may spur."

Refining the Theory

For their part, Boldrin and Levine recognize that work remains to be done to strengthen their theory. They have begun to look at the effect of uncertainty on their model, as Solow suggests, and they say the results still broadly obtain. The difference is that a large monopolist may be able to self-insure against risk, whereas competitors will need to create securities that allow them, said Boldrin, "to sell away some of the risk and buy some insurance."

As for pharmaceutical research development, Boldrin and Levine contend that it's largely a strawman argument, a misrepresentation of the industry's economics. Much of the high cost of pharmaceutical development, said Boldrin, is due to the inflated values placed on pharmaceutical researchers' time because they are employed by monopolists. Researchers are paid far less in the more competitive European drug industry.

In addition, pharmaceuticals aren't sold into a competitive market, said Levine. "They are generally purchased by large organizations such as governments and HMOs." If inflated drug prices are viewed more realistically, they argue, if pharmaceutical markets were truly competitive rather than protected by monopoly rights, the development costs of new drugs would not be nearly as insurmountable as commonly believed.

Moreover, copying a drug takes time and money, providing the innovative drug company with a substantial first-mover advantage. "It's not obvious that the other guys can imitate me overnight," said Boldrin. "The fact that you are the first . . . and know how to do it better than the other people . . . it may be a huge protection."

Still, they admit, there are cases of indivisibility where the initial investment may simply be too large for a perfectly competitive market. "We have argued that the competitive mechanism is a viable one, capable of producing sustained innovation," they wrote. "This is not to argue that competition is the best mechanism in all circumstances." If indivisibility constraints bind, some socially desirable innovations may not be produced; the problem is similar to a public goods problem. The authors suggest that contingent contracts and lotteries could be used in such cases, but "a theory of general equilibrium with production indivisibility remains to be fully worked out."

"All We Have Made . . ."

Some economists have already begun work on the next stages. Quah at the London School of Economics has taken their basic model, confirmed it and then pushed it in a number of directions to test its robustness and applicability. In one paper, he finds their model works well if he tweaks assumptions about consumption and production of the intellectual assets, but it falters if he changes time constraints.

In another paper, Quah contends that Boldrin and Levine's potential solutions to indivisibility constraints (through innovation lotteries, contingent contracts or entrepreneur coalitions) may not actually resolve the constraint. "What is needed," he wrote, "is the capability to continuously adjust the level of an intellectual asset's instantiation quantity." Which translates roughly to coming up with half an idea, more or less. So, that might be a problem. (Boldrin and Levine are already working on it.)

More studies like Quah's will be needed to poke, prod, refine, refute and extend Boldrin and Levine's theory. And empirical work will be needed to see whether it is, indeed, a more apt description of innovation. The theory is part of an intellectual thicket, and economists who work that thicket tend to render it impenetrable by adopting different terms or defining identical terms differently.

What is clear, though, is that Boldrin and Levine have mounted a formidable assault on the conventional wisdom about innovation and the need to protect intellectual property. That it has met with opposition or incredulity is to be expected. What matters are the next steps.

"The reaction for now is surprise and disbelief," reflected Boldrin. "We'll see. In these kinds of things, the relevance is always if people find the suggestion interesting enough that it's worth pushing farther the research. All we have made is a simple theoretical point."

 For Discussion:

1. What is "inappropriability"?
2. What is a monopoly? How do a copyright and a monopoly relate to one another? Based on what you understand about the difference, do you believe Boldrin is correct that "Patents and copyrights are NOT private contracts; they are monopoly rights given by governments"?

For Fact-Finding, Research, and Writing:

1. Using a newspaper database or Business Source Elite, find editorials expressing at least two different opinions about the Napster controversy.
2. Those opposed to music-sharing on the Internet have argued that recording sales decreased during the Napster years. Using a business database or Statistical Universe, find statistics that demonstrate whether or not this is actually true during the period in question.
3. Who introduced the legislation for the Digital Millennium Copyright Act of 1998? What was the stated purpose of this act?

F. Gregory Lastowka, "Search Engines Under Siege"

F. Gregory Lastowka is a lawyer who specializes in matters of intellectual property and the Internet. He has written widely on the subject in professional law journals. This essay originally appeared in the July 2002 issue of *Intellectual Property and Law Journal*.

Before You Read:

Do you think companies have a right to protect their trademarks from unauthorized use? What do you know about the way Internet search engines work?

Search Engines Under Siege:
Do Paid Placement Listings Infringe Trademarks?

F. Gregory Lastowka

CONSIDER THE FOLLOWING scenario: Your client is the purveyor of a soft drink called "Gnucola."[1] The Gnucola company has used your law firm to register the "Gnucola" mark with the US Patent and Trademark Office and has used your law

Reprinted/Adapted with permission from Aspen Law & Business, copyright © July 2002, F. Gregory Lastowka, *Intellectual Property & Technology Law Journal*, Search Engines Under Siege: Do Paid Placement Listings Infringe Trademarks, Vol. 14, No. 7, www.aspenpublishers.com.

firm to assist it in obtaining the registration of several Internet domain names, including the term "Gnucola." Your client has built a Web site at these domains from where it promotes and sells its flavorful amber beverage. Gnucola's customer base is rapidly expanding and its revenues are strong.

One day, during an idle minute, the president of Gnucola searches for "gnucola" on a popular Internet search engine, "E-Pointer." She finds, much to her surprise and chagrin, that the Web site for the archrival MicroCola is returned on the first page of results. The Gnucola Web site, on the other hand, is nowhere to be seen. It can be found only after clicking through several pages of results. The Gnucola president calls you for an explanation. You call the E-Pointer company only to have a sales representative politely inform you that, if you had paid attention to the fine print on its site, you would have seen that E-Pointer is a "paid placement" search engine. MicroCola has paid a substantial sum to appear prominently in the listings under the term "Gnucola." If Gnucola would like to appear on the first page of listings, E-Pointer tells you, it needs to pay for placement. You convey this to your client, who is outraged. She wants to know whether Gnucola can prevail against E-Pointer and MicroCola on a claim of trademark infringement.

Search Engines

Courts are not strangers to litigation over the use of Internet search engines.[2] Search engines are arguably the most important applications on the Internet. Although the Internet, as the Supreme Court has noted, is much like a "vast library," it is unfortunately a library with no card catalog.[3] When Internet users wish to explore the Web, they normally turn to search engines, which provide a quick, free, and reliable way to locate information or products available for purchase on the Web. Though the term "search engine" is most often associated with applications that index and query the entire World Wide Web, courts have used the term to describe other search applications (such as the search function of Napster) that index only a portion of the Internet or a private network.[4] Generally speaking, search engines provide a query window into which a user types a word or phrase, with the search engine returning a list of hyperlinks or results that, if selected, will direct the user to a specific Web site. Often, advertisements are interspersed with the results listings. These advertisements provide a source of revenue for the search engine.

The early Internet business giants, such as Yahoo and Excite, were predominantly search engines and owed their importance in the early Internet to their role as guides in the new cyberspatial environment. People turned to Yahoo and Excite to explore the Internet. Today, in the aftermath of the dotcom collapse, search engine companies are more aware of the need for workable business models to meet the substantial costs of maintaining the freshness of their databases and improving their search technologies. Advertising revenues, their prior mainstay, have grown scarce. As a result, many search engines have started to aggressively market their abilities to channel consumers to specific e-commerce locales, blurring the line between their "results" and their "advertisements."[5] Somewhat like tour guides who supplement their income by business arrangements with restaurants or gift shops, many search engines now actively direct users to those Web sites that pay for placement on results pages. As a business strategy, this model has been generally successful. E-commerce sites are hungry to connect with customers and are willing to pay search engines to appear in listings under popular search terms, such as "toys," "flowers," or "sex." Web users who are actively looking for the precise thing that a business sells are an ideal target audience.

Some, however, have criticized the paid placement business model. Last summer, Commercial Alert, a consumer protection organization associated with Ralph Nader, filed a complaint with the Federal Trade Commission alleging that the business of selling paid listings is deceptive to consumers, who assume search engine results to be unbiased.[6] A recently filed lawsuit against some paid placement search engines raises a private intellectual property variant of this same issue, namely: Can search engines freely sell placements in search results for terms that are protected as trademarks?[7] So far, no court has held a search engine liable for trademark infringement by selling paid placement listings. However, prior cases have explored the issue of trademarks and search engines in some detail and suggest that paid placement search engines may be vulnerable to legal attack.

Metatag Cases

One practice that raises concerns similar to paid placement is the use of trademarks in metatags. Keyword metatags are lines in a Web page's underlying code that can be used to describe the page's contents. Because a Web page's code generally is not visible when viewing the page through a standard browser (such as Microsoft's Internet Explorer), some courts have characterized keyword metatags as "invisible."[8] Some Web designers use keyword metatags to provide search engines with descriptions of the contents of their sites. In the past, search engines used these metatags to help determine the ranking of pages. Pages that claimed to be about Gnucola, for instance, would be ranked higher in searches for Gnucola. Some courts have noted the interesting symbiotic relationship between metatags, search engines, and domain names by suggesting that ownership of a particular trademark-related domain name (*e.g., gnucola.com*) may not be a practical necessity if a search engine can discover a business's Web site by typing the equivalent term into a search engine.[9]

Today, however, the majority of search engines claim that they do not recognize keyword metatags. This is because, on one hand, many Web site designers have failed to use metatags at all; on the other hand, many other Web site designers have used them improperly, claiming relevance to any search terms that afford them high traffic. This has not put an end to legal disputes over metatags, however, which still are frequent. In the vast majority of these disputes, a competitor has used a trademark holder's marks in metatags. MicroCola, for instance, might use "Gnucola" in its metatags to appear higher in the results for a "gnucola" query. Early decisions considering metatags generally found their use by competitors to be unlawful as trademark infringement. The search engines in these cases were characterized usually as passive conduits "duped" and "outwitted" by the infringing metatags. Notably, no recorded decision ever held a search engine liable for recognizing a Web site's metatags, despite the fact that all metatag cases involved search engines.

Two Influential Ninth Circuit Metatag Decisions: *Brookfield* and *Welles*

The leading case involving metatags is the Ninth Circuit's decision in *Brookfield Communications, Inc. v. West Coast Entertainment Corp.*[10] District courts prior to *Brookfield* had treated the issue of metatags fairly briefly, finding the use of trademarks in metatags to be especially pernicious evidence of trademark infringement under the standard likelihood-of-confusion analysis and frequently demonstrating a misunderstanding of the function of metatags. In *Brookfield,* Judge Diarmuid F. O'Scannlain treated the metatag issue much more carefully, adopting a pioneering initial-interest-confusion" analysis.

The facts in *Brookfield* presented some close questions. Brookfield Communications had obtained a federal registration of the term "MovieBuff" as a trademark for movie-related computer software. West Coast owned a prior federal registration on a phrase using the words "Movie Buff" for video products and had also registered the domain name *moviebuff.com.* West Coast intended to open a Web site at *moviebuff.com* with a movie database similar to Brookfield's. Brookfield brought suit seeking an injunction to stop West Coast from using the term "moviebuff" in commerce, including in West Coast's metatags.

The Ninth Circuit first concluded that West Coast was not permitted to use the *moviebuff.com* domain. The court then turned to West Coast's use of "moviebuff" metatags. The court noted that the issue of the metatags was quite different because it involved intermediary search engines. The court noted that search engines generally display results pages with a great number of listings, presenting their users with an array of choices. Because users would have the opportunity to select the Brookfield site, the court found that it was difficult to believe that a consumer would be likely to be confused about whose site he had ultimately reached or to think that Brookfield somehow sponsored West Coast's Web site.[11] Nevertheless, the Ninth Circuit found that the use of trademarked terms in metatags could be actionable as trademark infringement because the "moviebuff" metatags resulted in the ultimate diversion of consumers to West Coast's site based on an initial search for the "moviebuff" mark. In reaching this conclusion, the Ninth Circuit applied the doctrine of initial interest confusion.

The doctrine of initial interest confusion is of recent origin and essentially recognizes a trademark holder's right to prevent confusion that *diverts* consumer interest based on the holder's mark, even if such confusion is no longer present when a sale is consummated. For instance, if a bookseller uses a red and white crumpled hat (a trademark of Dr. Seuss) on the cover of its book, trademark infringement may occur when this generates initial consumer interest in the book based on the mark, even though consumers may be likely to realize, upon closer examination, that the book is not sponsored by or affiliated with Dr. Seuss.[12]

The Ninth Circuit reasoned that, if a "moviebuff" metatag placed West Coast's site among "moviebuff" results, this might divert consumers searching for Brookfield's products to West Coast's products instead. The court analogized the metatag to a misleading billboard that directed consumers to exit a highway at the wrong place or to posting a sign with another's trademark in front of one's store.

There were significant limits on the *Brookfield* decision, however. Despite finding that infringement existed, the Ninth Circuit noted that West Coast would be permitted to use the generic term "movie buff" in its metatags, which it found to be a "descriptive term . . . routinely used in the English language to describe a movie devotee." But this was not true for Brookfield's mark, which omitted the space between the two words. The court found that, in light of the fact that "MovieBuff" was not a word in the English language, when the term "MovieBuff" was employed, it was used to refer to Brookfield's products and services.[13] The court noted, however, that West Coast was not absolutely barred from using Brookfield's mark in its pages, as it would be fair use for West Coast to compare its services with Brookfield's product by name in the pages of its Web site. The court held, however, that it would not be fair use of the mark to use "moviebuff" in metatags to attract consumers to its Web site.

In a recent decision, *Playboy Enterprises, Inc. v. Welles,*[14] the Ninth Circuit further clarified that in certain circumstances a trademark can also be used in metatags by a competitor if the mark is used "nominatively" to describe characteristics of the competitor's site. In the *Welles* case, Terri Welles, a former Playboy model, had used several trademarks of Playboy Enterprises in her adult entertainment Web site's metatags. The Ninth Circuit found that Welles' use of Playboy's terms "accurately describe the contents of Welles' Web site, in addition to describing Welles. Forcing Welles and others to use absurd turns of phrase in their metatags . . . would be particularly damaging in the Internet search context." The Ninth Circuit agreed with the district court's decision that it would be both impractical and ineffectual for Welles to describe herself in her metatags without making reference to Playboy's marks, that is, to employ a metatag describing herself as "nude model selected by Mr. Hefner's magazine as its number-one prototypical woman for the year 1981." The court also suggested that the "playboy" metatag also might be used by Web sites that provide "critiques" of Playboy, affirming in *dicta* the results of several other district court cases allowing the use of trademarks in metatags of sites offering criticism of the trademark holder.[15]

Thus, *Brookfield* and *Welles* provide a general rule disallowing competitor use of trademarks in metatags, with significant broad exceptions for descriptive and nominative uses of trademarks. They suggest that although a competitor's use of trademarks in metatags may be actionable as infringement, use of trademark in metatags may be allowed if the term is (1) not used in its trademark sense (*i.e.*, "movie buff") or (2) used to fairly describe the actual contents of a site so that search engines might locate it.

Metatags v. Paid Placement: The *Nissan* Case

In terms of the behavior of MicroCola, there are strong similarities between the keyword metatag cases and the paid placement scenario. In both cases, MicroCola intentionally appears in the results listing for the search terms of the trademark holder. Indeed, to a consumer searching for Gnucola, the results of successful competitor metatags and the results of paid placements might look exactly the same. Because the test for trademark infringement looks to the consumer's likelihood of confusion, it is hard to see why the result of an infringement lawsuit should differ depending on whether metatags or paid placements were used to create the situation.

The first case to directly consider the issue of competitor purchases of paid placement listings was *Nissan Motor Co., Ltd. v. Nissan Computer Corp.*,[16] which essentially adopted an analysis of the issue similar to that in metatag cases. Nissan Motor Company had originally brought suit to evict the Nissan Computer Corporation from the domain name *Nissan.com*. This effort proved unsuccessful, probably because Nissan Computer's president was Uzi Nissan, who had been using his surname in relation to his businesses since 1980. Nissan Computer fired back with several counterclaims and later sought to amend those counterclaims to charge Nissan Motor with various state and federal trademark and unfair trade practice violations based on its purchase of paid placement search listings for Nissan and *Nissan.com*.

After a brief discussion of the function of search engines, the nature of intellectual property rights, and the application of trademark law to the Internet, Judge Dean D. Pregerson noted how prior decisions had found traditional trademark law to be applicable to Internet domain names and metatags. After discussing metatags, the court stated that there was no good cause for not extending the protections afforded in metatag cases to cases in which a company infringes a mark by purchasing a search term. However, the court found the *Nissan* case was not such a case, as Nissan could not infringe upon its own mark.[17]

The *Nissan* case suggests that the understanding of trademarks and search engines applies to metatag cases can be transferred without difficulty to paid placement cases. It thus provides some good authority for a lawsuit against a competitor who purchases search terms that the competitor could not use as metatags.[18] A lawsuit against MicroCola, therefore, may be promising for Gnucola, as MicroCola apparently is using the "gnucola" mark in its trademark sense and apparently has no "nominative use" defense for using the "gnucola" mark to describe the contents of its site.

A lawsuit against E-Pointer might, therefore, be premised on E-Pointer's complicity in placing MicroCola in the "gnucola" results listings and directly benefiting from MicroCola's infringement.[19] In the metatags cases, however, it is notable that search engines have *not* been sued or held liable; in fact, they have been generally perceived as the *targets* of the deceptive behavior. In the hypothetical presented, however, E-Pointer actively participated in placing MicroCola in the results listings for the Gnucola search. Is it possible that this involvement by the search engine might actually work against Gnucola's claims?

Playboy v. Netscape: Keyed Banners

The first trademark lawsuit directed at the search engines proved to be a disappointment for trademark holders and a substantial victory for search engines. The case, *Playboy Enterprises, Inc. v. Netscape Communications Corp.,*[20] involved not "results listings" but banner advertisements. A keyed banner advertisement is an advertisement that is displayed only alongside the results for certain search terms. In *Netscape,* the search engines sold advertisement banner placements in results listings for a group of 450 playboy- and playmate-related search terms. The advertisements were sold specifically to purveyors of adult entertainment. Thus, Playboy's competitors paid the search engine so that their advertisements appeared on the same page as results for the term "playboy." Playboy brought suit against the Excite and Netscape search engines, alleging trademark infringement and dilution.

Interestingly, the *Netscape* court did not seem to attribute much to the fact that the advertisements were not, strictly speaking, results. Perhaps this makes sense, because the *Brookfield* decision, upon which the district court arguably relied, seemed to find the legal harm from keyword metatag practices in the initial *diversion* of interest following a term search, not in any direct confusion based on the contents of results listings. The *Netscape* court noted that Playboy had *not* claimed that the search engines' results listings infringed and that the case was not literally a metatag case.[21] The decision came out in favor of the search engines based primarily on the *Brookfield* court's suggestion that the word "movie buff" was non-infringing because "movie buff" had a non-trademark meaning in the English language. Much of the court's opinion reflects an apparent conviction that because the search engines could never be sure that a user was looking for Playboy™ (and not for information on the generic word "playboy") that search terms, even when apparently sold to competitors for their trademark value, were incapable of possessing a trademark meaning.

The *Netscape* decision is currently under appeal in the Ninth Circuit. The International Trademark Association (INTA) has filed an *amicus* brief urging the Ninth Circuit to reverse or clarify the holding on appeal. INTA's argument is that the *Netscape* bright-line rule is contrary to established trademark law. It is undoubtedly true that a person might search for Nike or Apple in an effort to locate the Greek goddess or the fruit, not the footwear or computer companies. Yet *Netscape* suggests that terms that are English-language words can *never* be capable of trademark meaning in the context of search engines, an argument that goes too far and that would effectively deny protection to a vast number of marks.

If the term "apple" is sold to a fruit merchant, it is clear that the term is not sold for its trademark value. Selling the search term "apple" to IBM, however, is likely to be a sale based on the trademark function of the word, designed to divert Apple computer customers to IBM products.[22] Such diversion (under the initial interest theory of *Brookfield* at least) should be actionable under trademark law. Judge Stotler's opinion suggests that, because it will be practically impossible in most cases to determine whether a user's query is directed toward finding Apple™ or the fruit, the search term can never have a trademark meaning. However, what if a trademark holder, like Playboy, can produce evidence demonstrating that the vast majority of persons searching for "Playboy" are in fact searching for content associated with its mark and that the search engine's sales of the term "Playboy" are made exclusively toward its direct competitors in that market? Even if term sales in such a case do not infringe under a *Brookfield* analysis, what if Playboy produces evidence that the results of these sales create actual consumer confusion as to the sponsorship of the advertisements and Web sites displayed by the search engine? It is notable that Playboy apparently failed to produce such evidence.

Other Arguments for Search Engines

Other portions of the *Netscape* decision suggest alternative arguments a search engine might make to protect a pay-for-placement business model. For instance, the *Netscape* case suggested that a free speech argument exists for the search engines, observing that "First Amendment interests are at stake" and that a decision for the trademark holders risked "Internet users . . . losing their ability to obtain information about words which also happen to be trademarks."[23] In other words, if trademark holders can, through legal means, dictate how a search engine ranks its results listings, is this not analogous to telling newspapers what to say and how to order their headlines? Should trademark holders have the final say as to what must come first and what must be excluded in results listings? Certainly, most trademark holders would like to require search engines to place their own Web sites as the first listed result for associated search terms. But if a search engine does not wish to provide a link to Playboy's Web site, but wishes only to provide links to sites critical of Playboy or related to the dictionary meaning of "playboy," is this actionable as trademark infringement? Pay-for-placement search engines would probably counter that, in fact, markets for placement actually increase the relevance and usefulness of results listings.[24]

E-Pointer also might argue that trademark holders cannot expect search engines to direct customers to them for free. The Yellow Pages aren't forced to carry advertisements for local business without compensation, so why should search engines be forced to give prominent placement to Web sites without some compensation?[25] By extension, shouldn't the search engines have control over how they guide users who visit their proprietary pages? This "my property, my rules" argument has support in the *Netscape* decision, where the court grappled with the *Brookfield* analogy of a diverting sign and concluded (essentially) that "if the same entity owns the [page] on which both the [link to the trademark holder] and the competitor's [advertisement] stand, should that entity be liable to the [trademark holder] for diverting the [consumer]?"[26] The *Netscape* court answered in the negative.

Although courts may conclude that a trademark holder doesn't have an affirmative right to be listed by a search engine, there is a strong argument that a trademark holder is at least entitled to protection against a search engine working with its competitors, like MicroCola, who would purchase the company's own trademark to compete against it. Still, in many cases, it may be hard to establish that the search engine was aware a mark was purchased in bad faith, and thus the search engine might be characterized as an innocent infringer under 15 U.S.C. § 1114(2).

As an example of the practical difficulties involved in requiring a search engine to police term sales, what if a seller of yams or handkerchiefs wanted to purchase a placement under the "playboy" search term? Most people would assume this purchase might be unusual, but not actionable as trademark infringement. Yet, the *Netscape* court observed that valid trademark registrations exist for Playboy yams and sweet potatoes, Playboy handkerchiefs, and Playboy soft drinks. Should a search engine be required to perform trademark searches for all terms it sells and their variants? What of the many marks in use that are not registered? Outside cyberspace, identical trademarks often coexist by occupying different geographic locations or markets. The Playboy yams example demonstrates that requiring search engines to police search terms sales against every possibly infringing search term purchase would prove a difficult, perhaps impossible, administrative task.

Summary

Anecdotal evidence suggests that at least some search engines respond well to informal complaints about competitor purchases of search terms. Gnucola might therefore take the cost-effective initial step of sending a pointed letter to E-Pointer, making E-Pointer aware of Gnucola's potential legal claims and demanding that E-Pointer de-list MicroCola from its results for the "gnucola" search term. If such a letter would work in practice, it would certainly be less expensive than a lawsuit.

The viability of claims based on paid placement listing will only be worked out gradually. Hopefully, the Ninth Circuit may offer some guidance on the issue when the *Playboy v. Netscape* appeal is decided. Whatever the ultimate shape of the law, however, it will have a powerful effect on search engines, their business models, and Internet commerce generally. As e-commerce becomes more prevalent, users will turn to search engines as a primary source for locating products and information. Hopefully, the courts considering paid placement will be able to achieve a legal balance that protects the rights of trademark holders, ensures the public's access to reliable listings and diverse information, and promotes the integrity and usefulness of search engine results.

Notes

1. The names of the various parties in this hypothetical situation are wholly fictional, with any resemblance to real business entities being purely coincidental.
2. Nissan Motor Co., Ltd. v. Nissan Computer Corp., 204 F.R.D. 460 (C.D. Cal. 2001). *See, e.g.,* Florists' Transworld Delivery, Inc. v. Originals Florist & Gifts, Inc., 57 U.S.P.Q. 2d (BNA) 1079 (N.D. Ill. 2000) ("when Internet users wish to explore or 'surf' the Web, they normally turn to search engines"); Interstellar Starship Servs. v. Epix, Inc., 125 F. Supp. 2d 1269, 1279 (D. Or. 2001) ("Today's Internet user knows that search engines, such as 'Hotbot,' 'Lycos,' and 'Google,' provide a quick, free, and reliable way to locate a business' Web site when its exact Internet address is not known."): Imon, Onc. v. ImaginOn, Inc., 90 F. Supp. 2d 345, 352 n.2 (S.D.N.Y. 2000).
3. Reno v. ACLU, 521 U.S. 844, 853 (1997). Actually, of course, most libraries today use electronic databases and search engines to help their patrons search their contents. The idea of the card catalog is foreign to many younger patrons.
4. *See* A&M Records, Inc. v. Napster, Inc., 114 F. Supp. 2d 896, 920 (N.D. Cal. 2000) (Napster's "search engine" material in its finding of contributory infringement); Register.com v. Verio, 126 F. Supp. 2d 238, 242 n.2 (S.D.N.Y. 2000) (describing a domain name registry query as a "search engine"); A&H Sportwear Co., Inc. v. Victoria's Secret Stores, Inc., 134 F. Supp. 2d 668 (E.D. Pa. 2001) (describing an in-site query as a "search engine").
5. *See* Danny Sullivan, "Buying Your Way In To Search Engines," available at *http://searchenginewatch.com/webmasters/paid.html* (visited April 2, 2002).
6. *See* July 16, 2001, Letter from Gary Ruskin, available at *http://www.commercialalert.org/searchengines/searchengines.html* (visited April 2, 2002).
7. *See* Mark Nutritionals, Inc. v. Alta Vista Co., Civil Action No. SA-02-CA-0087 EP (W.D. Tex. 2002). Mark Nutritionals simultaneously filed three similar suits against other search engines: Findwhat, Kanoodle, and Overture (which was formerly GoTo.com).
8. *See* Bahari v. Gross, 119 F. Supp. 2d 309, 312 n.3 (S.D.N.Y. 2000).
9. *See, e.g.,* National A-1 Advertising, Inc. v. Network Solutions, Inc., 121 F. Supp. 2d 156, 179 (D.N.H. 2000); Chatam Int'l, Inc. v. Bodum, Inc., 157 F. Supp. 2d 549, 554 n.10 (E.D. Pa. 2001).
10. Brookfield Communications, Inc. v. West Coast Entertainment Corp., 173 F.2d 1036 (9th Cir. 1999). *See also* Eli Lilly & Co. v. Natural Answers, Inc., 233 F.3d 456 (7th Cir. 2000) (finding metatags strong evidence of deceptive intent and relying heavily on *Brookfield*).
11. *Brookfield,* 173 F.2d at 1062.
12. *See* Dr. Seuss Enterprises, L.P. v. Penguin Books USA, Inc., 109 F.3d 1394, 1405 (9th Cir. 1997).
13. *Id.* at 1066.
14. Playboy Enterprises, Inc. v. Welles. 279 F.3d 796 (9th Cir. 2002).
15. *See, e.g., Bahari,* 119 F. Supp. 2d 309 (metatags used in site complaining about mark holder); Bally Total Fitness Holding Corp. v. Faber, 29 F. Supp. 2d 1161 (C.D. Cal. 1998) (metatags used in site claiming that mark holder "sucks").
16. Nissan Motor Co., Ltd. v. Nissan Computer Corp., 204 F.R.D. 460 (C.D. Cal. 2001).

17. The court noted that, pursuant to Ninth Circuit precedent, "Nissan.com" was indistinguishable from "Nissan" as a matter of law and that Nissan Computer therefore had no separate intellectual property rights to the address *Nissan.com*. The court made short work of Nissan Computer's argument that people searching for *Nissan.com* would be misdirected, finding that the act of entering a domain name as a search term was analogous to calling a business to ask for its phone number.

18. *Cf.* DeVry/Becker Educ. Dev. Corp. v. Totaltape, Inc., No. 00 C 3523, 2002 U.S. Dist. LEXIS 1230 (N.D. Ill. Jan. 22, 2002) (finding that an order forbidding metatag uses did not encompass paid placement purchases, but clarifying its order to forbid paid placement purchases as well).

19. *See* Inwood Labs. v. Ives Labs., 456 U.S. 844, 854–855 (1982) (setting forth requirements of contributory trademark infringement).

20. Playboy Enterprises, Inc. v. Netscape. Communications Corp., 55 F. Supp. 2d 1070 (C.D. Cal. 1999).

21. *Id.* at 1072-1073, 1076.

22. The "apple/Apple" example is taken from the International Trademark Association's *amicus* brief filed in the appeal of *Playboy v. Netscape,* Nos. 00-56648, 00-56662 (9th Cir.).

23. *Netscape,* 55 F. Supp. 2d at 1083.

24. For instance, Overture.com states that its business method addresses "three fundamental problems . . . with Internet search[:] poor quality results, random ordering of listings and a weak advertising revenue model." Pay-for-performance "solves these problems by working directly with businesses to ensure relevant and up-to-date listings, and by creating a real-time market for consumer attention based on advertiser bidding." *See* "Overture's Corporate Overview," available at *http://www.averture.com/d/USm/about/company/vision.html* (visited April 2, 2002).

25. Danny Sullivan, the editor of a well-known publication, "Search Engine Watch," and expert witness in *Netscape,* has suggested this analogy will probably be employed. *See* "Lawsuit Over Paid Placements To Define Search Engines," available at *http://www.searchenginewatch.com/sereport/02/02-bodysolutions.html* (visited April 2, 2002).

26. *Netscape,* 55 F. Supp. 2d at 1075.

 ## *For Discussion:*

1. What are the "paid placement business model" and "metatags"?

2. Do you agree with the Ninth Circuit's analogy between placing misleading metatags in a web page and placing "a misleading billboard that directed consumers to exit a highway at the wrong place or to posting a sign with another's trademark in front of one's store"?

3. While this is an argument nominally about trademark placement and intellectual property rights, to what extent is this also about the control of information?

4. How have the concerns expressed in this essay changed since its publication? Are the technological issues still applicable?

For Fact-Finding, Research, and Writing:

1. How early can you find a first use of the term "metatag"? Where is this use and how do you know there is no earlier use?
2. Using either Congressional Universe or a government website, find the text of a specific federal law relating to trademarks. Explain the law in your own words.
3. Compare Lastowka's arguments about trademark infringements in the placement of metatags to Clement's claim that copyright and patent stifle innovation. How would Clement respond to Lastowka?
4. Compare Lastowka's arguments to Wil S. Hylton's in "Who Owns This Body?" How do the two texts treat the subject of the explosion of information access because of the Internet? How do the two texts approach the issue of how access to that information is controlled and affected?

Lawrence Lessig, "Privacy as Property"

Lawrence Lessig is currently Professor of Law at Stanford Law School, where he founded Stanford's Center for Internet and Society. Prior to joining the faculty at Stanford, he was Professor of Law at the Harvard Law School, a fellow at Wissenschaftskolleg zu Berlin, and Professor at the University of Chicago Law School. In addition to his law degree from Yale, Lessig also holds an MA in philosophy from Cambridge University in England. Adding to his distinguished legal career (he was called as an expert witness in the government's anti-trust case against Microsoft), he is the author of several books on the relationship between the Internet, intellectual property, and the "real world," most notably *Code And Other Laws of Cyberspace* (1999) and *The Future of Ideas* (2001). Most recently, Lessig has founded the Creative Commons Project, which is devoted to simplifying the process by which creators of original online content can license their work and protect it from misuse. This essay originally appeared in the journal *Social Research* in 2002.

 Before You Read:

What is privacy? How do we define it? Why is it important to us? How do you define property, and in what ways is it important or irrelevant?

Privacy as Property*

Lawrence Lessig

A SOCIETY PROTECTS its values in different and overlapping ways. The values of free speech in America are protected by a constitution that guards against speech abridging regulation (U.S. Constitution, First Amendment). They are supported by copyright regulation intended as an "engine of free expression" to fuel a market of creativity (*Harper & Row Publishers, Inc. v. Nation Enterprises*, 471 U.S. 539 (1985)). They are supported by technologies such as the Internet that assure easy access to content (Lessig, 1999: 164–185). And they are supported by norms that encourage, or at least allow, dissenting views to be expressed (Lessig, 1999: 164–185; 235–239). These modalities together establish cultural resources that to some degree support the right to speak freely within American society.

This is an essay about the cultural resources that support the values of privacy. My aim is to promote one such cultural resource—the norms associated with property talk—as a means of reinforcing privacy generally. In my view, we would better support privacy within American society if we spoke of privacy as a kind of property. Property talk, in other words, would strengthen the rhetorical force behind privacy.[1]

Such a view is not popular among privacy advocates and experts in the field of privacy law. It has been expressly rejected by some of the best in the field.[2] Thus it is my burden to demonstrate the value in this alternative conception.

This essay alone will not carry that burden. But my hope is that it will at least evince a benefit from our reconceiving privacy talk. I will address some of the objections to this form of speaking, but only after advancing the arguments in its favor.

The essay moves in six parts. I first introduce two stories that will frame my argument (parts I and II). I then consider one account by Professor Jonathan Zittrain that might explain the tension that is revealed between these two stories (part III). Part IV offers a different account from the one proposed by Professor Zittrain. In the final part, I offer a brief response to some of the criticisms that have been made of the privacy as property model. I then conclude.

I

At a public debate about the increasing scope of patent protection granted by U.S. law to software and business method inventors, Jay Walker, the president of Priceline.com and Walker Digital and a holder of many of these new, and controver-

*I am grateful to Jason Catlett for correction of and advice about parts of this essay. That is not to say he agrees.

From *Social Research*, Vol. 69, No. 1, "Privacy as Property" by Lawrence Lessig. Copyright © 2002 by New School University. Reprinted by permission.

sial, patents, was asked to justify them. Did we know, Walker was asked, whether increasing the scope of these new forms of regulation would actually increase innovation? Or would they, by requiring every developer to add to its team covens of lawyers, increase the costs so much as to chill or stifle innovation? ("Internet Society," 2000).

Walker did not have a strong answer. In the face of evidence that these patents harm innovation, he could cite no firm evidence to the contrary. Would it not make sense then, Walker was asked, to have a moratorium on this new form of patent protection until we learn something about its economic effects? Why not study the effect, and if it is not clear that they do any good, then why not halt this explosion of regulation?

Walker exploded in anger at the very suggestion. Grabbing the mic, he said to the questioner: "Does that mean if Microsoft takes *my property*, I can't bring a suit against them, is that what you're suggesting?" ("Internet Society," 2000; emphasis added).

II

Amazon.com is a collector of data. It sells books to collect that data. These data help it do an extraordinary job understanding its customers' wants. By monitoring their behavior, Amazon can build large and accurate profiles about its customers. And using powerful data-matching techniques, it can predict what books they are likely to want to buy.

Amazon had a privacy policy. The data it was collecting, Amazon said, would not be sold to others, at least if a customer sent Amazon an email asking that such data never be sold. The data was therefore collected only for Amazon's use. And for anyone who had used Amazon frequently, much of that use was obvious and familiar. Amazon watched its customers, and used the data from that watching to better serve its customers; relying on this policy, people gave Amazon years' worth of data from this watching.

At the end of 2000, however, Amazon announced a new policy.[3] From that point on, data from Amazon could be sold to or shared with people outside Amazon, regardless of a consumer's request that it not. The privacy policy would therefore no longer assure users that only Amazon would know what books they bought. Amazon, and anyone Amazon decided, could know their consumers' buying patterns.

The extraordinary feature of this announcement—and the one on which I want to focus here—was its retroactive effect.[4] Not only was Amazon announcing that from then on, data collected could be subject to sale. It also made that policy retroactive. Customers who had relied on Amazon's promise in the past and had indicated that they "never" wanted their information sold were now told their data could be sold. Amazon refused requests to delete earlier data; the consumers who had relied on its policy were told they had no right to remove the data they had given. Their data was now subject to sale.[5]

Amazon justified this change, and this retroactive effect, based on an escape clause built into the company's privacy policy. This policy, the clause explained, was always subject to change. Consumers were therefore on notice, Amazon explained, that the rules could change. They knew the risks they were taking.

III

In a recent essay, Harvard professor Jonathan Zittrain argued that there is no conceptual difference between the "privacy problem" and the "copyright problem" (Zittrain, 2000). Both, he argued, are examples of data getting out of control. In the context of privacy, it is personal data over which the individual loses control—medical records, for example, that find their way to a drug company's marketing department; or lists of videos rented, that before the protections granted by Congress, found their way to a Senate confirmation hearing. The problem with privacy is that private data flows too easily—that it too easily falls out of the control of the individual.

So understood, Zittrain argued, the problem of copyright is precisely the same. It too is a problem of data getting out of control. Music is recorded on a digital CD; that CD is "ripped" (that is, the audio extracted), and the contents are placed on a computer server; that content is then duplicated and placed on a thousand servers around the world. The data has thus gotten out of control. Copyright holders who would otherwise want to condition access to their data find the ability to condition access upon payment gone. Just as the individual concerned about privacy wants to control who gets access to what and when, the copyright holder wants to control who gets access to what and when. In both cases the presence of ubiquitous computing and saturating networks means that the control is increasingly lost.

Zittrain then considered the steps that have been taken to deal with each of these problems. These, not surprisingly, turn out to be quite different. In the context of copyright, technologists are developing many new technologies to re-empower the copyright holder—to assure that the use of his data is precisely as he wishes. Trusted systems, for example, will give the copyright holder the power to decide who can listen to what. A digital object with music inside can be released on the Internet, but it will only play if the possessor has a permitting key. It will then play just as the copyright holder wants—once, or ten times, or forever, depending on how the object is coded. Trusted systems promise to rebuild into the code an extraordinary system of control. It promises to use *code* to solve this problem of data getting out of control.

Changes in technology, however, are not the only changes that copyright owners have sought, and secured, to remedy the problem of data getting out of control. Copyright holders have also benefited from significant changes in law. In a series of significant acts of legislation, the U.S. Congress has increased the penalty for using copyrighted material without the permission of the copyright holder. It is now a felony to publish more than $1,000 of copyrights without the copyright holder's permission.[6] Congress has also added important rights and protections for copyrighted work online with the Digital Millennium Copyright Act (DMCA).[7] If a copyright holder uses technology to protect his copyright, then the DMCA protects that software with law by making it an offense to develop and distribute tools that circumvent that software. Software code thus increasingly protects copyrighted material. Legal code increasingly protects copyrighted material more strongly. And with the DMCA, law now protects code that protects copyright. These changes will thus balance the risk that copyrighted "data" will get out of control.

What about the response to the problem of privacy? Here the story is very different. We do not have a collection of new federal laws restoring control over their data to individuals. Law has been successfully resisted with a familiar rhetoric—that "we should let the market take care of itself." So far, these opponents have been quite successful. Congress has yet to pass an Internet privacy regulation, although it has passed regulation to protect financial privacy.[8]

Technology, too, has been slow to emerge. Not that there are not a host of creative technologies out there—technologies to anonymize transactions and presence, and technologies to facilitate control over the use of personal data.[9] But these technologies have not quite had the financial backing that copyright control technology has had. Germany, for example, requires that Internet service providers (ISPs) offer anonymous accounts.[10] That has spurred a market for providing such anonymity in Germany. But we have no such requirement in America, and hence we have not sufficiently spurred a market to provide this technology.

Zittrain puts these two stories together, and asks, What explains the difference? The same problem—losing control over our data—is raised in two very different contexts. In the one context, copyright, both law and technology (or we might say, "East Coast code" and "West Coast code") rally to defend the copyright holder against the users who would use it without control; in the context of privacy, both law and technology have been slow to respond. Same problem, two radically different responses. What explains the difference?

Zittrain offers a dark explanation: follow the money (Zittrain, 2000). If you want to understand why all controlled creativity in the world is allied on one side of this problem and only the public spirited, Marc Rotenberg-like are allied on the other, follow the money. When it pays to protect privacy—when it pays to build tools to protect privacy—you will see lots more privacy. But just now, it is Hollywood that pays, so it is copyright that gets protected.

IV

My aim in this essay is to explore a different account of why these two similar problems get fundamentally different treatment in Washington. This account focuses less on the dark motivations of dollars chasing policy. Instead, the difference I want to focus on is a difference in norms, or a difference in the ordinary understanding, or construction, or *social meaning* of the problem (see, e.g., Lessig, 1995: 943). This difference is seen in the two stories I began with at the start: the story of Jay Walker and Amazon.com.

Recall Walker's response to the suggestion that we investigate a bit more whether patents do any good before we issue more patents to protect software or business methods. And allow Microsoft, he asked, to steal "*my property?*" Focus on this term, "property." Jay Walker framed the question of proper patent policy within a familiar, and deeply American, discourse about property. The issue, so framed, is whether one is for property or not; the punishment for those who would question patents is thus the same as the punishment for questioning property: Are you or have you ever been a communist?

This move—as a matter of rhetoric—is brilliant, although the idea that "patents" should be spoken of as this sort of property would be strange to anyone with a sense of history. The framers of our constitution did not speak of patents as "property." Patents were understood as exclusive rights granted by the government for a public purpose, not natural rights recognized by the government as an aspect of natural justice. This was the import of Jefferson's famous description of patents,[11] and it explains in part why the term "intellectual property" did not enter our legal vocabulary until late into the nineteenth century.[12]

But ordinary people are not constrained by any sense of history. They instead are open to this more familiar way of speaking about patents. And Walker's use of the term "property" is an increasingly familiar way in which "intellectual property" is discussed. Thus, despite the dissonance with Jefferson, Walker can talk about "stealing" his "property" without anyone noticing anything funny in his speech. The debate then focuses on why people should be allowed to "steal" rather than on why a "patent" is "property."[13]

Yet had Walker been forced to use the language of the framers, his rhetorically powerful rhetorical question—"you want Microsoft to steal my property while you conduct your studies about what does what good?"—would have been the extremely weak rhetoric—"you want Microsoft to invade my monopoly while you conduct studies to determine whether the monopoly does any good?" In their language, the idea that Walker, or anyone, has a moral claim to a government-backed monopoly would seem odd. Had he been forced to express himself in just these terms, his question would have answered itself quite differently.

There is something in this story that we who would like stronger protection for privacy might learn. The story shows the different social resources that are available within our culture to claims that are grounded in property.

To see the point a bit more directly, think about the Amazon story with one fundamental change. Imagine that people spoke about their privacy as if privacy were a form of property. What constraints—social constraints—on what people can do to private data would exist then?

I know many want to resist this idea of speaking about privacy as property, and I certainly know that one must justify the usage if it is to be accepted (though I really do not recall reading the justification that transformed monopoly-speak in the context of patents and copyright into property-speak, but let us put that aside for a second). Before we get to justification, or even possibility, just imagine if we thought about our personal data the way we think about a car. And then think about this analogous case about a contract governing a car.

You drive into a parking lot, and the attendant hands you a ticket. The ticket lists a number of rules and promises on the back of the ticket. The lot is not responsible for damage to the car; the car must be picked up by midnight, etc. And then imagine, as with Amazon, that at the bottom of the ticket, the last condition is that this license can be modified at anytime by the management.

Imagine you walk up to the parking lot, hand him the ticket, and say, "I would like my car." And the attendant says to you, "Well, as you'll see at the bottom of your ticket, we reserved the right to change the conditions at any time. And in fact, I'm afraid we have changed the conditions. From here on out, we've decided to sell the cars we take in. And so we've decided to sell your very nice car. We therefore cannot return your car; the car is probably in New Jersey by now. We're sorry, but that's our policy."

Obviously, in ordinary property thought, this is an absurd idea. It would be crazy to interpret a condition in a license stating that the license could be changed to mean that the license might be changed to allow the parking lot to sell your car. One might well imagine a Jay Walker moment—"Hey, that's my property. You can't steal my property. You can't change the license and then run away with my car."

And yet, notice that these same intuitions are not excited when people hear the story about Amazon. I do not mean that there are not people who think what Amazon has done is awful—clearly there are such people, and perhaps most think what Amazon has done is awful. My claim is not that people agree with Amazon; my point is that because we do not think of privacy the way Hollywood has convinced us to think about copyright, we cannot easily invoke the rhetoric of property to defend incursions into privacy. If it were taken for granted that privacy was a form of property, then Amazon simply could not get away with announcing that this personal information was now theirs. That would be "theft," and this is my point: "theft" is positively un-American.

Property talk would give privacy rhetoric added support within American culture. If you could get people (in America, at this point in history) to see a certain resource as property, then you are 90 percent to your protective goal. If people see a resource as property, it will take a great deal of converting to convince them that companies like Amazon should be free to take it. Likewise, it will be hard for companies like Amazon to escape the label of thief. Just think about the rhetoric that surrounds Napster—where thousands are sharing music for no commercial gain. This practice is comfortably described by many—not me, but many others—as "theft." And more important, it is hard for the defendants to defend against this label of theft. The issue becomes whether the user has a right to steal—not the kind of case you would want to have to prove.

We could strengthen the cultural resources supporting the protection of privacy if we could come to think of privacy as property, just as the cultural resources available to Jay Walker have been strengthened by the happenstance of a legal culture that has come to refer to "patents" as intellectual property. Norms about property would support restrictions on privacy, just as norms about property resist limitations on Walker's "property."

That is the affirmative claim, but before I address objections, there are some qualifications I must offer to assure that certain confusions do not detain the debate.

1. To promote property talk is not to promote anarchism, or even libertarianism. "Property" is always and everywhere a creation of the state. It always requires regulation to secure it, and regulation requires state action. The DMCA is a law designed to protect what most think of as "property." That is regulation. Police are deployed to protect property. That too is regulation. Zoning laws regulate and control property. Rules regulating the market control how property is exchanged. And rules establishing privacy as property would govern when and how a privacy right can be traded. Property is inherently the construction of the state; and to confuse the promotion of property with the promotion of laissez-faire is to fall into the vision of the world that libertarians delude themselves with. There is no such thing as property without the state; and we live in a state where property and regulation are deeply and fundamentally intertwined.

2. Although property is often resisted by liberals because of the inequality that property systems produce, privacy as property could create less extreme inequality. If the privacy as property system were properly constructed, it would be less troubling from this perspective than, say, copyright or ordinary property. For if the law limited the ability to alienate such property completely—by permitting contracts about, for example, secondary uses but not tertiary uses—the owner of this property would be less likely to vest it in others in ways that would exacerbate inequalities.

3. Property talk is often resisted because it is thought to isolate individuals. It may well. But in the context of privacy, isolation is the aim. Privacy is all about empowering individuals to choose to be isolated. One might be against the choice to be isolated; but then one is against privacy. And we can argue long and hard about whether privacy is good or not, but we should not confuse that argument with the argument that property would better protect any privacy we have agreed should be protected.

4. To view privacy as property is not to argue that one's rights to use that property should be absolute or unregulated. All property law limits, in certain contexts, the right to alienate; contract law restricts the contexts in which one can make enforceable contacts. The state has a valid and important role in deciding which kinds of exchanges should be permitted. And especially given the ignorance about the Internet that pervades the ordinary user's experience, I would be wildly in favor of regulation of what people were allowed to do with "their prop-

erty." Indeed, I imagine there is no legislative recommendation of the Electronic Privacy Information Center (EPIC), for example, for regulating privacy that I would oppose (see <http://www.epic.org>).

Thus, to promote property talk is not to demote the role of regulation, or to believe that the "market will take care of itself," or to question the strong role the government should have to assure privacy. It is simply to recognize that the government is not the only, or often, most important protector of human rights. And that where norms can carry some of the water, my argument is that we should not be so quick to condemn these norms.

V

Privacy and property talk is resisted, however, by many in the privacy community. Their resistance is strong, and their arguments are good. I will not in this short essay be able to rebut these arguments in opposition. But I do hope to suggest how they might be resisted.

To make the criticism clearer and, obviously, to aid in the resistance of these criticisms, consider first a picture of what I imagine a property system protecting privacy to be.

In the world that I imagine, individuals interact online through machines that connect to other machines. My computer is a machine; it links across the Internet to a machine at Amazon.com. In this interaction, the machine could reveal to the other machine that a machine with a certain ID—for example, that a machine with an ID with characteristics A, B, and C purchased goods, X, Y, and Z after looking at pages k, l, m. This ID need not be linked back to a particular person, although it could be. The property right that I am imagining governs the terms under which one machine can access certain data from the other machine. It says that the party who would collect these facts cannot do so without permission from the ID. The default is that the facts cannot be collected, but that default can be negotiated around.

The negotiation occurs through technology that sets the terms under which facts A, B, and C may be collected. These facts then get wrapped in a digital envelope that in turn carries the terms with them. At this stage the problem is directly the problem of trusted systems in copyright law. And as with trusted systems, a system that trades these facts can only do so when dealing with a secure system that trades the facts according to the rules in the wrappers.

The terms on the wrapper could be many. I do not know which would be critical. Perhaps it is a permission for primary and secondary use, but not tertiary use. If so, after the secondary use, the fact would digitally "disappear." But access might also be granted on very different terms—conditioned on the promise that the fact will not be related back to the human who has control over the ID. Whatever the term, I assume the trusted system could implement it through secure trading technologies.

What are the problems with a regime so constituted?

"It would be unconstitutional." The strongest argument against the privacy as property position—if true—is that it would be unconstitutional for the government to grant property rights in privacy. This, the argument goes, would be just like granting property rights in facts, and facts, the Supreme Court has come very close to holding, cannot be secured by at least one particular form of property right—namely copyright (*Feist Publications v. Rural Telephone Service Co.,* 499 U.S. 340 (1991)). Thus, because copyright cannot protect facts, Congress cannot protect facts, and a property regime for privacy would therefore be unconstitutional.

But although I am a very strong believer in constitutional limitations on the intellectual property power, this argument moves too quickly. No doubt you could not grant an *intellectual property right* in private facts. It does not follow, however, that you cannot, through law, control the right to use or disseminate facts. Trade secret law protects certain "facts" from disclosure (Merges, Menell, and Lemley, 2000). Contract law can punish individuals for disclosing facts they have promised to keep secret (*Cohen v. Cowles Media Co.,* 501 U.S. 663 (1991)). These limitations on the right to distribute facts stem from regimes that are grounded on a constitutional authority other than the Copyright and Patent Clause.

For this privacy as property claim to be constitutional, it would require a constitutional source of authority other than the Copyright and Patent Clause. The most natural alternative source would be the Commerce Clause (U.S. Constitution, Art. 1, Sec. 8, Clause 3). There is a substantial body of evidence to suggest that fear about privacy inhibits online commerce. The same fear was said to undermine the use of wireless communications generally. Congress was able to regulate that communication under the Electronic Communications Privacy Act and the Wiretapping and Electronic Surveillance Act.[14] The same authority should support the construction of a stronger right through property.

No doubt there are limits on the ability to protect facts through property, especially in light of the important First Amendment interests that are involved. Those limits were well described in the most recent case considering the intersection between privacy and the First Amendment: *Bartnicki v. Vopper.*[15] But *Bartnicki* does not establish that private facts cannot be protected through law. It establishes only that the use of those facts illegally obtained cannot, in certain circumstances, be constitutionally restrained. The same limits would restrict privacy as property. They would not, however, render it unconstitutional per se.

Of course, other constitutional powers cannot, or should not, be relied on to support a privacy as property right if that right is of the kind that the Copyright and Patent Clause protects. But if trademarks are not the sort of right that the Copyright and Patent Clause protects (see, e.g., *Trade-Mark Cases,* 100 U.S. 82 (1879)), I do not believe privacy would be either. Thus, whether or not privacy as property is a good idea, it would not, I believe, be unconstitutional because of the Copyright and Patent Clause.

"It would queer intellectual property law." A second criticism is related to the first. Some fear that thinking of privacy as property would further strengthen property talk about intellectual property. Thus, increasing protection for privacy would perversely increase the already too expansive (in my view and the view of these critics) protection for intellectual property (see, e.g., Samuelson, 2000: 1140).

I share the concern about overprotecting intellectual property, so here again I think that if the criticism were correct, it would be strong. But I think the fear is overstated. Given the plethora of property talk that shoots through our society, it is fanciful at best to imagine that one more dimension of rights talk would tip any fundamental balance with intellectual property. If the power itself were grounded in the Copyright and Patent Clause, I would agree that it would create dangerous pressure on intellectual property law. I do not think that would be the source of any such power, and I therefore do not think that would be its effect.

"It would tend to promote the alienation of privacy, by encouraging a better, or more efficient, market in its trading." A third criticism is more pragmatic than the previous two. Its concern is with consequences. The fear is that increasing property talk would tend to increase the alienation of privacy. Property is associated with markets; markets associated with trade; trade is the alienation of this for the acquisition of that.[16]

It is certainly true that by thinking of privacy as property, one makes it easier to think about trading privacy within a market. But equally, if the essence of a "property right" is that the person who wants it must negotiate with its holder before he can take it, propertizing privacy would also reinforce the power of an individual to refuse to trade or alienate his privacy. Whether he or she alienates the property depends on what he or she wants. And while people who have pork bellies may well prefer cash for their property (and hence property facilitates the trade in pork bellies), it would not follow that family heirlooms would be better protected if we denied the current owner a "property right" in those heirlooms. Property defends the right of the farmer to alienate pork bellies as much as it defends my right to keep you from getting a mirror my grandmother gave me.

What property does do affirmatively is to allow individuals to differently value their privacy. It is the consequence of a property system that by protecting the right of an individual to hold his property until he or she chooses to alienate it, different individuals get to value different bits of privacy differently. I may be a freak about people knowing my birthday, and so would never "sell" access to that fact for any price, but someone else might be willing to sell access in exchange for 100 frequent flyer miles. The advantage of a property system is that both of our wishes get respected, even though the wishers are so different.

There is nonetheless a legitimate and residual concern that propertizing privacy will tend to facilitate "too much" alienation of privacy, and that we should therefore resist the move to propertize.

This criticism, however, must be divided into two distinct parts. For the criticism begs the question of how much alienation is too much? And also, from what perspective is the judgment of "too much" made?

For some critics, the only legitimate perspective is the individual. Under this view, the criticism must be that propertizing privacy would create market pressures for people to alienate privacy beyond what they otherwise would individually prefer. Or they may be pressured into alienating a kind of privacy they would not otherwise prefer. But if this is the complaint, then there is no reason it could not be met by specific, or targeted legislation. If there is some indignity in alienating a particular bit of privacy, then a law could make trading in that privacy illegal (as it does, for example, with facts about children).[17]

For others, the concern about "over alienation" is a kind of paternalism, though· by "paternalism" I do not mean anything derogatory. I am all for paternalism in its proper place. It would be the proper place here if we could rightly conclude that people would, if given the chance, alienate more privacy than they should.

The problem is knowing whether the amount they would alienate is more than they "should." I am skeptical about whether we can know that yet. If we narrow the focus of the privacy that we are concerned about to the "stuff" revealed between machines in the exchanges with others online, then at this stage in the life of the Internet, I believe we know very little about the harms or dangers this exchange will create. And in a context where we know little, my bias is for a technology that would encourage diversity.

That is precisely the aim of a market. A market would help us find a mix that reflected people's wants, and if, as I believe, people's wants were very different, then the range of different wants could be respected.

It may be that people have a very similar set of wants, and that the property system is an unnecessary expense in finding this common set of privacy preferences. This relates to the final criticism that I will survey here, but if true, then once we discover it is true, we may well choose to substitute a rule for a market. I am just not as convinced we know enough now to know what that rule would be.

"A property system for privacy would be difficult to implement." Property systems are not costless. They require real resources to make them work. A final line of criticism objects that the costs of making privacy property outweigh any benefit.

This last criticism may well be true, but we should be clear about the costs. The cost of a property system depends on the architecture that implements it. My assumptions about the value of a property system assume that the negotiations and preferences about privacy would be expressed and negotiated in the background automatically. This was the aspiration of the technology Platform for Privacy Protection (P3P) in its first description. It is a fair criticism of my position that the technology it depends on has yet to be developed.[18]

Yet technologies do not get invented in a vacuum. It was only after pollution regulations were adopted that innovative technologies for abating pollution were developed. And likewise here: establishing a strong property right in privacy and punishing the taking of that right without proper consent would induce technologies designed to lower the costs of that consent.

It may again in the end not lower the costs enough. The costs of a property rule may well exceed any benefits. And if that were so, then the alternative of a liability rule, which is pushed by privacy advocates who oppose privacy as property, would make most sense. But this, too, is not something we can know in the abstract.

I do not expect these responses to the criticism about privacy as property will convince. To answer the substantial criticism would require much more attention than I am permitted in these pages. But I do hope this is enough to identify the contours of a reply. My claim is not that the property view is right; it is the much less bold (much more balanced) claim that it could do some good, and that there is no obvious reason it is wrong.

VI

The law of privacy in America was born in a debate about property. In their seminal article giving birth to a "right to privacy," Brandeis and Warren related the need for that right to a change in how property was distributed. (Brandeis and Warren, 1890: 193, 198–199). They described an earlier time when property functioned as the protector of privacy: since one could not trespass, one could not invade the sanctity of the right to be left alone. That world had changed, Warren and Brandeis argued. Because property had become so unequal, protecting privacy through protecting property would no longer equally protect privacy. The landed may have had privacy; the person living in a tenement did not. Privacy should therefore be separated from property, they argued, so that privacy could be better protected.

Privacy advocates embrace this argument as a way of resisting the argument in favor of propertizing privacy. But notice an important conflation. The complaints Brandeis and Warren made about *physical property* would not necessarily apply to the *intangible property* I am describing here. Indeed, given the difference in the nature of such "property," very different conclusions should follow.

In my view, we should be as pragmatic about property as Brandeis and Warren were. But such pragmatism will sometimes mean that we embrace property to protect privacy, just as it sometimes means that we should resist property to protect privacy. Whether we should depends on the contingencies of the technologies for establishing and protecting property. And those, I suggest, cannot be known in the abstract.

Put another way, when invoking Brandeis and Warren's argument, it is important not to make Jay Walker's mistake. Real property is different from intangible property. Facts about real property do not necessarily carry over into the realm of intangible property. The physics of intangible property are different, and hence, so should be our analysis.

My claim is that in addition to the resources of law that Rotenberg and Catlett rightly advance (see <http://www.junkbusters.com>), and the resources of technology that Zeroknowledge et al. provide, and the mix of law and technology that

Zittrain describes, we need to think, in a less politically charged and politically correct way, about adding to the arsenal in support of privacy the favored weapon of Disney and Jay Walker: the ability to rely on the rhetorical force of—"you mean you want to steal my property?"

Notes

1. There are many others who have pushed the view that privacy be seen as a kind of property. Paul Sholtz (2001) has offered a transaction costs justification that closely tracks my own. His work, like mine, trades fundamentally on the distinction drawn in Guido Calabresi and Douglas Melamed's foundational work between property rules and liability rules (1972: 1089). See also Safier (2000: 6); Schwartz (2000: 743, 771–776). Other property-based arguments about privacy include "Developments in the Law" (1999); Kang (1998: 1193, 1246–94); Shapiro and Varian (1997).

   The view that law should push to property over liability rules is not limited to privacy (whether or not it should be). For a strong push, see Epstein (1997: 2091).

2. *Stanford Law Review*'s recent "Symposium on Privacy" has a strong collection of property's opponents. See, for example, Cohen (2000: 1373); Lemley (2000: 1545); Litman (2000: 1283); Samuelson (2000: 1125–1126) (there are "some reasons to doubt that a property rights approach to protecting personal data would actually achieve the desired effect of achieving more information privacy"). See also Rotenberg (2001).

3. For a summary of the facts surrounding these events, see <http://www.junkbusters.com/amazon.html>.

4. I do not mean it changed the rules that existed before. My claim is about expectations.

5. Under the policy before the change, Amazon permitted customers to send a message to an Amazon email address and be automatically removed from the list of customers who would permit their personal data to be disclosed.

6. *No Electronic Theft Act,* Public Law 105–147, 105th Cong., 1st sess. (16 December 1997): 111, 2678. This law, also known as the "NET Act," amended 17 U.S.C. § 506(a).

7. The anticircumvention provision of the DMCA was recently upheld in the Second Circuit. *See The Digital Millennium Copyright Act,* 17 U.S.C.S. § 1201; *Universal City Studios, Inc. v. Corley,* 2001 WL 1505495 (2nd Cir. 2001).

8. *Gramm-Leach-Bliley Act,* Public Law 106–102, 15 U.S.C. § 6801–6810 (1999).

9. See, for example, <http://www.zeroknowledge.com>.

10. See <http://www.iid.de/rahmen/iukdgebt.html#a2>.

11. As Jefferson wrote:

   If nature has made any one thing less susceptible than all others of exclusive property, it is the action of the thinking power called an idea, which an individual may exclusively possess as long as he keeps it to himself; but the moment it is divulged, it forces itself into the possession of everyone, and the receiver cannot dispossess himself of it. Its peculiar character, too, is that no one possesses the less, because every other possess the whole of it. He who receives an idea from me, receives instruction himself without lessening mine; as he who lites his taper at mine, receives light without darkening me. That ideas should freely spread from one to another over the globe, for the moral and mutual instruction of man, and improvement of his condition, seems to have been peculiarly and benevolently designed by nature, when she made them, like fire, expansible over all space, without lessening their density at any point, and like the air in which we breathe, move, and have our physical being, incapable of confinement, or exclusive appropriation. Inventions then cannot, in nature, be a subject of property.

   Letter from Thomas Jefferson to Isaac McPherson, 13 August 1813 (Jefferson, 1861: 175, 180).

12. Professor Fisher traces its origins to the late nineteenth century; see Fisher (1999: 2, 8).

13. But among lawyers, however, this does not mean patents cannot be considered "property." All property is held subject to public necessity; any property right is defined in relation to conceptions of the public good. What makes a right a "property right" is that the holder has the right to alienate that right, and the person wanting the right must negotiate with the holder before he or she can use that right. Among lawyers, what defines a right as a property right is that the law protects an individual's right to dispose of that right as he or she chooses.

14. *Electronic Communications Privacy Act,* 100 Stat. 1848 (1986), 108 Stat. 4279 (1994). See reference in *Bartnicki v. Vopper,* 121 S. Ct. 1753 (2001).

15. See *Omnibus Crime Control and Safe Streets Act,* Title III, 82 Stat. 211 (1968); *Bartnicki v. Vopper, supra.* See also *U.S. West v. FCC,* 182 F.3d 1224 (10th Cir. 1999) (striking certain privacy regulations of businesses on First Amendment grounds). *Bartnicki* is a centrally important case defining the future balance between privacy and First Amendment interests. In my view, the key distinction that would enable privacy regulations to survive is that they regulate a kind of access, and not the use of the facts accessed. I believe a property right could be so structured. For a careful and balanced (if skeptical) view toward the other side, see Singleton (2000: 97).

16. This view is well developed in Rotenberg (2001, ¶92).

17. Rotenberg rightly criticized my overly condensed treatment of his position in *Code* (Lessig, 1999: 161). His and EPIC's view is a far more subtle mix of policies that builds directly and strongly on an important tradition in privacy law that balances privacy interests that are to be kept out of the market with interests that can, properly, be within the market. I have little to criticize about that balance in the context of these traditional, and critical, privacy concerns. My focus here is on the emerging issue of informational privacy, and the particular issues the expanded capacity to manipulate those data creates.

18. For an extraordinary website that summarizes the debate on P3P exceptionally well, see "P3P Viewpoints" <http://www.stanford.edu/~ruchika/P3P/>. See also the World Wide Web Consortium <http://www.w3.org/>.

References

Brandeis, Louis, and Samuel Warren. "The Right to Privacy." *Harvard Law Review* 4 (1890).

Calabresi, Guido, and A. Douglas Melamed. "Property Rules, Liability Rules and Inalienability: One View of the Cathedral." *Harvard Law Review* 85 (1972).

Cohen, Julie. "Examined Lives: Informational Privacy and the Subject as Object." *Stanford Law Review* 52 (May 2000).

"Developments in the Law—The Law of Cyberspace." *Harvard Law Review* 112 (May 1999): 1647–48.

Epstein, Richard A. "A Clear View of the Cathedral: The Dominance of Property Rules." *Yale Law Journal* 106 (1997): 2091.

Fisher III, William W. *The Growth of Intellectual Property: A History of the Ownership of Ideas in the United States* (1999) <http://cyber.law.harvard.edu/ipcoop/97fish.1.html>.

Internet Society Panel on Business Method Patents <http://www.oreillynet.com/lpt/a/434>.

Jefferson, Thomas. *The Writings of Thomas Jefferson.* Vol. 6. Ed. H. A. Washington. 1861.

Kang, Jerry. "Information Privacy in Cyberspace Transactions." *Stanford Law Review* 50 (1998): 1193, 1246–94.

Lemley, Mark A. "Private Property." *Stanford Law Review* 52 (May 2000).

Lessig, Lawrence. "The Regulation of Social Meaning." *University of Chicago Law Review* 62 (1995).

———. *Code and Other Laws of Cyberspace.* New York: Basic Books, 1999.

Litman, Jessica. "Information Privacy/Information Property." *Stanford Law Review* 52 (May 2000).

Merges, Robert P., Peter S. Menell, and Mark A. Lemley. *Intellectual Property in the New Technological Age.* New York: Aspen Law and Business, 2000: 557–794.

Rotenberg, Marc. "Fair Information Practices and the Architecture of Privacy: (What Larry Doesn't Get)." *Stanford Technology Law Review* 1 (2001) <http://stlr.stanford.edu/STLR/Articles/ 01_STLR_1/>.

Safier, Seth. "Between Big Brother and the Bottom Line: Privacy in Cyberspace." *Virginia Journal of Law and Technology* 5 (Spring 2000).

Samuelson, Pamela. "Privacy as Intellectual Property?" *Stanford Law Review* 52 (May 2000).

Schwartz, Paul. "Beyond Lessig's *Code* for Internet Privacy: Cyberspace Filters, Privacy Control, and Fair Information Practices." *Wisconsin Law Review* (2000).

Shapiro, Carl, and Hal R. Varian. "U.S. Government Information Policy." School of Information Management and Systems, University of California, Berkeley. 30 July 1997 <http://www.sims.Berkeley. edu/~hal/Papers/policy/policy.html>.

Sholtz, Paul. "Transaction Costs and the Social Costs of Online Privacy." *First Monday* 6:5 (May 2001) <http://www.firstmonday.org/issues/issue6_5/sholtz/index.html>.

Singleton, Solveig. "Privacy Versus the First Amendment: A Skeptical Approach." *Fordham Intellectual Property, Media and Entertainment Law Journal* 11 (2000).

Zittrain, Jonathan. "What the Publisher Can Teach the Patient: Intellectual Property and Privacy in an Era of Trusted Privication." *Stanford Law Review* 52 (May 2000): 1201–1250.

For Discussion:

1. Do you agree with Jonathan Zittrain's argument that privacy and copyright are both essentially about the control of data?
2. Lessig argues that privacy and property are treated very differently by the law. What is his evidence? Do you agree with him that they are essentially the same?
3. Is Lessig correct in saying that "if you could get people . . . to see a certain resource as property, then you are 90 percent to your prospective goal"? What does that imply about our values and us?

For Fact-Finding, Research, and Writing:

1. Lawrence Lessig has published on a similar topic in the magazine, *American Spectator.* Find information that would lead you to identify the ideological perspective from which this magazine is published.
2. How would Lessig respond to Hylton's description of gene patenting? Into which of Lessig's categories does Hylton's discussion of gene patenting fall— privacy or property? Would Lessig even allow those categories?
3. Is your body your own property to do with as you wish? Is it "private"? What does the law say?

Oklahoma State University, "Academic Dishonesty: Definitions and Discipline Procedures"

"Intellectual property" is a relatively new concept and not universally accepted. Some cultures placing less value on private property find the idea peculiar, as do societies in which education is based on repeating the wisdom of those more learned or experienced than oneself. The student handbook of Oklahoma State University presents a typically American emphasis on the private ownership of ideas and information, and the importance of original thinking in education.

 Before You Read:

Why do you think some college students plagiarize?

"Academic Dishonesty: Definitions and Discipline Procedures"

from the 2002–03 Oklahoma State University Handbook
of Student Rights and Responsibilities

THE DEFINITIONS OF academic dishonesty and misconduct and the procedures to be followed are listed in the following sections.

A. Categories of Misconduct:

Students will be held accountable and face possible disciplinary action, should their behavior fall into one of the following categories.

1. Academic Dishonesty: Behavior in which a deliberately fraudulent misrepresentation is employed in an attempt to gain undeserved intellectual credit, either for oneself or for another person.
2. Academic Misconduct: Academic misconduct differs from academic dishonesty in that there is not intent to deliberately obtain undeserved intellectual credit by fraudulent means. Even unknowingly allowing other students to see examination answers, or to see term projects or papers, are possible acts of academic

misconduct. Students are required to actively protect their work against misuse by others.

B. Acts of Academic Dishonesty and Misconduct:

Any student found guilty of academic dishonesty or misconduct shall be subject to disciplinary action. Academic dishonesty and/or misconduct includes, but is not limited to, the following actions:

1. Plagiarism: The representation of previously written, published, or creative work as one's own. Wherever the wording, arguments, data, design, etc., belonging to someone else are used in a paper, report, oral presentation, or similar academic project, this fact must be made explicitly clear by citing the appropriate references or sources. The reference wording must fully indicate the extent to which any part or parts of the project are attributed to others. Paraphrased materials must be acknowledged in the same manner as material that is used verbatim.

2. Unauthorized Collaboration on Projects: The representation of work as solely one's own when in fact it is the result of an unauthorized joint effort.

3. Cheating on Examinations: The covert gathering of information before or during an examination from other students, or use of unauthorized notes or other unapproved aids. It is the responsibility of the instructor to indicate what testing aids, if any, are authorized for use during an examination.

4. Unauthorized Advance Access to Exams: The submission of materials prepared at leisure, as a result of unauthorized advance access to an examination or examination materials, as if the materials were prepared under the rigors of the exam setting.

5. Fraudulent Alteration of Academic Materials: The alteration of graded papers, research data, computer materials/records, course withdrawal slips and trial schedules, or the falsification of any academic documents in order to receive undeserved credit or advantage. This includes forging instructor's or advisor's signatures and altering transcripts.

6. Knowing Cooperation with Another Person in an Academically Dishonest Undertaking: Failure by a student to prevent misuse of his/her work by others. A student must actively protect his/her own work. Reasonable care must be taken that exam answers are not seen by others or that term papers or projects are not plagiarized or otherwise misused by others. Even passive cooperation in such an act is unacceptable.

7. Examples of academic misconduct:
   a. Failure to observe the rules governing the conduct of examinations through ignorance, carelessness, preoccupation, or psychological stress. (Specific examples: bringing study notes into a closed-book examination,

but without the intent or act of consulting them during the examination, failure to stop when time is called at the end of an examination.)

b. Failure to observe strict requirements for the proper identification and citation of sources and supporting ideas in reports and essays. (Specific example: inadvertently incomplete or erroneous attribution of ideas to bibliographically identifiable sources.)

c. Excessive reliance upon and borrowing of the ideas and work of others in a group effort. (Specific example: uncritical acceptance of calculations—perhaps erroneous—in joint laboratory reports in which it is understood that the reports will be prepared jointly.)

Faculty members have the authority to set reasonable standards in their classes within the definitions provided. Clearly communicated and consistently enforced standards regarding academic dishonesty and misconduct will be upheld by the Academic Appeals Board.

C. Academic Dishonesty/Misconduct Procedures:

Acts relating to alleged incidents of academic dishonesty or misconduct are responded to under a different disciplinary procedure as set forth in Oklahoma State University Policy and Procedures Letter 2-0822 (December 1984), entitled "Allegations of Academic Dishonesty or Misconduct," pp. 2-0822.1–2-0822.7. Academic dishonesty/misconduct is administered by the Executive Vice President. Copies of the detailed policies and procedures on academic dishonesty/misconduct can be obtained at the Office of the Executive Vice President, each college dean's office, or the Office of Student Conduct. (Also see, Section IX, Academic Policies, Rights and Responsibilities.)

D. Evidentiary Standards for Academic Dishonesty:

In the case of academic dishonesty, the burden of proof rests with the faculty member to demonstrate by "clear and convincing evidence" that the alleged act(s) occurred. "Clear and convincing evidence" requires a level of proof greater than a "preponderance of the evidence" but less than "proof beyond a reasonable doubt."

Experience of the Academic Appeals Board has indicated that the standard of proof requires more than a mere assertion that a student has been involved in dishonesty. Academic dishonesty requires an intent to deceive. However, even this represents a state of mind. A person's behavior in context can provide clear and convincing evidence of intent.

In most circumstances, evidence supporting the faculty member's assertion of academic dishonesty should be presented in the form of (1) documentary evidence, or (2) corroborating testimony from University faculty or staff, or other witnesses.

Only in instances in which no other supporting evidence is available should faculty members use other students as witnesses in support of an allegation of academic dishonesty. Because the student accused of academic dishonesty has the right to cross-examine the witnesses against him or her, written statements by persons not present at the Academic Appeals Board hearing normally will not be considered by the Board.

E. Alleged Academic Misconduct Procedures:

The factor distinguishing academic misconduct from academic dishonesty is the lack of intent to obtain intellectual advantage by fraudulently violating specific rules and accepted academic standards.

1. Instructor Procedure(s): If, after consultation with the student, the instructor of record decides to take academic disciplinary action, he/she may do one or both of the following:

    a. Require the student to complete a substitute assignment or examination.
    b. Award a reduced grade, a "zero," or an "F" for the assignment or examination.

    The student must be clearly notified in writing of any penalty within ten (10) working/school days of the discovery of the alleged act of misconduct. These penalties can be severe (a zero on an examination, for example) if the student has been properly instructed in the rules and warned of the consequences of violating them; such warning is of course the responsibility of the instructor and calls for care in the writing of the course syllabus.

2. Burden of Proof of Alleged Acts of Academic Misconduct: Grade reductions for reasons of academic misconduct make no allegation of moral shortcomings and require no further notification of University officials. Student appeals in such cases are to be seen as generally comparable to grade appeals. In this instance the burden of proof rests upon the student to establish his/her case. This may be done by showing that (1) the student was not clearly notified of the non-permissibility of the behavior in question, (2) the penalty was inconsistently administered, or (3) the non-permissible behavior did not occur. If the student wishes to argue the third alternative, he/she should be prepared to present corroborating evidence in support of the claim.

 For Discussion:

1. Note the difference between misconduct and dishonesty. Why do you agree or disagree with the distinctions made?

2. In what kinds of cases should expulsion be used as a penalty?
3. When George Harrison was convicted of unintentional copyright infringe-ment (his song, "My Sweet Lord," was judged to be excessively similar to the Chiffon's "He's So Fine"), was he committing misconduct or dishonesty? Compare copyright infringement to academic misconduct and dishonesty. Do you think one of these crimes is worse than the others?

 ### *For Fact-Finding, Research, and Writing:*

1. Find information about the famous case of the Kansas high school teacher who was fired for prosecuting plagiarism. Summarize the viewpoints given by the school board.
2. Read the discussion of plagiarism in *Keys for Writers* and find at least two other discussions that highlight cultural differences of opinion toward the question. Summarize your findings.
3. Using a newspaper or magazine database, find the facts about at least two famous American writers who have been accused of plagiarism.
4. Find a legal definition of plagiarism and cite the text. Compare this defini-tion to that found on high school and college websites.

Mike Godwin, "Hollywood vs. the Internet"

A graduate of the University of Texas School of Law, Godwin currently serves as a policy fellow for the Center for Democracy and Technology in Washington, DC. He is also Chief Correspondent for IP Worldwide and a columnist for *American Lawyer* magazine. He served on the Massachusetts Computer Crime Commission and appeared as co-counsel for the plaintiffs in the Supreme Court case, Reno v. ACLU. In addition to his 1998 book, *Cyber Rights: Defending Free Speech in the Digital Age,* he has published numerous articles on both legal and social issues raised in cyberspace communication. This selection was first published by *Reason,* a monthly magazine published by the Reason Foundation, a research and educational organization in Los Angeles.

 ### *Before You Read:*

Should there be different copyright standards for different communication venues such as print, broadcast, motion picture, and recording industries?

Hollywood vs. the Internet

Mike Godwin

IF YOU HAVE a fast computer and a fast Internet connection, you make Hollywood nervous. Movie and TV studios are worried not because of what you're doing now, but because of what you might do in the near future: grab digital content with your computer and rebroadcast it online.

Which is why the studios, along with other content providers, have begun a campaign to stop you from ever being able to do such a thing. As music software designer Selene Makarios puts it, this effort represents "little less than an attempt to outlaw general-purpose computers."

Maybe you loved Napster or maybe you hated it, but the right to start a Napster, or to infringe copyright and get away with it, is not what's at issue here. At some date in the near future, perhaps as early as 2010, people may no longer be able to do the kinds of things they routinely do with their digital tools today. They may no longer be able, for example, to move music or video files easily from one of their computers to another, even if the other is a few feet away in the same house. Their music collections, reduced to MP3s, may be movable to a limited extent, unless their hardware doesn't allow it. The digital videos they shot in 1999 may be unplayable on their desktop and laptop computers.

Programmers trying to come up with, say, the next great version of the Linux operating system may find their development efforts put them at risk of civil and criminal penalties. Indeed, their sons and daughters in grade school computer classes may face similar risks if the broadest of the changes now being proposed—a ban on software, hardware, and any other digital-transmission technology that does not incorporate copyright protection—becomes law.

Whether this scenario comes to pass depends mainly on the outcome of an emerging struggle between the content industries and the information technology industries. The Content Faction includes copyright holders such as movie and Tv studios, record companies, and book publishers. The Tech Faction includes computer makers, software companies, and manufacturers of related devices such as CD burners, MP3 players, and Internet routers. In this war over the future shape of digital technology, it's computer users who may suffer the collateral damage.

Digital television will be the first battleground. Unlike DVD movies, which are encrypted on the disk and decrypted every time they're played, digital broadcast television has to be unencrypted. For one thing, the Federal Communications Commission requires that broadcast television be sent "in the clear." (The rationale is that broadcasters are custodians of a public resource—the part of the electromagnetic spectrum used for television—and therefore have to make whatever they pump into that spectrum available to everyone.) Then, too, digital TV has to reach existing digital television sets, which cannot decode encrypted broadcasts.

The lack of encryption, coupled with digital TV's high quality, poses a problem for copyright holders. If a home viewer can find a way to copy the content of a digital broadcast, he or she can reproduce it digitally over the Internet (or elsewhere), and everybody can get that high-quality digital content for free. This possibility worries the movie and Tv studios, which repackage old television shows for sale to individuals as DVDs or videotapes and sell cable channels and broadcast stations the right to air reruns. Who is going to buy DVDs or tapes of TV shows or movies they can get for free online through peer-to-peer file sharing? And if everybody is trading high-quality digital copies of Buffy the Vampire Slayer or Law & Order over the Internet, who's going to watch the reruns on, respectively, Fox's F/X network or the Arts & Entertainment channel? What advertisers are going to sponsor those shows when their complete runs are available online to viewers, commercial-free, through some successor to Napster or Gnutella?

The Content Faction has a plan to prevent this situation from developing—a plan Hollywood's copyright holders hope will work for music and every other kind of content. The first part of the plan involves incorporating a "watermark" into digital TV signals. Invisible to viewers, the watermark would contain information telling home entertainment systems whether to allow copying and, if so, how much. But the watermark won't work without home entertainment equipment that is designed to understand the information and limit copying accordingly. Such a system has not been developed yet, but in theory it could apply to all digital media.

There are some problems with this scheme. If Princeton computer scientist Edward Felten is right, a watermark that's invisible to the audience yet easily detected by machines will be relatively easy to remove. To put it simply, if you can't see it, you won't miss it when it's gone. Which is why the components of new home entertainment systems probably would have to be designed not to play unwatermarked content. Otherwise, all you've done is develop an incentive for both inquisitive hackers and copyright "pirates" to find a way to strip out the watermarks. But if the new entertainment systems won't play content without watermarks, they won't work with old digital videos or MP3s.

The implications of a watermark system extend beyond the standard components of today's home entertainment systems: VCRs, CD and DVD players, TV and radio receivers, amplifiers, and speakers. What tech industry pundits call "convergence" means that one other component is increasingly likely to be part of home entertainment setups: the personal computer. Says Emery Simon, special counsel to the Business Software Alliance (an anti-piracy trade group), "That's the multipurpose device that has them terrified, that will result in leaking [copyrighted content] all over the world."

This prospect is what Disney CEO Michael Eisner had in mind when, in a 2000 speech to Congress, he warned of "the perilous irony of the digital age." Eisner's view of the problem is shared by virtually everybody in the movie industry: "Just as computers make it possible to create remarkably pristine images, they also make it possible to make remarkably pristine copies."

Because computers are potentially very efficient copying machines, and because the Internet is potentially a very efficient distribution mechanism, the Content Faction has set out to restructure the digital world. It wants to change not just the Internet but every computer and digital tool, online or off, that might be used to make unauthorized copies. It wants all such technologies to incorporate "digital rights management" (DRM)—features that prevent copyright infringement.

At stake in this campaign, according to Eisner, is "the future of the American entertainment industry, the future of American consumers, the future of America's balance of international trade." Lobbyists at News Corporation, Vivendi Universal S.A., and pretty much every other company whose chief product is content agree with Eisner, the Content Faction's acknowledged leader, about the magnitude of the issue (although foreign-based companies such as Bertelsmann A.G. are understandably less concerned about the U.S. balance of trade). All of them tend to talk about the problems posed by computers, digital technology, and the Internet in apocalyptic terms.

The companies whose bailiwick is computers, digital technology, and the Internet tend to take a different view. Of course, Tech Faction members, which include Microsoft, IBM, Hewlett-Packard, Cisco Systems, and Adobe, also value copyright. (Adobe, for instance, last year instigated the prosecution of a Russian computer programmer who cracked the company's encryption-based e-book security scheme.) And many of them—especially those who have been developing their own DRM technologies—want to see a world in which copyrighted works are reasonably well-protected. Yet if you ask them what they think of the Content Faction's agenda for the digital world, you invariably get something similar to the position expressed by Emery Simon of the Business Software Alliance (BSA), a group that includes the Tech Faction's major players: "We are strongly antipiracy, but we think mandating these protections is an abysmally stupid idea."

The two factions' agreement about the importance of protecting copyrighted works online makes them uncomfortable to be on opposite sides now. The Tech Faction and the Content Faction both supported the Digital Millennium Copyright Act (DMCA) of 1998, and both like it pretty much as it is. The DMCA prohibits the creation, dissemination, and use of tools that circumvent DRM technologies.

Where the two factions differ is on the issue of whether the DMCA is enough. The BSA's Simon views the DMCA as a well-crafted piece of legislation but thinks efforts to build DRM into every digital device are overreaching. And in taped remarks at a December business technology conference in Washington, D.C., Intel CEO Craig Barrett spoke out against a bill proposed (but not yet formally introduced) by Sen. Ernest "Fritz" Hollings (D-S.C.) that would mandate a national copyright protection standard. The Content Faction says it needs such a standard to survive.

A few companies are so big and diverse that they don't fall easily into either faction. Take AOL Time Warner. The movie studios and other content producers under its umbrella tend to favor efforts that lock down cyberspace, but AOL itself, along with some of the company's cable subsidiaries, tends to resist any effort to mandate universal DRM. "We like the DMCA," says Jill Lesser, AOL Time Warner's senior vice president for domestic public policy. "There isn't from our perspective a need for additional remedies." AOL's reluctance to embrace the Hollings legislation explains why the Motion Picture Association of America, of which AOL Time Warner is a prominent member, remains officially neutral on the bill.

But Lesser needs only to take a breath before she adds that something like the Hollings bill, at least with regard to digital TV, may be a good idea. Industry progress toward an agreement for copyright protection in digital television hasn't proceeded as quickly as the content companies would like. "Maybe a mandate is the way to get there more quickly," she says.

Napster is the specter that's haunting the Content Faction. Although the free version of Napster has been essentially wiped out by music-company litigation (a new version of the file sharing system is being developed by Bertelsmann A.G.), the Napster phenomenon still casts a long shadow. One technologist for News Corporation who is working on a watermark-based DRM scheme says he thinks Napster signals the end of the music industry. He argues that since record companies generally have most of their catalogs available on unprotected CDs, which can be "ripped" and duplicated with CD burners or distributed over the Internet as MP3 files, music lovers already have gotten out of the habit of paying for records, which means an end to big profits and thus an end to big record companies. "Within five years," he says, "the music industry will be a cottage industry."

Matthew Gerson, vice president for public policy at Vivendi Universal, which produces and sells both music (Universal Music Group) and movies (Universal Studios), is quick to dispute such predictions. "We know that if we build a safe, consumer-friendly site that has all the bells and whistles and features that music fans want, it will flourish," he says. "My hunch is that fans will have no trouble paying for the music that they love and compensating the artists who bring it to them—established stars as well as the new voices the labels introduce year after year."

But maintaining that model, in which big music companies play an important filtering role for audiences, depends both on large streams of revenue and on control of copyrighted works. The Internet and digital technology could change all that, cutting off the revenue stream by moving music consumers to a world in which trading music online for free is the norm. (Some recording artists, including Don Henley and Courtney Love, might welcome the change. They question whether the music companies truly serve artists' interests as well as they serve their own corporate interests.) At the same time, a technical/legal scheme that perfects control of digital content creates new revenue opportunities: The music companies, for example, could "rent" or "license" music to us in a protected format rather than sell copies outright.

The Hollings legislation, dubbed the Security Systems Standards and Certification Act, is designed to help content companies turn the potential peril of digital technology into profits. In the drafts available last fall, the bill would make it a civil offense for anyone to develop a new computer or operating system (or any other digital tool that makes copies) that does not incorporate a federally approved security standard preventing unlicensed copying. The bill would set up a scheme under which private companies met and approved the security standard. It would require that the standard be adopted within 18 months; if that deadline passed without agreement on a standard, the government would step in and impose one. In at least one version, the bill would also make it a felony to remove the watermark from copyrighted content or to connect a computer that sidesteps DRM technology to the Internet.

The Hollings bill applies to any digital technology, not just TV. It's clear why the bill's supporters want its scope to be so broad: If the watermark scheme works for digital TV, creating a system for labeling copyrighted works and for designing consumer electronics to prevent unlicensed copying, it should be possible to make it work for the rest of the digital world, including the Internet.

According to Capitol Hill sources, the Hollings bill was inspired by Eisner's 2000 speech to Congress. The people who had a hand in drawing up the legislation do not describe it in terms of protecting embattled copyright interests. Instead, they say it's a proactive measure designed to promote both digital content and increased use of high-speed Internet services. They note that consumer adoption of broadband services (such as cable modems and DSL) has been slower than predicted. Consequently, the cable and phone companies have too small a consumer base to justify building out their broadband capacity very quickly or very far. But if Hollywood could be assured that its content would be protected on the broadband Internet, the theory goes, it would offer more compelling online content, which would inspire greater consumer demand for high-speed service.

This theory, which assumes that what people really want from the Internet is more TV and movies, is questionable, but it has a lot of currency in Washington. And as the debate over broadband deregulation shows, Congress wants to find a way to take credit for a quicker rollout of faster Internet service.

It was the Hollings bill that brought the war between the Content Faction and the Tech Faction out into the open. And in the near term it's the Hollings bill that is likely to be the flash point for the debate about copyright protection standards. A congressional hearing on Hollings' proposal was held in late February, but no bill has been formally introduced.

One way to understand the conflict between the Content Faction and the Tech Faction is to look at how they describe their customers. For the content industries, they're "consumers." By contrast, the information technology companies talk about "users."

If you see people as consumers, you control access to what you offer, and you do everything you can to prevent theft, for the same reason supermarkets have cameras by the door and bookstores have electronic theft detectors. Allowing people to take stuff for free is inconsistent with your business model.

But if you see people as users, you want to give them more features and power at cheaper prices. The impulse to empower users was at the heart of the microcomputer revolution: Steve Jobs and Steve Wozniak wanted to put computing power into ordinary people's hands, and that's why they founded Apple Computer. If this is your approach—enabling people to do new things—it's hard to adjust to the idea of building in limitations.

In a basic sense, moving bits around from hard drives to RAM to screen and back again, with 100 percent accuracy in copying, is simply what computers do. To the Tech Faction, building DRM into computers, limiting how they perform their basic functions, means turning them into special-purpose appliances, something like a toaster. This approach is anathema to the user empowerment philosophy that drove the PC revolution.

The Tech Faction believes people should be able to do whatever they want with their digital tools, except to the extent that copyrighted works are walled off by DRM. The Content Faction believes the digital world isn't safe unless every tool also functions as a copyright policeman.

At the heart of this argument are two questions: whether computer users can continue to enjoy the capabilities computers have had since their invention, and whether the content companies can survive in a world where users have those capabilities. What's been missing from the debate so far has been the users themselves, although some public interest groups are gearing up to tackle the issue. Users may well take the approach I would take: If computers and software start shipping in a hamstrung form, mandated by government, I'll quit buying new equipment. Why trade in last year's feature-rich laptop for a new one that, while faster, has fewer capabilities?

The Content Faction may be right that what people really want is compelling content over broadband. It may even be the case that, if they were asked, most people would be willing to trade the open, robust, relatively simple tools they now have for a more constrained digital world in which they have more content choices. But for now, nobody's asking ordinary people what they want.

 For Discussion:

1. What is the difference between "consumers" and "users"?
2. What is DRM? What are the issues raised by the use of DRMs?

3. Godwin discusses the disagreements between the Tech faction and the Content faction. What is the third faction he acknowledges? Where does this third faction fit into the ongoing argument?
4. What action does Godwin suggest for computer owners? Will this action resolve the problems he has outlined?

 For Fact-Finding, Research, and Writing:

1. Locate a copy of the Hollings Bill and transcriptions of the debate it created. Who made the most effective argument for or against the bill? Why?
2. When were the first copyright laws enacted in the United States? Prior to that time, what rights of ownership did authors enjoy? What problems did authors face before copyright laws were enforced?
3. Find a list of contributors to the Center for Democracy and Technology. What can you infer from these funding sources?
4. Read the mission statement of the Reason Foundation. What are the implications of this organization's goals?

Don DeLillo, "Videotape"

Don DeLillo, a winner of the National Book Award and the PEN/Faulkner Award for fiction, is the author of twelve novels. Born in 1936, he worked at an advertising agency after graduating from Fordham University. In 1964, he became a freelance writer and published his first novel, *Americana,* in 1971. Although he was long a critically acclaimed author, *White Noise* (1985) was his first commercially successful work. "Videotape" first appeared in *Antaeus* in 1994, has been frequently reprinted and appears in the opening chapter of Part 2 of his novel *Underworld* (1997). He has described this short story as being "about reliving things. . . . Fiction is about reliving things. It is our second chance." Some of his work "relives" historical events such as the assassination of John F. Kennedy *(Libra).* DeLillo's work examines cultural production and the consumption of culture—how the world around us is presented and represented, and how we receive and use those representations. Although he may write about computers and other technological advances, he uses a manual typewriter to create his fiction.

Before You Read:

DeLillo writes, "You know about families and their video cameras." What do you know about camcorders in the hands of a family member? Why have some families scrapped their photo albums for video recordings?

Videotape

Don DeLillo

IT SHOWS A man driving a car. It is the simplest sort of family video. You see a man at the wheel of a medium Dodge.

It is just a kid aiming her camera through the rear window of the family car at the windshield of the car behind her.

You know about families and their video cameras. You know how kids get involved, how the camera shows them that every subject is potentially charged, a million things they never see with the unaided eye. They investigate the meaning of inert objects and dumb pets and they poke at family privacy. They learn to see things twice.

It is the kid's own privacy that is being protected here. She is twelve years old and her name is being withheld even though she is neither the victim nor the perpetrator of the crime but only the means of recording it.

It shows a man in a sport shirt at the wheel of his car. There is nothing else to see. The car approaches briefly, then falls back.

You know how children with cameras learn to work the exposed moments that define the family cluster. They break every trust, spy out the undefended space, catching Mom coming out of the bathroom in her cumbrous robe and turbaned towel, looking bloodless and plucked. It is not a joke. They will shoot you sitting on the pot if they can manage a suitable vantage.

The tape has the jostled sort of noneventness that marks the family product. Of course the man in this case is not a member of the family but a stranger in a car, a random figure, someone who has happened along in the slow lane.

It shows a man in his forties wearing a pale shirt open at the throat, the image washed by reflections and sunglint, with many jostled moments.

It is not just another video homicide. It is a homicide recorded by a child who thought she was doing something simple and maybe halfway clever, shooting some tape of a man in a car.

He sees the girl and waves briefly, wagging a hand without taking it off the wheel—an underplayed reaction that makes you like him.

It is unrelenting footage that rolls on and on. It has an aimless determination, a persistence that lives outside the subject matter. You are looking into the mind of home video. It is innocent, it is aimless, it is determined, it is real.

He is bald up the middle of his head, a nice guy in his forties whose whole life seems open to the hand-held camera.

But there is also an element of suspense. You keep on looking not because you know something is going to happen—of course you do know something is going to happen and you do look for that reason but you might also keep on looking if you came across this footage for the first time without knowing the outcome. There is a crude power operating here. You keep on looking because things combine to hold you fast—a sense of the random, the amateurish, the accidental, the impending. You don't think of the tape as boring or interesting. It is crude, it is blunt, it is relentless. It is the jostled part of your mind, the film that runs through your hotel brain under all the thoughts you know you're thinking.

The world is lurking in the camera, already framed, waiting for the boy or girl who will come along and take up the device, learn the instrument, shooting old Granddad at breakfast, all stroked out so his nostrils gape, the cereal spoon baby-gripped in his pale fist.

It shows a man alone in a medium Dodge. It seems to go on forever.

There's something about the nature of the tape, the grain of the image, the sputtering black-and-white tones, the starkness—you think this is more real, truer-to-life, than anything around you. The things around you have a rehearsed and layered and cosmetic look. The tape is superreal, or maybe underreal is the way you want to put it. It is what lies at the scraped bottom of all the layers you have added. And this is another reason why you keep on looking. The tape has a searing realness.

It shows him giving an abbreviated wave, stiff-palmed, like a signal flag at a siding.

You know how families make up games. This is just another game in which the child invents the rules as she goes along. She likes the idea of videotaping a man in his car. She has probably never done it before and she sees no reason to vary the format or terminate early or pan to another car. This is her game and she is learning it and playing it at the same time. She feels halfway clever and inventive and maybe slightly intrusive as well, a little bit of brazenness that spices any game.

And you keep on looking. You look because this is the nature of the footage, to make a channeled path through time, to give things a shape and a destiny.

Of course if she had panned to another car, the right car at the precise time, she would have caught the gunman as he fired.

The chance quality of the encounter. The victim, the killer, and the child with a camera. Random energies that approach a common point. There's something here that speaks to you directly, saying terrible things about forces beyond your control, lines of intersection that cut through history and logic and every reasonable layer of human expectation.

She wandered into it. The girl got lost and wandered clear-eyed into horror. This is a children's story about straying too far from home. But it isn't the family car that serves as the instrument of the child's curiosity, her inclination to explore. It is the camera that puts her in the tale.

You know about holidays and family celebrations and how somebody shows up with a camcorder and the relatives stand around and barely react because they're numbingly accustomed to the process of being taped and decked and shown on the VCR with the coffee and cake.

He is hit soon after. If you've seen the tape many times you know from the handwave exactly when he will be hit. It is something, naturally, that you wait for. You say to your wife, if you're at home and she is there, Now here is where he gets it. You say, Janet, hurry up, this is where it happens.

Now here is where he gets it. You see him jolted, sort of wire-shocked—then he seizes up and falls toward the door or maybe leans or slides into the door is the proper way to put it. It is awful and unremarkable at the same time. The car stays in the slow lane. It approaches briefly, then falls back.

You don't usually call your wife over to the TV set. She has her programs, you have yours. But there's a certain urgency here. You want her to see how it looks. The tape has been running forever and now the thing is finally going to happen and you want her to be here when he's shot.

Here it comes, all right. He is shot, head-shot, and the camera reacts, the child reacts—there is a jolting movement but she keeps on taping, there is a sympathetic response, a nerve response, her heart is beating faster but she keeps the camera trained on the subject as he slides into the door and even as you see him die you're thinking of the girl. At some level the girl has to be present here, watching what you're watching, unprepared—the girl is seeing this cold and you have to marvel at the fact that she keeps the tape rolling.

It shows something awful and unaccompanied. You want your wife to see it because it is real this time, not fancy movie violence—the realness beneath the layers of cosmetic perception. Hurry up, Janet, here it comes. He dies so fast. There is no accompaniment of any kind. It is very stripped. You want to tell her it is realer than real but then she will ask what that means.

The way the camera reacts to the gunshot—a startled reaction that brings pity and terror into the frame, the girl's own shock, the girl's identification with the victim.

You don't see the blood, which is probably trickling behind his ear and down the back of his neck. The way his head is twisted away from the door, the twist of the head gives you only a partial profile and it's the wrong side, it's not the side where he was hit.

And maybe you're being a little aggressive here, practically forcing your wife to watch. Why? What are you telling her? Are you making a little statement? Like I'm going to ruin your day out of ordinary spite. Or a big statement? Like this is the risk of existing. Either way you're rubbing her face in this tape and you don't know why.

It shows the car drifting toward the guardrail and then there's a jostling sense of two other lanes and part of another car, a split-second blur, and the tape ends here, either because the girl stopped shooting or because some central authority, the police or the district attorney or the TV station, decided there was nothing else you had to see.

This is either the tenth or eleventh homicide committed by the Texas Highway Killer. The number is uncertain because the police believe that one of the shootings may have been a copycat crime.

And there is something about videotape, isn't there, and this particular kind of serial crime? This is a crime designed for random taping and immediate playing. You sit there and wonder if this kind of crime became more possible when the means of taping and playing an event—playing it immediately after the taping—became part of the culture. The principal doesn't necessarily commit the sequence of crimes in order to see them taped and played. He commits the crimes as if they were a form of taped-and-played event. The crimes are inseparable from the idea of taping and playing. You sit there thinking that this is a crime that has found its medium, or vice versa—cheap mass production, the sequence of repeated images and victims, stark and glary and more or less unremarkable.

It shows very little in the end. It is a famous murder because it is on tape and because the murderer has done it many times and because the crime was recorded by a child. So the child is involved, the Video Kid as she is sometimes called because they have to call her something. The tape is famous and so is she. She is famous in the modern manner of people whose names are strategically withheld. They are famous without names or faces, spirits living apart from their bodies, the victims and witnesses, the underage criminals, out there somewhere at the edges of perception.

Seeing someone at the moment he dies, dying unexpectedly. This is reason alone to stay fixed to the screen. It is instructional, watching a man shot dead as he drives along on a sunny day. It demonstrates an elemental truth, that every breath you take has two possible endings. And that's another thing. There's a joke locked away here, a note of cruel slapstick that you are completely willing to appreciate. Maybe the victim's a chump, a dope, classically unlucky. He had it coming, in a way, like an innocent fool in a silent movie.

You don't want Janet to give you any crap about it's on all the time, they show it a thousand times a day. They show it because it exists, because they have to show it, because this is why they're out there. The horror freezes your soul but this doesn't mean that you want them to stop.

For Discussion:

1. DeLillo describes the videotape as, "more real, truer-to-life, than anything around you." What do you think such a statement implies about our world?
2. Why do you think this is a "famous murder"? Why might the young girl be called "The Video Kid"?
3. What might the videotape reveal if an adult had operated the camera? Why?
4. For what purpose would television stations air this video "all the time"?
5. How would you characterize the narrator and Janet as television news consumers? What do their responses suggest about American television audiences?

 For Fact-Finding, Research, and Writing:

1. Is there any "central authority" in the United States that monitors what video footage reaches an audience?
2. Using a newspaper or news magazine database, look up information about a specific instance of violent news footage aired in the United States. What was the public reaction to repeated broadcast of it?
3. What standards are in place for violent material broadcast on television? Print or copy the standards you locate and analyze the guidelines you have found. Are the goals ethical or commercial?
4. How has the federal government addressed the issues of representing violence on television? What government agencies would be concerned with this issue, and why?

CHAPTER THREE

What Is Cyberculture?

Introduction

Late twentieth century machines have made thoroughly ambiguous the difference between natural and artificial, mind and body, self-developing and externally designed, and many other restrictions that used to apply to organisms and machine. Our machines are disturbingly lively and we ourselves frighteningly inert.

—Donna Haraway
Simians, Cyborgs, and Women:
The Reinvention of Nature (1991)

In Ridley Scott's *Blade Runner* the earth is terrorized by cyborgs or "replicants" who look and act just like their human creators. To block the threat to humanity posed by the replicants, the government employs bounty hunters, or Blade Runners, to track down and execute the almost flawless human reproductions, and Rick Deckard is the best Blade Runner in the business. But, during his quest to eradicate the menacing presence, he falls in love with one of the machines, and it compromises his ability to retire the threatening cyborgs. *Blade Runner* points up a familiar conflict: on one hand, humans strive to create technology, which allows us to interact with the world in ways never dreamed of; on the other hand, they are fearful of their creations and strive to maintain control of the possible threat that machines pose to the human existence. Indeed, this premise continues to evolve as an important issue in contemporary life.

The mission of this chapter is to explore the increasing connection between humanity and technology, particularly as it affects issues of privacy, economy, politics, and gender. As our culture grows more and more dependent upon the Internet and its residual technologies, we must continue to investigate the developing concept of the cyberculture. Does technology isolate people, or does it provide for greater interaction? Does cyberculture threaten personal privacy? How does technology contribute to our sense of identity (or lack of it)? How do technology and power interact? The texts in this section explore these important questions and confront the world's love affair with its evolving technologies, as well as its fear of them.

185

Forest Pyle, "Making Cyborgs, Making Humans"

Forest Pyle is Associate Professor of English at the University of Oregon. Originally published in *Film Theory Goes to the Movies*, "Making Cyborgs, Making Humans" will appear as a chapter in the forthcoming book, *From Which One Turns Away: a Radical Aestheticism at the Limits of Culture*. Having written many essays on nineteenth- and twentieth-century literature, film, and painting, Pyle is also the author of *The Ideology of Imagination: Subject and Society in the Discourse of Romanticism* (1995).

 Before You Read:

What is a cyborg? How does it reflect our anxieties about the future?

Making Cyborgs, Making Humans

Of Terminators and Blade Runners
Forest Pyle

Bodies and Machines: Deconstruction at the Movies

CINEMA HAS A way of leaving the images of certain faces and bodies permanently inscribed in our memories: just as no one who has seen them is likely to forget the faces of Maria Falconetti in *The Passion of Joan of Arc* or Charles Bronson in *Once Upon a Time in the West,* no one is likely to forget the imposing body of Arnold Schwarzenegger moving relentlessly across the screen of *The Terminator.* Perhaps no aspect of the cinema is more powerful—or more potentially troubling—than its capacity to confront viewers with such moving bodies and faces, larger than life, images projected in motion and in time. Of course, the cinematic attention to the effects (special and otherwise) of bodies in motion stretches across film genres, from the action-adventure picture to the classical Western to hard-core pornography. But something curious happens when the bodies in motion turn out to be 'cyborgs'. This is the case for a subgenre of science fiction films that have achieved considerable critical and popular attention over the past decade, science fiction films which, often with distinctly dystopian tone and premise, make the 'cyborg'—hybrid of human and machine—their thematic and formal focus. What we find in such movies as *Blade Runner* (Ridley Scott, 1982) and the *Terminator* series (James Cameron, 1984; 1991) are unsettled and unsettling speculations on the borders that separate the human and the non-human.

The collisions—and collusions—between human and non-human do not originate with these films, of course: the opposition between human and cyborg is but a contemporary and more mechanical mutation of a motif that extends at least to *Frankenstein*. None the less, these films rework the opposition inherited from Romanticism in some important ways, drawing attention to a deep instability, by turns compelling and disorienting, present in our attempts to distinguish and define the human from its other. *Blade Runner* and the *Terminator* series not only reflect upon the threats to humanity posed by unchecked technological developments, they raise even more probing questions about the consequences of our definitions of the human. These films demonstrate that when we make cyborgs—at least when we make them in movies—we make and, on occasion, unmake our conceptions of ourselves.

To appreciate the stakes involved in the concern over the distinction between human and nonhuman in science fiction film, one could look to the often rancorous debates of contemporary cultural theory where the curricular role of the Humanities, the status of humanism, and the notion of the 'human' have revealed themselves to be tightly knotted and highly contentious issues. However removed these debates are from real life, including the curious real life of Hollywood production, the clamour and alarm that have accompanied them make it appear that much more than the value of the traditional Western Humanities curriculum is being questioned: indeed, if often seems as if humanity itself has been put at risk by a variety of critical methodologies—primarily imported, but with some domestic hybrids—oriented around a critique of humanism. Nowhere have the disputes and misunderstandings raged more than on the terrain of what is called 'deconstruction'.[1] None of the recent modes of analysis stands more accused of an anti-humanist nihilism, charged with a malevolent disregard for human agency, cast in the role of a 'terminator'.

In the context of these films, three pertinent aspects of deconstructive analysis should be emphasized. The activity most commonly identified with deconstruction is the location in a textual system of a decisive, even founding opposition, such as that between the 'organic' and the 'mechanical'. In the course of critical interrogation, the opposition is disclosed to be both asymmetrical and unstable, rendered 'undecidable' at some decisive if often unexpected moment: the presumed superiority of 'organic' over 'mechanical', for instance, is upset at a moment in the text which reveals that the 'organic' *needs* the 'mechanical' or proves them to be inextricable. The point of deconstruction, then, is not to decode a film's meaning or even to 'unmask' its 'ideologies'; decoding and unmasking presume a secure position of knowledge outside the unstable oppositions under consideration and immune from the effects they generate. Instead—and this is the second aspect of deconstruction to be stressed—the viewer finds the opposition between spectator and spectacle to be unstable, begins to acknowledge his or her complicity with the object under consideration, and acknowledges that the extent of the complicity may never be fully acknowledged, since there turns out to be no place free from the critical complications that ensue. In the case of a film such as *Blade Runner*, for example, we may start out with our assumptions of a clear distinction between human and machine intact; but through its representation of the hybrid figure of the cyborg, the film 'plays' on a borderline that we come to see as shifting and porous, one than begins to confuse the nature of the opposition and the values we ascribe to it.[2] In the course of the film, our own position as viewer does not remain unaffected. What results, as I will argue below, is the sense that we too have become implicated in the 'deconstruction' of the oppositions we have just witnessed.

It is by no means necessarily the case that a film (or its director, writers, actors, producers) conceives such a 'deconstruction' to be its overt or implicit project. Deconstruction—and this is the third point to be stressed—marks the moment in which aspects of the text's *performance* conflict with the themes it declares or develops.[3] A deconstructive analysis of film would confront the tensions and consequences generated by moments of visual or rhetorical excess that cannot be accommodated by the narrative demands of plot or reconciled with the film's thematies: the proliferation of point-of-view shots in a film, for instance, can establish a perspective that remains at odds with the development of the film's story or theme.

In *Blade Runner* we are confronted with a curious sort of visual excess: heavily allegorized shots (and scenes) which cannot be squared with the symbolic or mythological references they invite. When the cyborg Roy Batty impales his hand with a nail near the end of the film, the shot establishes a visual symbolic association to Christ on the cross, an association bolstered by other visual metaphors, such as the dove released to a suddenly blue sky at Roy's death. But though such images draw on that symbolic repertoire, the association with the Christian narrative inevitably conjured by the shots is invalidated by the film's own narrative logic: Roy inserts the nail into his palm solely in order to prolong his life, to defer his 'time to die'. Roy is in this and every regard far from Christ-like: he has, of course, just murdered the 'father' (Tyrell) who played his god and maker. What the film leaves us with are allegorical shots severed from their mythological sources, empty allegories that cannot be redeemed by the Christian narrative.

While the deconstructive attention to the rhetorical and performative capacities of language has been accused of dissolving all worldly matters into textual fictions, one can construe very differently deconstruction's emphasis on the 'text', on properties of language and the tendency of language to exceed human mastery. In the work of Paul de Man, for instance, the 'confusion of linguistic with natural reality' is held to be both a perpetual occurrence and another name for ideology. Deconstruction thus 'upsets rooted ideologies [such as the ideology of humanism] by revealing the mechanics of their workings', mechanics which are themselves textual (*RT*, 11). This may mean, for instance, opening the fundamental opposition between human and inhuman to such a deconstruction by stressing the cinematic 'languages' that form it in the first place. According to de Man, there are aspects and operations of language that are irreducibly mechanical and that disallow the organic models we traditionally attribute to it. That which we most want to be our own, that which we may believe to be most human—language—is thus from this deconstructive perspective an insistently *nonhuman* and even mechanical operation.

For an analysis of film and for the films under consideration this has particular relevance, because deconstructive analysis discloses the ways by which mechanical and rhetorical features of language always underwrite and potentially undermine our concept of the human. We can often discern an awareness of this aspect of cinematic language in the statements of some of the cinema's early practitioners, struggling as they were with formal and technical as well as theoretical matters. One of the founders of Soviet cinema, Lev Kulesov, in what has become a famous declaration, asserted that film must be regarded at its most basic level as a language: 'The shot must operate as a sign, a kind of letter.'[4] Deconstructive analysis works not only to recover the importance of the shot as 'a kind of letter', it attends to the instances at which this 'letter' may undo the narrative and thematic structures that are its effects, its 'projections'. What often gets obscured by the more hostile responses to deconstruction is its critical attention to the means and modes by which the recognition of such figural constitution, the insistence of the cinematic 'letter', is actively forgotten or recuperated by the course of the film. Indeed, we will find that the wavering balance between memory and forgetting is central to any understanding of *Blade Runner*. And certainly one measure of the massive popular success of the *Terminator* series is the effectiveness of its recuperations of the tensions and instabilities the films generate: their ability to recover an 'entertainment' by restoring the oppositions between human and machine that have been threatened.

There has been considerable and perhaps inevitable resistance to a theoretical approach that does not presume the 'human' to be a non-textual foundation, one that regards the 'human' as a concept/metaphor subject to the effects that befall all such elements of language: Derrida, de Man, and those influenced by their work have been accused of nothing less than 'inhumanity', as if the critique and displacement of certain governing concepts and assumptions were themselves a threat to the race. David M. Hirsch, a shrill and prominent voice in the chorus of denunciation, claims that deconstruction 'seek[s] to blind and deafen readers to all that is human'.[5] I mark the most inflammatory issue in the debates surrounding deconstruction, because it goes to the heart of matters that resonate with considerable visual and thematic complexity in *Blade Runner* and the *Terminators*.

It is important not to confuse deconstruction with destruction or nihilistic termination or even demystification: it is best understood in the context of film as the attempt to *read* moving pictures: such a reading is not to be confused with traditions of 'close reading' associated with the New Criticism which took both the subject and object of reading to be stable (if complex) entities. A deconstructive reading is itself an unstable but productive *activity,* one which forces us to confront the constructedness of certain concepts, such as the human, that we may have presumed to be stable essences and that we may have preferred not to look much into. The point is not, therefore, to 'deconstruct' movies 'from the outside' but to bring 'deconstructive' questions to bear upon them in order to understand how the films are *already* soliciting or working on the more significant oppositions. It is not, therefore, merely a matter of taking theory to the movies but of apprehending how movies project considerable theoretical light of their own on the screen of our concerns. It thus may be the case that when theory leaves the movie theatre, it does not leave unchanged—particularly when that theory is called deconstruction.

It is certainly the case that the issues raised by deconstruction regarding the instability of the concept of the human are evident in such films as *Blade Runner* and both *Terminators;* these films take the technological threat to the human as their narrative point of departure and make that threat into the occasion for a cinematic treatment and exploration of the status of the human. Each of the films takes up a consideration of the relationships between human and technology, moreover, not simply in the stories they tell but by their presentation of the spectacle of movies. Of all media, film would seem most likely to confirm de Man's insistence on the mechanical aspects of a text, for film foregrounds most insistently its reliance on the apparatus from the economics of production to the mechanics of projection. But this feature, the necessity of the apparatus, is through a variety of conventions susceptible to naturalization. Each of these films—and perhaps any of the recent science fiction dystopias—returns the problem of the apparatus to the viewer in the stories they tell and by the form of visual spectacle. And each of these films asks in its own way what happens when the status and fate of the human becomes intertwined with the technologically reproduced image of the cyborg.

'If You Want to Live'

Nothing less than the very fate of the human race is at stake in James Cameron's *The Terminator.* The film's justly celebrated and gruesomely nightmarish opening scene depicts a post-apocalyptic world in which the humans who have survived nuclear holocaust are engaged in a pitched battle for survival with machines that 'got smart' and now recognize all humans as threats to their existence. The machines send a combat-model cyborg back through time with the intention of 'terminating' the mother of John Connor, future commander of the human resistance. The humans follow suit by sending a 'lone warrior', Kyle Reese, back through time to protect Sarah Connor from the terminator and thus to preserve the inception of the rebellion.

The opposition between protagonist and antagonist is established early in the film by the depictions of their arrival to the present. Schwarzenegger's body and motion are a cluster of signs—sculpted 'Aryan' invulnerability—which immediately resonate historically as 'man-machine'. These signs must however be supplemented by crucial point-of-view shots: the terminator's apparent inhumanity must be confirmed not only by our seeing him (such looks could be deceiving), but by seeing for ourselves how he sees. This seals the distinction, for the point-of-view shots reveal that the terminator does not 'see' images but merely gathers 'information'.

If omnipotence is registered cinematically as inhumanness, the simplest of negative markings, relative physical weakness, identifies Kyle Reese as human (who doesn't need the point-of-view shot to establish any further identification). This empty marker is filled out in the course of the movie as the mechanical physical superiority of the cyborg is contrasted to the positive human capacity to improvise. Reese becomes distinguished by his ability to master or 'hotwire' technology through improvisation and *bricolage,* mobile forms of thinking and acting which the movie tells us are reserved for the human.[6] What *The Terminator* defines as fundamentally human is the routing of technological mastery into a rebellious subjectivity, a heroism capable of resistance and even self-sacrifice.

The Terminator is cluttered with images and elements of contemporary (and low) technology which, even when incidental to the plot, lend the film its visual density and contribute to the motif of a pervasive—and invasive—penetration of technology. The elements of contemporary technology that the film puts on display—answering machines, blow driers, phone systems, junked cars, toy trucks—are neither ominous nor advanced. What they collectively signify, however, is the interference these technologies pose to human communication and human agency. These are interferences that are open literally and figuratively to manipulation by the terminator and that must thus be recuperated by human vigilance.

Sarah Connor's initial bewilderment when confronted by this mechanized world made hostile functions both as a plot device which heightens the film's suspense and as an allegory of our potential enslavement to and possible liberation from technology. Constance Penley has challenged such an interpretation of *The Terminator,* arguing that the traces of technology that punctuate the movie do not support such an opposition: 'the film does not advance an "us against them" argument, man versus machine, a romantic opposition between the organic and the mechanical', says Penley, for this is a cyborg, 'part machine, part human'.[7] But if the film displays the thorough interpenetration of human and machine or depicts their hybridization, its narrative logic is bent upon fulfilling a fundamentally humanist fantasy, that of human mastery over the machine. Critics who have interpreted the film as politically progressive have stressed that it attributes the human capacity for mastery to the woman, Sarah Connor, who is not only the bearer of human potential, the mother of humanity's saviour, but the character that the film represents as achieving agency. When Sarah flattens the terminator between the plates of the hydraulic press, she does not become, as Penley claims, machine-like; rather, she gets to make good on what the film has constructed as our collective desire to crush the threatening technological other. The fantasy is thus a comprehensive one, for not only does it pose as two victories over the machine—ensuring the victorious *future* resistance (Reese suggests that humans in 2029 are poised to win) by achieving a human triumph in the present—it presents the possibility of human mastery over time itself, a theme which becomes a prominent motif in the sequel. *The Terminator* is in this sense about the reassertion of sheer and absolute human agency, 'the triumph of the will'.

We note during the course of this cinematic triumph the progressive physical revelation of the terminator's inhumanness. The movie proceeds to unmask the cyborg, to reveal visually that the semblance is indeed an illusion, that beneath the flesh and tissue there is nothing human. But in another sense, the machine that gets revealed is all-too-human, the embodiment of a host of human fears. This is played out in the film through the vehicle of suspense in the protracted ending. Reese's pipe bomb blows up the terminator's truck, and when the terminator is engulfed in fire, Reese and Sarah embrace in what looks like an ending. The relief is premature, of course, for the terminator emerges from the flames, metal frame intact, and the machine that we see resembles the murderous machines that haunted the film's opening scenes and that haunt Reese's 'flashbacks' of the future. The concluding scenes are the film's most harrowing in part because we suddenly recognize that this technological other is nothing less than our own quite 'human' images and fears. The war zone of the future is literally a nightmare. Reese's and our own, populated by pop cultural preconceptions of dinosaurs, mechanical Tyrannosaurus Rex and flying Pterodactyls, while the humanoid terminators stripped of their flesh spook us with the ghoulish childhood fears of the animated skeleton. At this moment the opposition between human and nonhuman established by the film is given a twist, for though we see the terminator as more inhuman than ever—all fleshly human resemblance seared away its 'inhuman' mechanical otherness is simultaneously felt to be a human projection.[8] When the human opposition to the machine finally triumphs in *The Terminator,* the opposition *between* human and cyborg begins to appear as the human projection it always was.

'Do Androids Dream . . .?'

Something much less apocalyptic than the fate of the race is at stake in Ridley Scott's *Blade Runner.* The execution, or 'retirement', of cyborgs or 'replicants' is portrayed as part of the business of law enforcement in the Los Angeles of 2019. Deckard is recruited back into service as a 'blade runner' when four replicants escape to earth after an 'off-world' skirmish in which a score of humans are killed. Though the replicants are depicted as ruthless and deadly, the threat is nothing of the order of *The Terminator;* this is but a minor slave uprising, and nothing suggests that the world is threatened. But from the outset, from the moment of Deckard's initial reluctance, the film conveys the sense that while 'retirement' may be more or less routine, it is a very messy business. The historical analogy is established when Deckard's boss describes the replicants as 'skin jobs', cop parlance which Deckard likens to the language which, as the 'history books' tell us, referred to black men as 'niggers'. Deckard is coerced into taking the assignment nonetheless, and begins to the job of detecting and terminating the replicants.

The film's action of detection and termination might appear on first sight as the mirror image of the logic we witness in *The Terminator:* 'blade runners' are, after all, 'terminators' of a sort who seek and destroy cyborgs, such as the terminator. But the depiction of the cyborg in *Blade Runner* takes us in a very different direction. Though the film's plot suggests that the cyborgs pose no real threat of extinction, the movie itself introduces a very real and troubling threat—not so much to the characters in the film, but to the stability of the notion of the human that underwrites our actions, beliefs, meanings. Everything in the course of Deckard's 'detection' of the replicants leads him—and his audience—to a self-detection of a different and disturbing sort: namely, the recognition of the undecidable nature of the opposition between human and its technological double.

The film thus begins to ask of humans what Walter Benjamin asked of the work of art in his highly influential essay of 1936. How, asked Benjamin, is the status of the work of art affected by the advent of its technological reproducibility? He argues that though the work of art has always been 'in principle' 'reproducible', the development of new technologies—most dramatically that of film—shattered the 'aura' and 'authenticity' which surrounded the 'original'.[9] One could indeed interpret the necessity of the replicants' extinction in light of this logic: they are too close, the very fact of their duplicity too disquieting, and because they pose a threat to the very 'aura' of the 'original'—the authentic human—the cyborg must thus be eliminated. Eric Alliez and Michel Feher describe the threat of replication in terms which, echoing Benjamin, bring to our attention the 'postmodern' condition of this relationship:

> *Thus it becomes imperative to maintain formal distinctions between men and machines even if the real differences tend to blur. Here we find the explanation for the four-year life span given to the replicants. As machines, they could remain efficient for more than four years. This time limit, then, does not represent a technological limit, but is rather an imposed level of tolerance beyond which the men/ machine interface becomes uncontrollable. . . . Beyond this threshold, that which allowed one to distinguish between model and copy, between subject and object, disappears.*[10]

The film itself, then, appears to confirm Benjamin's understanding of the fate of the 'original' and in the process confirms de Man's assertions with which we opened about the collapse of the foundational concept 'human': 'there is', de Man asserts extemporaneously, 'in a very radical sense, no such thing as the human' (*RT*, 96). *Blade Runner* delivers us to the point of such an awareness, one that is resisted in the name of 'humanism': that the 'human' is an *effect* of an opposition which at certain anxious and decisive moments cannot be sustained.

The film has attracted opposing interpretations, of course; most notably that it depicts the threat an autonomous technology poses to humanity. Thomas B. Byers, for instance, sees the film as a cautionary tale that 'warn[s] us against a capitalist future gone wrong, where such [human] feelings and bonds are so severely trun-

194 of 340 Chapter Three

cated that a quite literal dehumanization has become perhaps the gravest danger'.[11] While no one is likely to read *Blade Runner* as a celebration of late capitalism, it is not clear that the film reserves such a distinctly human space outside the logic of mechanization. Rather, technological reproducibility is taken by the film to be the condition of things. It would not seem, moreover, that 'dehumanization' is the 'gravest danger' proposed by the film, for much that is both grave and dangerous in *Blade Runner* goes by the name of the human. Far from preserving an essential and organic human dimension which can be opposed to the dehumanized replicants, the film tends to undo that opposition. This undoing is performed not by extending humanity to the replicants—their 'superhuman' and 'mechanical' qualities are visible to the end—but by disclosing the distinction to be unviable.

The blade runner's means of 'detecting' a replicant is significant in this regard: the 'Voight-Kampf' test examines the dilation of capillaries in the eye during interrogation. The detective's eye establishes the difference between human and replicant by looking into the eye of his subject, though judgement is made only by way of the mechanical device which measures what the detective cannot see for himself. The motif of the eye and its gaze runs throughout the movie: the eye superimposed over the city in the film's opening shot, the eye magnified in the 'Voight-Kampf', the eye of the owl perched in Tyrell Corporations Headquarters, the eyes genetically engineered and grown in the subzero lab, the lenses of various microscopes, the photograph enhancers, the gaze of panopticon devices and advertising projections, even the eyes of Tyrell himself, shielded by thick spectacles and blinded in the Oedipal inversion of Roy's dramatic patricide. All this literal and symbolic attention to eyes, this ubiquity of the gaze, only serves to underline the failures of seeing, for it turns out that one can never tell the difference by looking. Rachael's questions about the 'Voight-Kampf' test are pertinent: 'have you ever tried that thing on yourself?' she asks of Deckard, 'ever retired a human by mistake?'

But because one cannot see or detect a difference does not in and of itself prove that such difference is absent: there may well be internal differences unavailable to empirical detection. And the film presents the search for the most essential internal differences and distinctions—self-consciousness, emotion, memory—that would preserve the integrity of the human. Most crucial in this regard is the examination of time and memory, an examination that extends to every aspect of the film's visual and narrative logic. Most immediately, perhaps, the film addresses the memory of its *audience* by working in—and *with*—a style, *film noir*, that cannot help but evoke nostalgia. But the *film noir* effect of this hybrid of the 1940s and the early twenty-first century creates a curious effect, since the cinematic nostalgia played out in shadows and muted colours is projected onto the future. The 'noirish' resonances work against the grain of a Hollywood nostalgia that is most often the reassuring nostalgia for a morally unambiguous and comforting past. But this does not mean that nostalgia is banished: with *Blade Runner*, we are confronted by the nostalgia for memory itself, for a memory of something more than a film genre, and for a form of remembering that is something other than a cinematic projection.

The replicants' fascination with old photographs—'your beloved photos', as Roy tells Leon is initially treated by Deckard as a quirky eccentricity: 'I don't know why replicants would collect photos. Maybe they were like Rachael, they needed memories.' But his encounter with Rachael's simulated past modifies that judgement: for she too has 'photographs', documents that prove her past, give testimony. Though Deckard determines the photos to be 'fakes', supplied by Tyrell to shore up Rachael's memory 'implants' with the illusion of facticity, they prompt Deckard's own poignant reflection over his old photos—photos of absent women—photos that are clearly of another age, figures that within the time-frame of the film Deckard could never have 'known'. Deckard doesn't give voice here to the recognition we witness: his photos are also 'fakes'. Why, then, would anyone collect photos? Because photos *are* memories and the film tells us that, *exactly like the replicants,* we need memories to shore up the stories we tell of ourselves. There turns out to be a gap where we expect to find the core of the human; we need photographs to fill that gap, and 'humans' no more or no less than 'cyborgs' use the photographic image—which is always a stand-in, a 'fake'—to supplement what's missing.[12]

As spectators, our own relationship to the film and to its engagement with its *film noir* intertext functions similarly to undermine memory.[13] As we recognize the film's intertextual codes, we gain a sense of knowledge and mastery: 'Wary and world-weary detective, shadowy cinematography and shadowy characters, venetian blinds and ceiling fans, dark woman with a dark past: but, of course, it's *film noir.*'[14] On one level, then, this 'intertextual' reference or cross-generic play situates the viewer as knowledgeable, capable of mastering cinematic codes and generic traditions. But the security such knowledge should provide fades as we, alongside Deckard, are drawn by the allure of a past we could never know, a memory that could only be a borrowed one. The sense of a 'darkness' to Rachael's past that is invited by the *film noir* intertext is revealed not to be a sinister or disreputable act which veils her past in mystery, but a literal darkness. The film, in other words, does not merely deviate from the tradition of *film noir;* the film quotes the genre only to displace its thematic authority: the sense of 'mystery' is revealed to be an effect of our faith in the distinction between replicant and human. *Blade Runner* disrupts that faith by insisting on the inability of memory to restore the presence of what is past, an inability shared by all who live and remember in this movie.

The rhetorical question asked by Gaff near the film's end—'Too bad she won't live! But then again, who does?'—speaks directly to the matter of a movie that has, so it seems, effectively presented the deconstruction of its presiding opposition between the human and the machine. But it also seems that the movie cannot tolerate to conclude under the sign of such undecidability, at least not in its studio release, for the suspended conclusion—one which has suspended oppositions—is supplemented by Deckard's and Rachael's escape in the final scene. They have not only escaped the oppressive atmosphere and dangerous blade runners of the city, they have escaped the film's disorientations, to the liberating blue sky and romantic green world of the 'North'. It's the most transparent of gestures, of course, and however much it fails to respect the director's cut (the ending as well as Deckard's voice-over were demanded by the producers over Ridley Scott's objections), it demonstrates that the film has generated such a knot of visual and thematic intricacy that it can be 'stabilized' only by recourse to such a pastoral gesture. The film has thus reached a limit of sorts, a limit that reveals that in *Blade Runner*, when humans make cyborgs, it means the unmaking of the human through an anxious recognition that both were assembled in the first place.

'Trust Me'

When James Cameron returns to the distinction between human and cyborg in *Terminator 2: Judgment Day,* the opposition is given a new turn and new terminator, both of which initially appear designed to make '*T2*' more fully an action-adventure movie and to make the opposition between human and other more stable. In Cameron's sequel, a second terminator has been sent by 'Sky Net' to eliminate the young John Connor. Schwarzenegger returns in *T2* as a terminator, but one sent by Commander Connor in 2029 to protect himself from termination in 1991. The two warring terminators are neither identical nor equal, however, for as Schwarzenegger explains to the young John Connor, the second terminator, a 'T-1000', is technologically superior: no longer a cybernetic organism, 'living tissue over metal endoskeleton', the T-1000 is composed exclusively of liquid metal. *T2* thus gives us both a new terminator and a new opposition: the 'moving-parts' mechanism of the older terminator (to whom John endearingly refers at one point as 'lug nuts') is posed against the advanced technology of its amorphous and wholly inorganic adversary. The film replays Hollywood's apparently compulsive drive to up the technological ante and, by the same token, allegorizes the confrontation of a postmodern technology with a modernist one. That token is then given an interesting turn, for *T2* depicts a 'modernist' triumph over the very technology—dazzling, amorphous, uncanny, postmodern—that marks the film as different from its predecessor.

While the T-1000 is not technically a cyborg, it possesses the capacity to replicate any animate or inanimate object of its own mass, including a human, and to mimic the human voice. This ability provides the film with its violently uncanny moments of doubling, when the copy confronts and then kills the original. But *T2* backs away from the more radically disorienting possibility implicit in such technology: namely, that we might *never* know beforehand who the terminator is. Instead, the moments of such doubling punctuate the otherwise continuous (assumed) 'identity' of the terminator. This identity is not of course entirely reassuring, since the terminator 'is' an LA cop. The T-1000's capacity for 'shape-changing' establishes visually an opposition that recurs throughout the film thematically as well: the opposition between mechanical mimicry and genuine learning. While the T-1000 belongs purely and exclusively to the logic of machines, the older 'Cyberdyne Systems Model 101' comes equipped with a 'learning computer'. Early in the film, John Connor asks the terminator whether it could 'learn stuff [it] hadn't been programmed with, so [it] could be, you know, more human, and not such a dork all the time'. The terminator replies that the more contact he has with humans, the more he learns. There would seem to be nothing more human than 'learning'—particularly a moral and ethical learning—and *T2* cultivates further than its predecessor this humanist position.

The film even revises the equation of resistance with humanity implied in *The Terminator*: sheer resistance leads to the excesses of Sarah Connor, who has become physically formidable and has acquired from mercenaries, ex-Green Berets, contras, and other dubious sources the soldier and survival skills displayed by Reese in the first film. Her zeal leads her to attempt the execution of Myles Dyson, the computer engineer responsible for developing the computer chip recovered from the first terminator into the advanced Sky Net computer system that, in 'one possible future', becomes 'self-aware' and commits genocide. Poised to execute Dyson, she refrains, but must be taught by her son the same lesson he teaches the terminator: 'you can't go around killing people.' Nothing would appear more laudably 'humanist' than the film's emphasis on learning such lessons, its insistence on a human agency informed by moral principles, its rejection of a closed future: 'No fate but what we make' is the refrain passed from John to Reese to Sarah to young John and, perhaps, to the audience itself.

But though the film appears to deepen the distinction between human and machine, setting the moral and ethical principles of a human education against the threatening autonomy of a mutatable technology, it achieves this distinction by way of a hybrid intermediary that upsets the stability of the opposition. The cyborg can learn, and it seems to acquire—to earn—from its contact with humans nothing less than genuine human subjectivity. The film's overt humanist thematics are thus made tenuous when it is revealed that the cyborg terminator is indispensable to the opposition: both for the story of the human opposition *to* the machines and for the conceptual opposition *between* human and machine. In one sense, the cyborg is benevolent only because of its complete obedience; at the same time, however, the opposition between human and machine is placed at the mercy of the cyborg. The instability is suggested by Sarah Connor's rhapsody on the cyborg as she watches him play with her son. 'The terminator would never stop', she says, 'it would always be there, and it would die to protect him.' What had in the first film defined the terminator's terror, the sheer thoughtless relentlessness of its drive to terminate, is reinscribed here as trust and reliability: the terminator thus becomes in Sarah's estimation the 'best father'.

The cyborg has thus been 'humanized', capable of learning and, crucially, of dying. In the first film, as Sarah flattens the terminator in the hydraulic press, she declares, 'You're terminated, fucker!' She now gives voice to a belief in the capacity of the terminator not merely to be terminated but to experience 'death'. This is confirmed by the film's ending: after the spectacular extended meltdown of the T-

1000, one in which the history of its replicated victims reappear in a Dante-like procession, the Schwarzenegger terminator sacrifices himself in order to prevent the possibility that any prototypes or computer chips from this deadly technology would remain to provoke the catastrophe that has just been rescinded. Paradoxically, the act is his most fully 'human' act of the film, for to subject himself to the vat he refuses for the first time his master's order, who implores him to stay behind.[15] As Sarah lowers him into the vat—he cannot 'self-terminate'—the terminator's mechanical hand makes the rhetorical gesture of human triumph: the victorious 'thumbs up'. It is an easy visual cliché, of course, but is emblematic of the deep interweaving of human and machine. However much the film may want to extricate itself from the logic of machines, the knotting of human and cyborg is inextricable: in *Terminator 2,* the triumph of humans and humanism is made dependent on the humanizing of cyborgs.

Human Gestures, Mechanical Hands

I want to return in closing to the issues with which we opened, to the critical possibilities opened by a deconstructive reading and to the resistance it has provoked. I hope that it has become evident that far from seeking to 'blind and deafen its readers to all that is human' (Hirsch), deconstruction opens a critical questioning of the ways by which the sounds and visions of cinema operate, and the ways by which such sounds and visions get tangled up with our notions of the human. If the concept of the human proves to be less stable than before, it is not because of a nihilistic disregard for human beings, but because questions are raised by the films themselves that, if looked into, can only shake up the oppositions between human and machine that are deeply and problematically embedded in our culture.

An image from each of these films can serve as a coda to our discussion. In each film, the 'death' or 'termination' or 'retirement' of cyborgs is accompanied by gestures of the hand: the hand of the first threatening terminator extended towards Sarah's neck as she terminates him in the hydraulic press; the hand of Roy Batty in *Blade Runner* closing 'Christ-like' over the nail he has inserted as his 'time to die' approaches; the triumphant 'thumbs up' of the second terminator. Each is a 'human' gesture made by a mechanical hand, and each gesture points towards a humanism that the films may hope to affirm, but only by way of the insistence of mechanical hands which bind the human deeply to its other, even in termination.

Notes

One of the greatest pleasures about movie-going is the discussion it provokes. I would like to thank several people who have engaged me in discussion and debate over these films for some time and whose comments have been particularly helpful: C. Lee Taylor, Michael Stamm, Randal McGowen, Hilary Radner, Jim Collins and Ava Collins.

1. Deconstruction is the name given to a range of critical, philosophical, and literary inquiries and methodological procedures associated with the work of Jacques Derrida and Paul de Man. Their work, the work of those they have influenced, and the range of responses 'deconstruction' has provoked comprise an extensive body of discussion. Some of Jacques Derrida's most influential works include: *Of Grammatology,* trans. Gayatri Chakravorty Spivak (Baltimore: The Johns Hopkins University Press, 1976); *Writing and Difference,* trans. Alan Bass (Chicago: University of Chicago Press, 1982); *The Truth in Painting,* trans. Geoff Bennington and Ian McLeod (Chicago: University of Chicago Press, 1987). Paul de Man's books include: *Blindness and Insight,* 2nd ed., rev. (Minneapolis: University of Minnesota Press, 1983); *Allegories of Reading* (New Haven: Yale University Press, 1979); *The Rhetoric of Romanticism* (New York: Columbia University Press, 1984); *The Resistance to Theory* (Minneapolis: University of Minnesota Press, 1986). Further references to the latter will be included in the text, designated by the abbreviation *RT.*

   The body of secondary material on deconstruction is itself an extensive one. Some important book-length contributions to the discussion include: Lindsay Waters and Wlad Godzich (eds.) *Reading de Man Reading,* (Minneapolis: University of Minnesota Press, 1989); Jonathan Culler, *On Deconstruction* (Ithaca: Cornell University Press, 1982); Christopher Norris, *Paul de Man and the Critique of Aesthetic Ideology* (New York: Routledge, 1988). Perhaps the most succinct but scrupulous introduction to Derrida's work is Barbara Johnson's 'Translator's Introduction' to Jacques Derrida's *Dissemination* (Chicago: University of Chicago Press, 1981). For a lucid and rigorous essay-length introduction to the methods and implications of the work of de Man and Derrida, see Deborah Esch, 'Deconstruction' in Stephen Greenblatt and Giles Gunn (eds) *Redrawing the Boundaries of Literary Studies in English,* (New York: Publications of the Modern Language Association, 1992).

2. Much of my thinking about the theoretical, cultural and political importance of the cyborg has been inspired by Donna Haraway's compelling essay, 'A manifesto for cyborgs: science, technology and socialist feminism in the 1980s', *Socialist Review* 15:2 (1985), pp. 65–108. And see the 'Interview with Donna Haraway' conducted by Andrew Ross and Constance Penley for *Social Text* 26/26 (1990), pp. 8–23.

3. In this regard, deconstruction draws on and complicates the important work of so-called 'speech act theory', in particular the work of J. L. Austin. In *How To Do Things With Words* (Cambridge, Mass.: Harvard University Press, 1962), and in other writings, Austin draws attention to an aspect of language that does not state something about the world or represent existing conditions but that *performs* an act. When we make a promise or a wager, when we say 'I do' in a marriage ceremony, we are not referring to anything, we are accomplishing the act by saying it. For de Man and Derrida, this *performative* capacity of language cannot be rigorously distinguished from language's *constative* dimension, its capacity to 'state' things about the world. The result is a possibly permanent tension or conflict between these dimensions of language. Derrida has explored this most fully in *Margins of Philosophy,* pp. 307–29. De Man's treatments of this tension can be found in *Allegories of Reading,* pp. 119–35, 278–301.

4. Lev Kulesov, *Repeticionny metod v kino* (Moscow, 1922): as quoted in Roman Jakobson, 'Is the film in decline?', in Krystyna Pomorska and Stephen Rudy (eds) *Language in Literature* (Cambridge, Mass.: Harvard University Press, 1987) p. 459.

5. David M. Hirsch, *The Deconstruction of Literature: Criticism After Auschwitz* (Hanover: Brown University Press, 1991), p. 119. Hirsch's virulent denunciation of deconstruction, its philosophical lineage and its company of 'fellow travelers' takes off from the disclosures of Paul de Man's wartime writings. From 1939 to 1943, de Man, then in his early twenties, wrote reviews and cultural criticism, primarily for the Belgian newspaper *Le Soir* while under Nazi occupation. Of the many reviews and articles, one—'Les Juifs dans la littérature actuelle'—has come under particularly close scrutiny for its anti-Semitic expressions. For Professor Hirsch—and for many other critics of deconstruction—there exists an essential connection between de Man's early journalistic writings

and his mature critical and 'deconstructive' work: the disclosures of de Man's 'collaborations' in these early writings demonstrate, according to Hirsch, that de Man's entire career is one of 'prevarication'. For critics more sympathetic to the project of deconstruction—and even for many who are not so disposed—the mature work is discontinuous with or even implicitly critical of the formulations which appear in the wartime journalism. The debate over de Man's youthful writings and their possible relationship to deconstruction is itself too intricate to explore here, but it has prompted a substantial body of literature of its own. The reviews and articles Paul de Man published for *Le Soir* and *Het Vlaamsche Land* have been collected and published as W. Hamacher, N. Hertz, and T. Keenan (eds) *Wartime Journalism, 1939–1943, by Paul de Man*, (Lincoln: University of Nebraska Press, 1989).

6. On this aspect of the film, see Constance Penley's important essay, 'Time travel, primal scene and the critical dystopia', in Annette Kuhn (ed.) *Alien Zone: Cultural Theory and Contemporary Science Fiction Cinema* (London: Verso Books, 1990), pp. 116–27. See also Fredric Jamesons's Marxist analysis of the film: 'Progress versus Utopia: or, can we imagine the future?', *Science Fiction Studies*, 9:2 (1982). For a Marxist critique of humanism in the context of recent science fiction cinema, see James H. Kavanagh, 'Feminism, humanism, and science in *Alien*', in *Alien Zone*, pp. 73–81.

7. Penley, 'Time Travel', ibid., p. 118.

8. Slavoj Žižek has argued that the terminator is revealed to be nothing more than 'the blind mechanical drive' which is distinguished from the human 'dialectic of desire', *Looking Awry: An Introduction to Jacques Lacan through Popular Culture* (Cambridge, Mass.: MIT Press, 1991), p. 22.

9. Walter Benjamin, 'The work of art in the age of mechanical reproduction', *Illuminations*, ed. Hannah Arendt trans. Harry Zohn (New York: Schocken Books, 1969), pp. 217–52.

10. Eric Alliez and Michel Feher, 'Notes on the sophisticated city', *Zone 1–2* [n.d.], p. 52. The work of the French critic Jean Baudrillard is most responsible for defining the 'postmodern' in terms of the disappearance of the boundary between original and copy. See in particular *Simulations*, trans. Foss, Patton and Beitchman (New York: Semiotext(e), 1983).

11. Thomas B. Byers, 'Commodity futures', *Alien Zone*, p. 39. *Blade Runner* has been widely and well-written about. See in particular Peter Fitting, 'Futurecop: the neutralization of revolt in *Blade Runner*', *Science Fiction Studies* 14:3 (1987), pp. 340–54; Yves Chevier, '*Blade Runner*'; or, the sociology of anticipation', *Science Fiction Studies* 11:1 (1984), pp. 50–60.

12. Giuliana Bruno has written a valuable essay on the film's linking of history, photography and mothers. See 'Ramble city: postmodernism and *Blade Runner*', *Alien Zone*, pp. 183–95.

13. Gerald Prince usefully defines intertextuality as 'the relation(s) obtaining between a given text and other texts which it cites, rewrites, absorbs, prolongs, or generally transforms, and in terms of which it is intelligible'. *Dictionary of Narratology* (Lincoln: University of Nebraska Press, 1987), p. 46. In the case of *Blade Runner*, the generic patterns of *film noir* would constitute the 'intertext' which the film 'cites, rewrites, absorbs' and, importantly, 'transforms'. On the relationship between *Blade Runner* and *film noir*, see Susan Dell and Greg Faller, '*Blade Runner* and genre: film noir and science fiction', *Literature/Film Quarterly* 14:2 (1986), pp. 89–100.

14. Annette Kuhn ascribes the effect of 'knowing' recognition in *Blade Runner* to the film's processes of 'meta-enunciation': the film addresses its spectators doubly, about 'events in the narrative, but also about the history of cinema and the conventions of certain film genres' (*Alien Zone*, pp. 145–6).

15. In his important article on the *noirish* elements of *Blue Velvet* and *Terminator 2*, Fred Pfeil ('Home fires burning: family *noir* in *Blue Velvet* and *Terminator 2*, in J. Copjec (ed.) *Shades of Noir: A Reader*, London: Verso, 1993, pp. 227–60) describes the pivotal moment at which the Schwarzenegger terminator revives after he has been apparently terminated by the T-1000, a moment that tells us that he is indeed human because he has a 'soul': 'at this very moment of greatest extremity, a small red light begins to shine far, far back in his eye—the sign, we are told, of his back-up power supply kicking in. . . . [I]s it not clear that . . . Arnold, *our* new man, has a core-self—or, if you will, individual soul—and *just enough* of one . . . ?'

For Discussion:

1. With recent movies like *The Matrix and Matrix II,* why do you think the opposition between humans and machines continues to fascinate Hollywood filmmakers? Are machines and humans fundamentally different? Is it important to continue to control the progress of technology?
2. Put into your own words the theory Pyle uses to analyze the opposition between human and machine in the *Terminator* films and *Blade Runner.* What secondary sources does he draw upon to build this theoretical lens?
3. How does Pyle characterize the relationship between the human and the machine in these films? What evidence does he use to support his claim? How does the first *Terminator* differ from *T2*? What is the significance of the eye imagery in *Blade Runner*?

 ## *For Fact-Finding, Research, and Writing:*

1. The author makes many references to the concept of humanism. What is humanism, and how is it important to the argument and conclusions of this article?
2. Using the *Film/Literature Index,* look up either of the films discussed in this article and find five reviews of one of the films in the year of its release.
3. What are the differences between androids and cyborgs?

Jean Camp and Y.T. Chien, "The Internet as Public Space: Concepts, Issues, and Implications in Public Policy"

Jean Camp is Associate Professor of Public Policy at Harvard University's Kennedy School of Government. In her research, she focuses on the interaction of technology, society, and the economy, with a specific interest in electronic civil liberties. She is the author of *Trust and Risk in Internet Commerce* (2000). Y.T. Chien is Senior Staff Scientist at the Directorate for computer and Information Science Engineering at the National Science Foundation in Arlington, Virginia.

Before You Read:

Do you think the Internet is a site of primarily private or primarily public activity? How do you distinguish the two?

The Internet as Public Space: Concepts, Issues, and Implications in Public Policy

Jean Camp
Y.T. Chien

THE INTERNET HAS long been identified as an information agora (Branscomb, 1994). The role of the Internet as a public space for every citizen (as opposed to purely for professionals, for example) is being shaped by two seemingly contradictory characteristics: the Internet is both ubiquitous and personal. Cyberspace, unlike the traditional media types (broadcast, common carrier, publishing, distribution) and traditional public spaces in the physical world (Boston Common, Logan Airport, the city library, the train station, etc.) enables the citizenry to find new ways to interact economically, politically, and socially. This universal connectivity of the Internet is its potential for everyone and in everywhere. Yet the very nature of its ubiquity may also impinge on a variety of individual or organizational rights, thus hindering its overall usefulness.

Our goal is twofold. First to help clarify concepts—old and emerging, and to bring up important issues involved. Second, to consider how regulating the Internet as public space sheds light on public policies of the future regarding Internet governance. In particular, three issues must be considered when regulating electronic spaces: simultaneity, permeability, and exclusivity. Simultaneity refers to the ability of a person to be two places at once: at work and at a train station. Permeability is the ability of barriers between spatial, organizational, or traditional barriers to be made less powerful or effective with the adoption of information technology. The permeability of the work/home barrier is most clearly illustrated with telecommuting. Exclusivity is the nature of one space, perception, or activity to prevent others. Intranets may offer exclusive access through a variety of access control mechanisms. In the physical sphere, the walled private cities offer an excellent example of exclusivity.

© 2000 IEEE. Reprinted, with permission, from *Computers and Society* Vol. 30, No. 3, September 2000 by Jean L. Camp and Y.T. Chien, entitled "The Internet as Public Space: Concepts, Issues, and Implications in Public Policy," pp. 13–19.

In order to accomplish our goal, we begin by describing what the Internet is not: a new entrant into the media types paradigm. The media types approach fails with respect to the Internet. The failures of the media regulatory metaphor have lead to a spatial metaphor, which better addresses the subtly and complexity of virtual reality. However, the differences that prevent the spatial model from being mapped directly onto the Internet are issues of simultaneity and the permeability of boundaries on the Internet.

We address the fundamental policy issues that result from treating the Internet as public space. We delineate the types of public spaces that may be found on the Internet: libraries, clinics or hospitals, universities, marketplaces, international marketplaces or cultural exchange centers, schools, and a forum for political speeches or debate ("the digital stump"). For each public place, a subset of the previously discussed policy issues applies in a unique way.

We finally close with the implications with respect to public policy that are crucial to the continuing development of the Internet as a valuable viable public space. We argue in conclusion that the public space metaphor is flexible enough to encompass the equally vast Internet, yet sufficiently defined to offer guidance to public policy issues, while recognizing that the use of such a metaphor, and therefore policies based on the metaphor, is not without difficulties.

The Internet Is More than Multi-Media

There has been much recent debate about what the Internet really is—its role in society—as it rapidly moves from a pure academic interest into the public domain. Of particular interest when it comes to characterizing cyberspace is the way we look at the public services that are being created with the Internet. Naturally, since the Internet is part of the national and global telecommunications infrastructure, many tend to classify the Internet's services into traditional media types. One of the earlier voices in this debate (Camp and Riley, 1996) argues, however, that this classification hardly works well. In fact, previous work illustrates, using events at several universities, that attempts to fit media types to Internet services have led to incentives that neither create protected spaces nor encourage open dialogue. A different model, based on treating virtual spaces as their physical counterparts, would better serve both the organizations and the individuals (Camp and Riley, 1996). We extend this work by focusing on the Internet's public spaces, and the threats and promises of mapping physical spatial models onto virtual space.

Conceptually, media types have an advantage in drawing an analogy—the classification is based on technological determinism. There are four traditional media types: publisher, distributor, broadcast, and common carrier. It is easy to distinguish between these media types in daily life off the Internet. Once on the Internet, any individual may be all four and more: a customer, a merchant, a pamphleteer, a broadcaster, a publisher, and a distributor. The media type rubric fails, however, be-

204 — Chapter Three

cause it requires that the Internet be exclusive and technologically determinant, and that it fit into one of a small set of prescribed categories. Physical spaces, though also exclusive, are not technologically determinant and are not limited to a tiny set of prescribed categories.

To begin consideration, contrast the four media types and the Internet. Broadcasters use the commonly owned spectrum to transmit content. They do not own the spectrum but instead have a limited right to the spectrum based on a license. They initiate all that is sent over the airwaves licensed to them. The information they broadcast is centrally originated, one to many, and therefore subject to tight control—and stringent liability.

Common carriers are post and phone companies. A common carrier is required to transmit all information without discrimination based on content. Common carriers are expected to initiate only a trivial amount of that which they transmit (e.g., how many phone calls originate with AT&T?) and are therefore not liable for the contents of their wires.

Publishers create printed, audio, video, software, or multimedia material and transmit it to buyers through distributors. Publishers are liable for content, distributors less so. Broadcast is available over the air to all, and primary distribution of physical printed matter is easier to control. (Note that secondary distribution is an issue with publication as well.)

The Internet, on the other hand, can be all of the media types or more, and sometimes none of the above in the exclusive sense. It is inherently a mechanism for distribution—it connects networks through internetworking protocols and provides reliable distribution with the transmission control protocol and the user datagram protocol. These technical terms are meaningful in that they describe the basic function of the Internet—to provide transmission and to distribute user-generated data. In that way the Internet is a common carrier. Yet no one entity owns the Internet, and all who connect can create content. If the material distributed on the Internet was low volume, the media characterization of distributor might work in the legal sense. The days of a low volume Internet are long past, however.

On the Internet, everyone can be a publisher. At the same time, the method of publication can make the person a broadcaster as well. A Web page is one such publication. Similarly, the CU-CMe connection through the Web page is multicasting.

Because the information on the Internet is digital, Internet services are not truly common carriage. Digital information is subject to analysis with far greater ease than analog information. Firewalls are proof that the Internet is not a common carrier; yet both the volume that a modern firewall must handle and the imperfections of firewalls illustrate that the concept of distributorship is flawed.

There are evolutionary changes in conventional media types that preceded the Internet as a new entity. Cellular telephony and cable television began the breakdown between the media types with common carriage over the airwaves and broadcast over the wire. This was a sufficiently small change that the telephony/broadcast models could continue with limited legal adjustment. Yet on the Internet, this separation of media types completely fails.

As an alternative model, physical spaces are not technologically deterministic. It seems trivial to say that in architecture, function does not follow form, yet it is an important distinction between the media types model and the spatial model. The Internet is more like physical spaces in that the same generic technology defines things, which are very different—different spaces, locales, media, or forums. It may also seem trivial to note that physical spaces are separated by meaningful distance. They are exclusive—you can't be two places at once. Physical space is also synchronous. Thus there is work in going from one space to another and time passes linearly during transit. There are places that change nature over time. A public venue may have very different norms during a Bare Naked Ladies concert and a graduation ceremony. There is again an intrinsic separation—the passage of time. Similarly, the media types have appeared distinct to users. Users did not confuse buying a cellular phone with becoming Radio Free Arlington, and similarly a person knows that there is a change in place because of the usual need for travel. Unlike media types, physical spaces have the subtleties and shades of gray that exist on the Internet. Distinctions can be made in physical space under the rubric of time, space, and manner.

The properties of exclusion and determinism make the classification of the Internet as *a medium* tempting but incorrect. The Internet is neither exclusively one medium nor technologically determined. The concept of the Internet as a space mitigates, but does not remove, these characteristics. A new conception of the private, the public, and the personal must be a part of this new rule set. The Internet is also unique with respect to public spaces in that it was created in the workplace. The public space, the private sector space, and the personal spaces merge seamlessly. The next sections focus on these issues.

Digital Characteristics of a Public Space

Strolling in a park, hustling through a train station, or spending a quiet afternoon in a city library: Each of these activities has a unique way of giving us a physical space in the public domain. We claim a place in it and enjoy the rights associated with that space. In return, we are to adhere to the rules and responsibilities commonly declared in that space. Surfing the Internet as a public domain is a relatively new phenomenon, but clearly also needs a similar set of civic rules, intuitive or formal, governing its wide-ranging, information-based activities. Several concepts about the Internet as a public space come to mind when we look at its digital characteristics.

Each of these spaces has implicit, physical definitions of permeability or exclusivity. When applying the spatial models, the core that must be reconsidered is the relationship of one space to others. Physical spaces, and some electronic spaces, offer exclusivity. There is some parallel on the Internet, with the obvious being the battle over domain names—there can only be one "sun.com" on the Internet. The elements of electronic spaces that are exclusive may have public good parameters, as described in Nissenbaum, 1999. In contrast, as further explained in Shapiro, 1998, spaces are becoming more permeable. Home and work interact, and there are flows between them. Finally, at the far end, the experience of electronic spaces can be simultaneous—both on the company Intranet and in the public space. How spaces should be regulated should consider the case that every space exists across this continuum, with the elements of exclusivity, permeability, and simultaneity in different dimensions and situations. This is unlike physical spaces in that physical spaces all lie on the extreme end of the exclusive space. Thus the spatial metaphor is promising, but the assumptions of exclusivity can be neither completely rejected nor embraced as the only possible condition.

Public and Private. Unlike a physical space in most instances, the Internet that connects people, machines, and information resources is at once public and private. This is perhaps one of the most salient characteristics of the Internet—everyone works and lives in the same space, shares the same resources with the rest of the community, and yet each can carve out a part of the space and claim it to be his/her own. From the net we draw in shared resources and tailor them to personal use. Conversely, we put proprietary information (personal or business web sites, for example) on the net for public use.

Global vs. Local. An Internet space is by definition globally interconnected, but *localness* provides richness and extends its usefulness. Theoretically, it is just as easy to access the web site of a museum in Paris as one in Boston or the Smithsonian in Washington, DC. Beyond content, however, the Internet also invades the world politics, complicating the balance of power structure among nation states and globalization.

Trans-lingual and Cross-culture. While English is still the universal language of the digital age, the Internet is like New York City, cuddled in ethnic bits. Surfing the net is like walking in the streets of New York. Unless you shut your eyes or ears, hardly anything you see or hear that is interesting or relevant is rendered only in English.

Connections to the non-public. An Internet space, even in the public domain, may be connected, either inadvertently or by design, to spaces that are of a proprietary nature, e.g., workspace, marketplace. For example, a proprietary space, a proprietary commercial web site for a company (e.g., FedEx), can enhance its business efficiency by making it functionally public (every customer using its web site to check the status of package delivery effectively becomes an unpaid clerk for FedEx).

Control and/vs. Freedom. This is an external issue of governance. Yet the other characteristics of the Internet space described above makes it even harder to reach public consensus in this wired time. The public wants both unlimited access of information and a secure, protected electronic environment. The latest evidence of content control and related issues is best illustrated in the Digital Millennium Copyright Act, passed by the 105th Congress. This alters the balance between what is public, what is property, and thus what is controlled. For the fundamental right of the property owner is to exclude others from its use, whether the property is intellectual or physical.

Uses of Internet as Public Space: Opportunities and Barriers

As a public domain, the Internet challenges the average citizen's imagination for its function and power far beyond computing and communications. A variety of public uses of the Internet, which draw on one or more of the digital characteristics described above, are already upon us or emerging. Each of them brings to the fore a set of new opportunities, barriers, and policy issues:

DIGITAL LIBRARIES

Broadly speaking, a digital library deals with ubiquitous public access to digital collections and knowledge. It is open 24 hours a day and is accessible where the network is. Not a library by the traditional definition, the World Wide Web is the most visible instance of a digital library. New ones are coming on-line everyday. At the dawn of the next century, every school and home should own a piece of the Library of Congress from wherever they might be. This grand vision aside, however, there are serious issues concerning the public access of all digital materials. Nearly every public library is grappling with the problem of how to provide web access and protect the young readers from improper digital content at the same time.

The Internet as digital library brings to the fore connections to the private ownership of information, and control.

Content control is the single issue currently debated in terms of public interest and value. In both the 105th and 106th Congress Senator McCain proposed bills that would require filtering for any library that receives federal funds. The "Children's Internet Protection Act," with the title of section 2 of the bill, is more informative, "No universal service for schools or libraries that fail to implement a filtering or blocking technology for computers with Internet access."

There has been similar activity in the states, although one mandatory filtering requirement was found to violate the Constitution. In the courts, a federal judge rejected the mandatory filtering policy of the Loudon County, VA library system on the basis that mandatory filtering "impermissibly discriminates against protected speech on the basis of content and constitutes an unconstitutional prior restraint."

The issue of ownership of information is not one that has been discussed with the public interest in mind. The focus on ownership of information has intersected with the concept of digital libraries in the concern for the continuation of fair use into the digital age. Bills that would extend or apply (according to opponents and advocates, respectively) copyright into the digital age included the enabling legislation for the WIPO treaty, the Digital Millennium Bill, and bills to protect compilations of fact, usually called database bills. The American library and scientific communities were strongly opposed to the WIPO legislation, all database bills thus far presented, and certain components of the Digital Millennium proposal. The changes to allow reverse engineering and cryptographic analysis for engineering, research, and scientific purposes advocated by scientific societies were made in the Digital Millennium Bill, and it is now the Digital Millennium Act. WIPO enabling legislation and database bills have been defeated. Thus the physical libraries have successfully argued for continuation of fair use on the Internet, although there has been resistance to the idea among the owners of intellectual property.

Connections between the public and the private are brought forward with respect to privacy on the Internet. Forty-one states and the District of Columbia have specific statutes on the confidentiality of library circulation records. Library circulation records are records of reading patterns. Internet use patterns are also records of reading patterns. However, corporate library equivalents, such as Lexis/Nexis, are also on the Web. These and similar collections of information have been treated as databases and not as libraries. Yet a single uniform technologically agnostic law must treat all these collections of information as equal.

UNIVERSITIES

The internet is changing the landscape of education: Western Governors Virtual University makes 500 courses accessible to Internet users and community colleges, and aspires to serve beyond the local communities (Healy, 1998). Harvard's Extension School is expanding its distance education program via the Internet, with course offerings to anyone with Web access. On the other hand, many educators argue that overreliance on technologies, such as the Internet, threatens the essence of teaching (Banks, 1998). Very few, however, doubt the positive aspects of the Internet as a public tool for self-learning and instant access to material at minimal cost.

The primary issues of the Internet as a university are issues of access and certification. At the university level, issues of content control versus freedom of access are not crucial. Universities are by definition the learning spaces of adults, who are capable of evaluating content and taking their own risk.

At the university level, cross-cultural issues come to the fore. Should text-based translators fulfill their technical potential, information availability for those who do not speak English will not be an issue. Until and unless that happens, making content available in multiple languages is of critical importance. Making the Internet "interoperate" across cultures dwarfs the considerable technical cross-platform problem.

Global/local issues are also considerable. Universities are developed for use primarily by the citizenry, and are national and regional assets. Some universities have responded by closing much of the content from all outside the domain. An extreme example of this is Harvard's Business School, which has developed an intranet where students may only view those classes for which they are registered. Other universities make all course content (within the limits of copyright law) universally available. As universities begin to struggle with the abstract questions of access policies, the spatial model can offer guidance by changing the question from "What is our access policy?" to "What is our community?".

Of course, the Internet will simplify the proliferation of bogus universities and for-profit schools. Thus the issue of certification becomes significant. This is not an issue in the spatial comparison, as bricks and mortar are hard to falsify.

HOSPITALS

A grand example of the revolutionary change caused by the Internet is the new online digital Medline, by the National Library of Medicine. Other new technological advances in tele-medicine are also being made. The Internet will not cure the common cold, but the vast amount of medical data available on-line is changing the relationship between doctor and patient.

Consider this scenario. There is a historical record of discussion on alt.infertility at Deja News, which may reflect that the user posted about such things at work. Clearly making a phone call to a doctor or musing over one's medical problems at work is not actionable as an employee's loss of time. Certainly an employee seeking information in the library at lunch cannot be acted on by an employer, and the employer can not even know the subject of the employee's search. Obviously employers should always retain the right to evaluate performance. Employers have an interest in the actions of employers, which are identifiable to the employer through domain name. But what of the employees interest of privacy? When is the person a patient in the doctor's office and when are they employees at the job?

Cross-cultural issues are also important here. Information can be tailored to communities with different levels of access. Consider that lack of information is a leading cause of preventable death for children in the world: that caregivers do not know how to treat fluid losses in infants and children greatly increases the risk of fatality. How can such information be transmitted appropriately to communities? All the issues in the physical space carry over to the virtual one, and ignoring these questions by trying to fit the information to the medium rather than the many spaces where it may be read will have a predictably negative result.

INTERNATIONAL MARKETPLACES

Internet commerce will connect American consumers and small businesses to small vendors across the globe. Issues of business practice as well as business law will conflict. The most likely early adjudicators of business conflict are VISA, MasterCard, & American Express. However, the private sector may not take larger cultural issues into account when deciding on clearance and settlements. This may engender hostility, widespread friction, and, in the long term, abuse of electronic trust.

The answer to the question, "Where is this transaction?" is not necessarily "on the Internet." Or, if that is the answer, it will be increasingly meaningless. Spatial information can provide trust information, and alert consumers and merchants to possible misunderstandings as well as something as mundane as shipping costs.

SCHOOLS

Beyond the traditional ability to read and write, the skills of the digitally literate span a set of new core competencies, including the ability to evaluate critically what is found in cyberspace (Gilster, 1997). Digital literacy is becoming as important to the next generation of citizens in the 21st century as a driver's license to the 16-year-olds today.

All issues coincide at the school level. The possibility of global information will expose children to ideas, thus widening their minds. Conversely children can also be exposed to prejudices that narrow their minds. As the Internet is global, there is no way to remove what is hateful prejudice at one place, as it may be reasonable thought in another.

The issue of simultaneity occurs at the school. The Internet has very tight connections in public and private spaces. There is no way to get the Internet in schools without allowing banner adds. Commercialism in school has been consider unreasonable. Teaching children to be critical to commercials is a necessary part of bringing the Internet into schools. The classroom has traditionally been a place of trust, yet critical almost cynical thought is appropriate in the marketplace. Understanding that this collision of spaces and norms is occurring is possible with the spatial approach, but not if the Internet is merely the telephone on steroids.

THE DIGITAL STUMP

Like digital literacy, Web democracy means more than just reading a political document off the Internet (Norris, 1999). Educating the public (and leaders) to digest unfiltered on-line information and engage in political deliberations unrestrained by media control poses a critical test of the Internet as a tool of citizenship in a modern democratic society. (The recent release by Congress of the Independent Counsel's report over the Internet and its subsequent public response seems to be the first such test of both the Internet's technical capability and its potential role in the contemporary political process.)

What are the possibilities the Internet can create for democracy in the 21st century? Is the Internet providing a suitable space for the average citizen to more actively participate in public affairs? Or is it merely a conduit for hatred and intolerance? While media classifications for the Internet are falling with the advent of new communications technologies (Krattenmaker and Powe, 1998), exploring issues in civil rights in public electronic forums is critical to preserving them (Pool, 1983). Spatial concepts could make an important contribution here. The definition of public spaces and public roles are a critical step in re-defining civil liberties and other forms of freedom.

THE MARKETPLACE

Economic activities on the Internet will be a kind of universal shopping mall, farmer's market, and Wall Street put together—open, free, and blending the traditional and the modern (Camp, 2000). Transactions, large or small, will be accessible to all kinds of people for both new and old economic activities. Producers study demand from data on the Web. Smart consumers, on the other hand, use the Internet to access information about the goods or services before they buy. But can they trust the Internet to do business in cyberspace? To say the transaction is in cyberspace is almost meaningless: Is it a flea market (e.g., eBay), a major mail order company (e.g., L.L. Bean), a start-up (e.g., eToys.com), or an established brick and mortar store (e.g., Walden Hobbies)?

What are the barriers to economic participation? Again the spatial metaphor lends itself to the more complete discussion. For example, all auctions at Sotheby's are open to the public. Yet most of the public does not attend. What are the range of cultural and economic barriers? To answer this question requires a greater understanding of economic activity than can be found in CATV and POTS penetration rates.

Implications in Public Policy

Here we discuss how the spatial model would alter perceptions of public policy problems in comparison to the media types perspective. We describe how the differences in simultaneity, permeability, and exclusivity between virtual and real spaces affect governance.

GOVERNANCE OF INTERNET USE

Issues in Internet governance include security, protection of data and intellectual property rights, reliability, trust, standards, and global power interdependence (Hurley, Kahin & Varian, 2000; Spar & Bussgang, 1996). Much governance on these fronts has been delayed by the perception that what is required are multiple, fundamentally new and creative frameworks in which to seek answers. By using the already established framework of spaces, answers will come more easily.

In security, risk assessments determining the analysis between risk and threat will be more widely implemented. The security fallacy of security by obscurity appears properly absurd when using the spatial model; one does not simply hide valuable assets and call them secure.

Issues of privacy expectation can be more easily delineated with a spatial model than a media model. Those Internet spaces where medical information is provided should be defined by the type of information and transaction, not by the medium used to transport the information. The continuum possible with the spatial concept would provide greater flexibility with respect to privacy than the four discrete points on the media spectrum. What implications does the concept of Internet public spaces have to privacy? Using the Internet spaces metaphor, employees have a (private) desk drawer as well as a (public) desktop. Further issues of privacy in the public sphere could apply to public electronic spaces (Nissenbaum, 1999).

If local governments see themselves as points on the Internet, rather than as tangential to the Internet, cooperative governance may be more likely.

Understanding that the Internet is a global connected space may yield more fruitful talks, as the history of media is a history of national assets rather than shared connected space. The history of negotiations over common borders and shared resources yields richer and more varied models than the international history of media regulation.

IMPACT ON SOCIAL CAPITAL AND SOCIETY LEADERSHIP

The Internet enables the formation of "social capital," which refers to the features of social organization, such as networks, norms, and trust, which facilitates technology innovation (Fountain, 1998) due to increased coordination and interactivity for mutual benefits. On the other hand, some (Chapman, 1998) fear that as the new generation of political and civic leaders flock to the wealth created from economic growth, the society is loosing its leadership of sensitivity to the poor and disadvantaged. Understanding past concerns of spatial segregation enables building on a learning from experiments to foster equality in physical spaces. The media rubric lends nothing to such debates.

Another equally important issue is sociological impact. Heavy Internet home users may be vulnerable to social isolation, loneliness, and depression, according to a recent study by Carnegie-Mellon University (Kraut, et al, 1998). On the other hand, other surveys suggest Web users find the Internet a positive experience and they use it to build social networks and improve existing relationships. How do we steer society more in the positive direction with the Internet? The spatial concepts create openings for additional research to guide the policy debate beyond the traditional bounds of media studies.

IMPACT ON SOCIAL WELL-BEING

Many argue that, like at the beginning of Theodore Vail's era, the traditional concept of Universal Access needs a new definition (Brewer, 1997). The disputes over what is a "digital dial-tone" and the definition of broadband on the Internet have distracted policy-makers from the core issues. Beyond cross-subsidy between the haves and the have-nots, urban vs. rural, how do we bring the estimated 40 million citizens, with various requirements for access due to disability, on line? If the Internet consists of various spaces, including public spaces, there is a Constitutional imperative to ensure access, rather than a simple bargain with a turn of the century monopolist. The concept of universal access has shown its limitations, as the phrase is being twisted so that it has so many meanings as to be meaningless. The spatial metaphor will allow all the possible options to be addressed without such confusion, e.g. access to markets, access to credit, access to public debate, etc.

Conclusions

If a metaphor is to be used to describe the Internet, it must be a metaphor as rich as the Internet itself. Yet no metaphor will have the same set of boundaries as the Internet: What regulatory construct can protect the interests of the many Americans who can access the myriad electronic public spaces only from work? What actions properly balance the need for access as citizenry with the need of employers for control? Answering these questions requires a greater understanding of the characteristics of digital space and the resulting implications. Yet answering these questions can be assisted by understanding people as moving from one space to another.

The traditional roles of the government at various levels are still applicable. However, each has a special twist as the Internet takes the center stage. Defining these roles in spatial terms creates a better conception of the problem. For example, the media rubric suggest that it is necessary to keep pornography off the wires. Yet the spatial concept would argue for a market with content control that is competitive and non-exclusionary to ensure that all points of view can be easily protected or represented at the desktop.

Heading off the negative impacts of the Internet on society requires a better understanding of the social-behavioral issues at the intersection of technology and humanity. Supporting the research to gain this understanding requires the ability to pose the questions in the most full and rich language possible. Funding more research focused on human- or public-centered technologies requires understanding how technologies can be both public-centered and serve economic growth—just as the town square enables debate and supports commerce.

Finally, in terms of governance, the spatial metaphor will help to promote and coordinate work in standards, rules of governance, and ethics of Internet use. Speech, such as threats, are judged off-line by time, space, and content. The final judgement in the Jake Baker case on the threatening implication of his words was finally based on *where* the words were posted. Thus the courts found guidance in a difficult situation that balanced free speech and freedom from harm by using an implied spatial model.

A regulatory regime that is too extreme may result in employees limiting employers to private areas on the Internet. This may result in a decrease in the legitimate use of public space. The corporate investment in the Internet has vastly increased its value by increasing the utility through information and service availability. Similarly, the public square would be of little interest if it did not also house a marketplace, and were not surrounded by storefronts as well as government buildings. Spatial models offer a subtlety and complexity that are lacking in media models.

References

Aspen Institute, 1996, *Creating a Learning Society: Initiatives for Education and Technology*, a report of the Aspen Institute Forum on Communications and Society.

I. Banks, 1998, "Reliance on Technology Threatens the Essence of Teaching", *The Chronicle of Higher Education*, October 16.

A. Branscomb, 1994, *Who Owns Information?*, HarperCollins Publishers Inc., New York, NY.

L. Branscomb, 1990, "Public Uses of Information Systems: Principles for Design & Application", *International Journal on Human-Computer Interaction*, Vol. 2, No. 2, pp. 173–182.

J. Brewer, 1998, "World Wide Web Consortium's Accessibility Initiative: Report of Progress for 1997–1998". http://www.w3.org/WAI.

J. Camp, 1999, "Trust and Risk in Internet Commerce," *The MIT Press,* January.

J. Camp and D. Riley, 1996, "Bedrooms, Barrooms and Boardrooms on the Internet", *Selected Paper from the 1996 Telecommunications Policy Research Conference,* Lawrence Earlbaum Associates, NY, NY.

G. Chapman, 1998, "Digital Nation: Microsoft Trial Obscures Larger Inequality Issues", *Los Angeles Times*, October 12.

Y.T. Chien, 1997, "Digital Libraries, Knowledge Networks, and Human-Centered Information Systems", *Proceedings of the International Symposium on Digital Libraries*, Tsukuba, Japan, March, pp. 60–67.

Computer Science and Telecommunications Board (CSTB), 1997, "Advancing the Public Interest through Knowledge and Distributed Intelligence", National Research Council, Washington, DC.

J. Fountain, 1998, "Social Capital: A Key Enabler of Innovation", *Investing in Innovation: Creating a Research and Innovation Policy that Works* (Eds. Lewis Branscomb and James Keller), The MIT Press, Cambridge, MA.

P. Gilster, 1997, *Digital Literacy*, Wiley and Sons, New York, NY.

J. M. Healy, 1998, *Failure to Connect: How Computers Affect our Children's Minds for Better and Worse*, Simon and Schuster.

D. Hurley, B. Kahin, and H. Varian (Eds.), *Internet Publishing and Beyond: The Economics of Digital Information and Intellectual Property*, The MIT Press, Cambridge, MA; 2000.

D. Hurley and J. H. Kelly (Eds.), *The First 100 Feet: Options for Internet and Broadband Access*, The MIT Press, Cambridge, MA; 1999.

B. Kahin and J. Keller (Eds.), *Public Access to the Internet*, The MIT Press, Cambridge, MA; 1995.

B. Kahin and C. Nesson (Eds.), *Borders in Cyberspace*, The MIT Press, Cambridge, MA; 1997.

R. Kraut, et al, 1998, "Internet paradox: A Social Technology that Reduces Social Involvement and Psychological Well-Being?" *American Psychologist*, Vol. 53, No. 9. Also available at http://homenet.hcii.cs.cmu.edu/progess/HN.impact.10.htm.

R. O. Keohane and Joseph S. Nye, Jr., 1998, "Power and Interdependence in the Information Age", *Foreign Affairs*, Vol. 77, No. 5, September/October, pp. 81–94.

Krattenmaker and Powe, 1995, "Converging First Amendment Principles for Converging Communications Media", *Yale Law Journal*, Vol. 104, 1719–1744.

G. McClure, 1997, "Narrowing the Knowledge Gap: Today's Technology Can Either Unite or Divide Humanity", *International Journal of the W.K. Kellogg Foundation*, Vol. 8, No. 2.

W. J. Mitchell, 1995, *City of Bits: Space, Place, and the Infobahn*, The MIT Press, Cambridge, MA.

H. Nissenbaum, 1999, "The Politics of Search Engines—and Why It Matters," *IEEE Computer.*

P. Norris, 1999, "Who Surfs? New Technology, Old Voters, and Virtual Democracy in America", *democracy.com*, Hollis Publishing, Hollis, NH.

I.S. Poole, 1983, *Technologies of Freedom*, Harvard University Press, Cambridge, MA.

S. Shapiro, 1998, "Places and Space: The Historical Interaction of Technology, Home, and Privacy", *The Information Society*, No. 14, Vol. 4, pp. 275–284.

D. Spar and Jeffrey J. Bussgang, 1996, "Ruling the Net", *Harvard Business Review*, May-June, pp. 125, No. 133.

For Discussion:

1. How is it possible for the Internet to be "both ubiquitous and personal"? How does the combination of these traits differ from other types of media?
2. When discussing the issues that have arisen during attempts to regulate the Internet, the authors emphasize the concepts of simultaneity, permeability, and exclusivity. What are the meanings of these concepts and how do the authors use them?
3. How do Camp and Chien describe the spatial metaphor of the Internet? What examples do they use to explain their idea of the spatial metaphor? How does differentiating the Internet from other media types benefit the Internet?
4. Camp and Chien suggest that the "public wants both unlimited access of information and a secure, protected electronic environment." Can these demands co-exist? Does Camp's and Chien's spatial metaphor allow for their co-existence?

For Fact-Finding, Research, and Writing:

1. Find the text of the Digital Millenium Copyright Act. Using a few examples, explain how this Act of Congress attempts to control the content of the Internet.
2. If you live on campus and use the Internet, can the university find out which sites you've visited, or read the content of your e-mail? Find reliable sources you could cite, were you to make this claim in a research essay.
3. Use Camp and Chien's article as a lens through which to look at such contro- versial Internet issues as employee or student surveillance (see Introna's article on the subject), access to controversial materials, and the legal issues concerning the privacy of e-mail and other Internet documents in criminal prosecutions.

Esther Dyson "The Anonymous Voice"

The daughter of an English physicist and a Swiss mathematician, Esther Dyson graduated from Harvard in 1972 with a BA in economics. She began her career as a fact-checker for Forbes, became a reporter, and then an investor and commentator. Today, she is the chairperson of EDventure Holdings, a small company focused on emerging technology worldwide and on the emerging computer markets in Central and Eastern Europe. Dyson's first book, *Release 2.0: A Design for Living in the Digital Age* (1997), discusses the impact of the Internet on individuals' lives.

 Before You Read:

While in a chat room with people you don't know, do you prefer to remain anonymous? Why?

The Anonymous Voice

Esther Dyson

SOMETIMES PEOPLE ARE never so powerful as when they assume a mask of anonymity. They can say whatever they want to whomever they want, confident that they can escape accountability for their words and the effects of those words. Of course, anonymous communications did not begin with the Internet: people have been sending unsigned letters and messages for centuries, and anonymous telephone calls have been a fact of life for decades. Anonymous e-mail and chat-room messages are only the latest variant of this age-old phenomenon. As Esther Dyson points out in the following piece, there are sometimes legitimate reasons for Internet anonymity; but there are also opportunities for abuse and serious harm to people's reputations.

After earning a degree in economics from Harvard, Esther Dyson began her career as a fact checker and then a reporter for Forbes, *a business magazine. In 1974 she authored* Help Wanted: Minorities and Women in the Retail Industry, *a pamphlet published by the New York Council on Economic Priorities. Subsequently, Dyson became a researcher for Rosen Research, a company devoted to emerging information technology. In 1983, she bought the company from her employer and re-named it EDventure Holdings. EDventure publishes* Release 1.0, *a monthly computer-industry newsletter, and sponsors the annual PC Forum for important players in the high-tech industry. A frequent public speaker and a highly influential voice in the field of information technology, as it relates to venture capital and emerging markets, Dyson has published articles in* The New York Times, The Washington Post, Wired, Forbes, *and* Harvard Business Review. *The Following passage is from her book* Release 2.0: A Design for Living in the Digital Age *(1997). (Release 2.1 was published in 1998.)*

We were standing around the barbecue at a spruced-up country inn outside Lisbon, after a long day of discussions about anonymity, censorship, regulation, and the like. I took off my badge and quipped, "I'm anonymous now!"

"Well, I can think of many reasons to be anonymous," leered a bystander, "but I can't discuss them in polite company!"

That's the general attitude to anonymity: You've probably got something to hide, and it's probably disgusting. Good people don't need anonymity.

Well, good people wouldn't need anonymity if everyone around them were good, too, but there are too many people everywhere willing to take advantage of others' weaknesses, betray their confidences, or otherwise misuse a totally open world. (Of course, in a truly open world blackmail would be impossible.)

Socially, anonymity is a useful mechanism for people to let off steam, explore ideas or fantasies, and hide from social disapproval with a minimum of consequences. Whatever you think of this, it's probably better than the alternative, which is to explore those fantasies or face oppression in real life. It's not that you can't get hurt by emotions engendered online, but you're less likely to. A lot of the anonymous chatter is harmless because no one believes it anyway.

Anonymity may not be desirable in itself, but it is often a rational, best-of-a-bad-situation response to a less than perfect world. Or it may just be an outlet for a kid going through a phase.

My Other Self

Growing up in the fifties, I didn't know how to be a teenager around my parents, who had immigrated from Europe after I was born. They were reasonable and flexible, but they would have been nonplussed if I had talked about dating, asked to take driving lessons, started wearing makeup. There was just no concept of teenager in my family—only grown-ups and children. I left at the age of fifteen, although for the "respectable" reason of going to college, where I changed identity to become a teenager with a vengeance. It took about ten years for me to feel comfortable at home again.

Had the online world existed, I might have tried out being a teenager online and had less need to leave home—or perhaps the support from outside to stay home and change. I might not even have needed to be anonymous, since my parents probably wouldn't have been in the same circles online, but someone might have forwarded them something I wrote. I might have written something untrue, just because I didn't want to be burdened with my real identity of a slightly dumpy fifteen-year-old with braces and horn-rimmed glasses. I might have wanted to pretend my parents were wicked tyrants—or I simply might have wanted to discuss them in ways I wouldn't have wanted them to see.

That is one powerful reason for anonymity on the Net: You may be perfectly happy to be open in a specific community—a circle of your teenaged friends, for example—but you might not want to see your words copied out of context, or even read in full by someone outside that community. Think of all the banal or silly or indiscreet conversations you have had over the years at cocktail parties, in movie lines, at kids' soccer games, in locker rooms, among strangers on holiday . . . Imagine if all that were online and could be searched and retrieved. Haven't you ever told a stranger on a bus or airplane something you might not tell your best friend? Or your mother?

Why else would someone choose to be anonymous? Reasons range broadly:

- discussing personal problems (especially those involving a third party) with others. You could be an abused spouse, a parent with a rebellious teenager, or simply a government lawyer trying to decide if she really wants to stay in that career.
- testing ideas you may not want to be associated with. Are you a politician trying to float a trial balloon? Or perhaps a teenager wondering if there's a case for virginity?
- playing a harmless joke on a friend. This could backfire.
- complaining about anything from messy washrooms to a sexually abusive boss, a corrupt politician, or a tyrannical teacher. Or you could anonymously warn a friend that his job is in trouble, her loud music is annoying the neighborhood, or his kid is skipping school.
- asking dumb questions. One example offered by anonymity service provider Johan Helsingius was that of a C-language programmer who needed answers to some elementary questions and didn't want to reveal his ignorance to his boss.
- trying out a different identity—real or imagined. Many of these cases have to do with sexual orientation, but they could have to do with age or other aspects of identity. In less innocent cases, people pretend to be experts when they're not, and can cause considerable damage. (But this list is about *good* reasons.)
- rallying support and arousing political consciousness in an oppressive political regime. Often political dissent is crushed because dissidents don't know that others feel the same way. Repressive governments, of course, also *benefit* from anonymity: It hides the extent of dissatisfaction and makes people afraid to trust one another—which is a downside of anonymity.
- voting—perhaps the most widely recognized and approved form of anonymous behavior. The answer to "Who voted for the opposition?" is properly: No one knows. But their voices will be counted.

Anonymity in Practice

Many anonymous communities work perfectly well by their own standards. Those include a large variety of newsgroups where people discuss troubling subjects such as addictions, diseases, fantasies, fears, and other potentially uncomfortable topics.

Others simply revel in anonymity as part of their culture. For example, there's a strange thing called the Internet Oracle (formerly the Usenet Oracle), where anonymity is accepted and encouraged. People e-mail questions to the Oracle and other players supply the answers for their own and others' pleasure. That is, you e-mail in a question, and that question is forwarded to another person on the list, who answers it. The organizers cull the best of the questions and answers and post them for all to see. The underlying conceit is that the Oracle embodies the collective wisdom of all the players; he has his own crotchety whims, human frailties, and of course an ever-changing personality. The convention for contributors is anonymity, although it is not required. The system automatically removes people's return e-mail addresses, but the instructions say, "If you do not wish to remain anonymous, you may include a phrase in your answer like `incarnated as <insert your name and/or address here>.'" Fewer than 1 percent of the contributors identified themselves.

Consider it a giant party game played over the Net. Although it went through a rough spot for a couple of years as a large number of newcomers entered the fray without respect for the Oracle culture, they eventually dropped out and the Oracle retains its spirit of intellectual playfulness. The questions and answers are a mix of pseudomythology, programmer jargon, sophomoric jokes, and truly elegant irony. Entertainment on the Net isn't all virtual reality, video clips, and twitch games.

One of the organizers, veteran online user, editor, online columnist, and former English professor David Sewell, surveyed some of the participants about their perceptions of anonymity. He says, "Anonymity provides two crucial advantages: freedom of self-expression, and the shared aesthetic illusion of an Oracle persona. Like college professors who publish murder mysteries or romance novels under pseudonyms for fear of being thought unprofessional, Oracle writers sometimes feel safer when unidentified." In an article published by *First Monday,* an online internet journal, he quotes some participants and then goes on to explain further one lure of anonymity:

> *"I think [anonymity is] essential. I wouldn't have the guts to use the Oracle if I knew my name was going with everything I wrote."*

> *"It helps me to give answers which are much more uninhibited. If I knew my identity would be made public I might be a little reluctant to write, since I would not want co-workers to know how much I am involved."*

But the second reason for accepting anonymity more resembles that of the medieval author, who, in Hans Robert Jauss's words, wrote "in order to praise and to extend his object, not to express himself or to enhance his personal reputation." The "object" in this case is the collection of a corpus of work by a personality, the Oracle, whose characteristics derive from the collective efforts of contributors. . . . And in fact the Oracle has accreted an identifiable personality. Like a Greek god, he is polymorphous: now a crotchety old man, now a super-intelligent computer program, now a deity. A jealous, omniscient and omnipotent being, he is apt to strike with lightning supplicants who insult him or fail to grovel sufficiently. Nevertheless he is vulnerable to having his plug pulled by his creator Kinzler, his computer's system administrator, or an irate "god@heaven.com." Like Zeus, he has a consort: Lisa evolved from the cliché-geek's fantasy-fulfilling "net.sex.goddess" to the Oracle's companion. It may be that one reason for leaving Oracle submissions unsigned is generic constraint: like Scripture, Oracularities should seem to participants to proceed directly from the voice of God. As E. M. Forster once observed of unsigned newspaper editorials, "anonymous statements have . . . a universal air about them. Absolute truth, the collected wisdom of the universe, seems to be speaking, not the feeble voice of a man." A number of Oracle authors who responded to the questionnaire identified similar reasons for leaving their contributions unsigned:

> *"I'd put less effort into writing for the Oracle if [my identity] were public. I prefer the idea of an all-powerful Oracle rather than the various incarnations scenario. . . . Sometimes it would be nice to say, 'I wrote that!' but I prefer to just smile knowingly . . ."*

> *"I don't care who wrote it, but it sort of loses something when I see a signature line. Destroys the myth, so to speak."*

> *"When I read Oracularities . . . I prefer to think of a faceless deity in a cave somewhere, not joe@lharc.netcom.edu. I prefer anonymity."*

Why Anonymity Is Sometimes Not Such a Great Idea after All

Johan Helsingius, the Oracle and my teenage self all make a good case *for* anonymity. But why is it not something we want to promote in general?

First, because it can be done to excess and is not healthy for individuals, though this is a free country and a free Net. Second, because even good people tend to be "less good" when they're not recognized and building (or keeping) a reputation. And finally, because bad people can use anonymity to get away with truly harmful behavior.

Like alcohol, anonymity can be useful in moderation. For some people it's a harmless release and an outlet; others can overuse it and abuse it to avoid everyday responsibilities and challenges. No, you should not just go and live the rest of your life anonymously online, flitting from identity to identity. Nor should you drown yourself in alcohol, lose yourself in gambling, or escape into drugs. The Net can be an addiction like any other, although it is probably easier on your body than most of them.

It may not be nice to say it, but people are not all always nice, and therefore a little social pressure can be a good thing. For example, I consider myself basically "good," but I'm a lot less nice in airport lines (for instance) than in places where I know someone. Haven't you ever lost your patience with a clerk or a waiter and then been embarrassed when you found out someone you know was watching? Unfortunately, I have! (This is why people usually behave better in tight communities than in big cities, and tourists abroad behave in ways they wouldn't at home. Consider the well-known reprimand: "Would you do this in your mother's home?")

If you want to be scientific rather than moralistic about it, consider a variety of experiments in game and market theory. The basic finding of all of them is that people work together best by telling the truth, on any task from avoiding jail to setting prices for goods. Sometimes people can gain a short-term advantage by lying, but they usually can't benefit in the long run. Over time markets work better and produce better average outcomes, when people (1) tell the truth and (2) can earn a reputation for doing so.

When people operate anonymously, there's no incentive to tell the truth; dishonest people easily betray others for their own gain. Overall, anonymous markets don't work well. The wrong people get put into jail; the market prices are volatile and misallocate goods or investment; investment doesn't take place because no one can count on long-term gains. Overall, everyone is worse off on average, and the crooks do better than the honest people. However, they must always live in fear of encountering even bigger crooks. (This all sounds very much like the current situation in much of Russia to me. It has markets, yes, but it lacks the rules of disclosure and accountability that make them work.)

But the issue isn't just markets: Visibility leads to healthier communities in general. There should be occasions and places where anonymity is practiced but they should be clearly marked. The worst difficulties arise when you get something in-between—especially when people pretend to be other, known people rather than anonymous characters, as happened not long ago in one of the first online communities.

The Experience at the WELL

The WELL (perhaps too cutely, it stands for Whole Earth 'Lectronic Link) was started in San Francisco by Stewart Brand, also founder of the Whole Earth Catalogue. It attracted an elite crowd of early adopters. Brand had earlier been part of one of the first online services, called EIES (for Electronic Information Exchange System). On it was one small group of scientists and corporate people who were using it for an ongoing conference in the early '80s. That group had a brief but devastating encounter with anonymity. Recalls Stewart (by e-mail, of course): "They were all respected men and women with responsible positions in the world. Suddenly one was behaving like a 'you can't catch me' prankster. The whole discussion swerved to dealing with that. Amusement turned to resentment and then turned to distrust and distaste. The group fell apart online. The bad odor from that experience lasted for a long time."

That experience led Stewart to make personal identities required on the WELL. Besides, many of them already knew each other offline; others joined the community online and then met face-to-face. Over a couple of years, the few hundred members formed a tight little community, full of friendship and gossip, petty rivalries and deep affection, a few romances, some shared secrets . . . a normal community. Then a group of members decided to start a subgroup that allowed anonymity, over Brand's skepticism—but he figured the results might be different the second time around. They were not.

Strange things began to happen. First people posted unpleasant truths, attacking one another. In such a tight little community, it was pretty easy to figure out who was saying what—and trying to guess was fun. Then people started pretending to be one another, and it became harder to tell what was going on. Says Stewart in retrospect: "Because the people actually knew each other, they could pretend to be one another more convincingly. They could reveal secrets. It was far worse than a group of strangers could have been."

He continues: "Now, there were several conferences on the WELL where it was permitted, almost encouraged, for people to say absolutely vicious things about each other, and the strong WELL opinion against censorship made those conferences as sacrosanct as any other.

"But anonymous parody was apparently unacceptable where accountable viciousness was okay. Several people asked Cliff Figallo, who ran the WELL at the time [and who used to work at EFF] to shut down the Anonymous conference, and he promptly did. Nobody mourned. [The experiment] lasted at most two weeks with the world's most permissive online community.

"The two experiences add up to a proof for me. They were wholly separate—different systems, different people, different times. Both had fairly high-minded expectations of anonymity online. Both failed horribly. Different pathologies emerged and became decisive in the two occasions. On EIES, one of a close, trusted group turned into an unaccountable demon and never recanted. On the WELL, people pretended to be other people destructively. In both cases, trust was the casualty. It was easy to destroy; hard to rebuild."

Problems with Anonymity

Relatively speaking, the WELL was a mild case. Far worse than its tendency to foster bad behavior (and perhaps allowing people to work out their hostilities online rather than in real life), the fundamental argument against anonymity is the third one cited on page 266: lack of accountability for serious wrongdoing by seriously bad people. You might not want your neighbors to know you occasionally exercise your right to read pornography—or that you're the one who keeps correcting the school principal's grammar. But what if you're abusing children and posting the pictures online, then what?

Indeed, the possibility of anonymity is one of the scariest features of the Net—for parents, for law enforcement, for employers hiring new workers, for victims of nasty rumors, scams, and other misdeeds. It's troubling for merchants who want to know who their customers are, for debt collectors, and for others to whom obligations are owed.

On the other hand, anonymity is also a problem for repressive governments who want to know who is criticizing them, for maniacs who want to track and pester people they're obsessed with, for con artists trolling for new victims, and in general for people who want to know others' secrets. For anyone, anonymity can make it hard to assess the reliability and value of information.

Accountability

If society suspects someone (for whatever reason) of a crime, what right does it have to find out who it is and catch that person? Presumably, the same right online as offline. If it can find the person, following due process with appropriate search warrants and the like, society should be able to prosecute him. There is no ISP-client privilege similar to attorney-client privilege. But at the same time, people should not be forced to make it easy—just as the law doesn't force us to live without window shades or to use postcards instead of letters in envelopes.

In this sense, anonymity online is akin to conditions we take for granted in the terrestrial world. If we required each shopper to show an ID each time she entered a store, that would certainly both reduce crime and make it easier to catch criminals, but it is not likely (thank goodness!) that we will do so in the United States. Law-abiding citizens in the United States are not required to carry their documents with them, although they must do so when driving a car, buying a gun, passing a border, or getting on an airplane. All these are infringements on our liberty, but we accept them (or most of us do) because they reduce real risks. But I don't think the risk someone will do something bad is large enough or grave enough to require forcible identification of everyone online.

That means that anonymity in itself should not be illegal. There are enough good reasons for people to be anonymous that it should be considered part of the normal range of social behavior—at least in some places on the Net (again as in real life).

True-Life Experience

As I sit here writing this chapter on anonymity, I have just received a strange missive from a stranger, someone calling himself ******. I have no idea who he (?) is, but he knows a fair amount about me. Nothing he couldn't have read somewhere; it's probably not someone I know. But it's familiar enough: He knows the shape of my family, some of my background (Russia), and he's clever enough to make some inside jokes that only I could appreciate. How much do I want to say here? If he's obsessed with me, surely he'll be reading these words, too. As Carly Simon sings: "You're so vain, bet you think this song is about you." But it isn't, it's about the other one; take that! But he hasn't harmed me, asks nothing of me other than to read his quite clever ramblings.

What should I do? His e-mail comes from a commercial service; I could probably track him down if I wanted to. But why should I? To ask him to stop? Time enough to do that if he starts bothering me. First, I could filter and automatically delete everything he sends. If I got seriously unpleasant or threatening mail, I could go to his Internet service provider and ask it to ask him to stop. But the best approach is probably simply to ignore it.

Yet it feels creepy. And I have to compare it with several other anonymous messages, from a single different source, that I got after attending a conference last fall. They referred to two other people, one of whom was at the conference and one of whom wasn't. Could the messages have been from one of the people I had met there? Certainly, they spoiled my memory of the previous three days. These particular messages were quite obscene and offensive, but in some sense they were less troubling than the one I just received. This writer didn't seem to know much about me other than my gender; his comments were graphic and disgusting but they had nothing to do with me personally. And besides, I was one of three well known (in the Internet community) people he was attacking; the messages seemed to come *from him* rather than *to me*. It's invasion of privacy coupled with anonymity that's so creepy in this most recent message.

All these messages are the result of a trade-off I have made. I have become well known, and now strangers can write to me anonymously and disturb me. I could filter them out, taking mail only from people I know, but that would be ridiculous. As time passes, presumably I will become even more visible and get more e-mail, some of it helpful and enlightening, some of it wasteful of time, and some of it no doubt hurtful. That's the trade-off I'm making, and one I'm increasingly aware of. But I *do* have the choice.

Choice is what I want to preserve. Other people may choose differently. I would like the choice to have a secret e-mail account for my special friends. Perhaps I'd like to join some communities under a false name, if only to avoid the assumptions people will make when they hear my real one. While anonymity gives other people the opportunity to annoy me and others, it also gives me the opportunity to avoid those annoyers.

What will I do when they start posting lies, not just to me but to the world at large? That's when it gets more troubling.

I hope I'll have the fortitude to live by what I say here. At the same time, I hope people in general start to get wiser. It's one thing to read a lie about yourself in the *New York Times,* another to read it in the *National Enquirer.* It's one thing when it's said by a friend you know, another when it's said by someone who doesn't even dare to publish his name. Why honor him with attention?

For Discussion:

1. What are the benefits and drawbacks of anonymity, according to Dyson?
2. Dyson argues that "While anonymity gives other people the opportunity to annoy [her] and others, it also gives [her] the opportunity to avoid those annoyers." Does the Internet connect or estrange people?
3. The anonymity on the Net opens up a world of fantasies and illusions. Is this illusionary world a threat for one's real identity, or do you see it as harmless?
4. L. Jean Camp and Y.T. Chien discuss the implications of the Internet as a public space. Do you see any connections between their argument and Dyson's? Should the Internet be a private, anonymous space or a public one?

For Fact-Finding, Research, and Writing

1. Use academic databases (rather than a general reference like ProQuest) to locate three articles about the Internet as a private and/or public space. What main issues do those articles cover?
2. Some people claim to be addicted to Internet chat groups. Is this addiction recognized by the American Psychological Association as an actual disease? Use both the Psych Info database and a general Internet search engine. What differences do you observe in the kinds of sources you were able to access?

Mark Manion and Abby Goodrum, "Terrorism or Civil Disobedience: Toward a Hacktivist Ethic"

Mark Manion is Assistant Professor and Director of the Philosophy program at Drexel University. His scholarly work investigates the ethics and politics of risk assessment, the social effects of technology, engineering ethics, the philosophy of technology, and crisis management. He is the co-author of *Minding the Machines: Preventing Technological Disasters*. Abby Goodrum is Assistant Professor in the School of Information Studies at Syracuse University. Her research interests include multimedia information systems and the social, political, and economic impact of new media technology.

Before You Read:

What do you think cyber-activism might be? What about cyber-terrorism?

Terrorism or Civil Disobedience: Toward a Hacktivist Ethic

Mark Manion
Abby Goodrum

Introduction

In this era of global commerce via the Internet, strikes against the hegemony of bureaucratic capitalism and the commercialization of the Internet will inevitably be carried out on the World Wide Web. In fact, recent proliferation of hacking activity has shocked the commercial Internet world. On February 8, 2000, hackers attacked Yahoo, Amazon, eBay, CNN and Buy.com, closing them for several hours. Through "denial of service" attacks originating from dozens of independent computers, the sites were flooded with millions of simultaneous requests. This increase in fake service requests effectively blocked legitimate users from accessing the site.

These hacks have led to widespread speculation regarding the motivation of the perpetrators. Are they mere nuisance attacks perpetrated by malicious teenagers, more serious acts of cyberterrorism, or evidence of growing outrage over an increasingly commodified Internet? Although at present no individuals or groups have officially claimed responsibility, MSNBC reported receipt of an 18-page letter claiming responsibility by an individual who angrily criticized the sites for their "capitalization of the Internet" (Kirby, 2000). Numerous reports in the popular press have portrayed the hackers as vandals, terrorists, and saboteurs, yet no one seems to have considered the possibility that this might be the work of electronic political activists or "hacktivists."

Perhaps these attacks are evidence of a new form of civil disobedience, which unites the talents of the computer hacker with the social consciousness of the political activist. Adapting a variation of civil disobedience, with its practices of "trespass" and "blockade" to the electronic age, participants in what has been called electronic civil disobedience, or hacktivism, can attack the Web sites of any individual, corporation, or nation that is deemed responsible for oppressing the ethical, social, or

---

political rights of others. Through an investigation of hacktivism, this essay seeks to make clear the growing tensions between the cooperative and liberal ideology of the originators of the "electronic frontier," speaking in the name of social justice, political decentralization, and freedom of information, and the more powerful counteracting moves to reduce the Internet to one grand global "electronic marketplace."

Hacktivism has the potential to play an active and constructive role in the overcoming of political injustice, to educate, inform, and be a genuine agent of positive political and social change. However, there is the fear that cyber-activism could reduce to more radical and violent forms of cyber-terrorism (Arquilla & Ronfeldt, 1993). How governments and societies react to this new form of social activism has not been sufficiently addressed in the computer ethics literature. Researchers concerned with ethical issues in computing, policy makers, and computer professionals must come to terms with the complex set of issues surrounding the potential power of hacktivism.

Background

Hacktivism is defined as the (sometimes) clandestine use of computer hacking to help advance political causes. Hacktivist groups such as the Electronic Disturbance Theater, the Cult of the Dead Cow, and the Hong Kong Blondes have used electronic civil disobedience to help advance the Zapatista rebellion in Mexico, protest nuclear testing at India's Bhabba Atomic Research Center, attack Indonesian Government Web sites over the occupation of East Timor, as well as protest anti-democratic crackdowns in China. In addition, hacktivism has been used to inveigh against the corporate domination of telecommunications and mass media, the rapid expansion of dataveillance, and the hegemonic intrusion of the "consumer culture" into the private lives of average citizens.

These concerns give rise to two institutional forces that hacktivist protests aim to confront: the commodification of the Internet at the hands of corporate profiteers and violations of human rights at the hands of oppressive governments. Hacktivism thus poses a potential threat at two levels: the private industry/intellectual property level and the national government/national security level. Both of these issues will be discussed in this paper.

Electronic Civil Disobedience

Civil disobedience entails the peaceful breaking of unjust laws. It does not condone violent or destructive acts against its enemies, focusing instead on nonviolent means to expose wrongs, raise awareness, and prohibit the implementation of perceived unethical laws by individuals, organizations, corporations, or governments. In a civil society, it is the responsibility of all ethical individuals to take a stand against oppression, inequality, and injustice (Honderich, 1997). Civil disobedience is a technique of resistance and protest whose purpose is to achieve social or political change by drawing attention to problems and influencing public opinion. Breaking specific laws, which are unjust, constitutes *direct* acts of civil disobedience. *Symbolic* acts of civil disobedience are accomplished by drawing attention to a problem indirectly. Sit-ins and other forms of blockade and trespass are examples of *symbolic* acts of civil disobedience.

The Internet has created a brave new world of digital activism by providing forums for organizing, communicating, publishing, and taking direct action. The use of the computer as a tool of civil disobedience has been termed Electronic Civil Disobedience (ECD) (Wray, 1998). Electronic civil disobedience comes in many forms, ranging from conservative acts such as sending email and publishing Web sites, to breaking into computer systems. A distinction must be made between the use of computers to *support* ECD and the use of computers as an *act* of ECD. If a U.S. citizen wishes to speak out against the government's actions in Kosovo, it is legal to publish a Web site or host mailing lists or chat rooms for this purpose. This activity does not constitute an act of civil disobedience, electronic or otherwise. These types of activity are usually referred to as "electronic activism," which uses the Internet in fully legitimate ways to publish information, to coordinate effective action, and to directly lobby policy makers. Running a computer program such as FloodNet, however, that posts the reload command to a Web site hundreds of times a minute constitutes an act of symbolic ECD since the intended aim of such programs is to create an electronic disturbance akin to a sit-in or blockade.

The effect of hundreds of persons reloading targeted page on the Internet thousands of times effectively blocks entrance by outsiders and may even shut down the server, as occurred in the attacks on the commercial Web sites of Yahoo, Amazon, etc. In 1998, pro-Zapatista activists took this kind of action against Mexican government Web sites (Cleaver, 1999). This is easily seen as a symbolic act of ECD because it tries to draw attention to a perceived violation of rights, rather than attacking the suspected violator(s) directly. The purpose of most ECD is to disrupt the flow of information into and out of institutional computer systems. The point is not to destroy information or systems but to block access temporarily. This results in virtual sit-ins and virtual blockades. Since institutions today are no longer localized in physical structures but exist in the decentralized zones of cyberspace, electronic blockades can cause financial stress that physical blockades cannot (Critical Art Ensemble, 1994).

The changing nature of authoritative and repressive power has necessitated qualitative changes in resistance to this power. Power/Capital, having constituted itself in a new electronic form in cyberspace, requires that opposition movements have to invent new strategies and tactics that counter this new "nomadic" power of capital. This entails that certain old ways of trespass and blockade—such as street demonstrations—are being modified through electronic civil disobedience, or hacktivism, to meet the new conditions (Critical Art Ensemble, 1996).

Hacktivism and Electronic Civil Disobedience

Nothing has fired debate about ECD so heatedly as the issue of hacktivism. The central question is whether hacking can reasonably be defined as an act of civil disobedience. Now the refusal to obey governmental commands, even if it entails breaking the law, is often morally sanctioned if certain preconditions are met. Even though philosophers often disagree as to when the breaking of a law actually constitutes an act of civil disobedience, most would agree on the following set of core principles as forming the necessary conditions, and hence ethical justification, for acts considered civilly disobedient. They are:

- No damage done to persons or property
- Non-violent
- Not for personal profit
- Ethical motivation—i.e., the strong conviction that a law is unjust, unfair, or to the extreme detriment of the common good
- Willingness to accept personal responsibility for outcome of actions

Are acts of hacktivism consistent with the philosophy of civil disobedience? In order for hacking to qualify as an act of civil disobedience, hackers must be clearly motivated by ethical concerns, be non-violent, and be ready to accept the repercussions of their actions. Examined in this light, the hack by Eugene Kashpureff clearly constitutes an act of ECD. Kashpureff usurped traffic from InterNIC to protest domain name policy. He did this non-anonymously and went to jail as a result. Further evidence of ethical motivation for hacktivism can also be seen in the messages left behind at hacked sites (Harmon, 1998):

- "China's people have no rights at all, never mind human rights . . ."
- "Save Kashmir" overlaid with the words "massacre" and "extra-judicial execution."
- "Free East Timor" with hypertext links to Web sites describing Indonesian human rights abuses in the former Portuguese colony.

In order to justify hacktivism's direct action praxis and to legitimate its theoretical foundations, two things must be demonstrated. First, it must be shown that hacktivism is not the work of curious teenagers with advanced technical expertise and a curiosity for infiltrating large computer networks for mere intellectual challenge or sophomoric bravado. Moreover, the justification of hacktivism entails demonstrating that its practitioners are neither "crackers"—those who break into systems for profit or vandalism (Anonymous, 1998), nor are they cyberterrorists—those who use computer technology with the intention of causing grave harm such as loss of life, severe economic losses, or destruction of critical infrastructure (Denning, 1999). Hacktivism must be shown to be ethically motivated. Second, politicized hacking must be shown to be some form of civil disobedience—a form of civil disobedience that is morally justified. In order to determine the motivations of hacktivists, one place to look is what hacktivists *themselves* say is their motivation.

On October 12, 1998, the Web site of Mexican president Erenesto Zedillo was attacked. From all accounts, the Zedillo hack was not the work of bored teens. It was a political act, according to the Electronic Disturbance Theatre, to "demonstrate continued resistance to centuries of colonization, genocide, and racism in the western hemisphere and throughout the world" (Harmon, 1998). Earlier, in August of the same year, the hacktivist group "X-Ploit" hacked the Web site of Mexico's finance ministry, defacing it by replacing the contents with the face of the revolutionary hero Emiliano Zapata, in sympathy with the Zapatista rebellion in the Chiapas region of southern Mexico. These acts are political protests, which draw attention to what is perceived to be grave social injustice. The reason for these actions is clear. They are motivated by a socio-economic system that perpetuates discrimination, racism, and economic inequality, not the mere thrill and challenge of breaking into computer networks for fun.

In June of 1998, the hacktivist group "MilwOrm" hacked India's Bhabba Atomic Research Centre to protest against recent nuclear tests. Later, in July of that year, "MilwOrm" and the group "Astray Lumberjacks" orchestrated an unprecedented mass hack of more than 300 sites around the world, replacing web pages with anti-nuclear statements and images of mushroom clouds. Not surprisingly, the published slogan of MilwOrm reads: "Putting the power back in the hands of the people" (Hesseldahl, 1999). These examples seem to be motivated by belief in the positive forces of democracy and freedom rather than the mere thrill of vandalism or the nihilism of "cyberterrorism."

Mail-bombs were delivered and several Chinese government Web sites were hacked to protest the targeting of Chinese and Indonesian citizens for torture, rape, and looting during the anti-Suharto riot in May of 1998 (Hesseldhal, 1999). On August 1, the Portuguese group "Kaotik Team" hacked 45 Indonesian government Web sites, altering web pages to include calling for full autonomy of East Timor and the cessation of the harsh military crackdown on dissidents (Hesseldhal, 1999). Again, fighting for social justice and human rights is motivated by ethics, not anarchy. Many other hacktivist activities can be sited to demonstrate the ethical motivation behind this new form of political activism.

These messages, and many others like them, demonstrate a striking change from hacker messages of the past. Prior hacks have had little if any socio-political content and bear a closer resemblance to "tagging" and other forms of boasting graffiti. There has been a certain juvenile style to messages left by hackers in the past. The hacks listed above, however, represent a new breed of hacker, one who is clearly motivated by the advancement of ethical concerns and who believes such actions should be considered a legitimate form of (electronic) civil disobedience.

Hacktivism and Cyberterrorism

If hacktivism can be defined as an act of electronic civil disobedience, then the punitive outcomes must be brought into alignment with other forms of civil disobedience. Traditional penalties for civil disobedience are mild compared to penalties for hacking. Penalties for hacktivism are meted out with the same degree of force as for hacking in general, regardless of the motivation for the hack or the political content of messages left at hacked sites. Most governments do not recognize hacking as a political activity, and the penalties for breaking into computers can be extreme (Jaconi, 1999). For example, the hack of China's "Human Rights" Web site by the Hong Kong Blondes, attacks on Indonesian Government Web sites regarding policy in Kashmir, attacks on India's nuclear weapons research center Web sites to protest nuclear testing, as well as the hacks on the commercial Web sites of Yahoo, CNN, etc. are all subject to felony prosecution if apprehended. All of these examples provide convincing evidence in support of our thesis that hacktivism should be considered a legitimate form of civil disobedience, and not the work of "cybervandals" or "cyberterrorists." Under U.S. law, terrorism is defined as an act of violence for the purpose of intimidating or coercing a government or civilian population. Hacktivism clearly does not fall into this category, as it is fundamentally non-violent.

Since many acts of hacktivism have been perpetuated against government Web sites, however, hacktivism is increasingly being equated with acts of information warfare and cyberterrorism (Kovacich 1997, Furnell & Warren 1999). In August of 1998, the Center for Intrusion Control was established by a coalition of various government agencies to respond to these "cyber-warfare threats" (Glave 1998b). Similarly, organizations such as RAND and the National Security Agency (NSA) have categorically denied the existence of hacktivism as an act of civil disobedience and repeatedly refer to all acts of hacking as cyberwar or cyberterrorism in an attempt to push for stronger penalties for hacking, regardless of ethical motivations (Bowers 1998, Gompert 1998).

In order to determine the kinds and range of threats to its critical infrastructures posed by possible cyberterrorists, the U.S. government established the President's Commission on Critical Infrastructure Protection (PCCIP) in 1996. The PCCIP findings have led to the development of the National Infrastructure Protection Center (NIPC), the Critical Infrastructure Assurance Office (CIA), the National Infrastructure Assurance Council (NIAC), and the Joint Task-Force Computer Network Defense (JTF-CND), established by the Department of Defense. The development and findings of these research centers imply that the threat posed by cyberterrorism is very real. That much is clear. However, it is a mistake to identify hacktivism with cyberterrorism. As we have established above, acts of hacktivism are more akin to acts of civil disobedience than to acts of terrorism, and it is important to keep this distinction clear.

In fact, potential acts of cyberterrorism are explicitly condemned by hacktivists. During a December 1998 press conference, one member of a hacktivist group, which calls itself the Legion of the Underground (LoU), declared "cyberwar" on the information infrastructures of China and Iraq. This declaration of war prompted a coalition of hacktivist groups to condemn the "declaration or war" as "irresponsible." In a "Joint Statement by 2600, The Chaos Computer Club, The Cult of the Dead Cow, !Hispahack, LOpht Heavy Industries, Phrack and Pulhas," the leaders of the hacktivist community denounced the LoU declaration of war, saying

> *We strongly oppose any attempt to use the power of hacking to threaten or destroy the information infrastructure of any country, for any reason. Declaring 'war' against anyone, any group of people, or any nation is a most deplorable act . . . this has nothing to do with hacktivism or the hacker ethic and is nothing a hacker can be proud of (Hackernews, 12/29/98).*

This immediately prompted a quick response from the leaders of LoU who issued a statement saying that the declaration of war did not represent the position of the group. The letter states:

> *The LoU does not support the damaging of other nations' computers, network or systems in any way, nor will the LoU use their skills, abilities or connections to take any actions against the systems, network or computers in China or Iraq which may damage or hinder in any way their operations. (Hackernews, 01/ 799).*

Why is it, then, that a growing number of experts refuse to make this distinction, and insist on conflating hacktivism and cyberterrorism? It may be that describing hacktivists as criminals helps entrench a certain conception of, and control over, intellectual property, and obscures the larger critique about the ownership of information, and the legal system's need to protect the powerful economic interests of corporations attempting to dominate and completely commercialize the Internet. Moreover, labeling the hacktivist as a national security threat provides further legitimation for the erasure of individual privacy at the hands of the national security state, which compiles and stores vast databases on hundreds of thousands of citizens each year. The demonization of the hacker may also be an attempt to obscure the violation of our privacy at the hands of corporations. As one critic put it,

> *Through the routine gathering of information about transactions, consumer preferences, and creditworthiness, a harvest of information about an individual's whereabouts and movements, tastes, desires, contacts, friends, associates, and patterns of work and recreation become available in the form of dossiers sold on the tradable information market, or is endlessly convertible into other forms of intelligence through computer matching. Advanced pattern recognition technologies facilitate the process of surveillance, while data encryption protects it from public accountability" (Ross, 1998).*

Hence, one rationalization for the vilification of hacktivism is the need for the power elite to rewrite property law in order to contain the effects of the new information technologies. As a result of the newly evolving intellectual property laws, information and knowledge can now be held as capital. Since new information technology supports easy reproduction of information, the existence of these laws effectively curtails the widest possible spread of this new form of wealth. In addition, unlike material objects, information can be shared widely without running out. As two experts put it

> *Intellectual property is not a tangible, material entity. It is nothing more than a volatile pattern of electrons arrayed in patterns of open and closed gates to form intelligible numerical or textual symbols. Information, documents, and data reside inside computers in a form that can be 'stolen' without ever being removed, indeed without ever being touched by a would-be thief, or depriving the 'owner' from still using and profiting off of the 'property' (Michalowski and Pfuhl, 1991).*

Although the information inside of computers is clearly of value, the form of this value is both intangible and novel. According to Michalowski and Pfuhl, its character as "property" remained legally ambiguous until a rapid proliferation of computer crime laws took place in order to create the legal environment that helped define and delimit the debate over the nature of intellectual property. These laws and rulings ultimately served to protect the immediate financial interests of the corporate techno-elite and directed the state to protect the profit potential of telecommunications industries, financial investors, and entrepreneurs capitalizing on the Internet.

Ironically, the rapid proliferation of computer laws during the 1980s, which saw 47 states enact computer crime laws, as well as two Congressional pieces of computer crime legislation, which entered the legal system at the same time, resulted in relatively few arrests or prosecutions. For example, "Operation Sundial," the largest Secret Service sting on suspected hackers, which took place during the first week of May, 1990, led to no serious charges. A few hackers pled guilty and paid a total of $233,000 in fines, and spent 14 months in jail (Halbert, 1997). This rapid criminalization of computer abuse represents, moreover, an exception to the gradual and reformist nature of typical law formation in common law jurisdiction (Hollinger and Lanza-Kaduce, 1998). Michalowski and Pfuhl conclude from this that "the violations of computer security posed a broad challenge to the hegemonic construction of property and authority relations, and it was this challenge, more than the concrete losses resulting from unauthorized computer access, that created a climate of fear about computer crime that led to the swift and non-controversial passage of computer crime laws" (Michalowski and Pfuhl, 1991).

The power elite, often synergistically intertwined with the design and operation of information technologies, will always come to the aid and defense of technologies of control, making revolt difficult and reform hard. Intellectual property laws attest to this, as do the excessively stringent laws against hacktivism. Nevertheless, if we say we support civil disobedience as a legitimate form of social protest, then we must support the computerization of these efforts as well. This means bringing penalties for hacktivism, or electronic civil disobedience, in line with penalties for traditional mechanisms used for the breaking of what are perceived to be unjust laws.

Toward a Hacktivist Ethic

Every technology affords opposing possibilities towards emancipation or domination, and information technology is no different. The new information technologies are often portrayed as the utopian promise of total human emancipation and freedom. However, the promise of freedom from work, e-democracy, and global community, once hailed as the hallmarks of the computer revolution, are nowhere to be found. As critics are quick to point out, the only entities that seem to largely benefit from the Internet are large transnational business corporations.

For such critics, advanced information technology threatens to turn into an Orwellian nightmare of totalitarian domination and control, a dystopia of complete repression of free thought. They remind us that the Internet is quickly becoming subordinated to the pecuniary interests of the techno-elite, which merely pays lip service to the growth of electronic communities and participatory democracy. In reality, these interests are devoted to shutting down the anarchy of the Net in favor of virtualized commercial exchange. Hence, the power elite must destroy the public cyber-sphere for its own survival. This may account for the vilification of hacktivists, as well as why the charges against hacktivism are so high.

As is well known, however, the lifeblood of the hacker ethic has always been the freedom of information and the full democratization of the public sphere. The core principles of the hacker ethic were spelled out in Steven Levy's book, *Hackers: Heroes of the Computer Revolution* (Levy, 1984). Three of these principles are relevant here. They are:

1. Access to computers—and anything that might teach you something about the way the world works—should be unlimited and total. Always yield to the Hands-On Imperative!
2. All information should be free
3. Mistrust Authority—Promote Decentralization

Hacktivists prioritize freedom of information and are suspicious of centralized control over, or private ownership of, information. Hackers question why a few corporations can own and sell huge databases of information about others, as well as control information helpful to the public at large. Hackers are frustrated to discover that their coveted "electronic agora," a true marketplace for the free-play of ideas, which was the original ideal behind the formation of the Internet, has been invaded and taken over by avaricious and enterprising entrepreneurs who prefer dollars to the free-flow of information and knowledge. In sum, this ethic puts hackers in direct confrontation with the commercial-industrial complex who wish to own and control the Internet.

One of the most powerful positions against the panoptical intentions of the "Captains of Technology" is demonstrating that their system does not work. Every successful hack in some way reinforces the popular perception that the rise of the total panoptic surveillance society is not inevitable. Hence, the hacker ethic, libertarian and anarchist in its right-to-know principles and its advocacy of decentralized technology, is a principled attempt to challenge the tendency to use technology to form information elites.

The debate over the control of intellectual property demands that we address issues of social justice, such as wealth distribution and equality of opportunity. Politically, the resistance to corporate domination of the Internet must force not only the question of privacy and property, but it must also place the critique of the technological society itself into the center of pubic consciousness and debate. Hacktivist activities put theses issues of techno-control on the political agenda by performing acts of electronic civil disobedience.

Furthermore, resistance to political oppression and corporate manipulation must be embedded in a well-articulated theory, one that is morally informed and widely shared. Movements acting out of outrage often dissipate. They need to be durable and sustain a commitment, lasting through adversities of repression. This leads to the necessity of creating a form of technocultural activism that can bring to reality the ideals of human emancipation. Activism today is no longer a case of putting bodies on the picket line; it requires putting minds and virtual bodies "online." This is the promise of hacktivism, the fusion of the political consciousness of the activist with the technical expertise of the computer "hacker."

Conclusion

Hacktivism, is in its infancy, but, given the ubiquity and democratizing possibility of the Internet, we will certainly bear witness to the movement's growing pains and increasing maturity. One thing is sure, however. Incidents of cyberactivism are on the rise and will continue to be on the rise in the near future.

Never in the long and storied history of political and social activism have dissidents had at their disposal a tool as far-reaching and potentially effective as the Internet. Sadly, this inherently civil strategy of ECD is being deliberately and officially misconstrued through mis-information as cyberterrorism, which it is clearly not. Steps must be taken to separate political direct action in cyberspace from organized criminality or cyberterrorism.

When is it legitimate to practice direct action protest on the Internet? Some will inevitably argue that electronic civil disobedience is never justifiable, while others will argue that it is always justified. What are the limits of political protest in cyberspace? How far can activists go without infringing on the legitimate rights of the people and institutions against whom they are protesting? These questions demand a more extensive argument that extends beyond the scope of this essay. One thing is clear, however. In order for hacktivism to become a legitimate form of social protest, it must be provided sound ethical foundations. This, in turn, means expanding the ethical justification of civil disobedience to include acts of hacktivism.

References

Anonymous, (1998). "The language of hacking," *Management Review* 87 (9), pp. 18–21.

Arquilla, J. and Ronfeldt, D. (1993), "Cyberwar is coming," *Comparative Strategy*, Volume 12, no. 2, 141–165.

Bowers, S. (1998). "Information warfare: the computer revolution is altering how future wars will be conducted," *Armed Forces Journal International*, August, pp. 38–49.

Cleaver, H. (1998). "The Zapatistas and the electronic fabric of struggle," www.eco.utexas.edu/faculty/Cleaver/zaps.htm (accessed 5/18/99)

Critical Art Ensemble. (1996). *Electronic civil disobedience and other unpopular ideas*. Brooklyn, NY: Autonomedia.

Critical Art Ensemble. (1994). *The electronic disturbance*. Brooklyn, NY: Autonomedia.

Denning, Dorothy (1999). "Activism, Hacktivism, and Cyberterrorism: The Internet as a Tool for Influencing Foreign Policy," paper presented at the Internet and International Systems: Information Technology and American Foreign Policy Decisionmaking Workshop, Georgetown University, Washington, D.C.

Furnell, S. & Warren, M. (1999). "Computer hacking and cyberterrorism: The real threats in the new millennium," *Computers & Security*, 18, 28–34.

Glave, J. (1998). "Hacker raises stakes in DOD attacks," *Wired News*, available at: http://www.wirednews.com

Gompert, D. (1998). "National security in the information age," *Naval War College Review*, 51 (4), pp. 22–41.

Hackernews, available at http://www.hackernews.com/archive.html

Halbert, D. (1997). "Discourses of danger and the computer hacker," *The Information Society*, 13, 361–374.

Harmon, A. (1998). "Hacktivists of all persuasions take their struggle to the web," *The New York Times*, October 31, 1998, page I column 5.

Hollinger, R. and Lanza-Kaduce, L. (1988). "The process of criminalization: The case of computer crime laws," *Criminology* 26 (1), pp. 101–26.

Honderich, T. (1997). "Hierarchic democracy and the necessity of mass civil disobedience," in Bontekoe, R. ed. *Justice and democracy: cross-cultural perspectives*. University of Hawaii Press: Honolulu.

Hesseldahl, Arik (1999). "Hacking for Human Rights?," *Wired News*, 21 May. Available at: http://www.wirednews.com/news/news/politics/story/13693.html.

Jaconi, J. (1999). Federal cybercrime law, Section 1030 "Computer Fraud & Abuse Act," www.antionline.com (accessed 6/17/99)

Kirby, Carie (2000). "Net hackers strike again," *The San Francisco Chronicle*, February 9, p. A1.

Kovacich, G. (1997). "Information warfare and the information systems security professional," *Computers & Security*, 16, 14–24.

Levy, Stephen (1984). *Hackers: computer heroes of the computer revolution,* New York: Delta Trade Paperbacks.

Michalowski, R. and Pfuhl, E. (1991). "Technology, property and law: The case of computer crime," *Crime Law and Social Change* 15 (3), pp. 255–275.

Ross, Andrew (1998). "Hacking away at the counterculture," in *Technoculture,* Penley and Ross. Eds. Minneapolis: University of Minnesota Press.

Wray, S. (1998). "Electronic civil disobedience and the word wide web of hacktivism: a mapping of extraparliamentarian direct action net politics," available at: http://www.nyu.edu/projects/wray/wwwhack.html

 For Discussion:

1. How does this article change your perception of the hacker? Can hackers be agents of social change, or do they always represent a threat to the private and national security?

2. How do the authors define the Hacktivist? How do they differentiate the Hacktivist from the cyber-terrorist?

3. What is ECD? How does ECD unite the "talents of the computer hacker and the social consciousness of the political activist"? What are the methods and goals of ECD?

4. Manion and Goodrum refer consistently to the idea of the "corporate techno-elite," whom they see as more of threat to the Internet than hacktivists. What are the "corporate techno-elite" and what types of threat do they pose to information technology? How can hacktivists combat the power of the techno-elite?

 For Fact-Finding, Discussion, and Writing:

1. Using either an EBSCO or Proquest search, find a newspaper or magazine article that covers a recent hacker attack. Does the article portray the hacker attack as Hacktivism?

2. Find the actual text of a law referring to computer hacking.

3. Daniel Ellsberg committed acts of civil disobedience during the Vietnam War that could be considered that era's version of computer hacking. What were these acts? Do you think they were similar to hacking, as Manion and Goodrum define it?

Lucas Introna, "Workplace Surveillance, Privacy, and Distributive Justice"

Lucas Introna is currently Visiting Professor of Information Systems at the University of Pretoria. He is Associate Editor of *Information Technology & People*, and Co-Editor of *Ethics and Information Technology*. Introna is interested in the social dimension of information technology and its consequences for society, and in the way information technology mediates social interaction. His publications and academic papers cover topics such as virtual organizations, theories of information, and information technology.

 Before You Read:

What do you think about work surveillance? Does it impede on one's privacy?

Workplace Surveillance, Privacy, and Distributive Justice

Lucas D. Introna

Introduction

Surveillance has become a central issue in our late modern society. The surveillance of public spaces by closed circuit television, the surveillance of consumers through consumer surveys and point of sale technology, and workplace surveillance, to name but a few. As surveillance increases, more and more questions are being raised about its legitimacy. In this paper I want to focus on one of the more problematic areas of surveillance, namely workplace surveillance. There is no doubt that the extensive use of information technology in all organisational processes has created enormous potential for cheap, implicit, and diffused surveillance, surveillance that is even more 'close' and continuous than any human supervisor could be. The extent of current surveillance practices are reflected in the following indicators:

■   Forty-five percent of major U.S. firms record and review employee communications and activities on the job, including their phone calls, e-mail, and computer files. Additional forms of monitoring and surveillance, such as review of phone logs or videotaping for security purposes, bring the overall figure on electronic oversight to 67.3% (American Management Association 1999).

▪ Piller (1993) reported in a *MacWorld* survey of 301 business that 22% of the business have searched employee computer files, voice mail, e-mail, or other networking communications. The percentage jumped to 30% for business with 1000 or more employees.

▪ The International Labour Office (1993) estimates that some 20 million Americans may be subject to electronic monitoring on the job, *not including telephone monitoring.*

▪ In 1990 it was reported that up to one million jobs in Britain are subject to security checks (Lyon 1994, p. 131).

It would be reasonable to say that these formal surveys do not reflect the actual practice. It would also be reasonable to assume that organisations would not tend to publicise the degree to which they engage in systematic monitoring. Surveillance often functions as a resource for the execution of power, and power is most effective when it hides itself. One can imagine that the vast majority of organisations engage in anything from isolated incidents of specific monitoring to large-scale systematic monitoring.

The purpose of this paper is not to bemoan surveillance as such. I believe it is rather more important to understand the context and logic of surveillance in the workplace. In this paper I will argue that the real issue of workplace surveillance is justice as fairness. I will argue that it is the inherent political possibilities of surveillance that concerns employees, that they simply do not trust the interested gaze of management, and they have very good reason for such mistrust. Finally I will discuss the possibility of using Rawls' theory of justice to establish a framework for distributing the rights of privacy and transparency between the individual (employee) and the institution (the employer).

Resisting Workplace Surveillance

In the second half of the twentieth century, two major trends seem to create the background for our contemporary discussion of workplace surveillance. The first of these are the increasing challenges by the employees of their conditions of work, especially the normalising practices of discipline. The social revolution of Marxism and later of liberal democracy trickled into the production floor. Initially as labour became increasingly unionised, the debate about surveillance became articulated as a conflict between labour and capital in the Marxist idiom. Later workers demanded rights in the workplace they were already accorded elsewhere. Modern management increasingly needed to justify its surveillance practices. A second trend that intensified the debate was the rapid development of surveillance technology that created unprecedented possibilities for comprehensive surveillance. With the new technology, surveillance became less overt and more diffused. In fact, it became built into the very machinery and processes of production (workflow systems, keystroke monitoring, telephone accounting, etc.). This increasingly 'silent' and diffused potential of surveillance technology also started to concern policy makers, unions, social activists, and the like. However, in spite of their best efforts, and considerable progress in the establishment of liberal democracy in Western society, the balance of power is still firmly in the hands of the employer. The United States Congress' Office of Technology Assessment report (U.S. Congress 1987) into employee monitoring concludes that *"employers have considerable latitude in making use of new monitoring technologies; they have generally been considered merely extensions of traditional management prerogatives"* (p. 6). Even today there exists very little enacted legislation in Western democracies that articulate the fair use of workplace monitoring[1] (U.S. Congress 1987, Appendix A). I would argue that that one of the reasons for this lack of adequate protection may be the inappropriate way in which the workplace monitoring debate has developed (I will address this in detail in the next section).

In the United States, the right of the employer to conduct workplace surveillance as a means to protect the employer's interest to organise work, select technology, set production standards, and manage the use of facilities and other resources is recognised by the law. This means that there is no legal obligation on employees to ensure that "monitoring be 'fair', that jobs be well designed or that employees be consulted about work standards, except insofar as these points are addressed in union contracts . . ." (U.S. Congress 1987, p. 2). As less than 20% of office work in the US is unionised, it seems that decisions about work monitoring are made solely at the discretion of employers.

Recent legal developments seem to confirm this asymmetry of power. For example, in the area of e-mail monitoring, the right to use surveillance of communications technology supplied for business purposes has been confirmed in the Electronic Communications Privacy Act of 1986 ("ECPA"). Essentially the ECPA expanded preexisting prohibitions on the unauthorised interception of wire and oral communications to encompass other forms of electronic communications. However, the ECPA does not guarantee a right to e-mail privacy in the workplace because of three very important exceptions. I will just focus on two here. The first is the *business extension* or ordinary course of business exception. This exception allows the employer to monitor any communications that use communications technology supplied to the employee in the ordinary course of business for use in conducting the ordinary course of business. This means that the telephone or the e-mail account supplied to an employee to conduct their work can legally be monitored as long as the monitoring can be justified as having a valid business purpose (Dichter and Burkhardt 1996, p. 14). The second is the *consent exception*. This exception allows monitoring in those cases where prior consent has been obtained. It is important to note that implied consent is also recognised by the law. Employers who notify employees that their telephone conversations or e-mail is likely to be monitored will have the implied consent of their employees (Santarelli 1997). It also seems as if common law does not provide any correction in the balance of power. In common law the decision of permissibility hinges on the notion of a "reasonable expectation of privacy." This may mean, for example, that if an employee is provided with a space to store personal belongings, or a particular phone line for personal calls, it would be reasonable for them to expect it not to be monitored. Johnson (1995) and others have remarked that this expectation of privacy can easily be removed by an explicit policy that all communication using company equipment can and will be subjected to monitoring.

From this brief discussion it is clear that it would be fairly easy for employers to monitor all aspects of work and communications (on equipment made available for ordinary business use) as long as the employer explicitly communicates policy that monitoring can take place, and that the employer can justify it for a valid business purpose. It is hard to imagine what sort of monitoring—excluding some extreme cases—can not be defended as being for a valid business purpose (productivity, company moral, safety, etc). It is also hard to imagine what sort of resources an individual employee can use to generate a 'reasonable expectation of privacy' in a context where accepting an employment contract also means accepting the policies of the organisation and thereby relinquishing the right to a "reasonable expectation of privacy"—assuming there is an explicit monitoring policy. In the context of the typical asymmetry of power present in such employment situations, it is hardly a matter of choice. It is clear, and acknowledged by many, that the current US climate is heavily biased in favour of the employer.[2] The lack of legislation in other countries would also indicate that it would be reasonable to conclude that workplace monitoring is still largely viewed as a right of employers with the burden of proof on the employee to show that it is invasive, unfair, or stressful. It would seem that a legal correction in the imbalance of power is not likely to be forthcoming in the near future.

In spite of this imbalance of power, surveillance has not become a widespread practice, as one would assume (U.S. Congress 1987, p. 31). In addition, it seems that where surveillance is operating, it is not always challenged to the degree that one would assume (U.S. Congress 1987, p. 31). Why is this so? It seems that there is not sufficient evidence to suggest surveillance of *individuals* would lead to *long term* productivity improvements. To use Denning's well known quality dictum (revised accordingly): productivity is not merely a matter of surveillance, but is rather an emerging element of a system designed for productivity as a whole. There is also accumulating evidence that surveillance of *individuals* lead to stress, a lost of sense of dignity, and a general environment of mistrust. In this environment of mistrust employees tend to act out their employer's expectations of them—thereby eradicating any benefit that the surveillance may have had (Marx 1986; U.S. Congress 1987). Furthermore, I believe surveillance is not always challenged because we all at times benefit from its fruits. For example, the use of surveillance data for performance assessment can result in a more equitable treatment of employees. Such data can provide evidence to prevent unfair allocation of blame. It would be possible to think of many ways in which employees may use surveillance for their own benefit, such as "the boss can see on the CCTV that I do actually work many hours overtime," and the like.

Like power, surveillance "passes through the hands of the mastered no less than through the hands of the masters" (Foucault 1977). It does not only bear down upon us as a burden but also produces possibilities and resources for action that can serve multiple interests. Surveillance is no longer an unambiguous tool for control and social certainty, nor is it merely a weight that weighs down on the employee—rather its logic and its effects has become increasingly difficult to see clearly and distinctly. Surveillance, with modernity, has lost its shine.

In the next section, I want to consider the relationship between surveillance and autonomy and indicate its link with justice. This will provide the background for the following section where I will develop a framework for distributing the rights of privacy and transparency between the individual and the collective.

Privacy as a Matter of Justice

Privacy is by no means an uncontroversial issue. Some, like Posner (1978), tend to see the need for privacy as a way of hiding or covering up what ought to be exposed for scrutiny. He argues that exposure through surveillance would provide a more solid basis for social interaction because the participants will be able to discern all the facts of the matter for themselves. Privacy, for him, creates opportunities for hiding information that could render many social interactions "fraudulent." To interact with someone without providing that person with all information would be to socially defraud that person, or so he argues. This is a very compelling argument, which has made Posner's paper one of the canons in the privacy literature. As such, it provides a good starting point for our discussion.

At the root of Posner's argument—and the argument for surveillance in general—is the fundamental flaw of the modernity's belief in surveillance as a neutral gaze, as a sound basis for certainty—for knowing that we know. Surveillance can only fulfill its role as guarantor of certainty if it is complete and comprehensive—in short, omnipresent—and if it can be done from a vantage point where all things are of equal or no value—which is impossible. If these conditions can be fulfilled, then Posner's argument will be valid. However, once surveillance looses its omnipresent and value free status—which it never had in the first place—it no longer deals with facts but rather with values and interests. Science becomes politics—as it has been from the beginning (Latour 1987; Latour and Woolgar 1986 [1979]). Knowing is replaced by choosing. We have to select what to survey, and most importantly, we have to select how to value what we find in our surveillance.

Employees do not fear the transparency of surveillance, as such, in the way argued by Posner. It is rather the choices, both explicit and implicit, that the employers will by necessity be making that employees mistrust. They are concerned that these choices may only reflect the interests of the employer. They are rightly concerned that the employer will only have 'part of the picture', and that they may be reduced, in subsequent judgements, to that 'part of the picture' alone. They are also concerned that employers will apply inappropriate values when judging this 'part of the picture.' More than this, they will also be concerned by the fact that employers may implicitly and unbeknowingly bring into play a whole lot of other 'parts' of pictures that ought not be considered in that *particular context*—for example, judging a particular employee candidate for promotion or not because it is also known that the employee is a Muslim. They are concerned because we can not, contrary to the modern mind, separate out what 'pictures' we take into account or not when making judgements, *in the act of judging itself* (Merleau-Ponty 1962).

We are entangled and immersed in our values and beliefs to the point that they are merely there, available for use, part of the background that we do not explicitly attend to in making actual judgements (Heidegger 1962 [1937]). It is part of our thrownness (*Befindlichkeit*). It is therefore fruitless to posit that we should or should not apply particular data or particular values in making a particular judgment. We can simply not say to what degree we did or did not allow our judgement to become influenced by certain facts and certain value dispositions in making a particular judgement. The facts and values are not like fruits in a basket before us from which we can select, by rational choice, to take some and not others. We are immersed, engrossed, and entangled in our world in ways that would not normally make us explicitly attend to the particular facts, values, and interests that we draw upon in making particular judgements. We can of course attempt to make them explicit as bureaucracies and scientific management tried to do. However, Dreyfus (1992; 1986) has shown that skilled actors do not normally draw upon these explicit representations *in action*. Foucault (Foucault 1977) has also shown that these explicit representations are more important as resources for the play of power than resources for 'objective' judgements, which is exactly why employees mistrust them.

To conclude: It is the very political possibilities of surveillance, in the data selected, the values applied, the interest served, and the implicit and entangled nature of the judgement process, which makes employees—and persons in general—have a default position of mistrust rather than trust in 'exposing' themselves. It is this untrustworthy nature of judgements—of the products of surveillance—that moved Johnson (Johnson 1989) to define privacy as the right to the "freedom from the judgement of others." It is also this untrustworthy nature of judgements that made the OTA report argue that they view the issue of fairness as the most central issue of workplace monitoring. Fairness, as the levelling of the playing field, as serving all interests, not only the few.

Thus, the issue of workplace privacy is not merely a matter of 'bad' employees wanting to hide their unscrupulous behaviour behind a call for privacy (undoubtedly this is the case in some instances); it is rather a legitimate concern for justice in a

244 - Chapter Three

context in which the employees are, for the most part, in a relationship of severe power asymmetry. I would therefore argue that the development of the workplace privacy debate will be best served if it is developed along the lines of *fairness and organisational justice* rather than along the lines of a general notion of privacy as a matter of some personal space. The personal dignity and autonomy argument can so easily be seen as personal lifestyle choices that have no place in the public workplace as expressed by Cozzetto and Pedeliski (1999) in their paper on workplace monitoring: *"Autonomy embraces areas of central life choice and lifestyle that are important in terms of individual expression, but irrelevant to an employer and of no public concern."* I believe many employers and authors in the field find the concept of workplace privacy problematic because they link it to the general debates on privacy that are often cast exclusively in the mould of personal dignity and autonomy. This leads to claims of irrelevance. As one employer expressed it in the Canadian Information and Privacy Commissioner's (IPC) report (1993) on workplace privacy. *"The paper overstates this issue as a problem of pressing concern for employees and employers and the general public . . . the IPC is making more of an issue out of this, and looking for problems where none need exist" (p. 9).*

If we accept the general idea that workplace privacy and surveillance is a matter of justice, how should one go about structuring the debate? In the next section I will discuss the distribution of privacy and transparency as an issue of distributive justice using the work of Rawls (1972).

Privacy, Surveillance, and Distributive Justice

For the individual, privacy secures autonomy, creates social capital for intimacy, and forms the basis of structuring many diverse social relations (Introna 1997; Westin 1967). It is generally accepted that it is in the interest of the individual to have maximum control over her privacy—here taken to be the *freedom from the inappropriate judgement of others.* For the collective or institution, transparency secures control and thereby efficiency of resource allocation and utilisation, as well as creating mechanisms for disciplinary intervention (Foucault and Sheridan 1979). It is generally accepted that it is in the interest of the collective or institution to have maximum control over surveillance—here taken to mean *subjecting all individuals in the institution to reasonable scrutiny and judgement.* If the individuals are given an absolute right to privacy, they may act only in their own interest and may thereby defraud the institution. If the institution is given a complete right to transparency, it may strip the individual of autonomy and self-determination by making inappropriate judgements that only serve its own interest.

Thus, from a justice perspective we need a framework that would distribute the rights to privacy—of the individual (the employee in this case)—and right of transparency—of the collective (the employer in this case)—in a way that would be seen to be fair to all concerned. I would argue that wherever individuals and institutions face each other, the distribution of privacy and transparency rights will become an issue to be resolved. In this regard the institution can be as diverse as the family, the workplace, the community, the state, and so forth. At this stage I will exclude from my discussion the conflict of privacy and transparency rights between different institutions such as between the corporation and the state. Given this conflict between the individual employee and the institutionalised workplace, how can we decide on a fair distribution of privacy and transparency rights? I will propose that we may use the Rawlsian theory of justice as a starting point. Obviously one could use other frameworks. I am not arguing that Rawls is the only or even vastly superior perspective. Nevertheless, it does seem as if the Rawlsian framework is useful in this regard.

Rawls (in his seminal work *A Theory of Justice* of 1971) proposes a framework of justice as fairness in opposition to the leading theory of the day, viz. utilitarianism. For Rawls, utilitarianism puts no restrictions upon the subordination of some people's interests to those of others, except that the net outcome should be good. This would allow for any degree of subordination, provided the benefit to those advantaged was great enough. Rawls argues that a theory of justice cannot allow disadvantages to some to be justified by advantages to others. In our case this would imply a view that may posit the limited cost of the loss of individual privacy against the enormous economic benefit to the collective of securing effective control over productive resources. Such utilitarian arguments can easily make the individual's claim to privacy look trivial in the face of the economic prosperity of the whole. I would claim that it is exactly this utilitarian type of logic that continues to limit the legitimacy of the individual employee's claim to privacy in the workplace.

If this is so, how can we establish as set of rules that would ensure a fair distribution of privacy and transparency rights? Rawls (1972) argues that this can only happen behind a 'veil of ignorance' in the so-called original position. According to this formulation, a fair set of rules for this distribution would be a set of rules that *self-interested* participants would choose if they were completely ignorant about their own status in the subsequent contexts where these rules will be applied. What would be the rules for distributing privacy and transparency rights that may be selected from behind such a veil of ignorance?

As a starting point we need to outline the facts—about interests and positions—which we may assume to be available to those in the original position. This information will provide the force that may shape their choices. Obviously these need to be debated, but I would propose the following facts are known—first from the perspective of the individual, then from the perspective of the collective.

From the individual perspective:

- That there are no such things as neutral or objective judgements. Every judgement implies interests. Once data is recorded, it can in principle become incorporated into a judgement process that may not serve the individual's interests. It would therefore seem reasonable that the self-interested individual would try to limit all forms of capturing of data about themselves and their activities.

■ In the context of typical organisational settings, the employee is normally in a disadvantaged position—in a relation of severe power asymmetry. Thus, it is not possible for the individual, as an individual, to bargain for and ensure the fair use of data once it is captured. It would therefore be in the interest of the individual to limit all forms of capturing of data about themselves and their activities.

■ If data about themselves and their activities are captured, it is in their interest to have maximum control over it—what is captured, who sees it, for what purposes, and so forth.

From the perspective of the collective:

■ Without the capturing of complete and comprehensive information about the relevant activities of the individual, resources can not be efficiently and effectively allocated and control over the use of these resources can not be maintained. Without such control the collective would suffer. It would therefore seem reasonable to monitor all relevant activities of the individual. Relevant here would be understood to be those activities that imply the allocation and utilisation of collective resources.

■ Self-interested individuals would not always tend to use resources—allocated by the collective—for the sole purposes of furthering the aims and objectives of the collective. In fact they may use it completely for their own purposes. It would therefore seem reasonable to monitor all individual activities that allocate and utilise collective resources.

■ The collective needs to use data collected to coordinate and control the activities of the individuals for the good of the collective. It would be in the interest of the collective to have maximum control over the capturing and utilisation of relevant data about the individuals.

Given these facts—and other similar ones we may enumerate—what rules would those behind the veil of ignorance choose in distributing individual privacy and collective transparency rights? Before attempting to suggest some rules, it may be important to highlight Rawls' 'difference principle'—which he argues those behind the veil of ignorance would tend to choose. This principle states that an inequality is unjust except insofar as it is a necessary means to improving the position of the worst-off members of society. Without this principle it would be difficult for those behind the veil of ignorance to establish rules for distributing privacy and transparency rights, as its seems equally reasonable to grant and limit these rights both to the individual and the collective. However, we know, as indicated above, that in the context of the modern organisation the individual is in a position of severe power asymmetry. In the prevailing climate it would be difficult to argue that the individual employee is not 'the worst-off' with respect of securing a fair and reasonable level of privacy rights in the workplace. This would seem to indicate that most individuals behind the veil of ignorance would tend to want to argue for some bias towards securing the rights of the individual over and against that of the institution. With this in mind I will suggest—mostly for illustrative purpose—a set of fair 'rules' or guidelines that may be put forward by those behind the veil of ignorance. I would contend that they would acknowledge the following:

- That the collective (employer) does indeed have a right to monitor individuals' activities with respect to the allocation and utilisation of collective resources. The collective also has a right to use the data collected in a fair and reasonable way for the overall good of the collective as a whole.
- That the individual (employee) does have a legitimate claim to limit the surveillance of their activities in the workplace. The individual also has a right to secure a regime of control that will justify all monitoring and that will ensure that the data collected will be used in a fair and reasonable way.
- Based on the 'difference principle', it will be up to the collective (employer) to justify the collection of particular data in particular contexts. Furthermore, the regimes for controlling the collected data should be biased towards the individual.

Obviously one could develop these rules in much more detail. However, even this very limited, initial reflection would seem to suggest that the prevailing organisational practices that favour the collective (both in capturing and control) would seem to be unfair.

Obviously this analysis is still too crude and unsophisticated. However, it does illustrate that one may arrive at very different conclusions if one takes the issue of workplace privacy to be one of fairness rather than as a matter of working out the private/public distinction in the workplace—since it will always be relatively easy to argue that the workplace is a de facto public space, devoid of almost any privacy rights.

Conclusion and Some Implications

The potential for workplace surveillance is rapidly increasing. Surveillance technology is becoming cheap, silent, and diffused. Surveillance technology has created the potential to build surveillance into the very fabric of organisational processes. How should we concern ourselves with these facts? Clearly each workplace will be different. Some will be more bureaucratic, some more democratic. Nevertheless, the conflict between the individual right to privacy and the institutional right to transparency will always be there. In each individual case, different tactics will be used by the different parties to secure their interests.

In the case of workplace privacy, the prevailing legal and institutional infrastructure makes it difficult for the individuals to secure their interests, leaving them power-less, but by no means powerless. One of the major reasons for the unsuccessful challenge of modern workplace surveillance is the inappropriate manner in which the workplace privacy debate has evolved. In my opinion it incorrectly attached itself to the public/private distinction, which leaves the employee in a position of severe power asymmetry. In opposition to this debate I have argued that if one articulates the issue of workplace surveillance along the lines of competing, but equally legitimate claims (for privacy and transparency), needs to fairly distribute the possibilities for the individual to resist inappropriate workplace surveillance increases dramatically. Using the Rawlsian theory of justice I argued that those behind the veil of ignorance would tend to adopt a position that biases the right of the employee—the worst off—over that of the employer. This would suggest that a fair regime of workplace surveillance would tend to avoid monitoring unless explicitly justified by the employer. It will also provide mechanisms for the employee to have maximum control over the use of monitoring data. Both of these rules seem to suggest that most of the prevailing organisational surveillance practices are unfair. This, I believe, is the challenge to us: To set up the intellectual and organisational resources to ensure that workplace surveillance becomes and stays fair.

References

(ILO), International Labour Organisation. 1993. *Conditions of work digest: Monitoring and surveillance in the workplace.* Geneva: International Labour Office.

Association, American Management. 1999. *Workplace monitoring and surveillance:* American Management Association.

Commissioner/Ontario, Information and Privacy. 1993. *Workplace Privacy: The need for a Safety-Net,* http://www.ipc.on.ca/web_site.ups/matters/sum_pap/papers/safnet-e.htm: Information and Privacy Commissioner/Ontario.

Cozzetto, D and T.B. Pedeliski. 1999. *Privacy and the Workplace: Technology and Public Employement,* http://www.ipma-hr.org/pubs/cozzfull.html: International Personnel Association.

Dichter, MS and MS Burkhardt. 1996. Electronic Interaction in the Workplace: Monitoring, Retrieving, and Storing Employee Communications in the Internet Age. In *The American Employment Law Council: Fourth Annual Conference.* Asheville, North Carolina.

Dreyfus, Hubert L. 1992. *What computers still can't do: A critique of artificial reason.* Cambridge, MA: The MIT Press.

Dreyfus, Hubert L and Stuart E Dreyfus. 1986. *Mind over machine: The power of human intuition and expertise in the era of the computer.* New York: The Free Press.

Foucault, M. 1977. Truth and Power. In *Power/Knowledge: Selected Interviews & Other Writings 1972–1977,* ed. C. Gordon. New York: Pantheon Books.

Foucault, Michel and Alan Sheridan. 1979. *Discipline and punish: the birth of the prison.* Harmondsworth: Penguin.

Heidegger, Martin. 1962 {1937}. *Being and time.* Translated by John Macquarrie.

Edward Robinson. Oxford: Basil Blackwell.

Introna, L.D. 1997. Privacy and the Computer: Why We Need Privacy in the Information Society. *Metaphilosophy* 28, no. 3: 259–275.

Johnson, BT. 1995. *Technological Surveillance in the Workplace,* http://www.fwlaw.com/techserv.html: Fairfield and Woods P.C.

Johnson, J.L. 1989. Privacy and the Judgement of Others. *The Journal of Value Inquiry* 23: 157–168.

Latour, Bruno. 1987. *Science in action: How to follow scientists and engineers through society*. Cambridge, MA: Harvard University Press.

Latour, Bruno and Steve Woolgar. 1986 {1979}. *Laboratory life: The construction of scientific facts*. Princeton: Princeton University Press.

Lyon, David. 1994. *The Electronic Eye: the rise of the surveillance society*. Cambridge: Polity Press.

Marx, G.T. 1986. Monitoring on the Job: How to Protect Privacy as well as Property. *Technology Review*.

Merleau-Ponty, M. 1962. *Phenomenology of Perception*. Translated by Colin Smith. London: Routledge.

Piller. 1993. Bosses with x-ray eyes. *MacWorld*, no. July: 118–123.

Posner, R. 1978. The Right to Privacy. *Georgia Law Review* 12: 383–422.

Rawls, J. 1972. *A Theory of Justice*. Cambridge, Mass: Harvard University Press.

Santarelli, N. 1997. *E-mail Monitoring in the Work Place: Preventing Employer Liability*, http://wings.buffalo.edu/complaw/complawpapers/santarelli/html: Computers and Law Internet site.

U.S. Congress, Office of Technology Assessment (OTA Report). 1987. *The Electronic Supervisor: New Technology, New Tensions*. Washington DC: US Congress.

Westin, A. 1967. *Privacy and Freedom*. New York: Ateneum.

Notes

1. Sweden is the exception here. The Swedish Codetermination Act of 1976 require employers and employees to participate in decisions about electronic monitoring (U.S. Congress 1987, Appendix A).

2. There has been an attempt to change this in the unsuccessful Privacy of Consumers and Workers Act (PCWA) of 1993.

 For Discussion:

1. Do you see work surveillance as the right of the employer?
2. Although work surveillance is accepted by the law, privacy is considered by many to be a fundamental right. Where do you stand in this debate?
3. Do you agree with Introna's statement, "If the individuals are given an absolute right to privacy, they may act only in their interest and may thereby defraud the institution"? Why or why not?

 For Fact-Finding, Research, and Writing:

1. Introna's article revolves around privacy vs. transparency in the workplace. Compare and contrast his article with other articles that address the issue of privacy. Based on all these articles, formulate a definition of privacy.
2. Find three government documents on privacy in America. What main ideas do these documents cover?
3. Where does the Constitution actually affirm a right to privacy?
4. What Supreme Court decision first treated the issue of personal privacy?

5.   In what specific ways have issues of privacy been affected by the 2002 Home-
     land Security Act?

Laura Miller, "Women and Children First: Gender and the Settling of the Electronic Frontier"

Laura Miller is Senior Editor at *Salon,* an Internet magazine of arts and ideas,
and editor of *The Salon.com Reader's Guide to Contemporary* Author (2000). Prior
to joining *Salon,* Miller wrote about books, movies, and digital culture for the
San Francisco Examiner and such publications as *The New York Times Review of
Books, Harper's,* and *Wired.* This essay originally appeared in *Resisting the Virtual
Life: The Culture and Politics of Information* (1995).

Before You Read:

What kinds of dangers are posed by the Internet? Do you think women are
particularly endangered in any way by the Internet?

Women and Children First: Gender and the Settling of the Electronic Frontier

Laura Miller

WHEN *NEWSWEEK* (May 16, 1994) ran an article entitled "Men, Women, and Computers," all hell broke out on the Net, particularly on the online service I've participated in for six years, the WELL (Whole Earth 'Lectronic Link). "Cyberspace, it
turns out," declared *Newsweek*'s Nancy Kantrowitz, "isn't much of an Eden after all.
It's marred by just as many sexist ruts and gender conflicts as the Real World. . . .
Women often feel about as welcome as a system crash." "It was horrible. Awful, poorly
researched, unsubstantiated drivel," one member wrote, a sentiment echoed
throughout some 480 postings.

However egregious the errors in the article (some sources maintain that they were incorrectly quoted), it's only one of several mainstream media depictions of the Net as an environment hostile to women. Even women who had been complaining about online gender relations found themselves increasingly annoyed by what one WELL member termed the "cyberbabe harassment" angle that seems to typify media coverage of the issue. Reified in the pages of *Newsweek* and other journals, what had once been the topic of discussions by insiders—online commentary is informal, conversational, and often spontaneous—became a journalistic "fact" about the Net known by complete strangers and novices. In a matter of months, the airy stuff of bitch sessions became widespread, hardened stereotypes.

At the same time, the Internet has come under increasing scrutiny as it mutates from an obscure, freewheeling web of computer networks used by a small elite of academics, scientists, and hobbyists to . . . well, nobody seems to know exactly what. But the business press prints vague, fevered prophecies of fabulous wealth, and a bonanza mentality has blossomed. With it comes big business and the government, intent on regulating this amorphous medium into a manageable and profitable industry. The Net's history of informal self-regulation and its wide libertarian streak guarantee that battles like the one over the Clipper chip (a mandatory decoding device that would make all encrypted data readable by federal agents) will be only the first among many.

Yet the threat of regulation is built into the very mythos used to conceptualize the Net by its defenders—and gender plays a crucial role in that threat. However revolutionary the technologized interactions of online communities may seem, we understand them by deploying a set of very familiar metaphors from the rich figurative soup of American culture. Would different metaphors have allowed the Net a different, better historical trajectory? Perhaps not, but the way we choose to describe the Net now encourages us to see regulation as its inevitable fate. And, by examining how gender roles provide a foundation for the intensification of such social controls, we can illuminate the way those roles proscribe the freedoms of men as well as women.

For months I mistakenly referred to the EFF (an organization founded by John Perry Barlow and Lotus 1-2-3 designer Mitch Kapor to foster access to, and further the discursive freedom of, online communications) as "The Electronic Freedom Foundation," instead of by its actual name, "The Electronic Frontier Foundation." Once corrected, I was struck by how intimately related the ideas "frontier" and "freedom" are in the Western mythos. The *frontier,* as a realm of limitless possibilities and few social controls, hovers, grail-like, in the American psyche, the dream our national identity is based on, but a dream that's always, somehow, just vanishing away.

Once made, the choice to see the Net as a frontier feels unavoidable, but it's actually quite problematic. The word "frontier" has traditionally described a place, if not land then the limitless "final frontier" of space. The Net, on the other hand, occupies precisely no physical space (although the computers and phone lines that make it possible do). It is a completely bodiless, symbolic thing with no discernable boundaries or location. The land of the American frontier did not become a "frontier" until Europeans determined to conquer it, but the continent existed before the intention to settle it. Unlike land, the Net was created by its pioneers.

Most peculiar, then, is the choice of the word "frontier" to describe an artifact so humanly constructed that it only exists as ideas or information. For central to the idea of the frontier is that it contains no (or very few) other people—fewer than two per square mile according to the nineteenth-century historian Frederick Turner. The freedom the frontier promises is a liberation from the demands of society, while the Net (I'm thinking now of Usenet) has nothing but society to offer. Without other people, news groups, mailing lists, and files simply wouldn't exist and e-mail would be purposeless. Unlike real space, cyberspace must be shared.

Nevertheless, the choice of a spatial metaphor (credited to the science-fiction novelist William Gibson, who coined the term "cyberspace"), however awkward, isn't surprising. Psychologist Julian Jaynes has pointed out that geographical analogies have long predominated humanity's efforts to conceptualize—map out—consciousness. Unfortunately, these analogies bring with them a heavy load of baggage comparable to Pandora's box: open it and a complex series of problems have come to stay.

The frontier exists beyond the edge of settled or owned land. As the land that doesn't belong to anybody (or to people who "don't count," like Native Americans), it is on the verge of being acquired; currently unowned, but still ownable. Just as the idea of chastity makes virginity sexually provocative, so does the unclaimed territory invite settlers, irresistibly so. Americans regard the lost geographical frontier with a melancholy, voluptuous fatalism—we had no choice but to advance upon it and it had no alternative but to submit. When an EFF member compares the Clipper chip to barbed wire encroaching on the prairie, doesn't he realize the surrender implied in his metaphor?

The psychosexual undercurrents (if anyone still thinks of them as "under") in the idea of civilization's phallic intrusion into nature's passive, feminine space have been observed, exhaustively, elsewhere. The classic Western narrative is actually far more concerned with social relationships than conflicts between man and nature. In these stories, the frontier is a lawless society of men, a milieu in which physical strength, courage, and personal charisma supplant institutional authority and violent conflict is the accepted means of settling disputes. The Western narrative connects pleasurably with the American romance of individualistic masculinity; small wonder that the predominantly male founders of the Net's culture found it so appealing.

When civilization arrives on the frontier, it comes dressed in skirts and short pants. In the archetypal 1939 movie *Dodge City*, Wade Hatton (Errol Flynn) refuses to accept the position of marshal because he prefers the footloose life of a trail driver. Abbie Irving (Olivia de Haviland), a recent arrival from the civilized East, scolds him for his unwillingness to accept and advance the cause of law; she can't function (in her job as crusading journalist) in a town governed by brute force. It takes the accidental killing of a child in a street brawl for Hatton to realize that he must pin on the badge and clean up Dodge City.

In the Western mythos, civilization is necessary because women and children are victimized in conditions of freedom. Introduce women and children into a frontier town and the law must follow because women and children must be protected. Women, in fact, are usually the most vocal proponents of the conversion from frontier justice to civil society.

The imperiled women and children of the Western narrative make their appearance today in newspaper and magazine articles that focus on the intimidation and sexual harassment of women online and reports of pedophiles trolling for victims in computerized chat rooms. If online women successfully contest these attempts to depict them as the beleaguered prey of brutish men, expect the pedophile to assume a larger profile in arguments that the Net is out of control.

In the meantime, the media prefer to cast women as the victims, probably because many women actively participate in the call for greater regulation of online interactions, just as Abbie Irving urges Wade Hatton to bring the rule of law to Dodge City. These requests have a long cultural tradition, based on the idea that women, like children, constitute a peculiarly vulnerable class of people who require special protection from the elements of society men are expected to confront alone. In an insufficiently civilized society like the frontier, women, by virtue of this childlike vulnerability, are thought to live under the constant threat of kidnap, abuse, murder, and especially rape.

Women, who have every right to expect that crimes against their person will be rigorously prosecuted, should nevertheless regard the notion of special protections (chivalry, by another name) with suspicion. Based as it is on the idea that women are inherently weak and incapable of self-defense and that men are innately predatory, it actually reinforces the power imbalance between the sexes, with its roots in the concept of women as property, constantly under siege and requiring the vigilant protection of their male owners. If the romance of the frontier arises from the promise of vast stretches of unowned land, an escape from the restrictions of a society based on private property, the introduction of women spoils that dream by reintroducing the imperative of property in their own persons.

How does any of this relate to online interactions, which occur not on a desert landscape but in a complex, technological society where women are supposed to command equal status with men? It accompanies us as a set of unexamined assumptions about what it means to be male or female, assumptions that we believe are rooted in the imperatives of our bodies. These assumptions follow us into the bodiless realm of cyberspace, a forum where, as one scholar puts it "participants are washed clean of the stigmata of their real 'selves' and are free to invent new ones to their tastes." Perhaps some observers feel that the replication of gender roles in a context where the absence of bodies supposedly makes them superfluous proves exactly how innate those roles are. Instead, I see in the relentless attempts to interpret online interactions as highly gendered, an intimation of just how artificial, how created, our gender system is. If it comes "naturally," why does it need to be perpetually defended and reasserted?

Complaints about the treatment of women online fall into three categories: that women are subjected to excessive, unwanted sexual attention, that the prevailing style of online discussion turns women, off, and that women are singled out by male participants for exceptionally dismissive or hostile treatment. In making these assertions, the *Newsweek* article and other stories on the issue do echo grievances that some online women have made for years. And, without a doubt, people have encountered sexual come-ons, aggressive debating tactics, and ad hominem attacks on the Net. However, individual users interpret such events in widely different ways, and to generalize from those interpretations to describe the experiences of women and men as a whole is a rash leap indeed.

I am one of many women who don't recognize their own experience of the Net in the misogynist gauntlet described above. In researching this essay, I joined America Online and spent an hour or two "hanging out" in the real-time chat rooms reputed to be rife with sexual harassment. I received several "instant messages" from men, initiating private conversations with innocuous questions about my hometown and tenure on the service. One man politely inquired if I was interested in "hot phone talk" and just as politely bowed out when I declined. At no point did I feel harassed or treated with disrespect. If I ever want to find a phone-sex partner, I now know where to look but until then I probably won't frequent certain chat rooms.

Other women may experience a request for phone sex or even those tame instant messages as both intrusive and insulting (while still others maintain that they have received much more explicit messages and inquiries completely out of the blue). My point isn't that my reactions are the more correct, but rather that both are the reactions of women, and no journalist has any reason to believe that mine are the exception rather than the rule.

For me, the menace in sexual harassment comes from the underlying threat of rape or physical violence. I see my body as the site of my heightened vulnerability as a woman. But online—where I have no body and neither does anyone else—I consider rape to be impossible. Not everyone agrees. Julian Dibble, in an article for the *Village Voice,* describes the repercussions of a "rape" in a multiuser dimension, or MUD, in which one user employed a subprogram called a "voodoo doll" to cause the personae of other users to perform sexual acts. Citing the "conflation of speech and act that's inevitable in any computer-mediated world," he moved toward the conclusion that "since rape can occur without any physical pain or damage, then it must be classified as a crime against the mind." Therefore, the offending user had committed something on the same "conceptual continuum" as rape. Tellingly, the incident led to the formation of the first governmental entity on the MUD.

No doubt the cyber-rapist (who went by the nom de guerre Mr. Bungle) appreciated the elevation of his mischief-making to the rank of virtual felony: all of the outlaw glamour and none of the prison time (he was exiled from the MUD). Mr. Bungle limited his victims to personae created by women users, a choice that, in its obedience to prevailing gender roles, shaped the debate that followed his crimes. For, in accordance with the real-world understanding that women's smaller, physically weaker bodies and lower social status make them subject to violation by men, there's a troubling notion in the real and virtual worlds that women's minds are also more vulnerable to invasion, degradation, and abuse.

This sense of fragility extends beyond interactions with sexual overtones. The *Newsweek* article reports that women participants can't tolerate the harsh, contentious quality of online discussions, that they prefer mutual support to heated debate, and are retreating wholesale to women-only conferences and newsgroups. As someone who values online forums precisely because they mandate equal time for each user who chooses to take it and forestall various "alpha male" rhetorical tactics like interrupting, loudness, or exploiting the psychosocial advantages of greater size or a deeper voice, I find this perplexing and disturbing. In these laments I hear the reluctance of women to enter into the kind of robust debate that characterizes healthy public life, a willingness to let men bully us even when they've been relieved of most of their traditional advantages. Withdrawing into an electronic purdah where one will never be challenged or provoked, allowing the ludicrous ritual chest-thumping of some users to intimidate us into silence—surely women can come up with a more spirited response than this.

And of course they can, because besides being riddled with reductive stereotypes, media analyses like *Newsweek*'s simply aren't accurate. While the online population is predominantly male, a significant and vocal minority of women contribute regularly and more than manage to hold their own. Some of the WELL's most bombastic participants are women, just as there are many tactful and conciliatory men. At least, I think there are, because, ultimately, it's impossible to be sure of anyone's biological gender online. "Transpostites," people who pose as members of the opposite gender, are an established element of Net society, most famously a man who, pretending to be a disabled lesbian, built warm and intimate friendships with women on several CompuServe forums.

Perhaps what we should be examining is not the triumph of gender differences on the Net, but their potential blurring. In this light, *Newsweek*'s stout assertion that in cyberspace "the gender gap is real" begins to seem less objective than defensive, an insistence that online culture is "the same" as real life because the idea that it might be different, when it comes to gender, is too scary. If gender roles can be cast off so easily, they may be less deeply rooted, less "natural" than we believe. There may not actually be a "masculine" or "feminine" mind or outlook, but simply a conventional way of interpreting individuals that recognizes behavior seen as in accordance with their biological gender and ignores behavior that isn't.

For example, John Seabury wrote in *The New Yorker* (June 6, 1994) of his stricken reaction to his first "flame," a colorful slice of adolescent invective sent to him by an unnamed technology journalist. Reading it, he begins to "shiver" like a burn victim, an effect that worsens with repeated readings. He writes that "the technology greased the words . . . with a kind of immediacy that allowed them to slide easily into my brain." He tells his friends, his coworkers, his partner—even his mother—and, predictably, appeals to CompuServe's management for recourse—to no avail. Soon enough, he's talking about civilization and anarchy, how the liberating "lack of social barriers is also what is appalling about the Net," and calling for regulation.

As a newcomer, Seabury was chided for brooding over a missive that most Net veterans would have dismissed and forgotten as the crude potshot of an envious jerk. (I can't help wondering if my fellow journalist never received hate mail in response to his other writings; this bit of e-mail seems comparable, par for the course when one assumes a public profile.) What nobody did was observe that Seabury's reaction—the shock, the feelings of violation, the appeals to his family and support network, the bootless complaints to the authorities—reads exactly like many horror stories about women's trials on the Net. Yet, because Seabury is a man, no one attributes the attack to his gender or suggests that the Net has proven an environment hostile to men. Furthermore, the idea that the Net must be more strictly governed to prevent the abuse of guys who write for *The New Yorker* seems laughable—though who's to say that Seabury's pain is less than any woman's? Who can doubt that, were he a woman, his tribulations would be seen as compelling evidence of Internet sexism?

The idea that women merit special protections in an environment as incorporeal as the Net is intimately bound up with the idea that women's minds are weak, fragile, and unsuited to the rough and tumble of public discourse. It's an argument that women should recognize with profound mistrust and resist, especially when we are used as rhetorical pawns in a battle to regulate a rare (if elite) space of gender ambiguity. When the mainstream media generalize about women's experiences on line in ways that just happen to uphold the most conventional and pernicious gender stereotypes, they can expect to be greeted with howls of disapproval from women who refuse to acquiesce in these roles and pass them on to other women.

And there are plenty of us, as the WELL's response to the *Newsweek* article indicates. Women have always participated in online communications, women whose chosen careers in technology and the sciences have already marked them as gender-role resisters. As the schoolmarms arrive on the electronic frontier, their female predecessors find themselves cast in the role of saloon girls, their willingness to engage in "masculine" activities like verbal aggression, debate, or sexual experimentation marking them as insufficiently feminine, or "bad" women. "If that's what women online are like, I must be a Martian," one WELL woman wrote in response to the shrinking female technophobes depicted in the *Newsweek* article. Rather than relegating so many people to the status of gender aliens, we ought to reconsider how adequate those roles are to the task of describing real human beings.

For Discussion:

1. Explain Miller's reasons for arguing against the accuracy of the frontier as a metaphor for the Internet. What merits or faults do you see in her argument?
2. Do you agree with Miller when she contends: "But online—where I have no body and neither does anyone else—I consider rape to be impossible"?
3. Do you think that the flow of information on the Net should be controlled and regulated? If yes, do you think that women need protection?
4. Does Miller claim that the Internet is not particularly problematic for women, or does she argue that women should learn to live with the problems?

 For Fact-Finding, Research, and Writing:

1. Miller alludes to an article from *Newsweek*. Find the article, summarize its main points, and explain whether or not she has used it fairly.
2. Create an alternate email address (an alias) and log onto a chat room. (For you own protection, avoid chat rooms with offensive names). How are gender roles represented? How do your findings affect your reading of Miller's essay?
3. Using the Statistical Universe database, find current figures about the gender of Internet users.
4. In what specific ways would Esther Dyson ("The Anonymous Voice") agree with Miller's assertions? In what ways would Dyson's article work against Miller's?
5. Are there laws controlling Internet harassment? Are they adequate? Unnecessary?

CHAPTER FOUR

What's in the Future?

Introduction

It is certain that advances in information technology will influence our future. Unfortunately, determining the shape of this future is not as easy to predict. This section explores how current ideas may affect our future lives and ultimately the course of both humankind and the planet itself. There is no shortage of futuristic visions; speculation about the future comes not only from science fiction writers but from lawyers, chemists, engineers, and even plastic surgeons. The years 1984 and 2001 may have passed us by without fulfilling the fantasies wrought by Orwell and Kubrick, but the visions of the future examined in these readings seem to come nearer and nearer to the reality of our own present moment. Despite the divergences among their visions, the authors of these essays all share the same desire to know what tomorrow brings and to prepare for the outcome.

Our world continues to change as the information landscape evolves, as the ways we process, evaluate, and use information replace older methods. These solutions may lead to phenomenal advances, but as anyone who has ever felt a pang of dread during a science fiction film knows, there may be equally phenomenal risks, and sometimes those risks outweigh the rewards. The question we face as we advance deeper into the twenty-first century is not *if* we can do something, but *should* we? As the following readings show, this is a question of information. Information resides at the core of the future, and the future is decided today.

The Technology Timeline

TECHNOLOGICAL DEVELOPMENT is ever accelerating, bringing new products onto the market. To help understand the range of innovations emerging and their potential impacts, researchers at British Telecommunications began the Technology Timeline in 1991 under the direction of Paul McIlroy. Since then, futurist Ian Pearson of BTexact Technologies, BT's business division, has updated the timeline about once every two or three years.

The timeline presented here is drawn from the latest edition of the full timeline developed by Pearson with Ian Neild, which is available on BTexact's Web site. The timeline also incorporates several possible "wild cards," based on *Out of the Blue* by John L. Petersen of the Arlington Institute.

"What must be remembered by anyone preparing for the future is that technology change isn't very important in itself," says Pearson, "What matters is what this change enables or destroys." Thus, the timeline is potentially useful not only to BT's business customers, but also to government, the media, and private individuals.

"The intention of the timeline is to illustrate the potential for beneficial technologies," says Pearson. "We will have more variety of entertainment, better health, greater wealth, and probably better social well-being."

2005

ARTIFICIAL INTELLIGENCE AND LIFE	Toys with network based intelligence, 2004 Confessions to AI priest, 2004 Behavior alarms based on human mistake recognition, 2006 AI chatbots indistinguishable from people. 2005
BIOTECHNOLOGY: HEALTH AND MEDICINE	Retinal implants linked to external video cameras, 2004 Designer babies, 2005 All patients tagged in hospitals, 2005
BUSINESS AND EDUCATION	80% of U.S. homes have PCs, 2005 Virtual reality is used to teach science, art, history, etc. 2005
COMPUTING POWER	100-teraflop computer, 2004 **CAMERAS RECORD VISUAL EXPERIENCES BY 2004.**
ENVIRONMENT AND RESOURCES	Clothes collect and store solar power, 2005
HOME AND LEISURE	Smart paint containing computer chips is available, 2004 Fiber-optic plants used in gardens, 2005 Living rooms decorated with virtual reality scenes, 2005
MACHINE-HUMAN INTERFACE	Tactile sensors comparable to human sensation, 2004 Voice synthesis quality up to human standard, 2005 Voice control of many household gadgets, 2005
ROBOTICS	Robotic space vehicles and facilities, 2005
SECURITY, LAW, WAR	People's courts on Internet for minor disputes, 2004 VR routinely used in courtrooms for evidence presentation, 2005 Soldiers' weapons fired remotely, 2005
SPACE	Space tugs take satellites into high orbits, 2005 *Wild Card: Major genetic engineering accident, 2005*
TRAVEL AND TRANSPORTATION	Hydrogen-fueled executive jets (cryoplanes), 2005 Assisted lane-keeping systems used in trucks and buses, 2005
WEARABLE AND PERSONAL TECHNOLOGY	Cameras built into glasses record what we see, 2004 Polymer video screens built into clothes. 2005

2010

ARTIFICIAL INTELLIGENCE AND LIFE	Software is trained rather than written, 2006 Artificial nervous system for autonomous robots, 2010 25% of TV celebrities are synthetic, 2010
BIOTECHNOLOGY: HEALTH AND MEDICINE	Artificial heart (lab-cultured or entirely synthetic), 2010
BUSINESS AND EDUCATION	All government services delivered electronically, 2008
COMPUTING POWER	Optical neurocomputers, 2007 Quantum computer, 2007 Supercomputer as fast as human brain, 2010
ENVIRONMENT AND RESOURCES	Multilayer solar cells with efficiency of more than 50%, 2006 Effective prediction of most natural disasters, 2010
HOME AND LEISURE	Cybercommunity attains population of 100 million, 2010 Mood-sensitive light bulbs developed, 2010 Chips in packaging control cooking, 2010
MACHINE-HUMAN INTERFACE	Emotionally responsive toys and robots, 2006 Voice interface for home appliances, 2010
ROBOTICS	Robotic security and fire guards, 2008 Self-monitoring infrastructures use smart materials, sensors, 2010
SECURITY, LAW, WAR	First Net war fought between cybercommunities, 2007 Logic checkers highlight contradictory evidence, 2008
SPACE	Next-generation space telescope launched, 2007
TRAVEL AND TRANSPORTATION	Pollution-monitor chips are built into cars, 2008 Cars with automatic steering, 2008 GPS and engine-management systems limit speed automatically, 2010
WEARABLE AND PERSONAL TECHNOLOGY	Portable translation device for simple conversation, 2007 Video tattoos, 2010

Wild Card: Viruses immune to known treatments, 2010

2015

ARTIFICIAL INTELLIGENCE AND LIFE	Satellite location devices implanted into pets, 2015
BIOTECHNOLOGY: HEALTH AND MEDICINE	Some implants seen as status symbols, 2015 Shower body scan, 2015 Artificial lungs, kidneys, 2015
BUSINESS AND EDUCATION	Purely electronic companies exist with minimal human involvement, 2012 3-D video conferencing, 2015
COMPUTING POWER	DNA computer, 2012 Desktop computer as fast as human brain, 2015
ENVIRONMENT AND RESOURCES	Insect-like robots used for crop pollination, 2012 Commercial magma power stations, 2012
HOME AND LEISURE	Holographic windows redirect sunlight, 2015 Dual geo/cybernationality recognized internationally, 2015
MACHINE-HUMAN INTERFACE	COMPUTER SCREENS IN CLOTHES BY 2005.
ROBOTICS	Robots for almost any job in homes or hospitals, 2012 Reconfigurable buildings, 2015
SECURITY, LAW, WAR	ID cards replaced by biometric scanning, 2015
SPACE	First manned mission to Mars, 2015 Space hotel accommodates 350 guests, 2015 Near-Earth space tours, 2015
TRAVEL AND TRANSPORTATION	Wild Card: Self-aware machine intelligence, 2015
WEARABLE AND PERSONAL TECHNOLOGY	

2020

ARTIFICIAL INTELLIGENCE AND LIFE	Machine knowledge exceeds human knowledge, 2017 Electronic life form given basic rights, 2020 Artificial insects and small animals with artificial brains, 2025
BIOTECHNOLOGY: HEALTH AND MEDICINE	Artificial liver, 2020 Only 15% of deaths worldwide due to infectious diseases, 2020 Nanobots in toothpaste attack plaque, 2020
BUSINESS AND EDUCATION	
COMPUTING POWER	AI technology imitates thinking processes of the brain, 2018
ENVIRONMENT AND RESOURCES	Sensors widely used in countryside to monitor environment, 2020 Systems based on biochemical storage of solar energy, 2020
HOME AND LEISURE	Kaleidoscopic flowers using electronic inks, 2020 Digital image overlays enhance relationships, 2020 Bore filter screens dullards out of digital communications, 2020
MACHINE-HUMAN INTERFACE	Computers linked to biological sensory organs, 2018
ROBOTICS	Self-diagnostic, self-repairing robots, 2017 Robotic mail delivery, 2020
SECURITY, LAW, WAR	
SPACE	Regular manned missions to Mars, 2020
TRAVEL AND TRANSPORTATION	Driverless truck convoys using electronic towbar, 2020 Reservations required to use some key roads, 2020
WEARABLE AND PERSONAL TECHNOLOGY	Computer-enhanced dreaming, 2020

Wild Card: Rise of a global machine dictator, 2020

NEAR-EARTH SPACE TOURS BY 2015.

2025

ARTIFICIAL INTELLIGENCE AND LIFE	
BIOTECHNOLOGY: HEALTH AND MEDICINE	Fully functioning artificial eyes, 2024 Artificial peripheral nerves, 2025 Artificial legs, 2025
BUSINESS AND EDUCATION	Learning superseded by transparent interface to smart computers, 2025
COMPUTING POWER	
ENVIRONMENT AND RESOURCES	ROBOTS SURPASS DEVELOPED-WORLD POPULATION BY 2025.
HOME AND LEISURE	Holographic TV, 2025 VR becomes popular entertainment in nursing homes, 2025
MACHINE-HUMAN INTERFACE	Thought recognition becomes everyday input means, 2025
ROBOTICS	Cybernetic gladiators, 2025
SECURITY, LAW, WAR	Wild Card: Conscious networks won't cooperate, 2025
SPACE	Space factories for commercial production, 2025 Antimatter production and storage becomes feasible, 2025
TRAVEL AND TRANSPORTATION	
WEARABLE AND PERSONAL TECHNOLOGY	

2030

ARTIFICIAL INTELLIGENCE AND LIFE	Robots are physically and mentally superior to humans, 2030
BIOTECHNOLOGY: HEALTH AND MEDICINE	First Bionic Olympics, 2020
BUSINESS AND EDUCATION	
COMPUTING POWER	Library of Congress contents available in sugar-cube-sized device, 2030
ENVIRONMENT AND RESOURCES	Space solar power stations, 2030 Carbon dioxide fixation technologies for environmental protection, 2030
HOME AND LEISURE	
MACHINE-HUMAN INTERFACE	Full direct brain link, 2030
ROBOTICS	
SECURITY, LAW, WAR	Emotion control chips used to control criminals, 2030
SPACE	Start of construction of manned Mars laboratory, 2030 Use of human hibernation in space travel, 2030
TRAVEL AND TRANSPORTATION	
WEARABLE AND PERSONAL TECHNOLOGY	Dream-linking technology built for nighttime networking, 2030

Wild Card: Nanotechnology war, 2030

2040

ARTIFICIAL INTELLIGENCE AND LIFE	Living genetically engineered electronic toy/pet developed, 2040
BIOTECHNOLOGY: HEALTH AND MEDICINE	Artificial brain, 2035
BUSINESS AND EDUCATION	
COMPUTING POWER	ASTEROID DIVERSION TECHNOLOGY USED AS WEAPON BY 2040
ENVIRONMENT AND RESOURCES	Artificial precipitation induction and control, 2035 Wave energy provides up to 50% of UK requirements, 2040
HOME AND LEISURE	Experience-recording technology developed, 2035 Realistic nanotech toy soldiers are built, 2035
MACHINE-HUMAN INTERFACE	MOON BASE SIZE OF SMALL VILLAGE BUILT BY 2040
ROBOTICS	
SECURITY, LAW, WAR	Asteroid diversion technology used as weapon, 2040
SPACE	Moon base the size of small village is built, 2040
TRAVEL AND TRANSPORTATION	Wild Card: Electromagnetic communications disrupted, 2040
WEARABLE AND PERSONAL TECHNOLOGY	

Robert A. Weinberg, "Of Clones and Clowns"

> Winner of the 1997 National Medal of Science, Robert A. Weinberg is Professor of Biology at the Massachusetts Institute of Technology, one of the most renowned technical and scientific research universities in the world. In addition to hundreds of scientific papers, he has authored several books about cancer research for general audiences, including *Racing to the Beginning of the Road* (1996) and *One Renegade Cell* (1998).

Before You Read:

What do you think of when you think of cloning?

Of Clones and Clowns

Robert A. Weinberg

BIOLOGISTS HAVE BEEN rather silent on the subject of human cloning. Some others would accuse us, as they have with predictable regularity in the recent past, of insensitivity to the societal consequences of our research. If not insensitivity, then moral obtuseness, and if not that, then arrogance—an accusation that can never be disproved.

The truth is that most of us have remained quiet for quite another reason. Most of us regard reproductive cloning—a procedure used to produce an entire new organism from one cell of an adult—as a technology riddled with problems. Why should we waste time agonizing about something that is far removed from practical utility, and may forever remain so?

The nature and magnitude of the problems were suggested by the Scottish scientist Ian Wilmut's initial report, five years ago, on the cloning of Dolly the sheep. Dolly represented one success among 277 attempts to produce a viable, healthy newborn. Most attempts at cloning other animal species—to date cloning has succeeded with sheep, mice, cattle, goats, cats, and pigs—have not fared much better.

Even the successes come with problems. The placentas of cloned fetuses are routinely two or three times larger than normal. The offspring are usually larger than normal as well. Several months after birth one group of cloned mice weighed

72 percent more than mice created through normal reproduction. In many species cloned fetuses must be delivered by cesarean section because of their size. This abnormality, the reasons for which no one understands, is so common that it now has its own name—Large Offspring Syndrome. Dolly (who was of normal size at birth) was briefly overweight in her young years and suffers from early-onset arthritis of unknown cause. Two recent reports indicate that cloned mice suffer early-onset obesity and early death.

Arguably the most successful reproductive-cloning experiment was reported last year by Advanced Cell Technology, a small biotech company in Worcester, Massachusetts. Working with cows, ACT produced 496 embryos by injecting nuclei from adult cells into eggs that had been stripped of their own nuclei. Implanting the embryos into the uteruses of cows led to 110 established pregnancies, thirty of which went to term. Five of the newborns died shortly after birth, and a sixth died several months later. The twenty-four surviving calves developed into cows that were healthy by all criteria examined. But most, if not all, had enlarged placentas, and as newborns some of them suffered from the respiratory distress typical of Large Offspring Syndrome.

The success rate of the procedure, roughly five percent, was much higher than the rates achieved with other mammalian species, and the experiment was considered a great success. Some of the cows have grown up, been artificially inseminated, and given birth to normal offspring. Whether they are affected by any of the symptoms associated with Large Offspring Syndrome later in life is not apparent from the published data. No matter: for $20,000 ACT will clone your favorite cow.

Imagine the application of this technology to human beings. Suppose that 100 adult nuclei are obtained, each of which is injected into a human egg whose own nucleus has been removed. Imagine then that only five of the 100 embryos thus created result in well-formed, viable newborns; the other ninety-five spontaneously abort at various stages of development or, if cloning experiments with mammals other than cows are any guide, yield grossly malformed babies. The five viable babies have a reasonable likelihood of suffering from Large Offspring Syndrome. How they will develop, physically and cognitively, is anyone's guess. It seems unlikely that even the richest and most egomaniacal among us, intent on recreating themselves exactly, will swarm to this technology.

Biological systems are extraordinarily complex, and there are myriad ways in which experiments can go awry or their results can be misinterpreted. Still, perhaps 95 percent of what biologists read in this year's research journals will be considered valid (if perhaps not very interesting) a century from now. Much of scientists' trust in the existing knowledge base derives from the system constructed over the past century to validate new research findings and the conclusions derived from them. Research journals impose quality controls to ensure that scientific observations and conclusions are solid and credible. They sift the scientific wheat from the chaff.

The system works like this: A biologist sends a manuscript describing his experiment to a journal. The editor of the journal recruits several experts, who remain anonymous to the researcher, to vet the manuscript. A month or two later the researcher receives a thumbs-up, a thumbs-down, or a request for revisions and more data. The system works reasonably well, which is why many of us invest large amounts of time in serving as the anonymous reviewers of one another's work. Without such rigorously imposed quality control, our subfields of research would rapidly descend into chaos, because no publicly announced result would carry the imprimatur of having been critiqued by experts.

We participate in the peer-review process not only to create a sound edifice of ideas and results for ourselves; we do it for the outside world as well—for all those who are unfamiliar with the arcane details of our field. Without the trial-by-fire of peer review, how can journalists and the public possibly know which discoveries are credible, which are nothing more than acts of self-promotion by ambitious researchers, and which smack of the delusional?

The hype about cloning has made a shambles of this system, creating something of a circus. Many of us have the queasy feeling that our carefully constructed world of science is under siege. The clowns—those who think that making money, lots of it, is more important than doing serious science—have invaded our sanctuary.

The cloning circus opened soon after Wilmut, a careful and well-respected scientist, reported his success with Dolly. First in the ring was Richard Seed, an elderly Chicago physicist, who in late 1997 announced his intention of cloning a human being within two years. Soon members of an international religious cult, the Raëlians (followers of Claude Vorilhon, a French-born mystic who says that he was given the name Raël by four-foot-high extraterrestrials, and who preaches that human beings were originally created by these aliens), revealed an even more grandiose vision of human cloning. To the Raëlians, biomedical science is a sacrament to be used for achieving immortality: their ultimate goal is to use cloning to create empty shells into which people's souls can be transferred. As a sideline, the Raëlian-affiliated company Clonaid hopes to offer its services to couples who would like to create a child through reproductive cloning, for $200,000 per child.

Neither Seed nor the Raëlians made any pretense of subjecting their plans to review by knowledgeable scientists; they went straight to the popular press. Still, this wasn't so bad. Few science journalists took them seriously (although they did oblige them with extensive coverage). Biologists were also unmoved. Wasn't it obvious that Seed and the Raëlians were unqualified to undertake even the beginnings of the series of technical steps required for reproductive cloning? Why dignify them with a response?

The next wave of would-be cloners likewise went straight to the mainstream press—but they were not so easily dismissed. In March of last year, at a widely covered press conference in Rome, an Italian and a U.S. physician announced plans to undertake human reproductive cloning outside the United States. The Italian member of the team was Severino Antinori, a gynecologist notorious for having used donor eggs and *in vitro* fertilization to make a sixty-two-year-old woman pregnant in 1994. Now he was moving on. Why, he asked, did the desires of infertile couples (he claimed to have 600 on a waiting list) not outweigh the concerns about human cloning? He repeatedly shouted down reporters and visiting researchers who had the temerity to voice questions about the biological and ethical problems associated with reproductive cloning.

The American member of the team was Panayiotis Zavos, a reproductive physiologist and an *in vitro* fertilization expert at the Andrology Institute of America, in Lexington, Kentucky. "The genie is out of the bottle," he told reporters. "Dolly is here, and we are next." Antinori and Zavos announced their intention of starting a human cloning project in an undisclosed Mediterranean country. Next up was Avi Ben-Abraham, an Israeli-American biotechnologist with thwarted political ambitions (he ran unsuccessfully for the Knesset) and no reputable scientific credentials, who attempted to attach himself to the project. Ben-Abraham hinted that the work would be done either in Israel or in an Arab country, because "the climate is more [receptive to human cloning research] within Judaism and Islam." He told the German magazine *Der Spiegel,* "We were all created by the Almighty, but now we will become the creators."

Both Antinori and Zavos glossed over the large gap between expertise with established infertility procedures and the technical skills required for reproductive cloning. Confronted with the prospect of high rates of aborted or malformed cloned embryos, they claimed to be able to weed out any defective embryos at an early stage of gestation. "We have a great deal of knowledge," Zavos announced to the press. "We can grade embryos. We can do genetic screening. We can do [genetic] quality control." This was possible, he said, because of highly sensitive diagnostic tests that can determine whether or not development is proceeding normally.

The fact is that no such tests exist; they have eluded even the most expert biologists in the field, and there is no hope that they will be devised anytime soon—if ever. No one knows how to determine with precision whether the repertoire of genes expressed at various stages of embryonic development is being "read" properly in each cell type within an embryo. Without such information, no one can know whether the developmental program is proceeding normally in the womb. (The prenatal tests currently done for Down syndrome and several other genetic disorders can detect only a few of the thousands of things that can go wrong during embryonic development.)

Rudolf Jaenisch, a colleague of mine with extensive experience in mouse reproductive cloning, was sufficiently exercised to say to a reporter at the *Chicago Tribune,* "[Zavos and Antinori] will produce clones, and most of these will die in utero . . . Those will be the lucky ones. Many of those that survive will have [obvious or more subtle] abnormalities." The rest of us biologists remained quiet. To us, Antinori, Zavos, and Ben-Abraham were so clearly inept that comment seemed gratuitous. In this instance we have, as on other occasions, misjudged the situation: many people seem to take these three and their plans very seriously indeed. And, in fact, this past April, Antinori claimed, somewhat dubiously, that a woman under his care was eight weeks pregnant with a cloned embryo.

In the meantime, the biotechnology industry, led by ACT, has been moving ahead aggressively with human cloning but of a different sort. The young companies in this sector have sensed, probably correctly, the enormous potential of therapeutic (rather than reproductive) cloning as a strategy for treating a host of common human degenerative diseases.

The initial steps of therapeutic cloning are identical to those of reproductive cloning: cells are prepared from an adult tissue, their nuclei are extracted, and each nucleus is introduced into a human egg, which is allowed to develop. However, in therapeutic cloning embryonic development is halted at a very early stage—when the embryo is a blastocyst, consisting of perhaps 150 cells—and the inner cells are harvested and cultured. These cells, often termed embryonic stem cells, are still very primitive and thus have retained the ability to develop into any type of cell in the body (except those of the placenta).

Mouse and human embryonic stem cells can be propagated in a petri dish and induced to form precursors of blood-forming cells, or of the insulin-producing cells of the pancreas, or of cardiac muscle or nerve tissue. These precursor cells (tissue-specific stem cells) might then be introduced into a tissue that has grown weak from the loss of too many of its differentiated worker cells. When the ranks of the workers are replenished, the course of disease may be dramatically reversed. At least, that is the current theory. In recent months one version of the technique has been successfully applied to mice.

Therapeutic cloning has the potential to revolutionize the treatment of a number of currently untreatable degenerative diseases, but it is only a potential. Considerable research will be required to determine the technology's possibilities and limitations for treating human patients.

Some worry that therapeutic-cloning research will never get off the ground in this country. Its proponents—and there are many among the community of biomedical researchers—fear that the two very different kinds of cloning, therapeutic and reproductive, have merged in the public's mind. Three leaders of the community wrote a broadside early this year in *Science,* titled "Please Don't Call It Cloning!" Call therapeutic cloning anything else—call it "nuclear transplantation," or "stem cell research." The scientific community has finally awakened to the damage that the clowns have done.

This is where the newest acts of the circus begin. President George Bush and many pro-life activists are in one ring. A number of disease-specific advocacy groups that view therapeutic cloning as the only real prospect for treating long-resistant maladies are in another. In a third ring are several biotech companies that are flogging their wares, often in ways that make many biologists shudder.

Yielding to pressure from religious conservatives, Bush announced last August that no new human embryonic stem cells could be produced from early human embryos that had been created during the course of research sponsored by the federal government; any research on the potential applications of human embryonic stem cells, he said, would have to be conducted with the existing repertoire of sixty-odd lines. The number of available, usable cell lines actually appears to be closer to a dozen or two. And like all biological reagents, these cells tend to deteriorate with time in culture; new ones will have to be derived if research is to continue. What if experiments with the existing embryonic-stem-cell lines show enormous promise? Such an outcome would produce an almost irresistible pressure to move ahead with the derivation of new embryonic stem cells and to rapidly expand this avenue of research.

How will we learn whether human embryonic stem cells are truly useful for new types of therapy? This question brings us directly to another pitfall: much of the research on human embryonic stem cells is already being conducted by biotech companies, rather than in universities. Bush's edict will only exacerbate this situation. (In the 1970s a federal decision effectively banning government funding of *in vitro* fertilization had a similar effect, driving such research into private clinics.)

Evaluating the science coming from the labs of the biotech industry is often tricky. Those who run these companies are generally motivated more by a need to please stock analysts and venture capitalists than to convince scientific peers. For many biotech companies the peer-review process conducted by scientific journals is simply an inconvenient, time-wasting impediment. So some of the companies routinely bypass peer review and go straight to the mainstream press. Science journalists, always eager for scoops, don't necessarily feel compelled to consult experts about the credibility of industry press releases. And when experts are consulted about the contents of a press release, they are often hampered by spotty descriptions of the claimed breakthrough and thus limited to mumbling platitudes.

ACT, the company that conducted the successful cow-cloning experiment and has now taken the lead in researching human therapeutic cloning, has danced back and forth between publishing in respectable peer-reviewed journals and going directly to the popular press—and recently tried to find a middle ground. (For a fuller discussion of ACT's efforts, see "Cloning Trevor," by Kyla Dunn, beginning on page 31.) Last fall, with vast ambitions, ACT reported that it had conducted the first successful human-cloning experiment. In truth, however, embryonic development went only as far as six cells—far short of the 150-cell blastocyst that represents the first essential step of therapeutic cloning. Wishing to cloak its work in scientific respectability, ACT reported these results in a fledgling electronic research journal named *e-biomed: The Journal of Regenerative Medicine.* Perhaps ACT felt especially welcome in a journal that, according to its editor in chief, William A. Haseltine, a widely known biotech tycoon, "is prepared to publish work of a more preliminary nature." It may also have been encouraged by Haseltine's stance toward cloning, as revealed in his remarks when the journal was founded. "As we understand the body's repair process at the genetic level, we will be able to advance the goal of maintaining our bodies in normal function, perhaps perpetually," he said.

Electronic publishing is still in its infancy, and the publication of ACT's research report will do little to enhance its reputation. By the usual standards of scientific achievement, the experiments ACT published would be considered abject failures. Knowledgeable readers of the report were unable to tell whether the clump of six cells represented the beginning of a human embryo or simply an unformed aggregate of dying cells.

One prominent member of the *e-biomed* editorial board, a specialist in the type of embryology used in cloning, asked Haseltine how the ACT manuscript had been vetted before its publication. Haseltine assured his board member that the paper had been seen by two competent reviewers, but he refused to provide more details. The board member promptly resigned. Two others on the editorial board, also respected embryologists, soon followed suit. (Among the scientists left on the board are two representatives of ACT—indeed, both were authors of the paper.) Mary Ann Liebert, the publisher of the journal, interpreted this exodus as a sign that "clearly some noses were out of joint." The entire publication process subverted the potentially adversarial but necessary dynamic between journal-based peer review and the research scientist.

No one yet knows precisely how to make therapeutic cloning work, or which of its many claimed potential applications will pan out and which will not. And an obstacle other than experimental problems confronts those pushing therapeutic cloning. In the wake of the cloning revolution a second revolution has taken place—quieter but no less consequential. It, too, concerns tissue-specific stem cells—but ones found in the tissues of adults. These adult stem cells may one day prove to be at least as useful as those generated by therapeutic cloning.

Many of our tissues are continually jettisoning old, wornout cells and replacing them with freshly minted ones. The process depends on a cadre of stem cells residing in each type of tissue and specific to that type of tissue. When an adult stem cell divides, one of its two daughters becomes a precursor of a specialized worker cell, able to help replenish the pool of worker cells that may have been damaged through injury or long-term use. The other remains a stem cell like its mother, thus ensuring that the population of stem cells in the tissue is never depleted.

Until two years ago the dogma among biologists was that stem cells in the bone marrow spawned only blood, those in the liver spawned only hepatocytes, and those in the brain spawned only neurons—in other words, each of our tissues had only its own cadre of stem cells for upkeep. Once again we appear to have been wrong. There is mounting evidence that the body contains some rather unspecialized stem cells, which wander around ready to help many sorts of tissue regenerate their worker cells.

Whether these newly discovered, multi-talented adult stem cells present a viable alternative to therapeutic cloning remains to be proved. Many of the claims about their capabilities have yet to be subjected to rigorous testing. Perhaps not surprisingly, some of these claims have also reached the public without careful vetting by peers. Senator Sam Brownback, of Kansas, an ardent foe of all kinds of cloning, has based much of his case in favor of adult stem cells (and against therapeutic cloning) on these essentially unsubstantiated scientific claims. Adult stem cells provide a convenient escape hatch for Brownback. Their use placates religious conservatives, who are against all cloning, while throwing a bone to groups lobbying for new stem-cell-based therapies to treat degenerative diseases.

Brownback would have biologists shut down therapeutic-cloning research and focus their energies exclusively on adult stem-cell research. But no one can know at present which of those two strategies is more likely to work. It will take a decade or more to find out. Many biologists are understandably reluctant to set aside therapeutic-cloning research in the meantime; they argue that the two technologies should be explored simultaneously.

Precisely this issue was debated recently by advisory committees in the United States and Germany. The U.S. committee was convened by Bruce Alberts, the president of the National Academy of Sciences and a highly accomplished cell biologist and scientific educator. Quite naturally, it included a number of experts who are actively involved in exploring the advantages and disadvantages of stem-cell therapies. The committee, which announced its findings in January, concluded that therapeutic cloning should be explored in parallel with alternative strategies.

For their trouble, the scientists were accused of financial self-interest by Steven Milloy of Fox News, who said, "Enron and Arthur Andersen have nothing over the National Academy of Sciences when it comes to deceiving the public . . . Enter Bruce Alberts, the Wizard of Oz-like president of the NAS . . . On his own initiative, Alberts put together a special panel, stacked with embryonic-stem-cell research proponents and researchers already on the taxpayer dole . . . Breast-feeding off taxpayers is as natural to the NAS panel members as breathing."

The German committee, which reached a similar conclusion, was assembled by Ernst-Ludwig Winnacker, the head of his country's national science foundation. Winnacker and his colleagues were labeled "cannibals" by the Cardinal of Cologne. Remarks like the ones from Steven Milloy and the cardinal seem calculated to make public service at the interface between science and society as unappealing as possible.

President Bush, apparently anticipating the NAS panel's conclusion, has appointed an advisory committee all but guaranteed to produce a report much more to his liking. Its chairman, Leon Kass, has gone on record as being against all forms of cloning. (Earlier in his career Kass helped to launch an attack on *in vitro* fertilization.)

Meanwhile, a coalition of a hundred people and organizations recently sent a letter to Congress expressing their opposition to therapeutic cloning—among them

Friends of the Earth, Greenpeace, the Sierra Club, the head of the National Latina Health Organization, and the perennial naysayer Jeremy Rifkin. "The problem with therapeutic cloning," Rifkin has said, "is that it introduces commercial eugenics from the get-go." Powerful words indeed. Few of those galvanized by Rifkin would know that therapeutic cloning has nothing whatsoever to do with eugenics.

Usually progress in biology is held back by experimental difficulties, inadequate instruments, poorly planned research protocols, inadequate funding, or plain sloppiness. But in this case the future of research may have little connection with these factors or with the scientific pros and cons being debated earnestly by members of the research community. The other, more public debates will surely be the decisive ones.

The clashes about human therapeutic cloning that have taken place in the media and in Congress are invariably built around weighty moral and ethical principles. But none of us needs a degree in bioethics to find the bottom line in the arguments. They all ultimately converge on a single question: When does human life begin? Some say it is when sperm and egg meet, others when the embryo implants in the womb, others when the fetus quickens, and yet others when the fetus can survive outside the womb. This is a question that we scientists are neither more nor less equipped to decide than the average man or woman in the street, than a senator from Kansas or a cardinal in Cologne. (Because Dolly and the other cloned animals show that a complete embryo can be produced from a single adult cell, some biologists have proposed, tongue in cheek, that a human life exists in each one of our cells.) Take your pick of the possible answers and erect your own moral scaffolding above your choice.

In the end, politics will settle the debate in this country about whether human therapeutic cloning is allowed to proceed. If the decision is yes, then we will continue to lead the world in a crucial, cutting-edge area of biomedical research. If it is no, U.S. biologists will need to undertake hegiras to laboratories in Australia, Japan, Israel, and certain countries in Europe—an outcome that would leave American science greatly diminished.

 For Discussion:

1. How does Weinberg's article enlarge your sense of what cloning is?
2. What does Weinberg identify as the major problems aggravating the contentious debate about cloning? What solutions does he offer?
3. What's the difference between theraputic and reproductive cloning? Why do you think Weinberg speaks almost exclusively about the former? Do you have similar opinions about each type?

4. What does Weinberg think about government regulation of human theraputic cloning experiments? Do you think the government should stay out of the debate?

 For Fact-Finding, Research, and Writing:

1. Is Robert A. Weinberg also a science fiction author? How are you sure?
2. Using Public Agenda Online or a Gallup Poll, find statistics indicating American opinion on cloning. If possible, distinguish between therapeutic and reproductive cloning.
3. Have religious beliefs affected any other areas of bio-medical research?

Daniel J. Kevles, "Of Mice and Money: The Story of the World's First Animal Patent"

Daniel J. Kevles has taught at Princeton and Oxford, and is currently the Stanley Woodward Professor of History at Yale University. His articles have appeared in *The British Medical Journal, Discover, Contention,* and *The New Yorker.* He is the author of four books, including the forthcoming *Inventing America: A History of the United States.* In this piece Kevles investigates the legal, moral, and ethical issues surrounding patents on living organisms.

 Before You Read:

Can you think of any situation where owning a patent on an animal might be acceptable? What might be some of the far-ranging social and economic effects of being able to patent animals?

Of Mice & Money:
The Story of the World's First Animal Patent

Daniel J. Kevles

IN APRIL OF 1988, the United States Patent and Trademarks Office issued the first patent on a living animal in the history of the world's patent systems. Awarded to Harvard University, the patent covers a laboratory mouse that one of its scientists had genetically engineered to be supersusceptible to cancer. The Patent Office's adventurousness gratified biotechnologists, but it also disquieted many clerics. The World Council of Churches attacked animal patenting, declaring that it "removes the distinction between life and nonlife" and admonishing that "the gift of life from God . . . should not be regarded as if it were a chemical product." Other critics warned that animal patenting would spread beyond the laboratory to agriculture, where it would work harmful economic effects. The Patent Office, they said, had been high-handed in expanding the scope of patent protection to higher life forms on its own. So controversial a policy initiative was properly a matter for Congress.[1]

In a congressional hearing on genetically engineered animals the year before, Congressman Mike Synar, a wry Democrat from Oklahoma, remarked that few lawyers knew anything about patent law. "Everyone knows it is not part of the bar exam, so to hell with it."[2] But like many other branches of law—in the areas of, for example, business, regulation, and civil rights—patent law is also a branch of political economy. And in recent years, the part of it that concerns the patenting of life, especially animals and genes, has also become, for the first time, a branch of ethics.

What is patentable according to statute dates back to the patent law of 1793, which declared, in language written by Thomas Jefferson, that patents could be obtained for "any new and useful art, machine, manufacture, or composition of matter, or any new or useful improvement thereof." Jefferson's phrasing remained—and remains—at the core of the U.S. patent code, except for the eighteenth-century word "art," which was replaced in a 1952 congressional overhaul of patent law by the word "process."[3]

The code said nothing about patenting life, but a key precedent discouraging it was established in 1889, when, in a landmark ruling, the U.S. commissioner of patents rejected an application for a patent to cover a fiber identified in the needles of a pine tree. He noted that ascertaining the composition of the trees in the forest was "not a patentable invention, recognized by statute, any more than to find a new gem or jewel in the earth would entitle the discoverer to patent all gems which should be subsequently found." The commissioner added that it would be "unreasonable and impossible" to allow patents upon the trees of the forest and the plants of the earth.[4]

The commissioner's ruling formed the basis of what came to be known as the "product of nature" doctrine—that while processes devised to extract what is found in nature can be patented, objects discovered there cannot. They are not inventions, nor can they as a class be made anyone's exclusive property. In the Plant Patent Act of 1930, Congress granted patentability to one class of living products: plants that could be reproduced asexually. There was no other extension of patent law to vital entities for forty years, but then along came Ananda Chakrabarty, a biochemist at the General Electric Company, who in 1972, having bioengineered a bacterium to consume oil slicks, filed for a patent on the living, altered bacterium.

The U.S. Patent Office denied him a patent, arguing that no patent could be issued on a living organism, not least because it was a product of nature. Chakrabarty appealed his case through the courts, and at the end of 1979 it reached the United States Supreme Court under the rubric of *Diamond* v. *Chakrabarty,* in recognition of the fact that the position of the Patent Office was formally defended by Sidney Diamond, the current patent commissioner.

By the time the case arrived at the Court, it had become highly charged by the social and economic stakes that surrounded the swiftly accelerating commercialization of molecular biology. In the 1970s the new techniques of recombinant DNA were beginning to be exploited by adventurous startups such as Genentech. Companies were being founded at a rapid pace, while major pharmaceutical firms as well as several oil and chemical giants were plunging into work with recombinant DNA, initiating research programs of their own, giving research contracts to the startups, and even obtaining an equity interest in some of them. Biotechnology firms and firms eager to get into biotechnology sought connections with universities. In return, the universities could expect dividends from the biotechnology industry in the form of gifts, research grants, and license fees for the use of patents covering the valuable research products of their laboratories.

Chakrabarty had not used the technique of recombinant DNA to engineer his oil-eating bacterium, but the issue his case raised—the patentability of living organisms—spoke directly to the rapidly increasing stake in biotechnology patents. Ten *amicus* briefs were filed in the case. Most supported Chakrabarty and came from economically interested organizations including Genentech, the Pharmaceutical Manufacturers Association, the American Patent Law Association, the New York Patent Law Association, and the American Society for Microbiology. The University of California also submitted a friend-of-the-court brief. It was not more alive to the hopes of revenues from biotechnology than other universities, only more immediately interested, by virtue of the fact that Herbert Boyer, one of the inventors of recombinant DNA and a cofounder of Genentech, was a member of the faculty on its San Francisco campus.

The University of California's particular stake in the patenting of living products was echoed and generalized in a single *amicus* brief filed on behalf of the American Society of Biological Chemists, the Association of American Medical Colleges, the California Institute of Technology, and the American Council on Education as well as several faculty in biochemistry and molecular biology from Caltech and the University of California at Los Angeles. The brief was unabashedly frank in declaring the fundamental interest of each of these friends of the court in the outcome of the case:

> Some of the Amici *receive contract funds from commercial corporations whose future funding of research in this field is certain to be influenced by this Court's decision. All of the individual* Amici *receive or plan to receive indirect funding from royalties on patents which are held by their respective universities. . . . They fear that adoption of a* per se *rule excluding all living things from patentability will inhibit commercial development of the advances they are making in recombinant DNA research.*[5]

On June 16, 1980, the Court held, by the slim margin of 5 to 4, that whether the invention was alive or dead was irrelevant, that the bacterium was not a product of nature, that it was a product of Chakrabarty and hence deserved a patent. Chief Justice Warren Burger delivered the majority opinion, enthusing over the broad language that Thomas Jefferson had written into the patent law of 1793, calling it expressive of its author's "philosophy that 'ingenuity should receive a liberal encouragement'" and noting that all succeeding Congresses had left Jefferson's language virtually intact. Rejecting the contentions of the Patent Office, he found that the patent code as written was ample enough to accommodate inventions in areas unforeseen by Congress, including genetic technology, and to cover living microorganisms. Chakrabarty's bugs were new compositions of matter, the product of his ingenuity, not of nature's. As such, they were patentable under existing law.[6]

The principal inventors of the Harvard mouse were Philip Leder, a distinguished biomedical scientist who had been appointed to the university's medical school faculty in 1981, and Timothy Stewart, a young biologist who in 1982 had come to work in Leder's lab. Their construction of the mouse hinged on an experimental technique devised in 1980 at Yale University by Jon W. Gordon and Frank H. Ruddle, who expected that it could aid research into the genetics of development. Like cancerous growth, normal development occurs in a living organism, not in a tissue culture dish. Only in a living organism does the genetic program for cellular differentiation, its triggers keyed to the organism's developmental stages, play itself out over time to transform a single cell—the newly fertilized egg—into a mature animal of various specialized parts. Gordon and Ruddle expected that important features of the program might be exposed by introducing foreign DNA into the living mammalian system. The immigrant DNA would be detectable by conventional techniques in the tangle of DNA native to the organism; its behavior could thus be monitored, revealing information about the regulation of genes and the physiological functions of the proteins for which they coded.

With the techniques of recombinant DNA, any specific piece of DNA could be isolated for insertion into an animal. And then, if the DNA were introduced when the embryo consisted of just one cell, it could integrate into and then proliferate with the creature's native genome, eventually finding its way into every cell of the grown animal, including its sex cells. When the animal reproduced, the DNA would be transmitted to some fraction of its progeny, automatically supplying a large number of such genetically transformed animals.

Testing this research protocol, Gordon and Ruddle stitched together a plasmid from two different fragments of viral DNA, one containing a region involved in DNA replication, the other the code for a protein called thymidine kinase—an enzyme fundamentally involved in cellular growth—that was distinguishable from the version of the protein native to the mouse. They injected the plasmid into a pronucleus—that is, the nucleus of either the sperm or egg before one joins the other to form a single cellular nucleus—in several hundred newly fertilized mouse eggs, which were then inserted into females made psuedopregnant by coupling with vasectomized males. The females produced seventy-eight live offspring. Two of them possessed the plasmid DNA in all of their cells, indicating—a first in the annals of biology—that the two had incorporated the foreign gene and had thus been genetically modified. Gordon and Ruddle reported their experiment in December of 1980 in the *Proceedings of the National Academy of Sciences,* declaring their results to mean that "genetic transformation can be extended to whole mammalian organisms at a very early stage in their development."[7]

The creation of mice with foreign genes—"transgenic mice," to use the term that Gordon and Ruddle soon coined—attracted wide attention in the press (news stories appeared in *Time, Newsweek,* and *The New York Times*). However, the publicity did not stimulate a lot of immediate experimental commitment. Gordon and Ruddle noted that transgenic procedures, especially the insertion of foreign DNA into an early embryo, were difficult because newly fertilized mammalian eggs were delicate and small. In a conversation with Leder, I remarked that transgenic technology seemed simple. He bridled a bit, declaring, "It's very simple in the sense that someone will say that playing the violin is fairly simple." He pointed out that inserting the foreign DNA into an embryo, and then the embryo into a tiny opening in the mouse oviduct, which is thread-thin, requires not only some high-powered technology, particularly a very good microscope and very good micromanipulators, but also excellent hand-eye coordination. One of his post-doctoral fellows said that it's a good idea not to have more than one cup of coffee on a day that you're going to do microinjections, adding that otherwise your hand shakes too much and you can't manipulate the embryo.

The difficulties notwithstanding, Leder tried transgenic experiments before he arrived at Harvard, unsuccessfully, but then tried again once in Cambridge—this time with several constructions of different genes, including an oncogene called the *myc* gene. Timothy Stewart had come to Leder's Harvard group from the Institute for Cancer Research at Fox Chase, in Philadelphia, where he had collaborated in a transgenic experiment. Leder said, "Stewart was a very good biologist, an extremely talented young man, both gifted intellectually and very well coordinated."

Part of what Leder hoped to accomplish by creating a transgenic mouse was to see whether *myc* could be made to operate as an oncogene in a living animal, especially in its breast, and to test his hypothesis about how it worked as an oncogene—namely, by a deregulation that permitted the superproduction of its normal protein. Leder wanted to concentrate the expression of the *myc* gene at high levels primarily in the cells forming the animal's mammary tissue. So targeted, the gene would be little or unexpressed in male mice, since they do not develop mammary tissue, and expressed in females, making them a model for the study of breast cancer. Leder accomplished the targeting of *myc* by replacing some fraction of its promoter region by the DNA of the mouse mammary tumor virus that is activated in the breast.

In 1983, Leder and Stewart created a colony of ten transgenic mice that possessed and passed to their progeny various versions of a fused gene—a construction of mammary tumor virus DNA and the region of the mouse's normal *myc* gene that codes for its protein. From these founder ten, they established thirteen lines of *myc*-mice. By mid-1984, they had suggestive preliminary data, including a key set of results: Two of the ten founders, both females, developed cancer of the breast during an early pregnancy. One produced three daughters with the fused *myc* gene, each of which developed breast cancer in the course of a second or third pregnancy.

Leder proceeded to test whether superexpression—that is, high activation—of the fused *myc* gene in the mammary tissue was sufficient by itself to provoke malignancy. Scrutiny of the mouse breasts showed that it was apparently not sufficient: although the oncogene was expressed in all the mammary tissue, only some of the breast cells had turned tumorous. These observations were explainable by the multiple-hit theory of oncogenesis. The transformation of a normal cell into a cancerous one requires mutagenic hits that activate two or more oncogenes. Leder's results suggested that cells with elevated *myc* activity required a second hit to be made malignant—the kind of second hit that the two founder females with breast cancer and their three similarly diseased daughters had each presumably suffered.

Leder had not devised what came to be known as the "oncomouse" for the sake of producing a patentable product. But once the mouse was constructed, he recognized that it might have commercial possibilities. Indeed, his initial results indicated that it could serve a variety of different purposes, some purely scientific, others highly practical. Superexpression of the fused *myc* gene might be induced and controlled in any type of tissue by the administration of an appropriate amount of hormone, say, glucocorticoid. Leder and his collaborators thus expected that the mice could be deployed to investigate how different levels of *myc* activity influence normal development. They might also supply oncogenetic tissue from most any region of the body to laboratories for cell cultures. The tissue might be of the one-hit variety, containing just the fused *myc* oncogene, or it might be of the two-hit type, taken from tumors that might occur in any organ or cell of the mouse.

Most practical was the role that Leder's *myc* mouse could play in determining the power of a chemical to stimulate carcinogenesis or mutagenesis (genetic mutations). Leder explained:

> *Much carcinogen testing goes on in inbred strains of mice that have a very low incidence of malignancy. The test comes down to giving them varying doses of a mutagen or carcinogen and observing whether malignancies develop. Such experiments are very time-consuming—the mice may be held for two years or more— very hard, and very expensive. But if you want to use a chemical for some purpose—say, in crop dusting or fertilization—you want to have an answer to the question of whether it's carcinogenic as soon, as safely, and as sensitively as you can.*
>
> *Well . . . we know that the activation of the* myc *gene is necessary, but not sufficient, for carcinogenesis. It requires some additional hit. The likelihood of any gene in any cell suffering a mutational hit is roughly about one in a million— ten to the sixth power—per generation. The probability of any one cell's experiencing two such hits is the product of the probability of each occurring—or ten to the twelfth power. So that's six orders of magnitude difference in probability.*

Insertion of the fused *myc* gene into the mouse imposes a first carcinogenic hit on every cell in the animal. Although the probability that any one cell will experience a second hit is one in a million, the chance that such a hit will occur in the body is far higher: because the body contains millions of cells, at least one of them, somewhere, is likely to undergo a second hit. Leder said that animals with a built-in first hit will come down with malignancies at a faster rate than normal animals, explaining, "For example, if we start with a 100 percent tumor-free group of animals from some of our strains, 50 percent of them develop tumors by the age of 150 days. But we can provoke a quicker second hit by treating the animals with a chemical mutagen or a carcinogen. If we do that, 50 percent of our animals develop tumors in only 45 days. So our transgenic mouse provides a test for the mutagenicity or carcinogenicity of a chemical that is much faster than the conventional trial with ordinary mice."

In conjunction with Leder's recruitment to Harvard, the DuPont Corporation had given the university $6 million for support of Leder's research. The principal *quid pro quo* was simple: while Harvard would own any patents that might arise from Leder's investigations, DuPont would be entitled to an exclusive license on any and all such patented properties.

Under the circumstances, Leder considered himself required by Harvard to inform the university about any development in his laboratory that might be sufficiently useful and original to warrant a patent. He realized that no animal had ever been patented, but he knew that patent protection for living bacteria had recently been established in the *Chakrabarty* case. Indeed, after the *Chakrabarty* ruling, several critics had insisted that the decision appeared to leave no legal obstacle to the patenting of higher forms of life—plants, animals, and possibly human beings—or, by implication, to the genetic engineering of such life forms.

Leder wondered whether his mice might be eligible for patent protection because they formed a man-made model system for the study of cancer, including the testing of its causes and therapies. During his early work on the mice—about the end of 1983—Leder brought them to the attention of the Office of Technology Licensing and Industry Sponsored Research, the patents arm of Harvard Medical School. To explore the issue, the Office of Technology Licensing assembled a small group, including, along with Leder and several DuPont intellectual property lawyers, a patent attorney named Paul Clark, from the downtown Boston law firm of Fish & Richardson, Harvard's principal outside patent counsel. Clark later recalled in a conversation with me that "the work's most apparent and compelling manifestation was the animal itself," continuing, "it became clear immediately that it was important to claim the mice, to give Harvard and its licensee, DuPont, all the legal rights to which they were entitled. Claims on methods of using the mice, or on plasmids, although of some importance, would not have adequately protected the invention." Clark's reasoning was standard among patent lawyers: better to protect the product as well as the processes used to produce it; otherwise, competitors, using different processes, could develop similar products.

Clark also saw that Leder's transgenic animals were, like the bacteria in *Chakrabarty*, new compositions of matter made by man, and he knew that the Supreme Court had admonished in the *Chakrabarty* case that a court cannot properly consider the state of being alive when deciding whether something falls within the protection of patent law. Thus, Clark explained, "it was hard for me to see any legal basis for excluding claims on animals."

On June 22, 1984, on behalf of Harvard University, Clark filed an application for a patent on Leder and Stewart's invention. The main utilities that he claimed were straightforward, including the use of such animals as sources of malignant or protomalignant tissue for cell culture and as living systems on which to test compounds for carcinogenicity or—in the case of substances like vitamin E—power to prevent cancers. However, Clark was not at all conservative in what he claimed as the actual invention. It was not simply a transgenic mouse with an activated *myc* gene, which would have been extraordinary enough. It was any transgenic mammal, excluding human beings, containing in all its cells an activated oncogene that had been introduced into it—or an ancestor—at an embryonic stage.

The same year that Harvard filed for a patent on Leder's mouse, a marine biologist named Standish K. Allen and collaborators at the University of Washington applied for a patent on a version of *Crassostrea gigas,* a variety of the Pacific oyster, which they had improved by making it chromosomally triploid. The claim was partly for the triploidy process, which made the oyster more edible. However, it also covered the improved oyster as such, which challenged precedent.

The examiners in the U.S. Patent Office denied the claim, holding that neither *Diamond v. Chakrabarty* nor any other patent ruling authorized the grant of a patent on a higher animal, even if only an invertebrate. The examiners also found that the triploid oyster was not patentable on the technical ground that the innovation was obvious to anyone schooled in the art of oyster breeding. Allen and his colleagues appealed. In 1987, the Board of Patent Appeals and Interferences of the U.S. Patent and Trademark Office issued a decision, since known as *Ex parte Allen.* The Board upheld the examiners on the point that obviousness of art disqualified the oyster for a patent. However, it also declared that patents could in principle be granted on nonhuman animals.[8]

The ruling in *Ex parte Allen* did defuse one important public fear about law and biotechnology by stipulating that human beings cannot be patented by reason of the 13th Amendment to the U.S. Constitution. Since it outlaws slavery, it in effect prohibits one human being from holding a property right on another. But following *Ex parte Allen,* the patent examiners had no problem granting Leder and Stewart's claim on their mouse.

The ethical objections to the patenting of animals had been adumbrated at the time of the *Chakrabarty* case. During arguments in the case, vigorous objection to Chakrabarty's claim had come from the People's Business Commission (PBC), an activist group headed by Jeremy Rifkin. Rifkin was a social agitator and sleepless critic of biotechnology. The PBC's dissent was partly economic—patents on living organisms would foster monopoly in vital areas such as the food industry. It was quasi-religious, too, holding that "*the essence of the matter*" was that to permit patents on life was to imply that "life has no 'vital' or sacred property," that it was only "an arrangement of chemicals, or mere 'compositions of matter.'"[9] In its ruling on the case, the Supreme Court majority took note of these and other apprehensions, observing that they "present a gruesome parade of horribles" and "that, at times, human ingenuity seems unable to control fully the forces it creates." The majority observed, however, that genetic research with its attendant risks would likely proceed with or without patent protection for its products and that neither legislative nor judicial fiat as to patentability would "deter the scientific mind from probing into the unknown any more than Canute could command the tides."

The patenting of animals made the debate over the patenting of life more charged and brought into it new groups—notably animal rights activists, environmentalists, clerics, and farmers' representatives. Their objections were well aired in hearings held in 1987 and 1989 before the House Judiciary Subcommittee that dealt with patents, chaired by Congressman Robert Kastenmeier.[10] The objections raised to the patenting of animals tended to be specific to the groups raising them: animal rights activists contended that such patents would exacerbate the degradation of animals; environmentalists argued that genetically engineered animals would escape and threaten the integrity of wildlife; clerics claimed that patenting reduced God's creatures to mere material objects; and farm spokespersons worried about the economic effects of patented animals on small farmers.

Strong defenses of animal patenting came from other witnesses, notably representatives of the biotechnology industry and of major universities. Their arguments, echoing those advanced in the large majority of the *amicus* briefs submitted in the *Chakrabarty* case, emphasized the role of patents in stimulating biotechnological innovation, fostering American competitiveness, and advancing medical research, including diagnostics, therapies, and cures. No significant objection was raised against animal patenting by university representatives or scientists on grounds that such patenting would impede access to or use of transgenic research materials.

Kastenmeier and his subcommittee responded to the debate pragmatically— ignoring most of the objections raised by Rifkin and his allies but paying attention to those that touched directly on issues of public policy concerning the key interest groups involved, particularly agriculture. In 1988, Kastenmeier produced a bill that would exempt farmers from any restraint, including the restraint of royalty payments, on what they did with the progeny of their patented animals. It declared explicitly that human beings cannot be patented. The bill passed the House, but it was not taken up in the Senate before the end of Congress. Since then, no bill addressing animal patents has reached the floor of the House or Senate.

Moreover, advocates of biotechnology insisted on distinguishing between issues of political economy and issues of ethics. The former had a place in disputes over patent policy; the latter, at least in the United States, did not, even though they might be legitimate in principle. The appropriate venues for considering them were the legislative and regulatory arenas of government, not the Patent Office.

In contrast, the European Patent Convention—which was established in 1962 and governs the national patent systems of its adhering nations—specifically excludes two types of inventions from eligibility for patents. Article 53(a) prohibits patents on any invention that is contrary to public order or morality. And Article 53(b) prohibits them on plant or animal varieties, or anything produced by a natural biological process, except for microbiological products. Article 53(a) seems to have its roots in Roman law. Article 53(b) was adopted to prevent interference with the international system for the protection of breeders' rights—it is known acronymically as UPOV and was created in 1961—in new varieties of plants. At the time of the creation of UPOV, the extension of the exclusion to animal varieties was undoubtedly an afterthought.

However, both articles were brought into play when the European Patent Office (EPO), which administers the convention and which is headquartered in Munich, took up Harvard University's application, filed in 1984, for a European patent on its oncomouse. Ruling in June of 1989, the EPO found that oncomouse did not violate the public-order-and-morality clause of the convention, but it rejected Harvard's application on grounds that the mouse did violate Article 53(b). In the view of the EPO examiners, oncomouse was a new variety of animal, the product of a natural biological process, and, hence, ineligible for a patent under the convention.[11]

Harvard quickly appealed the rejection, insisting that its mouse was not a new variety but a new type of animal that transcended varietal classification, and that it was not a natural biological product but—echoing Chakrabarty's claim—a biological entity made by man. The appeal provoked an unprecedented degree of third-party filings. (Under the European Patent Convention, interested third parties can file comments for or against pending applications and appeals, an option that is unavailable in the American patent process.) Many of the filings were identical, the products of organized opposition to animal patenting in Europe from public-interest organizations concerned with animal rights, Third World agriculture, and environmental issues. The dissent mobilized by these public-interest groups appears to have been centered in England, where animal welfare groups are powerful, and in Germany, where opposition to genetic engineering and concern with environmental protection are vigorous. The arguments raised by these groups closely resembled those advanced in the United States against animal patenting. However, the European agricultural community appears to have been more profoundly split on patents for plants and animals than its American counterpart, with considerable opposition coming from countries where small-scale agriculture (as distinct from agribusiness) continues to flourish—for example, Denmark.

The third-party filings evidently contributed significantly to the decision of the appeals board, which in 1990 returned the Harvard application to the original examiners for reconsideration. The appeals board, agreeing with Harvard, declared that the rejection on grounds of Article 53(b) was without merit, but it held that the examiners had to review the application against Article 53(a), the morality clause. The examiners were compelled to reconsider issues raised by the third-party filings, particularly whether a patent on oncomouse would lead to animal suffering (mice with cancer) and environmental danger (the spread of oncogenes into the natural mouse population if the oncomice were to escape). However, the appeals board also instructed the examiners to weigh those matters against the likely benefit to human beings that might arise from research with oncomice.[12]

Harvard's lawyers in Europe contended that the mice would, of course, contribute to the battle against cancer, making them distinctly beneficial to human beings. They also argued that, since the mice were supersusceptible to the contraction of cancer, fewer of them would be required to test for carcinogens, and thus fewer mice would suffer in such testing. Finally, they pointed out that the mice posed only a minute environmental risk, because they were to be confined to the laboratory rather than released into the wild, and while unintended release might occur, the danger was surely a matter not for the patent system but for the agencies concerned with the control of hazardous materials.[13]

The Harvard lawyers' arguments persuaded the European Patent Office, which incorporated them in a ruling, issued in October of 1991, indicating that a patent on the mouse could and likely would be granted.[14] Under the terms of the convention, the ruling was liable to still further third-party objections; the comment period closed in February of 1993, having drawn many more filings of dissent, most of them advancing the same arguments and coming from roughly the same sources as in the first round.

The third-party dissidents did not prevail, just as the opponents to animal patenting have not prevailed in the United States. The biotechnology complex, having had its way politically on the western side of the Atlantic, had worked its will on the eastern side, too, given the pressures of high-technology competitiveness and the apparent lack of persuasiveness of the antipatenting arguments. However, even though American patent law continues to be literally amoral, anyone seeking a patent on a living organism in Europe will have to satisfy the requirements of Article 53(a). In the globalizing political economy of biotechnology, American innovators must now attend to the ethical features of their innovations.

Notes

1. Testimony of Jaydee R. Hanson . . . United Methodist Church, and Andrew W. Kimbrell . . . on Behalf of the Coalition on Animal Patenting, U.S. Congress, House, Hearings before the Subcommittee on Courts, Civil Liberties, and the Administration of Justice, Committee on the Judiciary. *Transgenic Animal Patent Reform Act of 1989*, 101st Cong., 1st Sess., September 13 and 14, 1989, 258–272.
2. U.S. Congress, House, Hearings before the Subcommittee on Courts, Civil Liberties, and the Administration of Justice, Committee on the Judiciary, *Patents and the Constitution: Transgenic Animals*, 100th Cong., 1st Sess., June 11, July 22, August 21, and November 5, 1987, 27.
3. Fritz Machlup, "Patents," *International Encyclopedia of the Social Sciences*, ed. David L. Sills (New York: Macmillan, 1968), XI, 461–464; Bruce W. Bugbee, *Genesis of American Patent and Copyright Law* (Washington, D.C.: Public Affairs Press, 1967), 152.
4. *Ex Parte Latimer*, March 12, 1889, C.D., 46 O.G. 1638, U.S. Patent Office, *Decisions of the Commissioner of Patents and of the United States Courts in Patent Cases . . . 1889* (Washington, D.C.: Government Printing Office, 1890), 123–127. See also H. Thorne, "Relation of Patent Law to Natural Products," *Journal of Patent Office Society* 6 (1923): 23–28.
5. *Brief Amicus Curiae of the Regents of the University of California*, January 1980; *Brief of Dr. Leroy Hood, Dr. Thomas Maniatis, Dr. David S. Eisenberg, the American Society of Biological Chemists, the Association of American Medical Colleges, the California Institute of Technology, the American Council on Education as Amicus Curiae*, January 28, 1980. The *amicus* briefs are with *Diamond* v. *Chakrabarty*, U.S. Supreme Court, Docket No. 79–136, 447 U.S. 303, January 1980.
6. *Diamond* v. *Chakrabarty*, 447 U.S. 303, 100 S. Ct. 2204 (1980), 2206–2212.
7. Jon W. Gordon, George A. Scangos, Diane J. Plotkin, James A. Barbosa, and Frank H. Ruddle, "Genetic Transformation of Mouse Embryos by Microinjection of Purified DNA," *Proceedings of the National Academy of Sciences* 77 (December 1980): 7380–7384.
8. *Ex Parte Allen*, United States Patent Quarterly (1987): 1425.
9. *Brief on Behalf of the People's Business Commission, Amicus Curiae*, 1979.

10. U.S. Congress, House, Hearings before the Subcommittee on Courts, Civil Liberties, and the Administration of Justice, Committee on the Judiciary, *Patents and the Constitution: Transgenic Animals,* 100th Cong., 1st Sess., June 11, July 22, August 21, and November 5, 1987; U.S. Congress, House, Subcommittee on Courts, Intellectual Property, and the Administration of Justice, Committee on the Judiciary, *Transgenic Animal Patent Reform Act of 1989,* 101st Cong., 1st Sess., September 13 and 14, 1989.
11. European Patent Office, Press Release No. 10/89, "EPO Refuses Patent Application for Oncogenic Mouse."
12. European Patent Office, "Decision of the Technical Board of Appeal 3.3.2 of 3 October 1990."
13. "European Patent Application No. 86 304490.7, President and Fellows of Harvard College, Response to the Official Letter of 11th December 1990. . . ."
14. European Patent Office, Press Release 3/92, "European Patent for Harvard's Transgenic Mouse."

For Discussion:

1. Technology leading to animal patenting could eventually be used in human cloning. Putting aside moral and ethical implications, what do we stand to lose or gain socially, economically, and/or politically as a result of animal patents or human cloning?
2. Kevles speaks of corporate investment and interests on patents for living organisms produced, primarily, on university campuses and in university libraries. What positive or negative outcomes might stem from such an investment?
3. Why do you think the EPO (European Patent Convention) was more conservative in its rulings on Harvard's genetically engineered oncomouse?

For Fact-Finding, Research, and Writing:

1. Investigate what patents are in dispute today. Are cases similar to those in this essay currently under review?
2. Kevles' essay cites two historic government documents. Locate Thomas Jefferson's patent law of 1793. Does Jefferson's language support the Kevles' argument? The 13th Amendment to the Constitution is also mentioned. Find the exact text of that Amendment. According to its language, is cloning oneself, in fact, unconstitutional?
3. Locate some of the original articles written on "transgenic mice" written by Gordon and Ruddle in the 1980s.

Lauren Slater, "Dr. Daedalus: A Radical Plastic Surgeon Wants to Give You Wings"

Lauren Slater is a writer and psychologist with degrees from Harvard and Boston University. In addition to her scientific papers, Slater has written many popular books on psychological issues and is most famous for her 1999 memoir, *Prozac Nation*. Her most recent book, *Love Works Like This: Opening One's Life to a Child*, details her reflections on motherhood; *Lying: A Metaphorical Memoir* (2001) echoes the ideas of the article offered here as she presents a deliberately contradictory and openly fictional tale as the story of her life.

 Before You Read:

If plastic surgery could enhance any one of your senses, which would you choose, and why? Given the opportunity to have surgically implanted wings, would you?

Dr. Daedalus

Lauren Slater

Part I: Beautiful People

JOE ROSEN, PLASTIC SURGEON at the renowned Dartmouth-Hitchcock Medical Center, and by any account an odd man, has a cold. But then again, he isn't sure it's a cold. "It could be anthrax," he says as he hurries to the car, beeper beeping, sleet sleeting, for it's freezing New England midwinter day when all the world is white. Joe Rosen's nose is running, his throat is raw, and he's being called into the ER because some guy made meat out of his forefinger and a beautiful teenager split her fine forehead open on the windshield of her SUV. It seems unfair, he says, all these calls coming in on a Sunday, especially because he's sick and he isn't sure whether it's the flu or the first subtle signs of a biological attack. "Are you serious?" I say to him. Joe Rosen is smart. He graduated cum laude from Cornell and got a medical degree from Stanford in 1978. And we're in his car now, speeding toward the hospital where he reconstructs faces, appends limbs, puffs and preens the female form. "You really wonder," I say, "if your cold is a sign of a terrorist attack?"

Joe Rosen, a respected and controversial plastic surgeon, wonders a lot of things, some of them directly related to his field, others not. Joe Rosen wonders, for instance, whether Osama bin Laden introduced the West Nile virus to this country. Joe Rosen wonders how much bandwidth it would take to make virtual-reality contact lenses available for all. Joe Rosen wonders why both his ex-wife and his current wife are artists, and what that says about his deeper interests. Joe Rosen also wonders why we insist on the kinds of conservative medical restraints that prevent him from deploying some of his most creative visions: wings for human beings; cochlear implants to enhance hearing, beefing up our boring ears and giving us the range of an owl; super-duper delicate rods to jazz up our vision—binocular, beautiful—so that we could see for many miles and into depths as well. Joe Rosen has ideas: implants for this, implants for that, gadgets, gears, discs, buttons, sculpting soft cartilage that would enable us, as humans, to cross the frontiers of our own flesh and emerge as something altogether . . . what? Something other.

And we're in the car now, speeding on slick roads toward the hospital, beeper beeping, sleet sleeting, passing cute country houses with gingerbread trim, dollops of smoke hanging above bright brick chimneys; his New Hampshire town looks so sweet. We pull into the medical center. Even this has a slight country flair to it, with gingham curtains hanging in the rows of windows. We skid. Rosen says, "One time I was in my Ford Explorer with my daughter, Sam. We rolled, and the next thing I knew we were on the side of the highway, hanging upside down like bats." He laughs.

We go in. I am excited, nervous, running by his bulky side with my tape recorder to his mouth. A resident in paper boots comes up to us. He eyes the tape recorder, and Rosen beams. Rosen is a man who enjoys attention, credentials. A few days ago he boasted to me, "You shouldn't have any trouble with the PR people in this hospital. I've had three documentaries made of me here already."

"Can I see them?" I asked.

"I don't know," Rosen answered, suddenly scratching his nose very fast. "I guess I'm not sure where I put them," and something about his voice, or his nose, made me wonder whether the documentaries were just a tall tale.

Now the resident rushes up to us, peers at the tape recorder, peers at me. "They're doing a story on me," Rosen says. "For *Harper's*."

"Joe is a crazy man, a nutcase," the resident announces, but there's affection in his voice.

"Why the beeps?" Rosen asks.

"This guy, he was working in his shop, got his finger caught in an electric planer . . . The finger's hamburger," the resident says. "It's just hamburger."

We go to the carpenter's cubicle. He's a man with a burly beard and sawdust-caked boots. He lies too big for the ER bed, his dripping finger held high in the air and splinted. It does look like hamburger.

I watch Rosen approach the bed, the wound. Rosen is a largish man, with a curly head of hair, wearing a Nordstrom wool coat and a cashmere scarf. As a plastic surgeon, he thinks grand thoughts but traffics mostly in the mundane. He has had over thirty papers published, most of them with titles like "Reconstructive Flap Surgery" or "Rhinoplasty for the Adolescent." He is known among his colleagues only second-arily for his epic ideas; his respect in the field is rooted largely in his impeccable surgical skill with all the toughest cases: shotgunned faces, smashed hands.

"How ya doin'?" Rosen says now to the carpenter. The carpenter doesn't answer. He just stares at his mashed finger, held high in the splint.

Rosen speaks softly, gently. He puts his hand on the woodworker's dusty shoul-der. "Looks bad," he says, and he says this with a kind of simplicity—or is it empa-thy?—that makes me listen. The patient nods. "I need my finger," he says, and his voice sounds tight with tears. "I need it for the work I do."

Rosen nods. His tipsiness, his grandiosity, seem to just go away. He stands close to the man. "Look," he says, "I'm not going to do anything fancy right now, okay? I'll just have my guys sew it up, and we'll try to let nature take its course. I think that's the best thing, right now. To let nature take its course."

The carpenter nods. Rosen has said nothing really reassuring, but his tone is soothing, his voice rhythmic, a series of stitches that promises to knit the broken together.

We leave the carpenter. Down the hall, the teenage beauty lies in still more se-rious condition, the rent in her forehead so deep we can see, it seems, the barest haze of her brain.

"God," whispers Rosen as we enter the room. "I dislike foreheads. They get in-fected so easily."

He touches the girl. "You'll be fine," he says. "We're not going to do anything fancy here. Just sew you up and let nature take its course."

I think these are odd, certainly unexpected words coming from a man who seems so relentlessly anti-nature, so visionary and futuristic in his interests. But then again, Rosen himself is odd, a series of swerves, a topsy-turvy, upside-down, smoke-and-mirrors sort of surgeon, hanging in his curious cave, a black bat.

"I like this hospital," Rosen announces to me as we leave the girl's room. "I like its MRI machines." He pauses.

"I should show you a real marvel," he suddenly says. He looks around him. A nurse rushes by, little dots of blood on her snowy smock. "Come," Rosen says.

We ride the elevator up. The doors whisper open. Outside, the sleet has turned to snow, falling fast and furious. The floor we're on is ominously quiet, as though there are no patients here, or as though we're in a morgue. Rosen is ghoulish and I am suddenly scared. I don't know him really. I met him at a medical-ethics conven-tion at which he discussed teaching *Frankenstein* to his residents and elaborated, with a little light in his eye, on the inherent beauty in hybrids and chimeras, if only we could learn to see them that way. "Why do we only value the average?" he'd asked the audience. "Why are plastic surgeons dedicated only to restoring our current notions of the conventional, as opposed to letting people explore, if they want, what the possibilities are?"

Rosen went on to explain other things at that conference. It was hard for me to follow his train of thought. He vacillates between speaking clearly, almost epically, to mumbling and zigzagging and scratching his nose. At this conference he kangaroo-leapt from subject to subject: the army, biowarfare, chefs with motorized fingers that could whip eggs, noses that doubled as flashlights, soldiers with sonar, the ocean, the monsters, the marvels. He is a man of breadth but not necessarily depth. "According to medieval man," Rosen said to the convention, finally coming clear, "a monster is someone born with congenital deformities. A marvel," he explained, "is a person with animal parts—say, a tail or wings." He went on to show us pictures, a turn-of-the-century newborn hand with syphilitic sores all over it, the fingers webbed in a way that might have been beautiful but not to me, the pearly skin stretched to nylon netting in the crotch of each crooked digit.

And the floor we're on now is ominously quiet, except for a hiss somewhere, maybe some snake somewhere, with a human head. We walk for what seems a long time. My tape recorder sucks up the silence.

Rosen turns, suddenly, and with a flourish parts the curtains of a cubicle. Before me, standing as though he were waiting for our arrival, is a man, a real man, with a face beyond description. "Sweeny,"* Rosen says, gesturing toward the man, "has cancer of the face. It ate through his sinus cavities, so I scraped off his face, took off his tummy fat, and made a kind of, well, a new face for him out of the stomach. Sweeny, you look good!" Rosen says.

Sweeny, his new face, or his old stomach, oozing and swollen from this recent, radical surgery, nods. He looks miserable. The belly-face sags, the lips wizened and puckered like an anus, the eyes in their hills of fat darting fast and frightened.

"What about my nose?" Sweeny says, and then I notice: Sweeny has no nose. The cancer ate that along with the cheeks, etc. This is just awful. "That comes next. We'll use what's left of your forehead." A minute later, Rosen turns to me and observes that pretty soon women will be able to use their buttocks for breast implants. "Where there's fat," Rosen says, "there are possibilities."

The coffee is hot and good. We drink it in the hospital cafeteria while we wait for the weather to clear. "You know," Rosen says, "I'm really proud of that face. I didn't follow any protocol. There's no textbook to tell you how to fashion a face eaten away by cancer. Plastic surgery is the intersection of art and science. It's the intersection of the surgeon's imagination with human flesh. And human flesh," Rosen says, "is infinitely malleable. People say cosmetic surgery is frivolous—boobs and noses. But it's so much more than that! The body is a conduit for the soul, at least historically speaking. When you change what you look like, you change who you are."

I nod. The coffee, actually, is too damn hot. The delicate lining of skin inside my mouth starts to shred. The burn-pain distracts me. I have temporarily altered my body,

---

Not his real name.

and thus my mind. For just one moment, I am a burned-girl, not a writer-girl. Rosen may be correct. With my tongue I flick the loose skin, picture it, pink and silky, on fire.

No, plastic surgery is not just boobs and noses. Its textbooks are tomes—thick, dusty, or slick, no matter—that all open up to images of striated muscle excised from its moorings, bones—white, calcium-rich—elongated by the doctor's finest tools. Plastic surgery, as a medical specialty, is very confusing. It aims, on the one hand, to restore deformities and, on the other hand, to alter the normal. Therefore, the patients are a motley crew. There is the gorgeous blonde with the high sprayed helmet of hair who wants a little tummy tuck, even though she's thin, and then there is the Apert Syndrome child, the jaw so foreshortened the teeth cannot root in their sockets. Plastic surgery—like Rosen, its premier practitioner—is flexible, high-minded, and wide-ranging, managing to be at once utterly necessary and ridiculously frivolous, all in the same breath, all in the same scalpel.

According to the American Society of Plastic Surgeons, last year more than 1.3 million people had cosmetic surgery performed by board-certified plastic surgeons, an increase of 227 percent since 1992. (These numbers do not include medically necessary or reconstructive surgeries.) The five most popular procedures were liposuction (229,588), breast augmentation (187,755), eyelid surgery (172,244), the just available Botox injections (118,452), and face lifts (70,882). Most cosmetic surgeries are performed on women, but men are catching up: the number of men receiving nose jobs—their most popular procedure—has increased 141 percent since 1997. The vast majority of patients are white, but not necessarily wealthy. A 1994 study found that 65 percent of cosmetic-surgery patients had a family income of less than $50,000, even though neither state nor private health insurance covers the cost of cosmetic surgeries. These figures alone point to the tremendous popularity and increasing acceptance of body alteration, and suggest that the slippery slope from something as bizarre as eyelid tucks to something still more bizarre, like wings, may be shorter than we think.

This medical specialty is ancient, dating back to 800 B.C., when hieroglyphics describe crude skin grafts. Rosen once explained to me that plastic surgery started as a means to blur racial differences. "A long time ago," he'd said, "Jewish slaves had clefts in their ears. And some of the first plastic-surgery operations were to remove those signs of stigma."

One history book mentions the story of a doctor named Joseph Dieffenbach and a man with grave facial problems. This man had the sunken nose of syphilis, a disease widely associated with immorality. Dieffenbach, one of the fathers of plastic surgery, so the story goes, devised a gold rhinoplasty bridge for this marginal man, thus giving him, literally, a Midas nose and proving, indeed, that medicine can make criminals kings.

As a field, plastic surgery is troubled, insecure. It is a lot like psychiatry, or dentistry, in its inferior status as a subspecialty of medicine. In fact, the first plastic-surgery association, started in 1921, was an offshoot of oral practitioners. Read: teeth people. Not to digress, but the other day I woke up with a terrible toothache and rushed in to see a dentist. I said to him, just to be friendly, "What sort of training do you need for your profession?" He said, "You need A LOT of training, believe me. I trained with the same guys who cure your cancer, but I don't get the same respect."

I wonder if Rosen ever feels like my dentist, and if that's why he's so grandiose, like the little boy who is a bully. Sander Gilman, a cultural critic of plastic surgery, writes that, in this group of doctors, there are a lot of big words thrown around in an effort to cover up the sneaking suspicion that their interventions are not important. One is not ever supposed to say "nose job"; it's called rhinoplasty. Gilman writes, "The lower the perceived status of a field . . . the more complex and 'scientific' the discourse of the field becomes."

Of course, I rarely meet a doctor who doesn't like jargon and doesn't like power. Rosen may be different only in intensity. "I'm not a cosmetic surgeon," Rosen keeps repeating to me. He says, "Really, there's no such thing as just cosmetic surgery. The skin and the soul are one." On paper, maybe, this comment seems a little overblown, but delivered orally, in a New England town when all the world is white, it has its lyrical appeal.

When Rosen cries out that he's not "just a cosmetic surgeon," he's put his finger on a real conflict in his field. Where does necessary reconstruction end and frivolous interventions begin? Are those interventions really frivolous, or are they emblematic of the huge and sometimes majestic human desire to alter, to transcend? If medicine is predicated upon the notion of making the sick well, and a plastic surgeon operates on someone who is not sick, then can the patient truly be called a patient, and the doctor a doctor? Who pays for this stuff, when, where, and how? These are the swirling questions. Over a hundred years ago Jacques Joseph, another of plastic surgery's founding fathers, wrote that beauty was a medical necessity because a person's looks can create social and economic barriers. Repairing the deformity, therefore, allows the man to function in a fully healthy way in society. Voilà. Function and form, utilitarianism and aestheticism, joined at the hip, grafted together: skin tight.

Perhaps we can accept Joseph's formulation. Okay, we say. Calm down. We say this to all the hopping, hooting cosmetic surgeons who want to stake out their significance. Okay, we respect you. I'd like to say this to Rosen, but I can't. Rosen's ideas and aspirations, not to mention his anthrax concerns, go beyond what I am comfortable with, though I can't quite unearth the architecture of my concerns. After all, he doesn't want to hurt anyone. Maybe it's because Rosen isn't just talking about everyday beauty and its utilitarian aspects. He is talking EXTREMES. When Rosen thinks of beauty, he thinks of the human form stretched on the red-hot rack of his imagination, which is mired in medieval texts and books on trumpeter swans. At its outermost limits, beauty becomes fantastical, perhaps absurd. Here is where Rosen rests. He dreams of making wings for human beings. He has shown me blue-prints, sketches of the scalpel scissoring into skin, stretching flaps of torso fat to fashion gliders piped with rib bone. When the arm stretches, the gliders unfold, and human floats on currents of air. Is he serious? At least partially. He gives lectures to medical students on the meaning of wings from an engineering perspective, a surgeon's perspective, and a patient's perspective. He has also thought of cochlear implants to enhance normal hearing, fins to make us fishlike, and echolocation devices so that we can better navigate the night. He does not understand the limits we place on hands. He once met a Vietnamese man with two thumbs on one hand. This man was a waiter, and his two thumbs made him highly skilled at his job. "Now," says Rosen, "if that man came to me and said, 'I want you to take off my extra thumb,' I'd be allowed, but I wouldn't be allowed to put an extra thumb on a person, and that's not fair."

We can call Rosen ridiculous, a madman, a monster, a marvel. We could dismiss him as a techno geek or a fool or just plain immature. But then there are the facts. First of all, Rosen is an influential man, an associate professor of surgery at Dartmouth Medical School and the director of the Plastic Surgery Residency Program at the medical center. He was senior fellow at the C. Everett Koop Institute from 1997 to 1998, and he has also served on advisory panels for the navy and for NASA's Medical Care for the Mission to Mars, 2018. Rosen consults for the American Academy of Sciences committee on the role of virtual-reality technology, and he is the former director of the Department of Defense's Emerging Technology Threats workforce. In other words, this is a man taken seriously by some serious higher-ups. "Echolocation devices," Rosen explains, "implanted in a soldier's head, could do a lot to enhance our military capacity." And this isn't just about the army's fantasies of the perfect soldier. Rosen travels worldwide (he gave over a dozen presentations last year) and has had substantial impact not only scalpeling skin but influencing his colleagues' ethics in a myriad of ways. "He has been essential in helping me to conceptualize medicine outside of the box," says Charles Lucey, MD, a former colleague of Rosen's at the Dartmouth Medical School. John Harris, a medical-ethics specialist in Manchester, England, writes in *Wonderwoman and Superman* that "in the absence of an argument or the ability to point to some specific harm that might be involved in crossing species boundaries, we should regard the objections *per se* to such practices . . . as mere and gratuitous prejudice." Rosen himself says, "Believe me. Wings are not way off. It is not a bad idea. Who would have thought we'd ever agree to hold expensive, potentially dangerous radioactive devices up to our ears for hours on end, day after day, just so we could gossip. That's cell phones for you," he says. And smiles.

Rosen has a nice smile. It's, to be sure, a little boyish, but it's charming. Sometimes Rosen is shy. "I mumble a lot," he acknowledges. "I don't really like people. I don't really like the present. I am a man who lives in the past and in the future only."

Now we leave the emergency room. The snow has stopped. The roads are membraned with ice. The sun is setting in the New Hampshire sky, causing the hills to sparkle as though they're full of little lights and other electric things. We drive back to his house, slowly. The emergencies are over, the patients soothed or suffering, he has done what can be done in a day, and still his nose runs. He coughs into his fist. "Truth be told," he says to me, "I didn't start out wanting to be a surgeon, even though I always, ALWAYS, had big ideas. In kindergarten, when the other kids were making these little ditsy arts-and-crafts projects, I was building a room-size Seventh Fleet ship." He goes on. As a child he wanted to be an artist. In high school he became obsessed with Picasso's *Guernica* and spent months trying to replicate it in the style of Van Gogh. As a freshman at Cornell, he made a robotic hand that could crack his lobster for him, and from then on it was hands, fingers, knees, and toes. His interests in the technical aspects of the body drew him away from the arts and eventually into medical school, which was, in his mind, somewhere between selling out and moving on.

We pull into his driveway. Rosen lives in a sprawling ranch-style house. He has a pet hen, who waits for us in the evergreen tree. His second wife, Stina Kohnke, is young and, yes, attractive. I'm afraid to ask how old she is; he looks to be at least fifty-three and she looks twenty-three, though maybe that's beside the point. Nevertheless, it all gets thrown into my mental stew: grandiose man, military man, medicine man, wants to make wings, young thing for a mate. Rooster and hen. Maybe there is no story here. Maybe there's just parody. All breadth, no depth. Except for this. Everyone I tell about Rosen and his wings, his *fin de siècle* mind, widens his or her eyes, leans forward, and says, "You're kidding." People want to hear more. *I* want to hear more. His ideas of altering the human form are repugnant and delicious, and that's a potent combination to unravel. And who among us has not had flying dreams, lifted high, dramatically free, a throat-catching fluidity in our otherwise aching form, above the ocean, all green, like moving marble?

Rosen and his wife have invited me for dinner. I accept. Stina is an artist. Her work is excellent. "Joe is an inspiration for me," she says. "He brings home pictures of his patients, and I sculpt their limbs from bronze." In her studio, she has a riot of red-bronze deformed hands clutching, reaching, in an agony of stiffness. She has fashioned drawer pulls from gold-plated ears. You go to open the breadbox, the medicine cabinet, the desk drawer, and you have to touch these things. It's at once creepy and very beautiful.

We sit at their stone dining-room table. Behind us is a seventy-gallon aquarium full of fish. Cacti, pink and penile, thrust their way into the odd air. Stina, homesick for her native California, has adorned the living room with paper palm trees and tiny live parakeets. We talk. Stina says, "Joe and I got married because we found in each other the same aesthetic and many moral equivalents. We found two people who could see and sculpt the potential in what others found just ugly."

"How did you two meet?" I ask.

"Oh, I knew Stina's sister, who was an art professor . . . That sort of thing," mumbles Rosen.

"I kissed him first," says Stina. She reaches across the table, picks up Rosen's hand, and wreathes her fingers through his. She holds on tightly, as if she's scared. I study Stina. She is conventionally pretty. She has a perfect Protestant nose and a lithe form, and a single black bra strap slips provocatively from beneath her blouse. Rosen, a man who claims to love the unusual, has picked a very usual beauty.

"Look!" Stina suddenly shouts. I jump, startled. "Look at her ears!" she says to Rosen.

Before I know it they are both leaning forward, peering at my ears. "Oh, my God," says Stina, "you have the most unusual ears."

Now, this is not news to me. I have bat ears, plain and simple. They stick out stupidly. In the fifth grade, I used to fasten them to the sides of my skull with pink styling tape in the hope of altering their shape. I have always disliked my ears.

Rosen uncurls his index finger and touches my left ear. He runs his finger along the bumpy, malformed rim. "You're missing the *scapha*," he says. "It's a birth defect."

"I have a birth defect?" I say. I practically shout this, being someone who desires deeply not to be defective. That's why I take Prozac every day.

"Joe," says Stina, "are those not the most amazing ears. They would be so perfect to sculpt."

"They're just a perfect example," Rosen echoes, "of the incredible, delectable proliferation of life-forms. We claim most life-forms gravitate toward the mean, but that's not true. Lots of valid life exists at the margins of the bell curve. You have beautiful ears," he says to me.

"I have nice ears?" I say. "Really?"

This is just one reason why I won't dismiss Rosen out of hand. Suddenly, I see my ears a little differently. They have a marvelous undulating ridge and an intricately whorled entrance, and they do not stick out so much as jauntily jut; they are ears with an attitude. Rosen has shifted my vision without even touching my eyes. He is, at the very least, a challenger of paradigms; he calls on your conservatism, pushes hard.

That night, I do not dream of wings. I dream of Sweeny and his oozing face. I dream he comes so close to me that I smell him. Then I wake up. Sweeny is very sick. He is going to die soon. Earlier in the day, I asked Rosen when, and Rosen said, "Oh, soon," but he said it as if he didn't really care. Death does not seem to interest Rosen. Beauty, I think, can be cold.

Part II: Monster and Marvels

Today, Rosen and I are attending a conference together in Montreal. Here, everyone speaks French and eats baguettes. The conference room is old-fashioned, wainscoted with rich mahogany, ornate carvings of creatures and angels studding the ceiling, where a single light hangs in a cream-colored orb. Around the table sit doctors, philosophers, graduate students: this is a medical-ethics meeting, and Rosen is presenting his ideas. On the white board, in bold black lines, he sketches out his wings, and then the discussion turns to a patient whose single deepest desire was to look like a lizard. He wanted a doctor to split his tongue and scale his skin, and then put horns on his head. "You wouldn't do that, would you?" a bespectacled doctor asks. "Once," says Rosen, dodging in a fashion typical of him, "there was a lady in need of breast reconstruction who wanted blue areolas. What's wrong with blue areolas? Furthermore, rhinoplasty has not reached its real potential. Why just change the nose? Why not change the gene for the nose, so that subsequent generations will benefit from the surgery. Plastic surgery, in the future, can be about more than the literal body. It can be about sculpting the genotype as well."

The bespectacled doctor raises his hand. "Would you make that man into a lizard?" the doctor asks again. "What I want to know is, if a patient came to you and said, 'I want you to give me wings,' or, 'Split my tongue,' would you actually do it?"

"Look," says Rosen, "we genetically engineer food. That's an issue."

"You're not answering my question," the doctor says, growing angry. Other people are growing angry, too. "Do you see any ethical dilemmas in making people into pigs, or birds?" another attendee yells out. This attendee is eating a Yodel, peeling off the chocolate bark and biting into a swirl of cream.

Rosen darts and dodges. "There is such a thing as liberty," he says.

"Yes," someone says, "but there's such a thing as the Hippocratic oath too."

This goes on and on. At last a professor of anthropology says, "Just tell us, clearly, please. Would you give a human being wings, if the medical-ethics board allowed it?"

Rosen puts down his black marker. He rubs his eyes. "Yes," he says, "I would. I can certainly see why we don't devote research money to it. I can see why the NIH would fund work on breast cancer over this, but I don't have any problem with altering the human form. We do it all the time. It is only our Judeo-Christian conservatism that makes us think this is wrong. Who here," he says, "doesn't try to send their children to the best schools, in the hopes of altering them? Who here objects to a Palm Pilot, a thing we clasp to our bodies, with which we receive rapid electronic signals? Who here doesn't surround themselves with a metal shell and travel at death-defying speeds? We have always altered ourselves, for beauty or for power, and so long as we are not causing harm what makes us think we should stop?"

For a group of intelligent people everyone looks baffled. What Rosen has said is very right and very wrong, but no one can quite articulate the core conflicts. After all, we seem to think it's okay to use education as a way of neuronally altering the brain, but not surgery. We take Prozac, even Ritalin, to help transform ourselves, but recoil when it comes to wings. Maybe we're not recoiling. Maybe wings are just a dumb idea. No one in his right mind would subject himself to such a superfluous and strenuous operation. Yet socialite Jocelyne Wildenstein has dedicated much of her life to turning herself into a cat, via plastic surgery. She has had her lips enlarged and her face pulled back at the eyes to simulate a feline appearance. An even more well-known case is Michael Jackson, who has whitened himself, slimmed his nose, and undergone multiple other aesthetic procedures. The essential question here is whether these people are, and forever will be, outliers, or whether they represent the cutting edge of an ever more popular trend. Carl Elliott, a bioethicist and associate professor at the University of Minnesota, recently wrote in *The Atlantic* about a strange new "trend" of perfectly healthy folks who desire nothing more than to have a limb amputated, and about the British doctor who has undertaken this surgery, believing that if he doesn't amputate the patients will do it themselves, which could lead to gangrene. Elliott wonders whether amputation obsession will morph into another psychiatric diagnosis, whether, like hysteria, it will "catch on." The metaphor of contagion is an interesting one. Multiple-personality disorder "caught on"; hysteria caught on. Why then might not an unquenchable desire for wings or fins catch on, too? In any case, we use medical/viral metaphors to explain trends, and, in the case of plastic surgery, we then use medical means to achieve the trend's demands.

Rosen himself now repeats to the conferees, "We have always altered ourselves for beauty or for power. The chieftains in a certain African tribe remove their left ears, without Novocain. Other tribes put their bodies through intense scarification processes for the sake of style. In our own culture, we risk our bodies daily to achieve status, whether it's because we're bulimic or because we let some surgeon suck fat from us, with liposuction. Wings will be here," Rosen says. "Mark my words."

He suddenly seems so confident, so clear. We should do this; beauty is marvelous and monstrous. Beauty is difference, and yet, to his patients in the ER just two weeks back, he kept saying, "Let nature take its course." Perhaps he is more ambivalent than he lets on.

Later that evening, over dinner, conferees gossip about Rosen. "He's a creep," someone says. "A megalomaniac," someone else adds. For a creep or a megalomaniac, though, he's certainly commanding a lot of attention. Clearly, his notions are provocative. "The problem with wings," says someone, "is that only rich people would have them, would be able to afford them. Our society might begin to see rich people as more godly than ever."

I order a glass of wine. The waitress sets it on the table, where it blazes in its goblet, bright as a tulip. With this wine, I will tweak not only my mind but all its neuronal projections as well. My reflexes will slow down and my inhibitions will lift, making it possible for me to sound either very stupid or very smart. Is this wine an ethical problem? I ask the group that.

"Wine is reversible," someone says. "Wings aren't."

"Well, suppose they *were* reversible," someone says. "Supposing a surgeon could make wings that were removable. Then would we be reacting this way?"

"It's a question of degree," a philosopher pipes up. He is bald and skinny, with bulging eyes. "Rosen is going to the nth degree. It's not fair to lump that in with necessary alterations, or even questionably necessary alterations. Without doubt, it is very clear, diagnostically, that wings are not necessary."

I think about this. I think about what Rosen might say to this. I can imagine that his answer might have something to do with the fluidity of the concept of necessary.

302 ■ Chapter Four

Four years ago, cell phones weren't necessary. Now they seem to be. Furthermore, he might say, if a person wants wings, if wings won't hurt a person, if they will help a person enjoy life and feel more beautiful, and if, in turn, the winged woman or man helps us to see beauty in what was before unacceptable, as we adjust and then come to love the sight of her spreading and soaring, then isn't this excellent? Later on, in my hotel room, I stand in front of the mirror, naked. My body contains eons. Once, we were single cells, then fish, then birds, then mammals, and the genes for all these forms lie dormant on their cones of chromosomes. We are pastiches at the cellular, genetic level. This may be why I fear open spaces, blank pages, why I often dream my house opens up into endless rooms I never knew were there, and I float through them with a kind of terror. It is so easy to seep, to be boundless. We clutch our cloaks of skin.

Back in Boston, I try to ascertain clearly, logically, what so bothers people about Rosen's ideas. At first glance, it might seem fairly obvious. I mean, wings. That's playing God. We should not play God. We should not reach for the stars. Myth after myth has shown us the dangers of doing so—Icarus, the Tower of Babel; absolute power corrupts absolutely. Bill Joy, chief scientist at Sun Microsystems, says, as our technological capabilities expand, "a sequence of small, individually sensible advances leads to an accumulation of great power and, concomitantly, great danger." Rosen's response to this: "So are we supposed to stop advancing? And who says it's bad to play God? We already alter the course of God's 'will' in hundreds of ways. When we use antibiotics to combat the flu, when we figure out a way to wipe smallpox off the very face of the earth, surely we're altering the natural course of things. Who says the natural course of things is even right? Maybe God isn't good."

The second objection might have to do with our notions of categorical imperatives. Mary Douglas wrote in her influential anthropological study *Purity and Danger* that human beings have a natural aversion to crossing categories, and that when we do transgress we see it as deeply dirty. In other words, shoes in themselves are not dirty, but when you place them on the dining-room table they are. When you talk about crossing species, either at the genetic or the anatomical level, you are mucking about in long-cherished categories that reflect our fundamental sense of cleanliness and aesthetics. Rosen's response to this, when I lob it at him in our next meeting: "Who says taboos are anything but prejudice at rock bottom? Just because it feels wrong doesn't mean it is. To a lot of people, racial intermingling and miscegenation feel wrong, but to me they're fine. I'm not a racist, and I'm not a conservative."

The third objection I can come up with has to do with the idea of proteanism. Proteus, a minor mythological figure, could shape-shift at will, being alternately a tiger, a lizard, a fire, a flood. Robert Lifton, one of, I think, the truly deep thinkers of the last century, has explored in his volumes how Proteus has become a symbol for human beings in our time. Lacking traditions, supportive institutions, a set of historically rooted symbols, we have lost any sense of coherence and connection. Today it is not uncommon for a human being to shift belief systems several times in a lifetime, and with relatively little psychological discomfort. We are Catholics, Buddhists, reborn, unborn, artists, and dot-commers until the dot drops out of the com and it all comes crashing down. We move on. We remarry. Our protean abilities clearly have their upsides. We are flexible and creative. But the downside is, there is no psychic stability, no substantive self, nothing really meaty and authentic. We sense this about ourselves. We know we are superficial, all breadth and no depth. Rosen's work embodies this tendency, literally. He desires to make incarnate the identity diffusion so common to our culture. Rosen is in our face making us face up to the fact that the inner and outer connections have crumbled. In our ability to be everything, are we also nothing?

For me, this hits the nail on the head. I do not object to Rosen on the basis of concerns about power, or of Mary Douglas's cross-category pollution theory. After all, who, really, would wings reasonably benefit but the window washers among us? And as for the pollution issue, protean person that I am, I could probably adjust to a little chimerical color. Rosen's ideas and aspirations are frightening to me because they are such vivid, visceral examples of a certain postmodern or perhaps, more precisely put, post-authentic sensibility we embrace and fear as we pop our Prozacs and Ritalins and decide to be Jewish and then Episcopalian and then chant with the monks on some high Himalayan mountain via a cheap plane ticket we purchased in between jobs and just before we sold our condo in a market rising so fast that when it falls it will sound like all of the precious china plates crashing down from the cabinet—a mess. What a mess!

Over and over again, from the Middle Ages on, when the theologian Pico wrote, in a direct and influential challenge to the Platonic idea of essential forms—"We have given you, Adam, no visage proper to yourself, nor endowment properly your own . . . trace for yourself the lineaments of your own nature . . . in order that you, as the free and proud shaper of your own being, fashion yourself in the form you may prefer. . . . [W]ho then will not look with awe upon this our chameleon . . ."— over and over, since those words at least, we as human beings have fretted about the question of whether there is anything fixed at our core, any set of unalterable traits that make us who we were and are and always will be. Postmodernism, by which I mean the idea of multiplicity, the celebration of the pastiche, and the rejection of logical positivism and absolutism as viable stances, will never die out, despite its waning popularity in academia. Its roots are too deep and ancient. And there has been, perhaps, no field like modern medicine, with all its possibilities and technological wizardry, to bring questions of authenticity to the burning forefront of our culture. At what point, in altering ourselves, would we lose our essential humanity? Are there any traits that make us essentially human? When might we become monsters or marvels, or are we already there? I vividly remember reading a book by a woman named Martha Beck. She had given birth to a Down syndrome child and she wrote in a few chilling sentences that because of one tiny chromosome, her child, Adam, is "as dissimilar from me as a mule is from a donkey. He is, in ways both obvious and subtle, a different beast." Is it really that simple, that small? One tiny chromosome severs us from the human species? One little wing and we're gone?

As for me, I am an obsessive. I like my categories. I check to make sure the stove is off three times before I go to bed. I have all sorts of other little rituals. At the same time, I know I am deeply disrooted. I left my family at the age of fourteen, never to return. I do not know my family tree. Like so many of us, I have no real religion, which is of course partly a good thing but partly a bad thing. In any case, last year, in some sort of desperate mood, I decided to convert from Judaism to Episcopalianism, but when it came time to put that blood and body in my mouth I couldn't go through with it. Was this because at bottom I just AM a Jew and this amness has profundity? Or was this because I don't like French bread, which is what they were using at the conversion ceremony? In any case, at the crucial moment of incorporation, I fled the church like the proverbial bride who cannot make the commitment.

I want to believe there is something essential and authentic about me, even if it's just my ears. And although my feelings of diffusion may be extreme, I am certainly not the only one who's felt she's flying too fast. Lifton writes, "Until relatively recently, no more than a single major ideological shift was likely to occur in a lifetime, and that one would be long remembered for its conflict and soul searching. But today it is not unusual for several such shifts to take place within a year or even a month, whether in the realm of politics, religion, aesthetic values, personal relationships. . . . Quite rare is the man or woman who has gone through life holding firmly to a single ideological vision. More usual is a tendency toward ideological fragments, bits and pieces of belief systems that allow for shifts, revisions, and recombinations."

What Lifton has observed in the psyche Rosen wants to make manifest in the body. I ask Rosen, "So, do you believe we are just in essence protean, that there is nothing fundamental, or core, to being human?"

He says, "Lauren, I am a scientist. My original interests were in nerves. I helped develop, in the 1980s, one of the first computer-grown nerve chips. The answer to your question may lie in how our nervous systems operate."

Part III: The Protean Brain

First, a lesson. In the 1930s, researchers, working on the brains of apes, found that the gray matter contained neural representations of all the afferent body parts. Ape ears, feet, skin, hands, were all richly represented in the ape brain in a series of neural etchings, like a map. Researchers also realized that when a person loses a limb—say, the right arm—this portion of the neural map fades away. Sometimes even stranger things happen. Sometimes amputees claimed they could feel their missing arm when, for instance, someone touched their cheek. This was because the arm map had not faded so much as morphed, joined up its circuitry with the cheek map, so it was all confused.

It was then discovered, not surprisingly, that human beings also have limb maps in their brains. Neurologists conceptualized this limb map as "a homunculus," or little man. Despite my feminist leanings, I am enchanted by the idea of a little man hunched in my head, troll-like, banging a drum, grinning from ear to ear. Of course the homunculus is not actually shaped like a human; it is, rather, a kind of human blueprint, like the drawing of the house in all its minute specificity. Touch the side of your skull. Press in. Buried, somewhere near there, is a beautiful etching of your complex human hand, rich in neural webwork and delicate, axonal tendrils designed to accommodate all the sensory possibilities of this prehensile object. Move your hand upward, press the now sealed soft spot, and you will be touching your toe map. Your eye map is somewhere in your forehead and your navel map is somewhere in your cerebellum, a creased, enfolded series of cells that recall, I imagine, ancient blue connections, a primitive love.

Today, Rosen is giving a lecture. I have come up to New Hampshire to hear him, and, unlike on the last visit, the day is beautiful and bright. Rosen explains how brains are truly plastic, which comes from the Greek root meaning to mold, to shape. When we lose a limb, the brain absorbs its map or rewires it to some other center. Similarly, Rosen explains, when we gain a limb, the brain almost immediately senses it and goes about hooking it up via neural representation. "If I were to attach a sonographically powered arm to your body," Rosen explains, "your brain would map it. If I were to attach a third thumb, your brain would map it, absolutely. Our bodies change our brains, and our brains are infinitely moldable. If I were to give you wings, you would develop, literally, a winged brain. If I were to give you an echolocation device, you would develop in part a bat-brain."

Although the idea of a brain able to incorporate changes so completely may sound strange, many neurological experiments have borne out the fact that our gray matter does reorganize according to the form and function of our appendages. Because no one has yet appended animal forms to the human body, however, no studies have been done that explore what the brain's response to what might be termed an "evolutionary insult" would be. Assuming, probably wrongly but assuming nevertheless, that human beings represent some higher form of species adaptation, at least in terms of frontal-lobe intelligence, the brain might find it odd to be rewiring itself to presumably more primitive structures, structures we shed a long time ago when we waded out of the swamps and shed our scales and feathers. Rosen's desire to meld human and animal forms, and the incarnation of this desire in people like the cat-woman and the lizard-man, raise some interesting questions about the intersection of technology and primitivism. Although we usually assume technology is somehow deepening the rift between nature and culture, it also can do the opposite. In other words, technology can be, and often is, extremely primitive, not only because it allows people a sort of id-like, limbic-driven power (i.e., nuclear weaponry) but also because it can provide the means to toggle us down the evolutionary ladder, to alter our brains, stuck in their rigid humanness, so that we become what we once were phylogenetically: tailed, winged, at last no longer landlocked.

All this is fascinating and, of course, unsettling to me. Our brains are essentially indiscriminate, able to morph—like the sea god Proteus himself—into fire, a flood, a dragon, a swan. I touch my brain and feel it flap. Now I understand more deeply what Rosen meant when he said, "Plastic surgery changes the soul." To the extent that we believe our souls are a part of our brains, Rosen is right. And, all social conflict about its place in the medical hierarchy aside, plastic surgery is really neurosurgery, because it clearly happens, at its most essential level, north of the neck. When a surgeon modifies your body, he modifies your oh-so-willing, bendable brain.

I get a little depressed, hearing this lecture. It seems to me proof at the neuronal level that we have the capacity to be, in fact, everything, and thus in some sense nothing. It confirms my fear that I, along with the rest of the human species, could slip-slide through life without any specificity, or "specificity." Last year, I had my first child. I wonder what I will teach her, what beliefs about the body and the brain and the soul I really hold. I think, "I will show her pictures of her ancestors," but the truth is, I don't have any pictures. I think, "I will teach her my morals," but I don't know exactly what my morals are, or where they came from. I know I am not alone. Like Rosen, perhaps, I am just extreme. Now I feel a kind of kinship with him. We are both self-invented, winging our way through.

Rosen comes up to me. He is finished with his talk. "So do you understand what I mean," he asks, "about the limitlessness of the brain?"

"Does it ever make you sad?" I say. "Does it ever just plain and simple make you scared?"

Rosen and I look at each other for a long time. He does seem sad. I recall him telling me once that when he envisions the future fifty years out, he hopes he is gone, because, he said, "While I like it here, I don't like it that much." I have the sense, now, that he struggles with things he won't tell me. His eyes appear tired, his face drained. I wonder if he wakes in the middle of the night, frightened by his own perceptions. Strange or not, there is something constant in Rosen, and that's his intelligence, his uncanny ability to defend seemingly untenable positions with power and occasional grace. In just three weeks he will travel to a remote part of Asia to participate in a group called Interplast, made up of doctors and nurses who donate their time to help children with cleft lips and palates. I think it's important to mention this—not only Bin Laden, bandwidth, anthrax, and wings but his competing desire to minister. The way, at the dinner table, he tousles his children's hair. His avid dislike of George W. Bush. His love of plants and greenery. Call him multifaceted or simply slippery, I don't know. All I do know is that right now, when I look at his face, I think I can see the boy he once was, the Seventh Fleet ship, the wonder, all that wonder.

"Do you and Stina want to go out for dinner? We could go somewhere really fancy, to thank you," I say, "for all your time."

"Sure," says Rosen. "Give me a minute. I'll meet you in the hospital lobby," and then he zips off to who knows where, and I am alone with my singular stretched self on the third floor of the Dartmouth-Hitchcock Medical Center. I wander down the long hallways. Behind the curtained cubicles there is unspeakable suffering. Surely that cannot be changed, not ever. Behind one of these cubicles sits Sweeny, and even if we learn to see him as beautiful, the bottomline truth is that he still suffers. Now I want to touch Sweeny's dying face. I want to put my hand right on the center of pain. I want to touch Rosen's difficult face, and my baby daughter's face as well, but she is far from me, in some home we will, migrants that our family is, move on from sometime soon. I once read that a fetus does not scar. Fetal skin repairs itself seamlessly, evidence of damage sinking back into blackness. Plastic surgery, for all its incredible advances, has not yet been able to figure out how to replicate this mysterious fetal ability in the full-born human. Plastic surgery can give us wings and maybe even let us sing like loons, but it cannot stop scarring. This is oddly comforting to me. I pause to sit on a padded bench. A very ill woman pushing an IV pole walks by. I lift up my pant leg and study the scar I got a long time ago, when I fell off a childhood bike. The scar is pink and raised and shaped like an *o*, like a hole maybe, but also like a letter, like a language, like a little piece of land that, for now, we cannot cross over.

 For Discussion:

1. Several times in this essay, Dr. Rosen tells his patients that it's best to "let nature take its course." Is there anything natural about the radical ideas Dr. Rosen possesses (about plastic surgery, genotyping, etc.)?
2. Dr. Rosen says at one point, "When you change what you look like, you change who you are." Is this true?
3. How far can we go in altering our physical body before we cease being human?

 For Fact-Finding, Research, and Writing:

1. Find out if any radical or nontraditional plastic surgeries are being performed in other countries around the world.
2. Investigate the idea of "neural representation." Is it true that the brain maps changes in the body? What are some of the implications of this?
3. Dr. Rosen has over thirty published articles. Using a scientific database, locate some of these. Do any of them deal with this particular subject matter?
4. Using Statistical Universe or a database of business statistics, locate some statistics about plastic surgeries from last year. How do they differ from the statistics in this essay?

Chris Hables Gray,
"Citizenship in the Age of Electronic Reproduction"

Chris Hables Gray received his B.A. from Stanford University and his Ph.D. from the University of California, Santa Cruz. Currently Associate Professor of Computer Science at the University of Great Falls, Gray is an internationally recognized scholar of cybernetics and cyberculture. A frequent consultant to the computer industry, he is the author or editor of four books: *Technohistory* (1996), *The Cyborg Handbook* (1996), *Postmodern War* (1997), and *Cyborg Citizen* (2002).

 Before You Read:

What traits do you believe must be present before someone can be considered human? In your view, are human rights different from the rights afforded to citizens of a nation?

Citizenship in the Age of Electronic Reproduction

Chris Hables Gray

[I]t is no longer enough to feel represented by a government (if it ever was); now a citizen of the cybernetic political world inhabits various bodies interfaced more or less intimately with various prosthetics, all models for political structures that subject and partially construct us.

—Chris Hables Gray and Steven Mentor

Who or What Is a Citizen?

IN AN EPISODE of *Star Trek: The Next Generation*, Data the android is put on trial to determine whether he is property or a citizen. *ST:TNG* is full of cyborgs: Geordi La Forge with his visor, Riker with his transporter clone, Worf with an artificial spine, Pecard with an artificial heart, various holographic characters who come to life, and, in several episodes, the ship itself. And there are the Borg, the evil, black-leather-clad cyborg group mind. But Data is a particularly interesting cyborg because his cyborgization is based on two very unrelated technologies. First, his skin is a biological construction. Second, his consciousness arises from patterns extracted from the memories of humans in the colony where he was built. Technically it is far from clear that Data is anything more than a very sophisticated robot with some borrowings from the organic world. But he longs to be human.

Data's trial results from the machinations of an ambitious scientist from the United Federation of Planets who wants to deconstruct Data to see how he works. Data's friends testify but they are far from convincing. Finally Data takes the stand. In his testimony he reveals that he keeps a hologram of Tasha Yar, the butch, blonde security chief who died engulfed in an evil ink blot on an earlier episode. Data confesses that he had sex with Tasha once when the whole crew was exposed to an aphrodisiac ("I am fully functional," he told her when she propositioned him), and so he is deemed a citizen after all.

The ability to have sex with a human may seem like a strange criterion for citizenship, but it is actually the ability to have sex *and talk about it* that saves Data. The definition of citizenship is freeing itself from gender-, race-, and class-based criteria and becoming an issue of competent participation in what some philosophers call a discourse community but what most of us would just label a meaningful conversation. The communication need not be speech or writing, as Helen Keller proved, but there must be communication for political participation. This perspective helps us think about cyborg citizenship just as it has helped define intelligence through the Turing test. We will return to the Turing test and the cyborg citizen below, but first a few more things need to be said about citizenship itself.

The idea of citizenship has been growing more powerful as the world transforms into a cyborged society. Consider the alternatives. Would you rather be a subject? An employee? A tribal member? The role of tribal member is much more nuanced than some might think and is quite different from "citizen." But while some coherent tribes remain strong institutions that people gladly subsume their individuality to because of long-standing blood ties and links to specific land, for most people being a tribal member is not an option. And for many tribal members it is an option that is refused. What is popular is citizenship.

The word "citizen" comes from "cities," and the first citizens were in the Greek city-states. They were male, adult, property-owning members who fought in the military; nonmembers, women, children, and the poor were not citizens and had few rights. Originally, in the Massachusetts Bay Colony, a citizen had to be a landowner or ranked as a master craftsman, a member of the Puritan Church, white, male, and an oath-swearer to the Crown. Even now, the U.S. Constitution says that the president must be a "natural-born citizen," which excludes "naturalized" citizens, of course; but does it also mean a test-tube baby cannot grow up to be president?

Some theorists still link the idea of citizenship to membership in a state and, like the Australian political scientist Jan Pakulski, they worry that the postmodern "weakening of the state and the erosion of state legitimacy will ultimately arrest the process of citizenship extension." Pakulski notes that more and more rights are being linked to a person's status as a human being (as in the UN's Declaration of Human Rights) and not to their membership in a state.

For me this is not a problem. I trace my citizenship to my consent to be governed, in the formulation of John Locke, and that stems from my ability to be part of the polis, the political entity that humans and cyborgs (and in the future who knows what else) share through our ability to communicate together about political issues, sex, and whether or not Madonna has talent. Let me stress that I reject the patriarchal and classist assumptions that mar Locke's work and that do not follow logically. But the fundamental premise of Locke (and of the American and French revolutions and many more besides) is that the governed must consent to be governed or the state is not legitimate. Postmodern citizenship is more diffuse and proactive, as consent and allegiance can be granted to more than just nation-states; (bio)regions, cities, and the world as a whole can claim part of the citizen's allegiance. This is not so much a matter of political theory as it is of political practice, and as long as enough of us are willing to put our lives and our sacred honor on the line for this idea of conscious and proactive citizenship, it will remain true.

Pakulski makes much of the state as "the monopolistic enforcer of rights," but it is my reading of history that individuals and groups have to struggle mightily, often against states, to acquire and defend their rights. Sometimes this is to establish or change states so that they are more amenable to human rights, but even then the natural tendency of even the most revolutionary and limited government is to grow in power (the iron law of bureaucracy) and start usurping people's freedoms. Thomas Jefferson stressed that it takes continual effort to keep our freedom. He phrased it in more colorful language, advocating perpetual revolutions every 20 years because: "The tree of liberty must be refreshed from time to time with the blood of patriots and tyrants." Such enthusiasm is probably why I am happy to call myself a Jeffersonian anarchist; after all, his disciple John L. O'Sullivan pointed out that "the government that governs least governs best," which has a nice logic to it.

Since nation-states are contingent, based on belief and history (some political scientists call them "imaginary communities"), there is no reason not to imagine a polity of the world. World citizenship makes much more political and ecological sense than does citizenship in nation-states. Aspects of national citizenship, such as those discussed by Bryan Turner in the premier issue of a journal called *Citizenship Studies*—legal rights, political rights, social rights—can be applied to world citizenship. But global citizenship offers the opportunity of combining human rights with these rights—and the concurrent obligations—of national citizens.

I am in sympathy with Pakulski's call for a "cultural citizenship" that expands the individual's rights and obligations to include economic and cultural dimensions as well as freedom and equality in the political process. Citizenship is clearly changing, as the very ground of politics shifts through the globalization of human culture and the other aspects of postmodernity that our ever-expanding technosciences are driving. But what will citizenship in the twenty-first century look like?

However citizenship may evolve, technology will play a major role. Langdon Winner, for one, has argued that technologies can be autonomous, that artifacts have politics of their own. Thus certain technologies may be inherently authoritarian, and real citizenship might be accorded only to those individuals who gain knowledge, control, or access as a result of their relationships to complex technologies. Those without are doomed to become "technopeasants" or, as my graduate student Katie Meyers wrote in an unpublished short story, "technotards." There is certainly the possibility that the expansion of citizenship might be reversed by differentiated access to technologies, especially health, information, and power. Cyborgization contains this danger as well. Yet the dynamics of cyborg citizenship are more complex than a simple accounting of haves and have-nots.

Engin Isin, a Canadian academic, has explored this issue in his article "Who Is the New Citizen?" He documents the rise of "new knowledge workers" and other shifts in the political landscape, including the development of a new "professional-citizen." This leads him to ask: What are the new political and moral obligations that will inevitably arise with new types of citizenship? The new citizenship must stem not just from the economic changes we are now experiencing but also from the actual changes our bodies are undergoing through cyborgization. We have to think in terms of the cyborg citizen, and that means we have to decide who qualifies.

The complications of cyborg citizenship call for a cyborg citizen Turing test to determine which entities can actually participate in our discourse community and which cannot. The Turing test is a very pragmatic exercise that has long been useful to scientists and writers trying to determine if a computer is intelligent. The test was first proposed by Alan Turing, the homosexual English computer scientist who died mysteriously in the 1950s after apparently biting a poisoned apple; whether it was suicide or the state solving a security risk we may never know. Turing, who played a fundamental role in developing the computer while he was building code-breaking machines during World War II, based his test on a party game called "the imitation game."

In the original "party" version, a man and a woman are given the same set of questions, which they then take to a separate room. One of them replies on a typed sheet, and the party guests try to guess if it is the man's or the woman's reply.

Turing proposed that a machine be substituted for one of the humans, and then argued that since intelligence is an operational concept, not an absolute, the best way to judge it is by testing whether or not the entity in question could carry on an intelligent conversation with an intelligent human for a serious length of time. If it could, then even a machine should be considered intelligent, at least as intelligent as many humans.

The value of Turing's test—and its use for determining cyborg citizenship—is its insight that intelligence, like citizenship, is a working idea, not an abstract universal value. Citizenship is based on assumptions about the consent of the governed, the relationship between responsibility and rights, and the autonomy of individuals. Historically, criteria for citizenship have ranged from gender and class, through literacy, to the current system in which birthright assures eventual citizenship unless it is abrogated through misdeeds. But beneath these shifting rules one can discern that the idea of a discourse community has always been the basic ground. Western political communities may have been limited in earlier days by political goals of racial, gender, or class domination, but among their approved citizens the ideal has always been equal discourse. The polis is a discourse community, after all, and every historical expansion of it has been predicated on arguments about the participation of new individuals in that discourse. Today, as we are faced with a whole range of complex and difficult decisions about who should be and who can be citizens, it seems wise to stay within this framework.

Currently, judgments about the suitability for citizenship of individual humans and cyborgs are made on the grounds of their ability to take part in the discourse of the polis, either by assumptions about age or by the evaluation of experts. Many of the more difficult cases are of actual cyborgs: humans linked to machines that keep them alive or humans who maintain autonomy only through drugs and other technointerventions. Instead of a jury of one's peers, the decision usually results from a negotiation between doctors, social workers, lawyers, and judges. Even in such cases, the criterion is operational. For example, in the United States, the National Council of State Boards of Nursing defines competence as "the application of knowledge and the interpersonal, decision-making, and psychomotor skills expected." If people are going to be judged on what is "expected," maybe that determination should be made by their peers.

Let us take such power away from the "soft" police and return it to the polis at large, in the form of juries of peers conducting their own rough Turing tests. An entity must convince a simple majority of twelve other citizens that it can be part of their conversation. This requirement should prevent refusals of citizenship on the basis of racism or other prejudices. The point is not to exclude those who are already citizens, as literacy and property laws were designed to do. And the point is not to include pets or fetuses or corporate entities. If such entities deserve rights and protection, they can be granted in other ways than citizenship.

The beauty of the Turing test is that it escapes the straitjacket of arbitrary standards and static definitions. Flexible though it is, it does not cast out all values; instead it focuses on the core of politics—communication—and enshrines that as the ultimate value. Also it implies strongly that citizenship is embodied, whether the body be organic, machinic, or both, ambiguous or not, constructed or not.

The Cyborg Bill of Rights

Donna Haraway's "A Manifesto for Cyborgs" is the founding document of cyborg politics. Republished dozens of times since 1985, it has inspired, outraged, and befuddled countless readers. Since then there has been a proliferation of cyber-manifestos. It almost seems as if most things written now about "cyber" anything are in the style of a manifesto. Which would be appropriate, since, according to Steven Mentor:

All manifestos are cyborgs. That is, they fit Donna Haraway's use of this term in her own "A Manifesto for Cyborgs"—manifestos are hybrids, chimeras, boundary-confusing technologies. They combine and confuse popular genres and political discourses, borrow from critical theory and advertising, serve as would be control systems for the larger social technologies their authors hope to manufacture.

Among the more interesting cyber-manifestos are the "Mutant Manifesto," Stelarc's "Cyborg Manifesto," "The Magna Carta for the Knowledge Age," and a number of proclamations from the Extropians. Many of these are based on earlier manifestos from the late 1700s. Other manifestos include "The Declaration of the Independence of Cyberspace" announced by cyber-libertarians in 1996, and the "Bill of Gender Rights" from the Second International Conference on Transgender Law and Employment Policy in 1993. This bill of rights includes "the right to control and change one's own body," the "right to medical and professional care," and the "right to freedom from psychiatric treatment." Manifestos seem to break the ground for new rights, which are sometimes then codified into texts that seem like technologies.

Bills of rights, and the constitutions they are prosthetics for, are technically called "written instruments" and they are indeed technologies. They are supposed to help us govern ourselves. While my particular Cyborg Bill of Rights is designed as amendments to the U.S. Constitution, the ideas in it are relevant to all postmodern democracies. Many constitutions draw from the U.S. version, as Japan's and South Africa's do. The U.S. Constitution comes out of English common law, French political thinking, and Greek, Roman, and Native American governing traditions. This is not a proposal aimed just at the United States. All cyborg citizens need their rights defended. So, in the hope of making a modest improvement in the human political condition, I propose this *Cyborg Bill of Rights*.

One last point. Despite some strange rulings in the past by the U.S. Supreme Court, it is explicitly stated in this new Bill of Rights that:

Business corporations and other bureaucracies are not *citizens or individuals, nor shall they ever be.*

As it is now, corporations have many of the rights of citizens but few of the obligations. In the future there might be "corporate" cyborgs with multiple or distributed intelligence. Without some level of unitary identity, such a cyborg will not have the ability to act coherently. But, perhaps some cyborg of the far future will be multiple but coherent enough to be capable of casting one vote. Still there is no reason to allow business corporations to keep their quasi-citizen status. Even without it they have too much power.

The ten amendments are as follows:

1. *Freedom of Travel.* Citizens shall have the right to travel anywhere, virtually or in the flesh, at their own risk and expense.
2. *Freedom of Electronic Speech.* Electronic and other nonphysical forms of transmitting information are protected by the Constitution's First Amendment.
3. *The Right of Electronic Privacy.* Electronic and other nonmaterial forms of property and personhood shall be accorded the protection of the Fourth Amendment.
4. *Freedom of Consciousness.* The consciousness of the citizen shall be protected by the First, Fourth, and Eighth Amendments. Unreasonable search and seizure of this, the most sacred and private part of an individual citizen, is absolutely prohibited. Individuals shall retain all rights to modify their consciousness through psychopharmological, medical, genetic, spiritual, and other practices, insofar as they do not threaten the fundamental rights of other individuals and citizens, and that they do so at their own risk and expense.
5. *Right to Life.* The body of the citizen shall be protected by the First, Fourth, and Eighth Amendments. Unreasonable search and seizure of this sacred and private part of an individual citizen shall be absolutely prohibited. Individuals shall retain all rights to modify their bodies, at their own risk and expense, through psychopharmological, medical, genetic, spiritual, and other practices, insofar as they do not threaten the fundamental rights of other individuals and citizens.
6. *Right to Death.* Every citizen and individual shall have the right to end their life, at their own risk and expense, in the manner of their own choice, as long as it does not infringe upon the fundamental rights of other citizens and individuals.
7. *Right to Political Equality.* The political power of every citizen should be determined by the quality of his or her arguments, example, energy, and single vote, not based on his or her economic holdings or social standing. Congress shall permit no electoral system that favors wealth, coercion, or criminal behavior to the detriment of political equality.
8. *Freedom of Information.* Citizens shall have access to all information held about them by governments or other bureaucracies. Citizens shall have the right to correct all information held on them by governments and other bureaucracies at the expense of these bureaucracies. Institutional and corporate use of information to coerce or otherwise illegally manipulate or act upon citizens shall be absolutely forbidden.
9. *Freedom of Family, Sexuality, and Gender.* Citizens and individuals have the right to determine their own sexual and gender orientations, at their own risk and expense, including matrimonial and other forms of alliance. Congress shall make no law arbitrarily restricting the definition of the family, of marriage, or of parenthood.

10. *Right to Peace.* Citizens and individuals have a right to freedom from war and violence. War shall be a last resort and must be declared by a two thirds vote of Congress when proposed by the president. The Third Amendment shall not be construed as permitting citizens and individuals to own all types of weapons. Freedom from governmental tyranny will not be safeguarded through local militia or individual violence. Only solidarity, tolerance, sacrifice, and an equitable political system will guarantee freedom. Nonetheless, citizens and individuals shall have the right to defend themselves with deadly force, at their own risk and expense, if their fundamental rights are being abridged.

These amendments are important, but alone they cannot protect us. We need active citizens and new political technologies to protect our rights from the relentless changes that cyborgian technoscience is producing.

I have assumed here that cyborg citizens are real political bodies and therefore they need real political rights instantiated in technologies such as constitutions and operational tests of citizenship. The individual needs real political protection in this age of new powerful technosciences and the systems they make possible. Without such protection, corporations, parties, bureaus of police, governments, and wealthy families will achieve hegemony, and the vast majority of us will lose all political power.

Citizenship will always be embodied in some sense, although not necessarily in living flesh. Many theorists, and I am one of them, think intelligence itself is inherently embodied. A disembodied intelligence, if it were even possible, might very well not be interested in our definition of citizenship. Our political system (indeed our existence) is based on embodiment.

It is feminist philosophy that has made the embodiment of citizenship undeniable in the postmodern era, through an examination of the dangers of disembodied philosophies that make hyperrationality the measure of all things and through many case studies of the role of bodies in real politics. For example, Elaine Scarry's *Bodies in Pain* details how bodies are the ground for both war and the coercive power of government. Different philosophies have put forward many other possible bases for political principles—the soul, the race, the nation—but in real terms it is the action of, and on, bodies that is the basis of politics. This explains the crucial political importance of cyborgs.

Donna Haraway points out that cyborg politics are not inevitably liberatory. Far from it. They offer a chance for sustaining, even extending, democracy, but also the equally real chance of ultimate oppression, especially if we subscribe to illusions of "total theory," "pure information," and "perfect communication" and deny the messy reality of machinic and organic bodies and their rights.

An example of where such illusions might lead can be found in Bruno Latour's political thinking, especially in his 1993 book *We Have Never Been Modern.* Latour, an aristocratic French scholar, has argued that science is a collaborative construction involving alliances between institutions, rhetorics, technologies, artifacts, and humans. On the surface it might seem that his argument parallels the one here. He denounces totalitarian rationality-is-everything narratives and urges a reconciliation between nature and technology. But Latour's advocacy for granting rights to nonhuman, nonliving objects and implementing a "Parliament of Things" is profoundly problematic on several levels. First, the argument is couched in abstract and symbolic terms. Secondly, it depends on a series of oversimplified dichotomies, such as the alienation of modernism from nature and the domination of human(ism) over the rest of reality. Finally, it is based on illusions about agency and causality that in actuality would make working politics impossible.

That artifacts have politics does not mean that they have agency. Certainly, cyborgs (or "hybrids," in Latour's formulation) demonstrate that organic embodiment is not the final arbitrator of agency, but that does not mean that anything can be an actor ("actant" for Latour). That everything can be called a system does not mean that all systems can think, or act, or practice politics in any real way.

The dangers of Latour's schema becomes apparent when one looks closely at his Parliament:

> *Let one of the representatives talk, for instance, about the ozone hole, another represent the Monsanto chemical industry, a third the workers of the same chemical industry, another the voters of New Hampshire, a fifth the meteorology of the polar regions; let still another speak in the name of the State; what does it matter, so long as they are all talking about the same thing, about a quasi-object they have all created, the object-discourse-nature-society whose new properties astound us all and whose network extends from my refrigerator to the Antarctic by way of chemistry, law, the State, the economy and satellites.*

All of this "speaking" for others reminds me of vanguard parties speaking for the working class. Elites have a funny way of helping themselves while they speak for others. This diffusion of representation based on Latour's totalizing theories about binary reality and his assumptions about perfect communication and pure information (both necessary for all this "speaking for," unless the meteorology of the polar regions suddenly does become articulate on its own) paves the way for the end of real representative government.

Citizens need representation, holes in the ozone layer and chemical companies do not. Chemical companies will look after themselves, unfortunately. That is why we have an ozone hole that threatens us, after all. It is living intelligence (whether human, cyborg, or purely artificial as may someday happen) that must be empowered, not every quasi-object we can count dancing on a pinhead.

"Lives are at stake," Donna Haraway reminds us, "in curious quasi-objects like databases. . . ." *Lives,* not objects, quasi or otherwise. Of course it is in the long-term interest of citizens to recognize how interdependent we all are, how much a part of nature we are. And it is in our interest to do more than theorize about old and new dichotomies. We have to get political, down and dirty, and mess with the cyborgian machinery of government. As Haraway also says:

Undoubtedly, we will have to do more than mutate the stories and the figures if the cyborg citizens of the third planet from the sun are to enjoy something better than the deadly transgressive flexibility of the New World Order.

Accepting ourselves as cyborgs can be liberating and empowering. We can choose how we construct ourselves. We can resist. But we must go beyond resistance. The long degradation of representation can be reversed if we reject calls such as Latour's for its elitist reconstruction. If autonomy is to avoid becoming automaton, we must make cyborg citizenship real, and defend it and expand it, in every way we can. Hence my ironic but serious proposal for a Cyborg Bill of Rights and a Turing test for citizenship. The threat to our freedoms and to justice from the megacyborgs of governments, corporations, and the superwealthy is very real indeed.

Cyborgian Justice: Panopticons Versus Cyborg Death Cults

I believe the fundamental bioethical imperative for behavioral scientists today is to have the courage to renounce all collaboration with forces seeking to "control" or "modify" or "engineer" human responses.

—Dr. Richard Restak

He would carry a gold-plated ice pick in a velvet case. After applying a mild local anesthetic, he would drive the ice pick into the patient's skull through the edge of one of the eye sockets, severing the nerve connections to the thalamus and producing, in many cases, zombielike behavior along with convulsive seizures, intellectual impairment to the point of severe retardation, and the loss of all emotions. He did this more than 3,500 times. He was Dr. Walter Freeman, a neurologist at George Washington University Hospital in Washington, D.C., and was, along with James Watts, the inventor of the lobotomy.

Controlling human behavior through psychosurgery or other means is an old dream dating at least back to the ancient Romans, who noticed that sword wounds in the head sometimes cured mental illness. But only in the late twentieth century did it become a massive industry with a tremendous amount of government support, often framed in the language of cybernetics, the science of control.

Ice picks and other surgical implements passed out of favor with the advent of powerful drugs that offered the potential for "chemical" lobotomies. Thorazine and other tranquilizers are used massively today to control violent or just annoying mental patients, even though their long-term effects are sometimes just as damaging as the gold-plated ice pick. Behavior modification scientists have gone much further, researching electrical brain implants, studying military brainwashing techniques to see how they can be applied to criminals, and even inventing their own torture devices.

In the 1960s, the staff at Atascadero and Vacaville, prisons for the criminally insane in California, used the drug succinylcholine to "modify" patient behavior. Since the drug paralyzes the whole body, including the lungs, but leaves the victim conscious as they suffocate, it was considered ideal for convincing prisoners to change their behavior.

Fortunately, legal interventions stopped these "experiments" and also ended other programs, such as the one where doctors coerced patients to agree to psychosurgery by administering brain shocks and then forcibly operated on them even though they had later recanted their earlier approval. The U.S. courts ruled that prisoners and patients could not be forced to undergo irreversible treatments and that in many cases noncoerced consent was impossible. However, reversible interventions, illegal experiments (some no doubt undertaken by the government), and studies outside North America and Europe, where patients' rights are protected to some extent, undoubtably continue.

In his book *Pre-Meditated Man,* Richard Restak reviews this history and looks at a number of other areas where biotechnology is impacting society, such a genetic engineering. The key issue, he decides, is power. Who has the power to decide? Transplant programs, kidney machine use, and behavior and genetic modifications "are not questions of 'ethics,' they are questions of power." As a physician and scientist himself, he stresses that we cannot rely upon scientists to be the ultimate judges. Society must decide in general, and individual patients must have the power in particular. And, he warns, we cannot assume the government is a disinterested mediator of what the people want. It has interests of its own. He also argues that the power of new technologies for behavioral and genetic modification and the ever-quickening rate of innovation in these areas means that the amount of time society has to respond to them grow shorter while the consequences of mistakes grows heavier. Every time we do not get it right there is a wave of deaths, deformations, and other horrific consequences, as with the thalidomide babies.

Some people just aspire to control people directly. Consider Dr. Jose M. R. Delgado, author of *Physical Control of the Mind.* A distinguished professor at Madrid University, UCLA, and Yale, he implanted electrodes in the brains of animals to control them. Donna Haraway describes Delgado's joint project with Nathan Kline and leading primatologists to manipulate gibbons through brain stimulation:

The proposed research was a straightforward extension of work Delgado had done for over twenty years. He had been instrumental in developing the multichannel radio stimulator, the programmed stimulator, the stimoceiver, the transdermal brain stimulator, a mobility recorder, chemitrodes, external dialtrodes, and subcutaneous dialtrodes. These were cyborg organs within cybernetic functionalism.

The cyborgs are animal-machines, experimental objects for perfecting cybernetic control. Along with the animals, the behavioral observations were automated as much as possible using a mobile telemetry system that, when analyzed by computer, would produce suggested medication levels. As Haraway notes, the "structure of a command-control-communication system pervades the discourse of Delgado and his community, whether or not explicit military metaphors or social ties appear." Command, control, and communication do not apply just to military units now; they are what governments want to exercise on citizen-subjects who otherwise might run out of control.

It is an old fear of rulers. How do we control the masses? More subtle approaches than those discussed here often work, but sometimes the powers-that-be feel that extreme measures are necessary. Technoscience has gifted us with incredible destructive powers. What do we do when they are used by small groups of clever nuts who have been driven insane by society's rapid transitions?

Today's body politic is clearly uncomfortable when it contemplates its progressing cyborgization. There is good reason to fear that there will be pathological reactions. The Aum group from Japan, famous around the world for its nerve gas attacks, was in many ways the first cyborg death cult. Along with the typical trappings of insane death cults (a guru, a bizarre eschatology, and an internal dynamic of oppression and conformity), cult members had also totally embraced the idea that they were cyborg supermen who would save the world from the apocalypse of the current world ecological crisis.

Aum's worldview was shaped equally by science fiction (the work of Isaac Asimov), Buddhism, and its leaders' dreams of commanding and controlling its members though perfect communication. World domination was their goal, nothing less. Aum devotees wore special six-volt electrode shock caps (four volts for children) that were meant to synchronize the wearers' brains to their guru's brain waves, which were continuously broadcast into their heads. They were called Perfect Salvation Initiation machines and they cost initiates about $7,000 dollars a month to use. Aum's security/medical team treated dissenters with electroshock and psychopharmacology. The executed were literally microwaved into ash. Cult members were told that they were superhumans capable of resisting nuclear blasts and plasma rays, thanks to a combination of cyborg technologies (such as the shock caps and drugs) and meditation. Aum's many young scientists not only manufactured small arms but also produced a wide range of biological and chemical weapons, including the sarin used in the Tokyo subway attacks that killed 12 and injured thousands. They had been trying to buy nuclear weapons and develop laser and microwave weapons as well. Fortunately, this particular cyborg microculture collapsed into self-destructive paranoia before it could effectively incorporate mass-death weapons.

The danger of groups like Aum is real. But perhaps the "cure" for such terrorism is just as dangerous as the disease. Using high technology to combat the threat of high-technology terrorism has tremendously corrosive effects on our freedoms, especially from government coercion and surveillance. Video systems have proliferated. They can be found in most stores now, in many workplaces, and on thousands of street corners. The government installs them not only to capture street crimes on tape, but traffic violations as well. Less obvious but perhaps even more intrusive is the explosive growth of databases full of information about the average citizen. A whole range of companies, from marketing to insurance, are creating profiles of millions of potential customers to maximize their advertising budgets or vet potential insurers. Much of this information is illegally acquired, inaccurate, or both.

Meanwhile, new surveillance technologies are introduced all the time. For example, police now possess a device that can detect electromagnetic radiation with such sensitivity that they can tell who is carrying a gun—or wearing a colostomy bag—without a direct search. There are also thermal-imaging devices that can track large mammals from the sky, gamma-ray scanners that can look inside trucks, X-ray technology and computer-aided metal detectors that can reveal items hidden under clothing up to 60 feet away, and ion sniffers that sample the air around someone's skin for chemical traces of cocaine and other naughty things.

Drug tests are used by many corporations and government agencies, from the short-term and inaccurate (but cheap) urine tests to the expensive hair analysis that can detect drug use from years before. Despite the many false-positives such tests produce (do not eat poppy-seed muffins before hand!), their popularity is increasing. Managers find the superficial clarity of such measures reassuring, and for this same reason they have begun to use various personality profiles to cull potentially bad employees and even resort to lie-detector tests for important positions.

A universal infallible lie detector such as the one imagined in James Halperin's novel *The Truth Machine* might seem like a beneficial development at first glance, but not upon reflection. No machine would be 100 percent accurate, only 99.999 percent at best, because there will always be a few sociopaths who can beat it. In the story, the inventor, who programmed it, can also outsmart it. Who watches the watcher? Then there is always the problem of people who are mistaken. They think they are telling the truth but they are wrong, which actually happens with many eyewitness identifications today. Even if the machine were perfectly accurate, is it really what we want? Sure, most of the criminals would be caught and most of the innocent freed, and most politicians and lawyers would be out of a job. But every insincere compliment, every stray politically incorrect thought, every incomplete self-deception could potentially be exposed. In the novel no wedding, no hiring, no contract, no graduation takes place without a truth test, and it fundamentally reorganizes society.

While a perfect truth machine might never be possible, more accurate lie detectors will eventually be built because our understanding of cognition and physiology continues to improve. Do we want a lie detector of 98 percent accuracy, for example, admitted into court? There is always that 2 percent, but most people do not seem to care. Even now, the use of our current horribly inaccurate lie detectors is spreading. Society loves technological solutions to political problems; look at the popularity of "electronic" arrest.

Since 1983 many convicted minor criminals, such as habitual drunk-driving offenders, have been held under "house" arrest by electronic "leashes" that are cuffed to their wrists or ankles and linked to their phones. A simple call from the probation department can verify if the convict—or at least the leash—is at home.

The system is being adapted for more dangerous criminals, such as Wesley Miller, who killed and mutilated a high school classmate in 1982. Three different systems monitor Miller: the ankle cuff, a global positioning system (GPS) satellite link on his other ankle, and a pager that he must answer immediately so that a computer can verify his identity with voice-recognition software. The satellite link insures that he will not go to any forbidden locations. Texas monitors over 1,000 high-risk parolees using these systems, but Miller is the first to have all three. He will not be the last.

A whole range of such cyborg containment technologies are being developed, including chips to be implanted in the flesh. They give the government and other big bureaucracies unprecedented power to control the population. Private security firms sell much of the actual equipment and expertise to the highest bidder, so we are beginning to experience a privitized version of *1984*. "I want to thank George Orwell for having the depth and foresight to plan my career," remarked Richard Chace of the Security Industry Association, an organization that promotes closed-circuit television security systems.

But is privacy overrated? David Brin, a physics professor and brilliant science-fiction writer, has explored the idea that privacy may be a problem. In his novel *Earth*, the nations of the world have attacked Switzerland in a nuclear Helvetian War to expose the secrets and the fruits of governmental and corporate abuse hidden in Swiss banks. His novel explores the politics of privacy in great detail (along with a dozen other fascinating themes, some of them quite cyborgian), and, to his credit, he does not simplify the issues. Surprisingly, he comes down unequivocally *against* privacy. He argues that "secrecy has always favored the mighty." Today the powerful benefit from secrecy; they can buy the most impenetrable privacy and they can also "get around whatever pathetic barriers you or I erect." So "privacy laws and codes will protect those at the top."

His answer is not "more fog, but more light: transparency." He admits that the average citizen would sacrifice something, but "we'll have something precious to help make up for lost privacy: freedom." Brin proposes to do away aggressively with privacy altogether. No secret bank accounts, no hidden files, free access by anyone to any camera anywhere! If the police have a surveillance system, the citizen should be able to view it. The weakness of this proposal is that it would take a world war to implement. Until then, do we really want to live in a totally surveilled society, inside the panopticon?

Jeremy Bentham coined the term "panopticon" for a prison he designed with his brother in which jailers could always observe the inmates. A key to the success of the panopticon is that the inmates would not know if they were being watched or not, just that they might be. The same can be said of the ubiquitous video cameras spreading through contemporary society. You can never know if someone is watching the monitor or might view the tape later.

The effect of this uncertainty is very wearying. Have you ever been watched? During my years as a political organizer, I was photographed at scores of demonstrations, visited by the FBI and Secret Service, had my phone tapped more than I probably know, and was jailed 10 times. Once, when asked how it felt to get out of jail, I replied: "It feels the same out here"—which was an exaggeration, of course. Still, I have seldom felt that the outside world was fundamentally different from jail. Our culture disturbingly resembles *The Truman Show,* where the unsuspecting Truman had his whole life broadcast live on television. As the actor who plays the actor playing Truman's best friend explains, the set of the Truman Show is "real, it is merely controlled." Our real world seems quite controlled. It is becoming more and more like the panopticon designed by the Bentham brothers. The difference between the two is shrinking at an alarming rate.

Is this what cyborg society inevitably leads to—a commanded and controlled body politic? A consumer-friendly police state? Do cyborg technologies offer only potential threats to our freedoms? Many people would argue that the reverse is true. Cyberdemocracy is true democracy, they claim. We shall see.

 ### *For Discussion:*

1. Gray begins his essay by introducing definitions of citizenship. What forms of citizenship besides "membership in a state" does he suggest? Which ones seem most important to you?

2. Using the example of Mr. Data, Gray argues that one's right to citizenship should be based on what abilities? Do you agree? What could happen if some people have greater access to the means of discourse, while others remain "technopeasants"?

3. According to what criteria are citizen's rights, human rights, and the rights of non-human life defined in futuristic fiction novels and films with which you are familiar? Are there conflicting definitions?

4. What dangers does Gray see in "cyborg containment technologies"? Will enhanced privacy laws protect us sufficiently? Compare his vision of the future with Lucas D. Introna's analysis of privacy issues in the present.

5. Some of Gray's sentences require slow, careful reading. Choose a sentence you found difficult and work through it with a partner or as a class to establish a clear paraphrase.

For Fact-Finding, Research, and Writing:

1. The library catalog and online booksellers such as amazon.com can provide helpful lists of other books on the subject you are researching if you begin your search by entering the name of an author or book with which you are already familiar. Take one of the writers used by Chris Hables Gray and search his or her name in the library catalog and an online bookseller. What other titles do you find? What categories of subject matter are listed for further searching?

2. Find the U.N. declaration on human rights. Which points are similar to those proposed by the Cyborg Bill of Rights and the Turing test for citizenship? In the rights it defines and the persons to whom they apply, is the U.N. declaration broader or narrower?

3. As of May 1, 2003, the United States was still holding more than 650 prisoners ranging in age from thirteen to ninety-eight at a military prison in Guantanamo Bay. Does the United States military recognize them as citizens of any country? In what ways does their status compare to or contrast with U. S. citizens who have been arrested and/or convicted? Is there any governing body or declaration that protects their human rights?

4. Gray mentions the Extropians in his discussion of the Cyborg Bill of Rights. What is Extropianism? Find an article by an Extropian that is related to one of the issues raised by Chris Hables Gray.

Sherry Turkle, "Cyberspace and Identity"

Sherry Turkle is Abby Rockefeller Mauzé Professor in the Program in Science, Technology, and Society at the Massachusetts Institute of Technology (MIT). She is also the founder and director of the MIT Initiative on Technology and Self. She is considered one of the foremost experts on the psychological and sociological impacts of computational technology. Her books include *Psychoanalytic Politics: Jacques Lacan and Freud's French Revolution* (1978), *The Second Self: Computers and the Human Spirit* (1984), and *Life on the Screen: Identity in the Age of the Internet* (1995), from which this essay is excerpted.

Before You Read:

Do you have different personalities you use to handle certain people or occasions? Do you ever wish you were someone else? What might change about you if you had a different name, or even a different face or body? If you chat online, what are some differences between your real identity and your online identity? If you have never chatted online, what might you leave out of a personal description?

Cyberspace and Identity

Sherry Turkle

What we think of as our <u>identity</u> is generally our <u>unique inner self</u>—that core personality that makes us different from our friends, our brothers or sisters, even our identical twin. Not only do we like to think of our identity as unique, but we also see it as unified and whole. People who have <u>multiple personalities</u>, like those we read about in the cases of The Three Faces of <u>Eve</u> *or* Sybil *are <u>clinical aberrations</u>. Increasingly, however, this view of the <u>unitary self</u> is being challenged. We have long known that personalities can fragment; but it is only recently that the concept of fragmented or "decentered" selves has been seen not only as normal, but actually as psychologically healthy. Certainly, in some extreme cases, the personality can fragment to the point where the individual cannot function normally (particularly if one personality is not aware of the existence of the others). But if Superman and his alternate identity Clark Kent can healthfully coexist in the same body, then why not DrJane and Hellraiser as two different screen names of a single Internet subscriber?*

It is not that one side of the self excludes the other; it is rather that both (or in fact several) sides are aspects of the same individual, and there is no reason why one cannot "cycle through" the various sides of oneself while remaining a balanced, functioning member of society. In the following article, sociologist Sherry Turkle explores this concept of multiple identity, as it has been fostered by the development of cyberspace communication.

Sherry Turkle did her undergraduate work at Radcliff and earned a joint doctorate in sociology and personality psychology from Harvard in 1976. A <u>licensed clinical psychologist</u>, Turkle is Professor of the Sociology of Science in the Program in Science, Technology, and Society at the Massachusetts Institute of Technology. One of the most highly regarded authorities in the field, Turkle has written numerous articles on computer technologies and virtual commu-

---

For a fuller discussion of the themes in this essay, see Turkle (1995).

nities in such periodicals as The Utne Reader, Sociological Inquiry, Social Research, Sciences, American Prospect, Signs, *and* Daedalus. *Her books include* Psychoanalytic Politics: Jacques Lacan and Freud's French Revolution *(1981),* The Second Self: Computers and the Human Spirit *(1984), and* Life on the Screen: Identity in the Age of the Internet *(1995). In 1995 she was selected by* Newsweek *as one of the "50 For the Future: the Most Influential People to Watch in Cyberspace." Turkle has been featured on the cover of* Wired *(April 1996) and* Technology Review *(February/March 1996). She has also been profiled in* Scientific American *(April 1998) and* The New York Times *(18 June 1998). This article, originally entitled "Looking Toward Cyberspace: Beyond Grounded Sociology: Cyberspace and Identity," first appeared in* Contemporary Sociology *in November 1999.*

WE COME TO SEE ourselves differently as we catch sight of our images in the mirror of the machine. Over a decade ago, when I first called the computer a "second self" (1984), these identity-transforming relationships were most usually one-on-one, a person alone with a machine. This is no longer the case. A rapidly expanding system of networks, collectively known as the Internet, links millions of people together in new spaces that are changing the way we think, the nature of our sexuality, the form of our communities, our very identities. In cyberspace, we are learning to live in virtual worlds. We may find ourselves alone as we navigate virtual oceans, unravel virtual mysteries, and engineer virtual skyscrapers. But increasingly, when we step through the looking glass, other people are there as well.

Over the past decade, I have been engaged in the ethnographic and clinical study of how people negotiate the virtual and the "real" as they represent themselves on computer screens linked through the Internet. For many people, such experiences challenge what they have traditionally called "identity," which they are moved to recast in terms of multiple windows and parallel lives. Online life is not the only factor that is pushing them in this direction; there is no simple sense in which computers are causing a shift in notions of identity. It is, rather, that today's life on the screen dramatizes and concretizes a range of cultural trends that encourage us to think of identity in terms of multiplicity and flexibility.

Virtual Personae

In this essay, I focus on one key element of online life and its impact on identity, the creation and projection of constructed personae into virtual space. In cyberspace, it is well known, one's body can be represented by one's own textual description: The obese can be slender, the beautiful plain. The fact that self-presentation is written in text means that there is time to reflect upon and edit one's "composition," which makes it easier for the shy to be outgoing, the "nerdy" sophisticated. The relative anonymity of life on the screen—one has the choice of being known only by one's chosen "handle" or online name—gives people the chance to express often unexplored aspects of the self. Additionally, multiple aspects of self can be explored in parallel. Online services offer their users the opportunity to be known by several different names. For example, it is not unusual for someone to be BroncoBill in one online community, ArmaniBoy in another, and MrSensitive in a third.

The online exercise of playing with identity and trying out new identities is perhaps most explicit in "role playing" virtual communities (such as Multi-User Domains, or MUDs) where participation literally begins with the creation of a persona (or several); but it is by no means confined to these somewhat exotic locations. In bulletin boards, newsgroups, and chat rooms, the creation of personae may be less explicit than on MUDs, but it is no less psychologically real. One IRC (Internet Relay Chat) participant describes her experience of online talk: "I go from channel to channel depending on my mood. . . . I actually feel a part of several of the channels, several conversations . . . I'm different in the different chats. They bring out different things in me." Identity play can happen by changing names and by changing places.

For many people, joining online communities means crossing a boundary into highly charged territory. Some feel an uncomfortable sense of fragmentation, some a sense of relief. Some sense the possibilities for self-discovery. A 26-year-old graduate student in history says, "When I log on to a new community and I create a character and know I have to start typing my description, I always feel a sense of panic. Like I could find out something I don't want to know." A woman in her late thirties who just got an account with America Online used the fact that she could create five "names" for herself on her account as a chance to "lay out all the moods I'm in—all the ways I want to be in different places on the system."

The creation of site-specific online personae depends not only on adopting a new name. Shifting of personae happens with a change of virtual place. Cycling through virtual environments is made possible by the existence of what have come to be called "windows" in modern computing environments. Windows are a way to work with a computer that makes it possible for the machine to place you in several contexts at the same time. As a user, you are attentive to just one of the windows on your screen at any given moment, but in a certain sense, you are a presence in all of them at all times. You might be writing a paper in bacteriology and using your computer in several ways to help you: You are "present" to a word processing program on which you are taking notes and collecting thoughts, you are "present" to communications software that is in touch with a distant computer for collecting reference materials, you are "present" to a simulation program that is charting the growth of bacterial colonies when a new organism enters their ecology, and you are "present" to an online chat session where participants are discussing recent research in the field. Each of these activities takes place in a "window," and your identity on the computer is the sum of your distributed presence.

The development of the windows metaphor for computer interfaces was a technical innovation motivated by the desire to get people working more efficiently by "cycling through" different applications, much as time-sharing computers cycle through the computing needs of different people. But in practice, windows have become a potent metaphor for thinking about the self as a multiple, distributed, "time-sharing" system.

The self no longer simply plays different roles in different settings—something that people experience when, for example, one wakes up as a lover; makes breakfast as a mother; and drives to work as a lawyer. The windows metaphor suggests a distributed self that exists in many worlds and plays many roles at the same time. The "windows" enabled by a computer operating system support the metaphor, and cyberspace raises the experience to a higher power by translating the metaphor into a life experience of "cycling through."

Identity, Moratoria, and Play

Cyberspace, like all complex phenomena, has a range of psychological effects. For some people, it is a place to "act out" unresolved conflicts, to play and replay characterological difficulties on a new and exotic stage. For others, it provides an opportunity to "work through" significant personal issues, to use the new materials of cybersociality to reach for new resolutions. These more positive identity effects follow from the fact that for some, cyberspace provides what Erik Erikson ([1950] 1963) would have called a "psychosocial moratorium," a central element in how he thought about identity development in adolescence. Although the term moratorium implies a "time out," what Erikson had in mind was not withdrawal. On the contrary, the adolescent moratorium is a time of intense interaction with people and ideas. It is a time of passionate friendships and experimentation. The adolescent falls in and out of love with people and ideas. Erikson's notion of the moratorium was not a "hold" on significant experiences but on their consequences. It is a time during which one's actions are, in a certain sense, not counted as they will be later in life. They are not given as much weight, not given the force of full judgment. In this context, experimentation can become the norm rather than a brave departure. Relatively consequence-free experimentation facilitates the development of a "core self," a personal sense of what gives life meaning that Erikson called "identity."

Erikson developed these ideas about the importance of a moratorium during the late 1950s and early 1960s. At that time, the notion corresponded to a common understanding of what "the college years" were about. Today, 30 years later, the idea of the college years as a consequence-free "time out" seems of another era. College is pre-professional, and AIDS has made consequence-free sexual experimentation an impossibility. The years associated with adolescence no longer seem a "time out." But if our culture no longer offers an adolescent moratorium, virtual communities often do. It is part of what makes them seem so attractive.

Erikson's ideas about stages did not suggest rigid sequences. His stages describe what people need to achieve before they can move ahead easily to another developmental task. For example, Erikson pointed out that successful intimacy in young adulthood is difficult if one does not come to it with a sense of who one is, the challenge of adolescent identity building. In real life, however, people frequently move on with serious deficits. With incompletely resolved "stages," they simply do the best they can. They use whatever materials they have at hand to get as much as they can of what they have missed. Now virtual social life can play a role in these dramas of self-reparation. Time in cyberspace reworks the notion of the moratorium because it may now exist on an always-available "window."

Expanding One's Range in the Real

Case, a 34-year-old industrial designer happily married to a female co-worker, describes his real-life (RL) persons as a "nice guy," a "Jimmy Stewart type like my father." He describes his outgoing, assertive mother as a "Katharine Hepburn type." For Case, who views assertiveness through the prism of this Jimmy Stewart/Katharine Hepburn dichotomy, an assertive man is quickly perceived as "being a bastard." An assertive woman, in contrast, is perceived as being "modern and together." Case says that although he is comfortable with his temperament and loves and respects his father, he feels he pays a high price for his own low-key ways. In particular, he feels at a loss when it comes to confrontation, both at home and at work. Online, in a wide range of virtual communities, Case presents himself as females whom he calls his "Katharine Hepburn types." These are strong, dynamic, "out there" women who remind Case of his mother, who "says exactly what's on her mind." He tells me that presenting himself as a woman online has brought him to a point where he is more comfortable with confrontation in his RL as a man.

Case describes his Katharine Hepburn personae as "externalizations of a part of myself." In one interview with him, I used the expression "aspects of the self," and he picked it up eagerly, for his online life reminds him of how Hindu gods could have different aspects or subpersonalities, all the while being a whole self. In response to my question "Do you feel that you call upon your personae in real life?" Case responded:

> Yes, an aspect sort of clears its throat and says, "I can do this. You are being so amazingly conflicted over this and I know exactly what to do. Why don't you just let me do it?" . . . In real life, I tend to be extremely diplomatic, nonconfrontational. I don't like to ram my ideas down anyone's throat. [Online] I can be, "Take it or leave it." All of my Hepburn characters are that way. That's probably why I play them. Because they are smart-mouthed, they will not sugarcoat their words.

In some ways, Case's description of his inner world of actors who address him and are able to take over negotiations is reminiscent of the language of people with multiple-personality disorder. But the contrast is significant: Case's inner actors are not split off from each other or from his sense of "himself." He experiences himself very much as a collective self, not feeling that he must goad or repress this or that aspect of himself into conformity. He is at ease, cycling through from Katharine Hepburn to Jimmy Stewart. To use analyst Philip Bromberg's language (1994), online life has helped Case learn how to "stand in the spaces between selves and still feel one, to see the multiplicity and still feel a unity." To use computer scientist Marvin Minsky's (1987) phrase, Case feels at ease cycling through his "society of mind," a notion of identity as distributed and heterogeneous. Identity, from the Latin *idem*, has been used habitually to refer to the sameness between two qualities. On the Internet, however, one can be many, and one usually is.

An Object to Think with for Thinking about Identity

In the late 1960s and early 1970s, I was first exposed to notions of identity and multiplicity. These ideas—most notably that there is no such thing as "the ego," that each of us is a multiplicity of parts, fragments, and desiring connections—surfaced in the intellectual hothouse of Paris; they presented the world according to such authors as Jacques Lacan, Gilles Deleuze, and Felix Guattari. But despite such ideal conditions for absorbing theory, my "French lessons" remained abstract exercises. These theorists of poststructuralism spoke words that addressed the relationship between mind and body, but from my point of view had little to do with my own.

In my lack of personal connection with these ideas, I was not alone. To take one example, for many people it is hard to accept any challenge to the idea of an autonomous ego. While in recent years, many psychologists, social theorists, psychoanalysts, and philosophers have argued that the self should be thought of as essentially decentered, the normal requirements of everyday life exert strong pressure on people to take responsibility for their actions and to see themselves as unitary actors. This disjuncture between theory (the unitary self is an illusion) and lived experience (the unitary self is the most basic reality) is one of the main reasons why multiple and decentered theories have been slow to catch on—or when they do, why we tend to settle back quickly into older, centralized ways of looking at things.

When, 20 years later, I used my personal computer and modem to join online communities, I had an experience of this theoretical perspective which brought it shockingly down to earth. I used language to create several characters. My textual actions are my actions—my words make things happen. I created selves that were made and transformed by language. And different personae were exploring different aspects of the self. The notion of a decentered identity was concretized by experiences on a computer screen. In this way, cyberspace becomes an object to think with for thinking about identity—an element of cultural bricolage.

Appropriable theories—ideas that capture the imagination of the culture at large—tend to be those with which people can become actively involved. They tend to be theories that can be "played" with. So one way to think about the social appropriability of a given theory is to ask whether it is accompanied by its own objects-to-think-with that can help it move out beyond intellectual circles.

For example, the popular appropriation of Freudian ideas had little to do with scientific demonstrations of their validity. Freudian ideas passed into the popular culture because they offered robust and down-to-earth objects to think with. The objects were not physical but almost-tangible ideas, such as dreams and slips of the tongue. People were able to play with such Freudian "objects." They became used to looking for them and manipulating them, both seriously and not so seriously. And as they did so, the idea that slips and dreams betray an unconscious began to feel natural.

In Freud's work, dreams and slips of the tongue carried the theory. Today, life on the computer screen carries theory. People decide that they want to interact with others on a computer network. They get an account on a commercial service. They think that this will provide them with new access to people and information, and of course it does. But it does more. When they log on, they may find themselves playing multiple roles; they may find themselves playing characters of the opposite sex. In this way, they are swept up by experiences that enable them to explore previously unexamined aspects of their sexuality or that challenge their ideas about a unitary self. The instrumental computer, the computer that does things for us, has revealed another side: a subjective computer that does things *to* us as people, to our view of ourselves and our relationships, to our ways of looking at our minds. In simulation, identity can be fluid and multiple, a signifier no longer clearly points to a thing that is signified, and understanding is less likely to proceed through analysis than by navigation through virtual space.

Within the psychoanalytic tradition, many "schools" have departed from a unitary view of identity, among these the Jungian, object-relations, and Lacanian. In different ways, each of these groups of analysts was banished from the ranks of orthodox Freudians for such suggestions, or somehow relegated to the margins. As the United States became the center of psychoanalytic politics in the mid-twentieth century, ideas about a robust executive ego began to constitute the psychoanalytic mainstream.

But today, the pendulum has swung away from that complacent view of a unitary self. Through the fragmented selves presented by patients and through theories that stress the decentered subject contemporary social and psychological thinkers are confronting what has been left out of theories of the unitary self. It is asking such questions as, What is the self when it functions as a society? What is the self when it divides its labors among its constituent "alters"? Those burdened by posttraumatic dissociative disorders suffer these questions; I am suggesting that inhabitants of virtual communities play with them. In our lives on the screen, people are developing ideas about identity as multiplicity through new social *practices* of identity as multiplicity.

With these remarks, I am not implying that chat rooms or MUDs or the option to declare multiple user names on America Online are causally implicated in the dramatic increase of people who exhibit symptoms of multiple-personality disorder

(MPD), or that people on MUDs have MPD, or that MUDding (or online chatting) is like having MPD. I am saying that the many manifestations of multiplicity in our culture, including the adoption of online personae, are contributing to a general reconsideration of traditional, unitary notions of identity. Online experiences with "parallel lives" are part of the significant cultural context that supports new theorizing about nonpathological, indeed healthy, multiple selves.

In thinking about the self, *multiplicity* is a term that carries with it several centuries of negative associations, but such authors as Kenneth Gergen (1991), Emily Martin (1994), and Robert Jay Lifton (1993) speak in positive terms of an adaptive, "flexible" self. The flexible self is not unitary, nor are its parts stable entities. A person cycles through its aspects, and these are themselves ever-changing and in constant communication with each other. Daniel Dennett (1991) speaks of the flexible self by using the metaphor of consciousness as multiple drafts, analogous to the experience of several versions of a document open on a computer screen, where the user is able to move between them at will. For Dennett, knowledge of these drafts encourages a respect for the many different versions, while it imposes a certain distance from them. Donna Haraway (1991), picking up on this theme of how a distance between self states may be salutory, equates a "split and contradictory self" with a "knowing self." She is optimistic about its possibilities: "The knowing self is partial in all its guises, never finished, whole, simply there and original; it is always constricted and stitched together imperfectly; and therefore able to join with another to see together without claiming to be another." What most characterizes Haraway's and Dennett's models of a knowing self is that the lines of communication between its various aspects are open. The open communication encourages an attitude of respect for the many within us and the many within others.

Increasingly, social theorists and philosophers are being joined by psychoanalytic theorists in efforts to think about healthy selves whose resilience and capacity for joy comes from having access to their many aspects. For example, Philip Bromberg (1994) insists that our ways of describing "good parenting" must now shift away from an emphasis on confirming a child in a "core self" and onto helping a child develop the capacity to negotiate fluid transitions between self states. The healthy individual knows how to be many but to smooth out the moments of transition between states of self. Bromberg says: "Health is when you are multiple but feel a unity. Health is when different aspects of self can get to know each other and reflect upon each other." Here, within the psychoanalytic tradition, is a model of multiplicity as a state of easy traffic across selves, a conscious, highly articulated "cycling through."

From a Psychoanalytic to a Computer Culture?

Having literally written our online personae into existence, they can be a kind of Rorschach test. We can use them to become more aware of what we project into everyday life. We can use the virtual to reflect constructively on the real. Cyberspace opens the possibility for identity play, but it is very serious play. People who cultivate an awareness of what stands behind their screen personae are the ones most likely to succeed in using virtual experience for personal and social transformation. And the people who make the most of their lives on the screen are those who are able to approach it in a spirit of self-reflection. What does my behavior in cyberspace tell me about what I want, who I am, what I may not be getting in the rest of my life?

As a culture, we are at the end of the Freudian century. Freud, after all, was a child of the nineteenth century; of course, he was carrying the baggage of a very different scientific sensibility than our own. But faced with the challenges of cyberspace, our need for a practical philosophy of self-knowledge, one that does not shy away from issues of multiplicity, complexity, and ambivalence, that does not shy away from the power of symbolism, from the power of the word, from the power of identity play, has never been greater as we struggle to make meaning from our lives on the screen. It is fashionable to think that we have passed from a psychoanalytic culture to a computer culture—that we no longer need to think in terms of Freudian slips but rather of information processing errors. But the reality is more complex. It is time to rethink our relationship to the computer culture and psychoanalytic culture as a proudly held joint citizenship.

References

Bromberg, Philip. 1994. "Speak that I May See You: Some Reflections on Dissociation, Reality, and Psychoanalytic Listening." *Psychoanalytic Dialogues* 4 (4): 517–47.

Dennett, Daniel. 1991. *Consciousness Explained.* Boston: Little, Brown.

Erikson, Erik. [1950] 1963. *Childhood and Society,* 2nd Ed. New York: Norton.

Haraway, Donna. 1991. "The Actors are Cyborg, Nature is Coyote, and the Geography is Elsewhere: Postscript to 'Cyborgs at Large.'" In *Technoculture,* edited by Constance Penley and Andrew Ross. Minneapolis: University of Minnesota Press.

Gergen, Kenneth. 1991. *The Saturated Self-Dilemmas of Identity in Contemporary Life.* New York: Basic Books.

Lifton, Robert Jay. 1993. *The Protean Self: Human Resilience in an Age of Fragmentation.* New York: Basic Books.

Martin, Emily. 1994. *Flexible Bodies: Tracking Immunity in American Culture from the Days of Polio to the Days of AIDS.* Boston: Beacon Press.

Minsky, Martin. 1987. *The Society of Mind.* New York: Simon & Schuster.

Turkle, Sherry. [1978] 1990. *Psychoanalytic Politics: Jacques Lacan and Freud's French Revolution.* 2nd Ed. New York: Guilford Press.

——— 1984. *The Second Self: Computers and the Human Spirit.* New York: Simon & Schuster.

——— 1995. *Life on the Screen: Identity in the Age of the Internet.* New York: Simon & Schuster.

For Discussion:

1. Turkle writes that "your identity on the computer is the sum of your distributed presence." Using yourself as an example, list some ways that you see yourself fragmented in this way. What does this mean? If you cannot come up with any, what do you think this says about your identity?
2. Turkle argues that healthy people use multiple identities to deal with a variety of situations. She further argues that these people differ from those with multiple-personality disorder (MPD) because their various selves never disassociate them from the whole. Do you agree or disagree with this idea?
3. A writer might create a story, poem, or song from the perspective of someone other than him or herself. What's different about doing that and speaking from multiple identities in the way Turkle describes? Or is there a difference?

For Fact-Finding, Research, and Writing:

1. In discussing the concept of *multiplicity*, Turkle cites five other sources that deal with the topic. Using the library, locate two of the sources she mentions and paraphrase how they define the term *multiplicity*. To what extent do you agree with these definitions? How would you modify them?
2. Turkle builds her argument on the ideas of the influential psychologist Erik Erikson. Who is he, and what ideas is he best known for?
3. In what ways are Turkle's ideas related to Dyson's argument about anonymity? In what ways does it echo Plato's argument about the need to come out of the cave?